The AMERICAN COVENANT

ONE NATION UNDER GOD

THE CONSTITUTION,
THE CIVIL WAR, AND
OUR FIGHT TO PRESERVE
THE COVENANT TODAY

The AMERICAN COVENANT

ONE NATION UNDER GOD

THE CONSTITUTION, THE CIVIL WAR, AND OUR FIGHT TO PRESERVE THE COVENANT TODAY

Timothy Ballard

DIGITAL LEGEND

New York

Send inquiries to:

Digital Legend Press and Publishing
4700 Clover Street
Honeoye Falls, NY
14472

To see the complete Digital Legend library, visit www.digitalegend.com
For info write to: info@digitalegend.com or call toll free: 877-222-1960

ISBN: 978-1-937735-12-8

Printed in the United States of America First Printing: December 2011 (V1)

Cover design and book interior layout by Alisha Bishop

PRAISE FOR *THE AMERICAN COVENANT*

An absorbing read into the nature of the American Covenant, how the world's history, with its many philosophical and religious movements, serves to inform and sometimes define the Restoration that crowns the Covenant. This book compels honest scholars to open their minds and hearts to the cumulative effect of history on the Restoration.... Rather than being some new religion revealed by an angel and taught by a prophet, Mormonism is actually the crowning achievement of a long historical record. By rereading American history in light of the Restoration, Ballard has given readers a clear path to follow in understanding just how God has guided history, resulting in the ushering in of the Dispensation of the Fullness of Times.

- Jeffrey Needle
Book Review Editor, *The Association for Mormon Letters*

Tim Ballard has shown great skill in compiling and researching all that has been written or spoken concerning this covenanted land of America. Many a reader has read different quotes regarding the destiny of America. The American Covenant *by Ballard brings all of this information and more together in one book. This book will be a valuable resource in every home. I highly recommend this book.*

- Vicki Jo Anderson
Author of *The Other Eminent Men of Wilford Woodruff*

Tim Ballard's The American Covenant *is an inspiring and thought-provoking work that will cause Latter-day Saints to think more profoundly about their role in America's destiny, and better understand America's place in God's plan. The American Covenant will stir any God-fearing patriot to reflect anew on the divine origin and destiny of this remarkable nation.*

- Mayor Mike Winder
Author of *Presidents and Prophets:*
The Story of America's Presidents and the LDS Church

ACKNOWLEDGEMENTS

First and foremost I thank my wife, Katherine. Se alone has faithfully accompanied me throughout the entirety of this almost decade-long project. Against an already overbearing schedule (raising six children, all but one born during the production of this work), she read, discussed, then read and discussed again, every page of the manuscript with me. This book is rightfully dedicated to her. I thank my children as well for at least acting interested in the countless stories of American History they have been forced to endure.

I thank all my friends and family, particularly my parents and siblings (both sets), who I mentioned in Volume I: Dennis, Melanie, Brent, Sue, Shauna, Todd, Julianne, Mark, Craig, Kim, Emily, Justin, Richard, Tamra, Tevya, Rich, Rico, Amy, Elisa, Kris, Cristol, Rhett, and Dale. Additionally, I want to give special thanks to a group of people who read all or most of the Volume II manuscript and went above and beyond in assisting me with suggestions, edits, and advice: Todd Reynolds, Dennis Ballard, Craig Ballard, Stephen Fairbanks, Tevya Ware, Brandon Wood, Matthew Cooper, David Rozsa and Karen Rozsa. I am very appreciative of two great legal minds who helped me navigate some of the more difficult constitutional material—Don Marshall and John Holliday. Though I relied heavily upon this much needed help, I alone am responsible for any errors in the final product. I would also add that the arguments and conclusions made in this book do not necessarily represent the official doctrine or position of the Church of Jesus Christ of Latter-day Saints.

For Katherine

CONTENTS

The Eminent Men and Women of Wilford Woodruff, by Matthew Grant
Courtesy of Reid Moon

INTRODUCTION

In August 1877, the Founding Fathers appeared on two consecutive nights to the apostle Wilford Woodruff. According to Elder Woodruff, they "pled" with him, "as a man pleading for his life," demanding that their temple ordinances be performed. These noble spirits justified their request to the apostle, declaring, "We laid the foundation of the government you now enjoy, and we never apostatized from it, but we remained true to it and were faithful to God."[1] They had indeed laid the foundation for the government that would protect the very temple blessings they now sought—they had laid the foundation for the restoration of the gospel.

When these Founders told Elder Woodruff that they had accomplished this great task in "faithful[ness] to God," they were not merely reflecting upon their mortal lives as beings who had finally come to a realization of what they had been a part of on earth. No, they were telling him something that they *knew*—and knew deeply—while they walked on earth. They knew they had laid the foundation under the direction of God. But more than that, they knew, even in mortality, something that we as Americans are beginning to forget: that God had established the American government through them by way of a *national covenant*. It was a covenant with specific blessings (*liberty, protection,* and *prosperity*) and obligations (obey and serve God). It was a covenant that, with those blessings, created the socio-political foundation necessary for God's Church to flourish. It was the *American Covenant*.

As discussed in Volume I of this book, the Founders understood certain fundamental ideas about this covenant. They called themselves the "New Israel" and comprehended that their national covenant was connected to the covenants of Israel. What they felt concerning this covenant is more specifically articulated and enhanced, for us today, through the scriptures and through modern revelation. For we now know that Jacob of old (Israel) had pronounced the American Covenant blessings upon his son Joseph; and that Joseph's posterity, through his son Ephraim, had carried these blessings into Western Europe and delivered them (through the Pilgrims and other early settlers) to the Promised Land of America. We also know that ancient American prophets, who had also carried Joseph's national covenant, had prophesied that this national covenant would form the foundation for latter-day America.* It was this covenant, and the Founders' understanding of their obligations under this covenant, that explain the vast miracles that occurred in our nation's early history. This is what explains how God prepared His children for the final restoration of His Church and Kingdom on the earth.

That the American Covenant had been foreseen and foreordained thousands of years before it arrived upon the earth should be of little surprise. For the Almighty has always directed that national covenants precede his gospel restorations. Indeed, He had offered this covenant to the ancient Israelites in preparation for their gospel restoration (as detailed in the Old Testament) and to the ancient Americans in preparation for theirs (as detailed in the Book of Mormon). And He would do so again for the United States of America in its equally divine mission.

The explanation for why these national covenants are so important to God's work has its beginning in the pre-mortal existence, even in that great War in Heaven. According to the scriptures, "Michael and his angels fought against the dragon; and the dragon fought and his angels, and prevailed not" (Revelation 12:7-8). "Wherefore," stated the Lord, "because that Satan rebelled against me, and sought to *destroy the agency of man*...I caused that he should be cast down" (Moses 4:3-4, emphasis added). During the pre-mortal existence, Satan proposed a "plan of salvation" for God's children that would take away agency and replace it with forced

---

* These prophecies and their fulfillment are discussed at length in Volume I, Chapters 1 and 2.

obedience. Satan was so adamantly against any opposing plan that included agency, that when his own plan was rejected, he responded by waging a war in heaven, which he would ultimately lose.

The relevant question in all this is, *Why would Satan work so hard just to deny us our agency?* The answer is simple: Satan understood that free agency in its fullness was the only way to achieve eternal progression in its fullness—and he certainly did not want God's children to progress beyond his self-perceived grandeur. And so he would fight for a system of governance that oppresses, compels, and makes choices for its subjects, thus making the true steps of eternal progression impossible to achieve. Indeed, his system would deny us the liberty to be tested, to face adversity, to fail, to learn from mistakes, to find and employ faith, to fully repent, to seek and find truth, to change within, to longingly make and keep covenants, to succeed, then to grow, and thus "work out [our] own salvation" (Philippians 2:12), as God has outlined it (2 Nephi 2:11; Alma 62:41; D&C 122:1-9).

If Satan forced us into taking these steps, our personal drive and righteous desires necessary for their fulfillment would be dissolved, thus rendering void the entire process. If he simply withheld aspects of this process, such as true principles of faith, repentance, covenants, etc., the effect would be the same. Either way, his choice-impeding, freedom-less plan of governance would deny us the gospel as we know it and thus withhold from us our fullest potential. In short, though Satan's plan would offer some sort of "salvation," without the invaluable environment provided by a fullness of agency, man—mired in a stagnant state—would, as Satan devised, lack the resources to become worthy of exaltation with the Father.

On the other end of the spectrum was Jesus Christ, whose plan glorified the Father and allowed mankind, through agency, to be "free to choose...eternal life through the great Mediator" (2 Nephi 2:27). This freedom would ultimately allow God's children the ability to employ all the above-outlined essential steps of faith unto progression. Most importantly, it would allow them the opportunity to choose Christ and, through His atoning power, perfect themselves and share in His glory.

The righteous children of God who accepted and fought for His plan of agency in the pre-mortal existence are now on earth. However, their opponents in that fight, even Satan and his followers, are also here, albeit without physical bodies (see Moses 4:1-3; D&C 29:36-37; 76:25-38). With these two forces for good and evil together again—this time in mortality—it naturally follows that the same war over agency unto salvation would continue to rage. Satan and his followers, once "cast down" to earth, would certainly continue to employ their *modus operandi,* and do all in their power to influence those they could—from kings and their armies to tyrants and their navies—to rule and reign with blood and horror on the earth. They would attempt to control man, thus limiting his choices and thwarting his God-given agency. This would allow them the opportunity to frustrate man's eternal advancement, which they have clearly done.

It is estimated that less than five-percent of all people who have ever lived on earth have enjoyed a life of "freedom."[2] In other words, less than five-percent of all Heavenly Father's children have enjoyed the fulness of agency required to access the fullness of the gospel. A mere glimpse into just our recent world history (say, the last couple hundred years) reveals the Evil One's influence over governments. (Consider, for example, monarchical Europe, Nazi Germany, the Soviet Union, Saddam's Iraq, and even highly-oppressive factions within our own dear nation—just to name a few.) Backed by armies and navies, men susceptible to Satan's influence have undoubtedly turned to tyranny and have attacked precious freedom and liberty, and thus have attacked God's plan of salvation.

And this is where the national covenant comes in. For, as this adversarial influence created a very real and *physical* affront to God's plan for the full salvation of His children (again, we are talking about the adversary's influence over literal armies and navies, etc.), a very real and *physical* response from Heaven would be required. To be sure, if God could counter Satan by forming a government, set forth on a national covenant complete with the necessary *liberty, protection,* and *prosperity,* then this nation could, under the guidance of Heaven, fight and destroy these kings and tyrants, these armies and navies, and thus enforce and maximize the divine agency of man. These three blessings fight evil so effectively because they collectively develop the antidote to, and the counter-attack against, the adversary; indeed, these three blessings produce a fullness of moral agency. Only with this ultimate blessing could mankind receive the opportunity to fully and freely worship the one true God and thereby find salvation.

The members of God's Church, who would administer the gospel upon the earth, could not alone defeat such a physical threat. But a righteous nation, of which they were a part, certainly could. Once such a nation and government under God was in place, with agency unto salvation enhanced, the eternal progression of God's children would be facilitated and the Kingdom of God, even the Church of Jesus Christ, could exist and prosper.

It should be noted, however, that though the gospel in its fullness is the crowning purpose of God's national covenants, this does not exclude non-Church members as beneficiaries of it. As implied above, these national covenants, which provide and enhance agency, can benefit *all* children of God by allowing them an opportunity to choose freely, employ personal responsibility, and thus learn and grow from their successes and failures—whether in or out of the gospel. As any positive progression brings these children closer to God and His eternal plan for them, they too have claim and interest in the national covenant. Indeed, the eternal outcome of *all* God's children is attached to this national covenant, which is why we need a national covenant today and always.

As detailed in Volume I, whenever God (in preparation for a gospel restoration) established His national covenant among His children, this national covenant was, naturally, always the same. As the nations adhered, the same blessings of *liberty, protection,* and *prosperity* abounded. We see these same three blessings clearly defined in the Old Testament for the nation of ancient Israel, and we see them clearly defined again in the Book of Mormon for those chosen nations in ancient America. And, as proven in Volume I, when both ancient Israel and ancient America failed, the national covenant was (after God had prepared the way) delivered to the United States in preparation for the final Restoration.

Christ knew his churches in ancient Israel and ancient America would fall; and he knew that, in each case, the fall would begin with broken national covenants. He knew that a broken nation —which inevitably crushes moral agency—could not support His church for long. So He told ancient Israel that the "Kingdom of God shall be taken from you, and given to a *nation* [latter-day America] bringing forth the fruits thereof (Matthew 21:43, emphasis added).* He similarly told his ancient American covenant-makers—who, by prophecy, would eventually fall (1 Nephi 12:20-23)—that "it is wisdom in the father that they [referring to the latter-day inhabitants of America] should be established in this land, and be set up as a free people by the power of the Father, that the covenant of the Father may be fulfilled which he hath covenanted with his people, O house of Israel" (3 Nephi 21:4).

Some of the greatest evidence of this covenant-transfer is based in the fact that the United States of America, with its abundance of *liberty, protection,* and *prosperity,* has taken on—and defeated—the most tyrannical nations and movements (such as those listed earlier). Indeed, America has conquered those very nations and movements that sought to carry out Satan's plan of oppression against God's children. It has literally *saved* the cause of the gospel in these latter-days.

Volume I detailed this transfer of the national covenant to latter-day America and laid out the stunning proofs of this covenant in the history of our land, from its discovery through its Revolution.

---

* The LDS King James Bible cross-references this scripture with 1 Nephi 13:26 and D&C 90:1-5, both of which support the claim that the new "nation" Christ referred to was, in fact, America.

But if we, as a nation, are to fully grasp the power and meaning of the covenant, that we might use it to assist God in His latter-day work and glory, we must understand its place in post-revolutionary America as well. For at the end of the Revolution, the covenant story had only just begun.

We will now continue the narrative and, in so doing, will provide astonishing answers to questions such as: *Why was James Madison the chosen one to bring forth the Constitution? Why did Joseph Smith love this document so much that he was willing to die for it? And why did the Prophet of the Restoration feel compelled to run for the presidency of the United States? What deep connection did the Prophet share with Abraham Lincoln, and what powerful relationship did Lincoln establish with the God of this land? Was the Civil War really a reflection of the covenant relationship? Why did Lincoln check out a Book of Mormon during the darkest days of his presidency? What evidence exists that his purported reading of the Book of Mormon influenced his conversion to the American Covenant? Was the Union's General Order No. 11 really a direct fulfillment of Joseph Smith's prophecy? And did the Prophet really know — and did Lincoln and his people come to learn — that this national calamity would restore the national covenant and build up the Kingdom of God? What other historical figures (even in our more modern-day history) were profoundly connected to God's covenant and purposes? And finally, Where do we stand today as a nation under this covenant?*

Many valiant and noble spirits had indeed appeared to Wilford Woodruff in the St. George Temple. Though, by the end of Volume I, we had yet to identify them all. They, too, were there for a reason. Their stories must also be told.....

ENDNOTES

1 Wilford Woodruff Journal, 7:367-69, as quoted in Vicki Jo Anderson, *The Other Eminent Men of Wilford Woodruff* (Malta: Nelson Book, 1994), 420-1; Wilford Woodruff, as quoted by Truman G. Madsen, *The Presidents of the Church*, recorded lecture series (Salt Lake City: Bookcraft), tape/track 4, "Wilford Woodruff;" Wilford Woodruff, *Conference Report*, April 1898, 89-90, as quoted in Anderson, Appendix.

2 Chris Stewart and Ted Stewart, *Seven Tipping Points That Saved the World* (Salt Lake City: Shadow Mountain, 2011), 12.

The Scene at the Signing of the Constitution of the United States
by Howard Chandler Christy
Courtesy of the Architect of the Capitol

CHAPTER 1

THE CONSTITUTION:
A HEAVENLY BANNER

*It is impossible for the pious man not to recognize in [the Constitution]
a finger of that Almighty Hand which was so frequently extended to us
in the critical stages of the evolution.*

—James Madison

*The Constitution of the United States is a glorious
Standard…. It is a heavenly banner.*

—Joseph Smith

Though the American War for Independence had ended, the
greater war with evil that had begun in our pre-mortal existence
continued to rage. It is true that with American independence, the
adversary had lost some ground in his efforts to obstruct America's
spiritual destiny. However, his evil designs to thwart freedom and
agency—and thus to snuff out the opportunity for eternal salvation
—continued to march forward. As such, the Lord would deliver a
most inspired document—one which would direct and guide the

newly independent nation in its fight against the adversary. It would be a document that would uphold and support God's gift of free agency unto eternal salvation. These next two chapters will show that the Constitution of the United States was and is this document, and that it was and is inspired by the Almighty to serve as yet another building block of the American Covenant.

Why God Sent the Constitution

That the Constitution was given by God, for the reason stated above, is evidenced by His own words. Said the Lord:

> That every man may act in doctrine and principle pertaining to futurity, according to the *moral agency* which I have given unto him, that every man may be accountable for his own sins in the day of judgment. Therefore, it is not right that any man should be in bondage one to another. And for this purpose have I established the Constitution of this land, by the hands of wise men whom I raised up unto this very purpose (D&C 101:78-80, emphasis added).

Satan's fight against man—both in the War in Heaven, and in the extension of that war, here on earth—has largely been over liberty and agency. For the Evil One has "sought to destroy the agency of man" (see Revelation 12:7-8 and Moses 4:3-4). This he does to thwart mankind's ability to progress unto eternal life.

We cannot emphasize enough that the scriptural definition of Satan's target, as just cited, is man's "agency;" and that the scriptural explanation, as also just cited, of why God sent the United States Constitution, includes the preservation of this "moral agency." Indeed, the Constitution stares down Satan's plan to attack freedom and agency, and promises to defeat it.

It should be noted that the Constitution, in its effort to counter-strike at the adversary, is fulfilling the exact goal and purpose of the American Covenant, as particularly described in

2

Volume I. As the Constitution shares the same ultimate goal as the American Covenant—and as they were both inspired by God for His eternal purposes—it naturally follows that the Constitution is a part of the American Covenant. In fact, the Constitution even sets out to achieve this heavenly goal the same way the American Covenant does. As we will see in the next chapter, the Constitution fulfills ancient prophecy by providing America with the same national covenant blessings promised by father Jacob to latter-day America through his son Joseph, and through his grandson Ephraim. And it promises to provide the same blessings Lehi and his people projected for latter-day America.* Indeed, the Constitution does nothing less than provide the divine and foreordained precursor blessings necessary for a fullness of "moral agency"—it specifically provides *liberty, protection,* and *prosperity.*

If deserved and thus delivered, not only would these national covenant blessings of the Constitution protect our ability to progress through personal choice (regardless of what we choose), but would, at the same time, protect a vast array of choices from which to choose. For example, the national covenant/Constitution would protect the existence of God's Church and Kingdom, thus making available the opportunity for man to join God's Church and Kingdom. And so, the ability to achieve eternal life would be safeguarded.

Of course, under the national covenant structure, these blessings leading to eternal life are activated upon worthiness. Some will be surprised to see in the pages and chapters to follow, that this covenant relationship is acknowledged and configured in the Constitution itself.

It should also be noted that the Lord certainly had more than just America in mind when He influenced the creation of the U.S. Constitution. For not only would the Constitution facilitate the development of God's restored gospel in America (which gospel

---

* See Volume I, Chapters 1 and 2, for a full analysis of how these ancient Biblical and Book of Mormon promises were directed at latter-day America.

would eventually reach the world), but the Constitution would be the template for the nations of the world, that they might have for themselves a government that could receive and protect this gospel once it arrived. A seven-volume study produced by the University of Virginia details how this constitutional influence occurred. Its introduction muses at how we "pay so little attention to the historical relationship...of the U.S. Constitution and other constitutions in Asia, Africa, Europe and Latin America."[1] This University of Virginia study predates the creation of the constitutions in the newly liberated nation-states of the Former Soviet Union and in Iraq. These budding countries also follow the pattern of the U.S. Constitution and, therefore, promise to protect those rights that support the existence of the restored gospel.

Many of these foreign constitutions have practically copied the U.S. Constitution's structure. This U.S. influence, more often than not, was a result of positive action by the U.S., such as diplomacy, economic incentive, and (when necessary) war. Today, these nations enjoy three branches of government, checks and balances, and balance of powers. They also enjoy unprecedented human rights protections such as religious freedom. Remember, the U.S. Constitution came first. The other governments of the world, most of which were bogged down by tyranny and oppression, watched and then followed in turn. And these foreign governments have found success in this constitutional endeavor. Evidence of this success is reflected in the fact that in those countries that adopted a U.S.-type constitution, there exist today temples dedicated to the Lord. (Those newly liberated countries, whose inspired constitutions are only beginning to congeal, possess a solid hope and potential to enjoy such temples in the future.)

To be sure, there was more divine and global purpose in God's creation of the Constitution than many realize. God did, after all, reveal that He created the U.S. Constitution to preserve "the rights and protection," not only of Americans, but "of all flesh" (see D&C 101: 77). Elder Dallin H. Oaks recently confirmed that the Constitution is "this nation's most important export."[2] Indeed, there is powerful truth to the declaration by President Ezra Taft Benson that America is "the Lord's base of operations" in these latter-days.[3]

Having presented a broad-brush explanation for why God sent us the Constitution, we will now take a closer look at the world as it existed just prior to the creation of the Constitution, that we might witness up-close the eternal struggle over agency and observe the power the Constitution would bring to secure it. Indeed, we will witness how the Constitution shattered the dark and apostate gloom that covered and threatened the earth.

It is true that after winning its independence, America seemed an unlikely victim of the adversary's assault on liberty and moral agency. After all, the very blessed and inspired nation had just witnessed the heaven-sent chain of events which, through its national covenant with God, had brought victory along with other blessings. So blessed was America during these post-war days (yet prior to the Constitution) that Thomas Jefferson commented, even during this transitional time, on the greatness of America's "equality, liberty, laws, people & manners." He declared, "My God, how little my countrymen know what precious blessings they are in possession of, and which no other people on earth enjoy."[4] So then, could this great nation not have secured and preserved man's rights of moral agency without a constitution? Each state, after all, possessed its own constitutional laws full of protections and rights. Was a national constitution really necessary? History has taught us that indeed it was.

Consider, for example, the case of Michael Servetus, who in 1553 was burned at the stake in Geneva, Switzerland, for no other reason than his alternative and outspoken view of Christianity. The reason this execution stands out among the millions of equally unjust acts against free thought, is that it was ordered by none other than the great religious reformer, John Calvin.[5] Calvin, like other inspired reformers responsible for freeing people from the chains of intolerance, was now, ironically, acting as intolerant towards others as his Catholic oppressors had acted toward him and his people. Even Martin Luther insisted that his religious views be enforced by his government, stating in 1536 that "secular authority is held to reprimand blasphemy, false doctrines and heresy and to inflict corporal pain on those who support such."[6] And Luther was one of the chosen ones. He had led the way in breaking the chains of religious oppression, thus rightfully meriting himself a place at Wilford Woodruff's St. George Temple miracle.[7]

The spine-chilling lesson is all too clear: If even the most inspired among us can be influenced to assist the adversary's plan to thwart agency through violently enforcing religious intolerance, anybody can—even the inspired American Founders. As such, a broad-reaching, national, God-given protection against such adversarial attacks on moral agency would certainly be required before a fullness of religious truth could be restored and accepted. The U.S. Constitution provided precisely this type of protection.

To understand how important and timely the U.S. Constitution was in the grand plan of the Almighty, consider the adversary's assault on freedom and agency in the world leading up to the creation of America. In 1401, for example, the king of England issued a national edict, which called for the immediate arrest and punishment of anyone who preached religious thought contrary to the king's religion. If found guilty of a second offense of the same, the decree called for immediate death by hanging.[8] Then, of course, there were the similarly violent and seemingly endless atrocities surrounding the Catholic Inquisition, which was responsible for the torture and death of tens of thousands of non-believers from Spain to Asia and from Central to South America.[9] So successful were Satan's efforts to deny moral agency in the Old World, that even the "faithful" members of the state church had to risk life and limb just to pick up a Bible and read it. Such was forbidden by the clergy, who desired to control "God's law."[10] Furthermore, a large portion of seventeenth-century Europe was scarred by the horrific Thirty Years

War, a conflict which claimed hundreds of thousands of lives mostly over religious intolerance. Finally, by 1685, the king of France, in the same evil spirit, demanded that all those unwilling to accept French Catholicism were to be immediately exiled or put to death.[11] Sadly, these examples represent only a portion of the religious intolerance that permeated the world during this era.

It is no surprise, then, that the adversary would take this evil influence, derived from his long-lasting war against freedom and agency, to the shores of America. The adversary certainly knew this was the land set apart and foreordained for the Restoration. Though America had gained footing against this evil plan through achieving independence from the Old World—which was tainted by the apostasy—the adversary had still managed to maintain his presence in the Promised Land. He did this by way of his earlier introduction of two practices that threatened to destroy the divine purposes of America.

First was slavery, which codified all that the adversary stood for and which permitted a spirit in the land and among the people that could not coexist with the restored gospel. This evil and oppressive practice made it difficult for the Lord to bless America under its covenant (as the blessings were contingent upon national worthiness).

The second evil practice that persisted in America, even after independence had been gained, was direct (and legal) religious intolerance and persecution. This grew out of the colonial American tradition of allowing state and local governments to favor and support the more popular religious sects, thus encouraging the persecution of the less popular, minority sects. As the restored gospel would clearly be counted among such minority sects in America, this obstacle to God's work had to be eliminated before the fullness of the gospel could flourish.

The Constitution of the United States would work to fight both of these evil influences in support of God's gospel purposes for America. In the next several chapters we will discuss how the creation, development, and proper application of the Constitution, over many years, drove out these evil inhibitors of man's moral agency, making America a worthy safe-haven for personal progression unto eternal salvation. Later chapters will deal with the more complicated issues surrounding how the Lord would develop the Constitution into a tool to rid the nation of its most stubborn national sin—slavery. This chapter and the next will focus on how the Constitution first provided the basic tools necessary to stomp out oppression and intolerance, as particularly related to religious freedom, in supporting moral agency and paving the way for the Restoration.

The story of this fight over the destiny of moral agency upon American soil begins with the many religious "dissidents" from Europe who eventually made their way to the land of America, so that they might find a place to worship freely. Ironically, like Calvin, Luther, and others, even these did not always abandon the very spirit of intolerance they themselves had sought refuge from. As many American victims of religious intolerance soon learned, the European influence of the apostasy hovered over the New World as well. Indeed, many of the colonists were forced to pay taxes for the state-managed religions, were forced to attend church services, and could legally be whipped for not knowing the religious doctrines. Many people in New England were even executed for their nontraditional beliefs.[12]

Even after America had miraculously secured its independence, no national protection from religious intolerance had been put in place. To be sure, the British evacuation of America did little to immediately usher in religious freedom. Though the war had inspired a refreshing sense of liberty in America—which would eventually inspire the nation to adopt a policy of greater religious freedom—the war was not fought directly for religious freedom, and therefore did not immediately produce such blessings. As detailed in Volume I, the colonists entered the War for Independence on principles of political rights and property rights—religious rights were mostly sidelined.[13] In fact, among the many grievances against the Crown listed in the Declaration of Independence, issues related to religious freedom or religious intolerance were nowhere to be found. The colonists mostly enjoyed religious freedom under Britain. Many, including Washington, even chose to be members of the Church of England. This is not to say British rule was benign. For it did make things hard on minority religious thought (just not enough to compel the majority to go to war). Its monarchical system could too easily have served as a tool of oppression for the adversary against the gospel restoration. Britain had to go. But, again, British evacuation of the Promised Land did not mean America was yet ready for the Restoration.

It should be understood that—like the British—the colonists themselves practiced religious intolerance against these minority religions. The colonists continued this persecution well after the British had packed up and left. Simply put, religious intolerance was not much of an issue for the colonists at the time. It is not why they fought. However, as the restored gospel would one day be carried by one of these minority religions in need of protection, the Lord utilized the Revolution to send a new spirit of liberty that would, apart from freeing the nation from Britain, also open the national heart to pursue a policy of enhanced religious freedom. Indeed, though the colonists did not generally articulate religious freedom as a justification for war, the Lord, who sees the end from the beginning, knew the crowning fruit of the conflict would be religious freedom. And so, He influenced events toward that inspired end. However, this inspired end would take additional time and revelation, even after independence had been gained.

And so, without religious freedom immediately at the forefront of the revolutionary mind, we can see how, even after independence had been won, many states still controlled aspects of religion—something which sadly led to further persecution of minority religions. For example, even during the height of the Revolution, some states maintained control over minority religious thought by requiring that certain preachers attain licenses in order to preach. Since minority sects, such as Baptists, were unable or unwilling to attain state licenses to preach, it was not unusual for them to be subjected to public whippings and floggings, even at the hands of local, American law enforcement. Between 1765 and 1778, for example, over forty-five Baptist ministers were jailed in Virginia alone for nothing more than preaching.[14]

Such injustices were not limited to the South. During this same period (even during and after the Revolution) religious minorities in New England suffered equally under laws and customs of religious oppression. Baptist preachers in Connecticut, for example, were not authorized to perform marriages, were faced with continuous harassment, and were barred from preaching in certain locations. Its members were also forced to pay taxes in support of the state-sponsored religion.[15]

In Massachusetts, members of the New Light Baptist Church were likewise forced to pay taxes to benefit the state church, which was the Congregational Church (the successor of the Puritan Church). This was done upon punishment of imprisonment or seizure of property. And these laws were enforced. The New Light Baptists even had to deal with a state law which required infant baptism—something this Baptist sect believed to be a false doctrine.[16] The endurance of this unrighteous power over religious minorities wielded by the New England states is further witnessed by the fact that both Connecticut and Massachusetts persisted in maintaining a state-sponsored religion, even after the U.S. Constitution had been ratified. (More on how this happened will be discussed later.)[17] In fact, the complaints and allegations made by these persecuted religious minorities continued into the eighteen hundreds—well after the establishment of the Constitution.[18]

Sadly, these were not isolated incidents; they reflected an element of American culture that persisted throughout the land and affected other religious minorities such as Quakers, Mennonites, Jews, and Catholics. Several members of the Continental Congress even wanted to prohibit Catholics from fighting in the Revolutionary War. Additionally, many colonies disallowed Catholics from holding public office. Only three colonies permitted Catholics to vote, all but one of the colonies banned Catholic schools, and at least one of the colonies would have priests arrested just for crossing its borders.[19]

Such was the tragic state of affairs in America, even at that inspired time of the Revolution. During this crucial period in history, it became an American problem that required an American solution. Though independence had been gained, America had yet to fill the measure of its creation. As one scholar of American religious rights recently noted: "The birth of religious freedom [in America] was not inevitable."[20]

The Lord certainly had more to accomplish in preparation for His latter-day work. For, if Baptists, Quakers, Mennonites, Jews, Catholics, and other religious minorities suffered religious persecution under American culture and law, how would the "Mormons" have fared under this environment? With such wicked cultural elements filling the world and spilling into America, even affecting the most inspired leaders, how could the Prophet Joseph and his very "nontraditional" religion stand a chance? How would these other sects tolerate a "new" religion, which by "revelation from God" declared that "their creeds were an abomination"?[21] Such hard truth could not abound anywhere in the world during this era —not even (as of yet) in America. A miraculous intervention would no doubt be required to root out this influence of the adversary.

This intervention was on its way. The stage had already been set. For, the victory over the British had at last rid the nation of a dangerous monarchical regime and had also given birth to a new sense of liberty in America. Both of these fruits of the Revolution would have a profound effect on furthering God's work. But in light of the above, while God's work in the war for American independence was a necessary step, it was nonetheless a preliminary one. Certain wicked elements, even the aforementioned oppressors of religious freedom, still roamed the countryside and held positions of public trust. But now with the war won, and the land free from European interference, the Lord had a clean slate with which He could finally influence a new formula of government, one that would effectively deal with these remaining wicked elements. As such, within a decade after independence was achieved, the Lord would initiate the next phase of His prelude to the Restoration by providing the crowning element of the American Revolution. He would provide the Constitution of the United States—another building-block of the American Covenant.

In an effort to recognize God's hand in the Constitution, thus seeing it for what it is—an essential element of the American Covenant and a tool unto salvation—these next two chapters are dedicated to analyzing its creation and content.

James Madison and the Commencement of a Plan

Though we now know the Constitution was created to protect religious freedom—and thus God's Kingdom on the earth—its creation (even right after America gained its independence) was by no means a foregone conclusion. Its blessings were not inevitably bound for the Promised Land. It would take God's influence to make this happen.

At about the time the flogging and unjust imprisonment of preachers was occurring in America (not to mention the even greater religious violations abroad), the newly independent America was dealing with a slew of other problematic issues, which dominated the public's attention. Since independence had been officially recognized in 1783, the individual states had seen little reason to remain as "united" with each other as they had been during the war (and even during the war they struggled with unity). As such, the national treasury fell to almost nothing, making it impossible for the nation to pay its sizable debt to its European creditors; and having to default on the loans meant poor credit for the new nation—something it could not afford to have.

As the bickering states continued to act more like individual countries than a united nation, other negative externalities emerged. For example, the colonies could not agree on a unified tariff schedule, nor was there any person or group (like a *national* customs service) assigned to enforce such a tariff (even if it had existed). Foreign countries, therefore, brought their goods in for free, while the Americans were forced to pay tariffs on their own exports.

Furthermore, with the standing army having been all but abolished since the war, there was no national security beyond the uncoordinated, understaffed, and underpaid state militias. This was an alarming notion, considering that France and Spain were gaining territory in the South while Great Britain still remained in the North.[22] Highlighting the embarrassing fact that the colonies had no national security was an incident in 1783, when an armed mob of ex-Continental soldiers came knocking on the Continental Congress' door, looking for the money the national government owed them. The delegates, without any defense, were forced to flee for their lives. Some of the states even felt so threatened and insecure that they were entering into negotiations with foreign governments, and in some cases even favored a reunification policy with the British.[23]

The problem turned violent when several unscrupulous factions within the individual states assumed control over the local governments. (Again, there was no federal system with the power to temper such corruption.) These events resulted in policies that burdened farmers and the working class. Unable to pay their mortgages and taxes, many rose up in mob violence and burned public buildings. The local governments stood by and watched, having inadequate resources to control the mobs. (Again, there was no federal system with the power to help control the mobocracy.) One of the most famous of these uprisings is known today as Shay's Rebellion. The governments' inability to make good policy and control mob-rule emphasized the need for some drastic political changes. Though America was still a land of hope, and though it still boasted of the freedom and liberty inherited by its independence, things were heading down the wrong path.

Fortunately, one young and highly inspired statesman from Virginia watched in horror as this social, economic, and political powder-keg waited to explode. He understood better than anyone that the individual states were, by nature, incapable of dealing with these *national* social ills, and that the current structure of the national government (composed of the Continental Congress and its Articles of Confederation) was far too weak to be effective. After all, the Articles of Confederation required a super-majority vote in Congress for binding policy, which was rarely achieved. Even if consensus *was* achieved, the delegates' respective state governments would often disregard the national congressional acts and do as they pleased. For, there was no national entity to enforce the national policy. (This is similar to how the United Nations functions today.)[24]

But this young Virginian decided he would no longer stand idly by, watching his government fail to provide the protections and services necessary for the pursuit of happiness. Heaven had moved him. After all, how could the Lord set up his "base of operations" in such a messy and insecure environment? His name was James Madison, and he was beginning to devise a divine plan—he was beginning to formulate, in his mind, the blueprints for the United States Constitution.

Before examining his plan and how it was carried out, we must first understand something about Madison's background; for in it we find the underpinnings of God's design for him and America. Born in 1751, Madison—who was generally described throughout his life as shy, small, and frail—was raised in the typical fashion of the American upper-class, graduating with high marks from the College of New Jersey (now called Princeton). Before his 30th birthday, he was elected as a delegate to the Continental Congress, from whence he made his above-mentioned observations at very close range. He would go on to serve as both a state and a national congressmen, secretary of state, and eventually he would serve as president of the United States. However, it was these initial and inspired stirrings within him, occurring shortly after the war had ended, that produced the greatest fruit of his public life—the Constitution.

History books state that Madison's passion for writing the Constitution's blueprints stemmed from the observations he made, as noted above: no national security, no national treasury, no unified tariff schedule, general disunity among the states, and so on. This is certainly a correct view. Through a gospel lens, we also see how such issues needed resolution in order to provide a secure political foundation prior to the Restoration. However, the more specific and relevant goal of the Constitution, which God appeared to be working toward above all else pursuant to His plans for America, was to secure, within the government, total religious freedom, or as the Lord put it, to secure man's *moral agency* (see D&C 101:78-80).

It is here where we see God's hand over the advent of the Constitution. We have already emphasized (particularly in Volume I) how the Revolution had (as God designed) begun changing hearts and opening up American minds to understand the importance of making religious liberty part of the new government. This was, of course, an essential reason that America eventually adopted policies supporting religious freedom. However, the movement toward full religious liberty still grew slowly, not having been a generally articulated justification, among the colonists, for independence or war (see Volume I). Furthermore, as seen above, the most pressing issues of the day were unrelated to religious freedom. Again, victims of religious persecution were still "merely" the minority sects, and could easily be overlooked. However, James Madison would not overlook them. In fact, James Madison was perhaps the greatest champion in American history of religious rights, particularly for the religious underdog. He would keep the spirit and importance of religious freedom alive, reminding his fellow Americans what they had learned and felt as a result of their recent Revolution.

The miracle of it all is that the one person most responsible for creating the Constitution was also the most passionate about religious freedom. This did not necessarily need to be the case, for there were many other prominent promoters of a national government who might have easily overlooked the religious issue, and marginalized it in the Constitution. Again, we should note the scholarly consensus that "[t]he birth of religious freedom [in America] was not inevitable."[25] Madison's placement in history, therefore, was no coincidence. The Lord had prepared him early on and raised him up to be "the father" of the Constitution. He would carry the true spirit of the Revolution with him and not neglect the indispensable blessing of religious liberty. God had led the nation toward the path of religious freedom through the war He had presided over. And He made sure His servant Madison was front and center on the scene, in the aftermath of this war, to ensure the nation did not get distracted from this heaven-lit path toward full religious freedom.

Madison's sensitivity to religious liberty developed at an early age. By the time he was twenty, he had witnessed and became appalled at the aforementioned discrimination and persecution against the Baptists in his state of Virginia, even though he himself was a devout member of the Church of England. Madison's sensitivity would soon be anchored by intellectual and spiritual conviction upon studying under the president of the College of New Jersey, Reverend John Witherspoon. (This is the same divinely-inspired Witherspoon mentioned in Volume I, Chapter 7, who prophesied of the hand of God in the Revolutionary War.)

Madison soaked up Witherspoon's ideas on the importance of religious freedom: "The magistrate ought to defend the rights of conscience," Witherspoon wrote, "and tolerate all their religious sentiments that are not injurious to their neighbor." After graduating under the tutelage of Witherspoon, Madison felt inclined to continue with him an extra year to study Hebrew and ponder the meaning of the Scriptures.[26] At this point in his life, he seriously considered entering the holy ministry, but in the end, and for inspired reasons, he chose politics.[27]

Upon returning to Virginia, Madison (at the age of twenty-five) participated in the state convention to write Virginia's Declaration of Rights, which, as he had desired, set in motion the eventual termination of the religious persecution over minority religions. While the original language called for religious "toleration," it was Madison who changed the language to include a broader protection of man's most precious and inherent right. He declared "that all men are equally entitled to the free exercise of religion, according to the dictates of conscience, unpunished, and unrestrained by the magistrate."[28] Fittingly, this work began in 1776, while America was in the middle of its war for independence.[29] And though it was not immediately applied as Madison desired, it would set a foundation that would one day influence future documents and policies of America by changing the standard of religious freedom from mere toleration to full-fledged liberty.[30]

Years later, in 1784, Madison would again work to protect freedom of religion by fighting against a proposal in Virginia that would have allowed the state government to raise taxes in benefit of those whom the state determined were "Christian" clergy. Madison feared this would allow the government to wield too much power over private religion, thus setting a precedent which the government could one day expand upon. He feared government could eventually begin dictating to the churches, defining religions, and (while perhaps helping some) hurting minority religions that the local and state governments deemed unworthy. Imagine, for example, how such a law might have led to government abuses against new religious movements, like the soon-to-be delivered Church of Jesus Christ of Latter-day Saints. In his plea against the measure, Madison inspiringly argued: "The Religion then of every man must be left to the conviction and conscience of every man; and it is the right of every man to exercise it as these may dictate." He further argued that "[i]f this [religious] freedom be abused, it is an offense against God, not against men. To God, therefore, not to man, must an account be rendered." Madison won the argument, and the bill was rejected.[31]

Madison's observation that religious intolerance is an "offense against God" is perhaps more accurate than he could have understood at the time. For, in order for God's gospel plan to unfold, and in order for the enterprise and prospect of the Restoration to develop, God needed disciples willing to open their hearts and minds to the mysteries and commandments of His kingdom. As Madison had pointed out years earlier, "Religious bondage shackles and debilitates the mind, and unfits it for every noble enterprise, every expanded prospect."[32] Madison seemed to understand something of what God required, and he worked tirelessly to achieve it.

With this legislative victory under his belt, Madison felt encouraged to expand religious freedom even further. And so, in 1785—almost immediately after defeating the clergy tax—he pulled out an old 1779 bill-proposal originally put forth by his friend, Thomas Jefferson. It was the Virginia Statute for Religious Freedom. Whereas the recently defeated clergy tax proposal halted only one particular aspect of religious intolerance, this statute utilized the same basic principles, but made them permanent and thus applicable to any future threat to religious freedom. The statute declared, "Almighty God hath created the mind free, [and] all attempts to influence it by temporal punishments... are a departure from the plan of the holy author of our religion."[33] The statute goes on to say— and imagine how the Prophet Joseph would have loved the full application of this principle

James Madison, by Thomas Sully
Courtesy of the Library of Congress

in his day—that "no man shall be...enforced, restrained, molested, or burthened in his body or goods, nor shall otherwise suffer on account of his religious opinions or belief, but that all men shall be free to profess...their opinions on matters of Religion, and that the same shall in no wise diminish, enlarge or affect their civil capacities."[34]

When Jefferson had originally proposed the statute in the middle of the Revolutionary War, his countrymen had not yet felt enough of the revolutionary "spirit of liberty" to adopt the policy, and so it was temporarily shelved. However, a few years after the war, once the nation was sufficiently prepared, Madison brought it back (Jefferson was serving the country overseas at the time) and ushered it into law.[35] A new standard for religious freedom had been set.

Madison was a born champion of religious freedom. It was an issue passionately near and dear to him. His unique contributions to the cause of religious freedom become even more pronounced and inspiring when considering the following commentary put forth by Judge John Noonan:

> James Madison was, so far as I know, the first statesman who, himself a believer, had enough empathy with the victims of persecution to loathe the idea of enforced religious conformity and to work to produce law that would forever end it. It is easy to be tolerant if you don't believe. To believe and to champion freedom—that is Madison's accomplishment.[36]

Such was the man Madison. And his passion for religious freedom would not be restrained to the borders of Virginia. He knew and felt that more must be done to protect religious freedom on the national level as well. Indeed, he understood, perhaps more than anybody, that it was religious freedom that, as he declared, "promised a lustre to our country."[37] He also understood, perhaps more than anybody, that *national* legislation would be the key to stomping out any state or local abuses over such rights.

And so, without downplaying his equally impassioned desire to deal with the many other more immediate national ills plaguing early America, Madison took his solutions for religious intolerance to the national level. On one occasion, just before heading to the national congress to do just that, Madison assured one leader of a minority religious sect that he would achieve "the most satisfactory provisions for all essential rights, particularly the rights of Conscience in the fullest latitude."[38]

But bringing religious freedom to the national level would not be easy, especially in light of the fact that no solid national venue for such national policies even existed at the time. Yet, undeterred by his daunting responsibility, Madison set out to create the national venue (even the national government) he would need in order to create protections for religious freedom, nationwide. At last, by 1787, he had convinced the bickering states to send delegates of the Continental Congress one more time to a convention at Philadelphia. There, he would see if, by some miracle, their many national social problems could at last find resolution. Those problems included disunity on taxes and tariffs, national debts, foreign threats, and, most importantly for the purposes of God (though underrated at the time), injustices related to *religious freedom*. Mr. Madison had a plan, and he greatly desired to share it with his fellow delegates.

Madison's plan carried the name of the state from whence its author hailed: The Virginia Plan. It proposed the abolishment of the weak Articles of Confederation and the adoption of a new national (or federal) government. Within it was the skeleton of our familiar political structure, rife with the oft-referenced ideas like "checks and balances," "separation of powers," "natural rights," and "three branches of government." In it was the recipe for a new national government to fulfill that which is the only real responsibility of any good government: to identify social ills (like those listed above) plaguing the people and fix them. Yet, the final product included so much more than just these catch phrases. As we will see in the following chapter, Madison's proposal set the stage for one of the most inspired systems for protecting liberties, particularly religious liberties, that the world has ever known. So powerful were these protections, that Madison originally did not feel the need to even add the First Amendment (the religious freedom amendment) to the Constitution, though he eventually gave in and drafted it himself.[39]

When he finally did draft and propose the First Amendment, Madison was so forward-thinking that he even wanted to include more powerful constitutional language to ensure that all states would respect religious freedom.[40] Unfortunately, his more powerful language was rejected, thus causing God's restored church unnecessary pains in the future (more on this in later chapters).

Clearly, Madison possessed inspired insight beyond his years, and his involvement in securing such significant freedoms have been far too underrated in the annals of history. His efforts and successes were reminiscent of an ancient statesman documented in the Book of Mormon. Having witnessed religious persecution among his people, the Jaredite king, Shule, "did execute a law throughout all the land, which gave power unto the prophets that they should go withersover they would" without fear or threat of being beaten, imprisoned, or executed (see Ether 7:24). It was this law in ancient America, as it would be in latter-day America (particularly after the Restoration), that fulfilled the purposes of God. For, as the above-referenced scripture concludes, "by this cause the people were brought to repentance" (Ether 7:24).

Though little, if anything, is said of King Shule's personal religious testimony or belief, he is called "righteous." Madison was clearly of similar caliber, and both seemed to have received inspiration from the same benevolent source. They both ultimately received this inspiration, though in separate eras, under the same American Covenant. Indeed, they were both ultimately working for the same eternal purposes of God.

Speaking of his work in creating American religious freedom, William Bennett commented that "perhaps it was Madison's... unwillingness to beat his own drum that has caused us to fail to appreciate his great achievement."[41] But whatever the reasons may be that we have forgotten many aspects of this inspired and underrated founder, we will attempt now to resurrect his memory, complete his story, and learn of his plan for religious freedom; for all this is integral to the American Covenant.

It should be noted that, notwithstanding his most prominent role in applying such great ideas to a national government in America, Madison was not working in a vacuum. In fact, many political philosophers, including some in Europe, had theorized over similar models, and much smaller governments in much earlier days had even attempted to apply some of them. Even in Colonial America, John Adams had implemented many of these political concepts in his writing of the Massachusetts Constitution, which (for the most part) is still intact today. Madison himself modestly stated, after being lauded as the writer of the Constitution, that it was actually "the work of many heads and many hands."[42] And many of these heads and hands belonged to those inspired delegates who accepted Madison's invitation to Independence Hall in Philadelphia and came to the *Glorious Convention*.

The Glorious Convention

As the delegates shuffled into Independence Hall during that hot Philadelphia summer of 1787, Madison was tense and uneasy. After all, he had *intentionally* failed to mention to them the real cause for calling the convention: to present his Virginia Plan—even to present a new national constitution. With the exception of his closest circle of friends, Madison was virtually the only one that had any idea that this meeting could become what would famously go down in history as the *Constitutional Convention*. Madison knew that if the delegates had understood his true intention, they may not have participated. For they had come to Philadelphia under the impression (and under strict instructions from their respective states) that they *might* amend certain aspects of the Articles of Confederation. They had no idea that they would be asked to form an entirely new national system.

Understandably, when Madison's plan was proposed, the delegates, fearful of a strong central authority, immediately protested. Some even threatened to leave the Convention, and others actually made good on the threat. Had it not been for the fact that America's two most inspired and respected citizens, George Washington and Benjamin Franklin, sat in council with them, and vigorously promoted the plan, the entire Convention might have ended before it began. With such foresight, Madison had worked tirelessly in the preceding months to secure Washington's commitment to chair the Convention.

But even among those who were willing to discuss Madison's plan, the dissension and contention became almost unbearable, as the details of his plan were hammered out (the most contested detail being how state representation in the new national congress would be configured). If the delegates had only understood how significant this work would be, perhaps they would not have allowed, as Benjamin Franklin pointed out, the interference of "all their prejudices, their passions, their errors of opinion, their local interests, and their selfish views."[43] God's kingdom, after all, was the issue at stake. Perhaps it was Franklin himself who understood better than anyone else that something bigger than anything they could imagine was behind the Convention. It was the eighty-one-year-old Franklin who, after weeks of virtual stalemate in the Convention, humbly offered the last and only solution. In one of the most powerful improvised speeches of all time, Franklin declared:

> The small progress we have made after 4 or five weeks close attendance & continual reasonings with each other – our different sentiments on almost every question, several of the last producing as many noes as ays, is methinks a melancholy proof of the imperfection of the Human Understanding. We indeed seem to *feel* our own want of political wisdom, since we have been running about in search of it. We have gone back to ancient history for models of Government, and examined the different forms of those Republics which, having been formed with the seeds of their own dissolution, now no longer exist. And we have viewed Modern states all around Europe, but find none of their Constitutions suitable to our circumstances.

In this situation of this Assembly, groping as it were to find political truth, and scarce able to distinguish it when presented to us, how has it happened, Sir, that we have not hitherto once thought of *humbly applying to the Father of lights to illuminate our understandings?* In the beginning of the Contest with G. Britain, when we were sensible of danger, we had daily prayer in this room for the divine protection.—Our prayers, Sir, were heard, and they were graciously answered. All of us who were engaged in the struggle must have observed frequent instances of a Superintending providence in our favor. To that kind Providence we owe this happy opportunity in consulting in peace on the means of establishing our future national felicity. *And have we now forgotten that powerful friend? Or do we imagine we no longer need his assistance? I have lived, Sir, a long time, and the longer I live, the more convincing proofs I see of this truth—that God governs in the affairs of men.* And if a sparrow cannot fall to the ground without his notice, is it probable that an empire can rise without his aid? We have been assured, Sir, in the sacred writings, that "except the Lord build the House, they labour in vain that build it." I firmly believe this; and I also believe that without his concurring aid we shall succeed in this political building no better than the builders of Babel: We shall be divided by our little partial local interests; our projects will be confounded, and we ourselves shall become a reproach and bye word down to future ages. And what is worse, *mankind* may hereafter from this unfortunate instance, despair of establishing Governments by Human Wisdom and leave it to chance, war and conquest.

I therefore beg leave to move—that henceforth prayers imploring the assistance of Heaven, and its blessings on our deliberations, be held in this Assembly.[44]

Washington, as we have previously demonstrated, certainly understood Franklin's sentiments as well as anyone at the

Convention, and therefore would happily add his own endorsement to such counsel. Standing before the Convention, during a heated debate, Washington declared: "If to please the people, we offer what we ourselves disapprove, how can we afterward defend our work? Let us raise a standard to which the wise and honest can repair; *the event is in the hand of God!*" Historian John Fiske commented that *"from that moment* the mood in which [the delegates] worked caught something from the glorious spirit of Washington."[45] Indeed, the testimony from such spiritually powerful men seemed to change the entire environment, as a spirit of brotherhood and compromise, at last, entered Independence Hall. The Lord had intervened once again.

The key players at the Convention certainly felt the Lord's hand over them. For example, New York delegate Alexander Hamilton, the soon-to-be first secretary of the Treasury and, outside of Madison, the strongest proponent for a national government, would declare that the "sacred rights" placed within the Constitution were "written, as with a sunbeam, in the whole volume of human nature, by the hand of Divinity itself, and can never be erased or obscured by mortal powers."[46] Hamilton further stated, "I sincerely esteem it a system, which without the finger of God, never could have been suggested and agreed upon by such a diversity of interest."[47]

Another very active delegate at the Convention, Charles Pinckney, said the following of the Constitution: "When the great work was done and published, I was struck with amazement. Nothing less than the superintending Hand of Providence, that so miraculously carried us through the war...could have brought it about so complete, upon the whole."[48]

Madison, who was obviously closest to the entire Convention and its development, and whose notes are the preeminent source of the Convention's inter-workings, would, in the same spirit, declare the following:

It is impossible for the pious man not to recognize in it [the Constitution] a finger of that Almighty Hand which was so frequently extended to us in the critical stages of the evolution....No people ought to feel greater obligations to celebrate the goodness of the Great Disposer of events and the Destiny of Nations than the people of the United States....And to the same Divine Author of every good and perfect gift we are indebted for all those privileges and advantages, religious as well as civil, which are so richly enjoyed in this favored land.[49]

The congressional invoker of prayer, Ben Franklin, referenced the miracle of the final product when, just before putting his name to the document, he stated that it "astonishes me, Sir, to find this system approaching so near to perfection as it does." He further added, referring to the image of the sun carved into the back of Washington's chair, how painters find it difficult to distinguish between a rising and setting sun. "I have," he declared, "often in the course of the session...looked at that behind the President without being able to tell whether it was rising or setting. But now at length I have the happiness to know that is a rising and not a setting sun."[50] On another occasion, Franklin further revealed his deep spiritual feelings towards the Constitution, when he declared:

I have so much faith in the general government of the world by Providence, that I can hardly conceive a transaction [referring to the creation of the Constitution] of such momentous importance to the welfare of millions now existing, and to exist in the posterity of a great nation, should be suffered to pass without being in some degree influenced, guided, and governed by that omnipotent, omnipresent, and beneficial Ruler.[51]

Another witness at the Convention, Benjamin Rush, stated his belief that "the hand of God was employed in this work, [just] as...God had divided the Red Sea to give a passage to the children of Israel" or had delivered "the ten commandments on Mount Sinai!"[52] Rush's analogy was especially poignant considering that the very Constitution he was making reference to was a part of the American Covenant, which had its origins in ancient Israel.[53]

Even the commoners of America sensed the deeper meaning of their new Constitution. "I am convinced [the Constitution] is the Lord's doing, and it is marvelous in our eyes," said a Connecticut farmer, as quoted in his local paper soon after the Convention.[54] Other newspapers of the day captured a similar feeling, which swept the new nation. For example, the *Massachusetts Sentinel* projected a hope of what the Constitution should mean to the country: "May the GREAT IDEA fill the mind of every member of this honourable body that Heaven on this auspicious occasion favours America...."[55]

But the most credible testimony of all, concerning the Lord's hand over the Convention and the Constitution, stems from none other than the Lord Himself, who declared that it was He Himself who "established the Constitution of this land, by the hands of wise men whom I raised up unto this very purpose" (D&C 101:80). "Therefore, I, the Lord, justify you and your brethren of my church, in befriending that law which is the constitutional law of the land" (D&C 98:6). The Prophet Joseph expounded on this revelation, teaching that "the Constitution of the United States is a glorious standard;"

> it is founded in the wisdom of God. It is a heavenly banner; it is to all those who are privileged with the sweets of liberty, like the cooling shades and refreshing waters of a great rock in a thirsty and weary land. It is like a great tree under whose branches men from every clime can be shielded by from the burning rays of the sun.[56]

Then, in an almost startling indication of the apparent level at which he held the Constitution, the Prophet Joseph bore the following testimony:

> We say that God is true; *that the constitution is true*; that the
> Bible is true; that the Book of Mormon is true; that the
> Book of Covenants is true; that Christ is true; that the
> ministering of angles sent forth from God are true, and that
> we know that we have an house made with hands eternal
> in the heavens, whose builder and maker is God.[57]

Based on the scriptures, and on accounts and testimonies referenced throughout this chapter, it is clear that the Lord created the Constitution as part of His national covenant with America. It is also clear that He raised up inspired American Covenant-makers to deliver this Constitution to the world. All this He did for a wise and eternal purpose. And thus, the American Covenant was strengthened once more under God.

ENDNOTES

[1] Kenneth W. Thompson, ed, *Constitutionalism: Founding and Future*, Volume I (Lanham, University Press of America, 1989), viii. The entire seven volume study is entitled The Miller Center Bicentennial Series on Constitutionalism, and is produced by the University of Virginia's Miller Center of Public Affairs. The volumes, published by the same publisher listed above, include the titles *The U.S. Constitution and the Constitutions of Asia, The U.S. Constitution and Constitutionalism in Africa, Constitutionalism and Human Rights: America, Poland and France,* and *The U.S. Constitution and the Constitutions of Latin America.*

[2] Dallin H. Oaks, "Religious Freedom is at Risk," speech given at BYU Idaho, as reported in *Church News*, Week Ending October 17, 2009, 6.

[3] Ezra Taft Benson, "The Lord's Base of Operations." Talk given at the 132nd Annual General Conference of the Church of Jesus Christ of Latter-Day-Saints, 8 April. *The Improvement Era* 65, no.6 (1962): 454-56.

[4] Thomas Jefferson (1786), as quoted in John Ferling, *Adams vs. Jefferson* (New York: Oxford University Press, 2004), 33.

[5] David Pigott, "What We Hold So Dear," *Prelude to the Restoration* (Salt Lake City, Deseret Book, 2004), 149-150.

[6] Pigott, 148.

[7] Vicki-Jo Anderson, *The Other Eminent Men of Wilford Woodruff* (Cottonwood: Zichron Historical Institute, 1994), preface.

[8] David Whitchurch, "Thomas Bilney, A Prelude to the Restoration," *Prelude to the Restoration* (Salt Lake City: Deseret Book, 2004), 253-254.

[9] Paul Kengor, *God and Ronald Reagan* (New York: Regan Books, 2004), 147.

[10] Tad Callister, *The Inevitable Apostasy and the Promised Restoration* (Salt Lake City: Deseret Book, 2006), Chapter 17.

[11] Pigott, 151.

[12] Linda Monk, *The Words We Live By* (New York: Stonesong Press, 2000), 128.

[13] See Volume I, Chapters 5 and 8.

[14] Michael Novak, *On Two Wings: Humble Faith and Common Sense at the American Founding* (San Francisco: Encounter Books, 2002), 52.

[15] Steven Waldman, *Founding Faith: Politics, Providence and the Birth of Religious Freedom in America* (New York: Random House, 2008), 173.

[16] Waldman, *Founding Faith*, 52-53.

[17] Waldman, *Founding Faith*, 136, 173.

[18] Waldman, *Founding Faith*, 173-4.

[19] Waldman, *Founding Faith*, 49.

[20] Waldman, *Founding Faith*, xvi.

[21] Joseph Smith History 1:9, from The Pearl of Great Price. 1986. Salt Lake City: The Church of Jesus Christ of Latter-day Saints.

[22] John Ferling, *Adams vs Jefferson* (New York: Oxford University Press, 2004), 43.

[23] Milton Cummings and David Wise, *Democracy Under Pressure*, 9th edition (Belmont: Wadsworth Publishing, 2003), 38.

[24] Cummings and Wise, 38.

[25] Waldman, *Founding Faith*, xvi.

[26] Novak, *On Two Wings*, 52.

[27] John C. Mcollister, *God and the Oval Office* (Nashville: W Publishing Group, 2005), 24.

[28] Waldman, 114.

[29] Novak, *On Two Wings*, 53.

[30] Waldman, 114-115.

[31] Waldman, 119-123; McCollister, 25.

[32] Madison, as quoted in Waldman, 106.

[33] Waldman, 124-125; full transcript available at *Library of Virginia*, www.lva.virginia.gov/whatwedo/k12/bor/vsrftext.htm.

[34] As quoted from Virginia Statute for Religious Freedom, available at *Library of Virginia*, www.lva.virginia.gov/whatwedo/k12/bor/vsrftext.htm.

[35] Waldman,124.

[36] John Noonan, *The Lustre of Our Country: The American Experience of Religious Freedom* (California: University of California, Berkeley, 1998), 4.

[37] William Bennett, *America: The Last Best Hope,* Vol. I (Nashville: Thomas Nelson, 2006), 130.

[38] Novak, *On Two Wings*, 53.

[39] Waldman, 138-9.

[40] Waldman, 155.

[41] Bennett, *America, The Last Best Hope*, Vol.I, 130.

[42] Linda Monk, *The Words We Live By* (New York: Hyperion, 2003), 119.

[43] Benjamin Franklin, as quoted in Dallin H. Oaks, "The Divinely Inspired Constitution," Ensign, Feb. 1992, 68.

[44] Benjamin Franklin, as quoted in William J. Bennett, *The Spirit of America* (New York: Simon and Schuster, 1997), 384-385.

[45] John Fiske, *The Critical Period of American History*: 1783-1789 (Boston and New York: Houghton, Mifflin &Co., 1898), 231-232, emphasis added.

[46] Novak, Michael, and Jana Novak, *Washington's God* (New York: Basic Books, 2006), 3.

[47] Alexander Hamilton, as quoted in Paul L. Ford, *Essays on the Constitution of the United States*, 1892, 251-2; and quoted in Ezra Taft Benson, *"Our Divine Constitution, "Ensign*, Nov. 1987, 5-6.

[48] Paul L. Ford, 251-2; and quoted in Ezra Taft Benson, *"Our Divine Constitution, "Ensign*, Nov. 1987, 5-6.

[49] James Madison, as quoted in James D. Richardson, *A Compilation of the Messages and Papers of the Presidents* (Washington D.C.: by Authority of Congress, 1899), Vol. I, March 4, 1815, 561; also available at www.americandestiny.com.

[50] Walter Isaacson, *Benjamin Franklin, An American Life* (New York: Simon and Schuster, 2003), 457-459.

[51] Ben Franklin, as quoted in Jon Meacham, *American Gospel: God, the Founding Fathers, and the Making of a Nation* (New York: Random House, 2006), 88.

[52] Benjamin Rush, as quoted in Meacham, *American Gospel*, 91.

[53] Refer to Volume I, Chapter 2 of this book.

[54] Meacham, *American Gospel*, 99-100.

[55] Meacham, *American Gospel,* 94.

[56] Joseph Smith, as quoted in Bruce R. McConkie, *Mormon Doctrine* (Salt Lake City: Bookcraft, 1995), 160.

[57] McConkie, *Mormon Doctrine*, 160 (emphasis added).

The Constitution (original)
Displayed at the U.S. National Archives

The Constitution As Covenant

*The constitution came forth to prepare the way for
the restoration of the gospel, the fulfilling of the
covenants God made with ancient Israel, and the
organization of the Church and Kingdom of God
on earth in the last days.*

—Elder Bruce R. McConkie

Thus far we have demonstrated why and how the Lord inspired the creation of the Constitution. However, up until now we have only pointed out bits and pieces of what it actually says, particularly in the context of its mandate to further the Lord's work. Based on the testimonies from founders, prophets, and the Lord Himself, the spiritual offerings of the Constitution must certainly be significant. So what does it say? What are the blessings and safeguards within the document responsible for soliciting such powerful endorsements? How does it fulfill the most profound mission of providing and protecting the *moral agency* necessary for progression unto eternal life, and why did the Lord declare that it contained "holy principles" (see D&C 101:77-80)? These questions will be answered in the pages below, as we come to see how the Constitution is nothing less than an extension and representation of the American Covenant. In fact, so united are the two that the most prominent blessings of the Constitution are the same American Covenant blessings of *liberty, protection,* and *prosperity.*

The skeptic might argue that things like liberty, protection, and prosperity are the goals of any government, and therefore their existence in the Constitution is not exceptional. However, it must be understood that during the time of the Founders, these constitutional goals were not sought (for the most part) by other governments of the world. Indeed, the governments of the world were not striving very hard to make these blessings available to their citizenry. The idea was new and revolutionary.

But more than being unique ideals, these blessings were directly connected to ancient prophecy concerning latter-day America. For these specific blessings, which the Founders sought after and included in their Constitution, were the *exact* blessings designated by God in the Old Testament for Joseph's American posterity in the latter-days. They were also the *exact* blessings that were prophesied by Book of Mormon prophets for latter-day America.[1] This certainly makes their existence in the Constitution something exceptional. It makes the Constitution a fulfillment of prophecy. Recall that in the history of mankind, less than five-percent of God's children ever reaped the blessings of freedom—so few enjoyed the necessary foundation to receive the fullness of the gospel.[2] It is no wonder the ancients received a vision of latter-day America—even that nation which would usher in unprecedented freedoms in preparation for the Dispensation of the Fullness of Times. Of such is the importance of the Constitution.

More remarkable still is the fact that the Founders *intentionally* sought and received these blessings; for the covenant was, as Jeremiah prophesied, "written in their hearts" (Jeremiah 31:33; see Volume I, Chapter 2, for how we know this prophecy applies to latter-day American Covenant-makers). It is a testimony of who they were and of the covenant they knew and loved. The prophet Nephi, who saw them in vision, thought it was significant that these Founders came to latter-day America with "a book [that]

34

...was carried forth among them." This book—the Bible—contained, according to Nephi, "the covenants of the Lord, which he hath made unto the house of Israel" (see 1 Nephi 13:20-23). It contained the national covenant, which the Founders needed, sought, and clearly applied to their Constitution. The connection they felt to these covenants of the House of Israel was so strong that they regularly invoked the national covenant through their authority as the "New Israel," which name they consistently assumed (see Volume I).

That the Founders took seriously their connection to this Biblical covenant, particularly in relation to their building the nation and its Constitution, is evidenced in the findings of a 1973 study directed by political scientist Donald Lutz. Dr. Lutz and his team set out to evaluate everything published in America during the time of nation-building (between 1760 and 1805). They sought to settle the long-standing debate about which of the Enlightenment writers most influenced the creation of America. (Was it Montesquieu? Locke? Hume? Hobbes? Or perhaps it was the more ancient writers, such as Plutarch or Cicero.) The answer stunned them all. It was, overwhelmingly, the writers of the Biblical covenant.[3]

Further connecting the Constitution and its blessings to the covenant is the manner in which the Constitution came into being. For, as the Founders themselves readily admitted, these constitutional blessings were not sought after and achieved in a vacuum. They emerged as the fruit of a history overwhelmingly characterized by a miraculous connection to God and covenant. We have seen this (largely in Volume I) through analyzing the truth behind the discovery and settlement of the land, through detailing the history behind the Revolution, and through examining the creation of the Constitution. And now, we will see this once more through exploring the content of the Constitution. Such powerful things should not be trivialized. Let us make no mistake: The Constitution is a direct fulfillment of ancient American Covenant prophecy. In fact, the Constitution is nothing less than the American Covenant codified in the land!

We will begin our discussion of the Constitution's content by detailing the American Covenant blessings found within the document, and then we will outline the American Covenant obligations associated with the document. These obligations, as we shall see, are (fittingly) the same obligations of the American Covenant, as detailed in the Old Testament and the Book of Mormon. As we see that the Constitution does, in fact, carry with it the covenant blessings and obligations of the national covenant (and this is in addition to the many other scriptural and miraculous elements surrounding it, as mentioned above), it will open our eyes to the profound nature of the document. More than just a political paper, it becomes a spiritual text, derived from the Almighty for His eternal purposes.

However, before launching into this discussion, we should note that the mere existence of divine and holy principles within the document did not mean the new nation would necessarily apply them all immediately, or apply them all correctly. As will be pointed out in later chapters, many of these constitutional principles would unfortunately take years—and at times would require blood, sweat, and tears—to fully develop and become the powerful blessings they were intended to be. Notwithstanding America's inability to always apply them in the real world, however, these principles and blessings always had a firm foundation in the Constitution.

Covenant Blessings in the Constitution

In analyzing the great blessings found in the Constitution, we will begin with those outlined in the Preamble.

> *We the People of the United States, in Order to form a more perfect Union, establish Justice, insure domestic Tranquility, provide for the common defense, promote the general Welfare, and secure the Blessings of Liberty to ourselves and our*

Posterity, do ordain and establish this Constitution of the United States of America.

Surely, the Preamble should inspire confidence in any person (including Latter-day Saints) or organization (including Christ's restored church) desiring to live and prosper unmolested. After all, what else is needed for such progression other than *justice, tranquility, defense, welfare,* and *liberty?* These blessings make fertile ground for man's agency and thus for his eternal salvation.

The main body of the Constitution then proceeds to describe how such lofty goals, set forth in the Preamble, are to be obtained. It describes how the new national government will work to eradicate the social ills that obstruct *justice, tranquility, welfare,* and *the blessings of liberty.* First, it explains how it will create public policy through the legislative branch (Article I). Second, it explains how it will enforce this policy through the executive branch (Article II). And third, it explains how it will check the validity of government action through an independent judicial branch (Article III). Subsequent articles include, among other things, certain ground-rules for how states will interact with the federal government, how amendments will be added, and how general ratification of the Constitution will be conducted. The Constitution is rounded out with a list of very specific rights—known as amendments—held by the people, which the government, in administering its duties, is obligated to respect.

Yet the Constitution says so much more than just that. And so, in an effort to present the fullness of the Constitution and to reveal its direct connection to the American Covenant, we will now analyze its content by exploring eight of its most inspired principles.

Bill of Rights

The Amendments to the Constitution secure moral agency for both individuals and for private institutions, such as the Church. They guarantee the right to express ourselves freely through word and press (vital to the missionary effort); to gather with those we choose (essential for church and temple meetings/ordinances to be safeguarded); to be secure against unreasonable searches and seizures; to be free from arrest without probable cause; to have access, if needed, to an impartial jury; and to not be deprived of life, liberty, and property without due process of law. It is easy to imagine the many ways Satan could influence the fight against agency and Christ's church if such protections did not exist (or, as was the case with the first generation of the Church, if these protections were not properly enforced). But with the existence and proper enforcement of such rights, how could God's work be stopped?

It is perhaps the following clause in the First Amendment, authored by Madison himself, that does more than any of the others to secure God's work on the earth: "Congress shall make no law respecting an establishment of religion, or prohibiting the free exercise thereof." Such freedom of religion would be paramount for the Restoration.

Though we will discuss this matter further in later chapters, it is important to note that many secularists today try to interpret this amendment's *Establishment Clause*—that there shall not be a government "establishment of religion"—as meaning that God should have no place in government. However, this entire book (including Volume I) provides irrefutable evidence that the Founders believed God had (and has) a very prominent place in government. *The Establishment Clause* certainly does not take God out of American government, but instead, it rightfully prohibits the government from supporting and favoring (i.e. *establishing*) a particular religious domination. Religious favoritism could, and probably would, eventually be used as a political tool of oppression. And so, in a manner quite the opposite of detracting from God's place in America, this amendment secures our ability to worship Him freely and unobstructed, thus allowing truth to be restored and practiced. It truly delivers the *moral agency* God intended the Constitution to provide (see D&C 101: 78-80).

God certainly reserved this land and government as the designated venue for such blessings unto salvation. For these few constitutional words concerning religious freedom are, as Judge John Noonan put it, an "American invention."* He continued, "How foolish it would be to let a false modesty...obscure the originality."[4] It was, in fact, of singular origination. But then again, it was, after all, designed for a singular purpose. As former justice of the Utah Supreme Court and now apostle, Dallin Oaks, explained: "Without the free exercise of religion, America could not have served as the host nation for the restoration of the gospel."[5]

So significant was the principle behind this amendment that the Lord specifically endorsed it in the Doctrine and Covenants, which states that "governments were instituted of God for the benefit of man," and that such governments should "secure to each individual the free exercise of conscience," and not "mingle religious influence with civil government" (D&C 134: 2; 9). In at least this instance, it can safely be said that this constitutional clause is nothing short of scriptural. Of course, that God inspired and endorsed this governing principle should be of no surprise. He commanded the same under His ancient American Covenant, as reflected in the Nephite and Jaredite governments (see Alma 30: 7-11 and Ether 7:24). He did so for the same glorious purpose of saving souls.

Not only is the divine nature of these constitutional rights corroborated by the Book of Mormon, but also by that most famous national covenant—and precursor to the American Covenant—even that covenant of ancient Israel. For ancient Israel also applied such rights of liberty and protection to its citizens for the same reason the American Covenant offers these blessings today.[6]

---

* It should be noted that certain state governments had codified religious freedom prior to this national Bill of Rights. The most famous of these was the Virginia Statute for Religious Freedom, authored by Thomas Jefferson. However, and as future events would reflect, a national amendment supporting religious freedom, which naturally would cover *all* the states, was an inspired necessity.

Checks, Balances, and Separation of Powers

The religion clause is not the only political safeguard the Lord revealed to both His ancient and modern Americans. To the ancients of the Book of Mormon, He revealed the divine system of government whereby government officers would be checked and balanced, "higher judges" by "lower judges" and "lower judges" by "higher judges," so that "if these people commit sins and iniquities they shall be answered upon their own heads" (Mosiah 29: 29-30). Indeed, the people could not blame the government for forcing them to act a certain way, as under this system, individual moral agency was far from the reach of oppressive hands. By protecting personal freedom and accountability, God's children could be tested and thus could progress towards eternal life.

To His modern Americans, the Lord revealed the same system, even a system with separate branches of government, all with independent powers, and all with clear constitutional responsibilities to keep the others in check. With such a system, one government entity could not easily misapply the inspired constitutional principles, such as the First Amendment, without receiving some form of legal censure from the others. For example, the legislative branch can withhold funds from, or even impeach, a wicked executive and/or judicial branch; the executive branch can veto wicked laws from the legislative branch; and the judicial branch can censure both for violating their constitutional trusts and duties. These are just a few of the built-in checks and balances.

Perhaps the adversary could reasonably gain influence over a segment of the government (say, one of the branches, or at least a part of one). But under this American system, in order for the adversary to have any prolonged negative effect on the political foundations that support God's purposes, he would have to gain all three branches—a highly improbable proposition. Therefore, the whole system is virtually safe for moral agency and for God's church and kingdom to reside in confidence. As the lawyer, political scientist, and apostle, J. Reuben Clark, commented: "It is this union of independence and dependence of these branches—legislative, executive and judicial—...that constitutes the marvelous genius of this unrivaled document....As I see it, it was here that the divine inspiration came. It was truly a miracle."[7]

A Living Document

In 1816, Thomas Jefferson wrote: "Some men look at constitutions with sanctimonious reverence, and deem them like the ark of the covenant, too sacred to be touched."

> They ascribe to men of the preceding age a wisdom more than human, and suppose what they did to be beyond amendment. I knew that age well; I belonged to it, and labored with it...But I know also, that laws and institutions must go hand in hand with the progress of the human mind. As that becomes more developed, more enlightened, as new discoveries are made, new truths disclosed, and manners and opinions change with the change in circumstances, institutions must advance also.[8]

The Constitution is a living document, open to change when such change is needed. Just as the Lord provides continuous revelation to His prophets for His church, so He can provide the same to His American Covenant-makers for His chosen land.

Even from the beginning, there were constitutional problems that needed attention. For example, the Constitution placed restrictions on certain segments of the population (based on sex and race), denying many Americans full participation in government. Furthermore, Article IV, Section 2 required that all states return fugitive slaves to their original owners. Thankfully, an inspired amendment process was also established (defined in Article V), whereby such immoralities could be purged, as they eventually were. As will be detailed in the next chapter, this constitutional purging would become indispensable for the Lord's ultimate purposes with America.

Though inspired, this amendment process would need to be kept in check in order to prevent an over-zealous (and perhaps less than virtuous) mere majority from getting carried away. And so, the Lord inspired a built-in protection (also defined in Article V) for minorities—for His Saints would almost always be counted among such minorities. Elder J. Reuben Clark explained:

> The Constitution was framed in order to protect minorities...In order that the minorities might be protected in the matter of amendments under our Constitution, the Lord required that the amendments should be made only through the operation of very large majorities—two-thirds for action in the Senate [and the House], and three-fourths as among the states. This is the inspired, prescribed order.[9]

A First Republic

A republican form of government is one whereby the people, through their representatives, remain the source of all power. As Abraham Lincoln put it, it is a "government of the people, by the people and for the people."[10] We live in a day when most nations enjoy such a political structure, and often we take for granted the uniqueness of this concept. But, as few may know, America was the first to implement a republic over such a vast expanse of land and over such a great population. It is true that republican systems had been tried with relative success in small geographical and demographical regions, such as in Greek city-states and in Swiss cantons. But nothing like what the Constitution presented had ever been successfully attempted and achieved.[11]

The Old World, even the ever-enduring monarchists, mocked the new document, saying that the people could never govern themselves and that eventually anarchy would emerge and that the states would become separate nations unto themselves. They argued that it was only under strict central control, where power was derived not from people, but from kings and rulers, that the needed discipline for stability could be found. This, critics continued, was necessary, even at the cost of personal freedoms, including freedom of religion. Satan most certainly had blinded the Old World.

But God, through His grace and power during the Revolution, had eradicated such oppressive ideals of governance from America, paving the way for a new order abounding in popular sovereignty. And why was this so important to the Lord? Why inspire the discovery and settlement of a new land, followed by war and nation building, just to establish this principle? The Book Mormon illuminates the answer, when it commands us to "choose you by the voice of this people, judges, that ye may be judged according to the laws which have been given you…which are correct, and which were given them by the hand of the Lord."

> Now it is not common that the voice of the people desireth anything contrary to that which is right; but it is common for the lesser part of the people to desire that which is not right; therefore this shall ye observe and make it your law —to do your business by the voice of the people (Mosiah 29:25-26).

Through the Book of Mormon, the Lord reveals to us today that inspired laws (like the First Amendment), which were given to the United States, even by "the hand of the Lord," are well protected as long as the majority of the people remain in power—as long as the United States remains a true republic.

The idea that such governmental ideas are of divine origin is further corroborated by the fact that the national covenant of ancient Israel—equally inspired by God for the same eternal purposes— included these very principles. The people of ancient Israel were instructed under their national covenant to elect leaders and pass new laws under the common consent of the people (see 2 Samuel 2:4; 1 Chronicles 29:22; for the dismissal of a leader, see 2 Chronicles

10:16; for the people's approval and consent of new legislation, see Exodus 19:8).[12] Furthermore, the government under Moses boasted of separate branches of government.[13] In 1788, while the Constitution was being debated for final ratification, colonial leaders, including Samuel Langdon and Benjamin Franklin, pointed out how God, through the Constitution, had resurrected the government of ancient Israel in latter-day America.[14] And indeed He had.

Federalism

The Constitution introduces us to a strange concept we call *federalism*, which is defined as the division of powers between state and federal governments. Today we abide by two separate books of law (state and federal). We elect officers to represent us in two separate capital cities (state and federal). And we pay taxes to two separate jurisdictions (both state and federal). Though we all accept it, as it's the only thing we have ever known, we must acknowledge its uniqueness. We live, work, and play under two governments. And while there is both dependence and independence between them, each functions with its own legislative, executive, and judicial branches. Elder Dallin Oaks stated that this system which "divides government powers between the nation and the various states…was unprecedented in theory or practice." Some may even argue that it is so unusual that only an outside source—like Heaven itself—could have brought it forth to the minds of men. Yet despite its uniqueness, it would prove to be the best form of government to date, and the nations of the world would even begin to emulate it. Though structurally strange, Elder Oaks concluded that federalism was (and is) most certainly an "inspired fundamental."[15]

The inspiration behind *federalism* represents itself in the many blessings it produces. For example, two separate governments facilitate a powerful diffusion of power. While state and local governments can focus on local issues, which they are most familiar with and can best deal with (like crime or pollution in its cities), the federal government can handle broader issues that affect every state (like interstate commerce or foreign policy). Additionally, with two separate concentrations of power, the people have two sources to appeal to. This limits the ability of one single government from becoming overbearing and perhaps oppressive—a common occurrence in the annals of history. This is particularly important for the preservation of liberty and moral agency.

It is worth noting here that the idea of political protection emerging out of both small, concentrated governmental groups, and simultaneously out of a larger, more centralized governmental head, stems from divine origin. For Moses revealed to ancient Israel that such should be the case for its early governmental structure under its respective national covenant (see Exodus 18: 13-26). Such connections reinforce the Constitution as an embodiment of the national covenant, which God has repeatedly designed and delivered for His gospel purposes.

In terms of the U.S. Constitution, one of the most inspired dimensions to this division of powers is the existence of the Tenth Amendment, which ensures that the state governments focus on what they do best and that the federal government focuses on what it does best. "The powers not delegated to the United States by the Constitution," declares the amendment, "are reserved to the States respectively, or to the people." Here is yet one more check and balance built in for our protection.

However, as beneficial as the Tenth Amendment is, too many have over-interpreted it to mean that unless the Constitution specifically grants a power to the federal government, then the federal government has no right to intervene at all. The truth is, the Constitution tempers the Tenth Amendment with certain provision— for example, the Preamble and the Necessary and Proper Clause in Article I, Section 8—which allows federal intervention on any number of issues, when it is "necessary and proper" in fulfilling the federal government's mandate. An overly strict interpretation of the Tenth Amendment, for example, would have barred the very necessary intervention of the federal government on issues of equal and civil rights. For the Constitution does not explicitly state (only implies) that a national Civil Rights Act, so essential to the protection of the Church, could be created. But in the cause of civil rights (like in other cases) the individual states were either unable to help or were themselves the problem, which left no other hope than federal intervention. The Constitution's Preamble, after all, mandates the federal government to "secure the blessings of liberty," and civil rights legislation was certainly "necessary and proper" to fulfill that mandate. It was ultimately federal intervention mandated by this federal legislation that arguably saved both the Union and the restored gospel. (This will be explained in later chapters.)

Certainly we must respect and support the Tenth Amendment and states' rights. Through the years there has, no doubt, been abuses of federal authority over the states. However, as we seek the appropriate balance between the two governments, we must also recognize the many divine fruits that the federal government has produced.

A New Promise of Liberty

As established throughout this book, one of the most significant blessings of the American Covenant is *liberty*. Throughout Volume I of this book, we saw how this governmental principle is defined in the scriptures as a powerful element of the American Covenant. These scriptural references include, but are not limited to, the Book of Mormon prophecies that *latter-day* Americans would be "set up as a free people by the power of the Father" (3 Nephi 21:4), that these Americans were destined to be "free from bondage" (Ether 2:12), and that "it shall be a land of liberty unto them" (2 Nephi 1:7). We also witnessed, in Volume I, how these promises and scriptures also applied to ancient American Israelites (e.g. the Nephites). We also examined how that most prominent national covenant with ancient Israel promised this same *liberty* (see Exodus 14, Leviticus 26), and provided as its basic tenet: "Proclaim liberty throughout all the land unto all the inhabitants thereof" (Leviticus 25:10). We have further witnessed how Jacob of old prophesied that his descendants (through Joseph) in latter-day America would also have claim on such political freedom (JST Genesis 48:11). And finally, we have made clear, throughout this two-volume book, that all these blessings were given as a support for God's kingdom on the earth.[16]

If such prophecies and promises are really part of the American Covenant, and if the Constitution really is a reflection of this covenant, it follows that an abundance of *liberty*—even a new promise of *liberty*—would be offered through the Constitution. And it would be offered in a way to support God's kingdom and gospel purposes. We have already outlined some of these principles of *liberty* found within the Constitution, such as the republican form of government it promotes and the First Amendment protections it offers. Yet there is infinitely more. For the Constitution came equipped with a new and powerful formula for preserving *liberty*.

From the beginning, the inspired Madison knew just how his proposed constitution would supply this formula for *liberty*, and he would strive to teach this formula to his fellow countrymen. After Madison's plan for a new national government was submitted to the congressional delegates, they immediately balked. They argued that conventional wisdom suggested that small governments, like those of the individual states, were better because they were closer to the needs of the people and permitted more accessibility to government. Though Madison would not have dreamed of scrapping state governments for those very reasons, he did turn conventional wisdom on its head regarding governments that govern over a small geographic/demographic region versus larger governments that govern over vast geographic/demographic regions. Madison stood and boldly asserted that it is only through a comprehensive, national government that a fullness of liberty could ever be secured. The delegates listened in awe as Madison expounded on this new and peculiar political theory.

He explained that every nation on earth was composed of interested parties seeking power over one another. These parties, which he referred to as "factions," are in constant political battle— the rich against the poor, the religionists against the atheists, industrialists against agriculturalists, races against races, families against families, and so on. In a small government, argued Madison, where a lesser population allows for only a limited amount of these "warring factions," there is naturally less political competition. Reduced competition facilitates an eventual victor, who would likely take the political reigns, and rule tyrannically over the remaining minority factions. The delegates could not deny that, in each of their states, they had seen such a faction do just that, and they had seen the corruption, the dishonesty, and the subversion of minority rights that inevitably follows.

But under this *new* system, Madison explained, there would exist a second government, and one which would include not just the citizenry from one state, but from all states—indeed, from the entire nation. This would naturally open up the playing field for vast participation, allowing so many factions into the political battle, that it would be next to impossible for one or a few oppressive factions to dominate the stage.

Hence, Madison sought to maximize the Book of Mormon principle of popular sovereignty by creating the largest possible arena where the inspired "voice of the people" could come together to thwart the minions of Satan that seek to oppress. Again, "it is not common that the voice of the people desireth anything contrary to that which is right" (Mosiah 29:26). This same aforementioned Book of Mormon scripture further justifies Madison's reasoning by identifying these few dangerous factions as "the lesser part of the people," then declaring that "it is common for the lesser part of the people to desire that which is not right"(Mosiah 29:26). But under a new *national* system, the "voice of the people" would simply swallow up the wicked "lesser part."

An analogy of this concept (popular with my political science students) is as follows. Imagine there are two separate mile-long running races being prepared side by side. Participants are filing in at the two starting lines to run for the reward of political power and control. As the racers are waiting for the gun to sound, you notice that only five people have lined up for one of the races, while five thousand have lined up for the other. Then you look up and notice a familiar face walking up to register for one of the two races. Complete with high riding jogging shorts and an unsightly tank top, you realize that it is none other than Adolf Hitler! The registrar turns to you and asks, "Which race should I put him in?"

Madison would argue that, under a system of small governments, where only smaller races exist, Hitler must, by necessity, be given the chance to run in the race of five, thus allowing him a good chance to win, wrest control, and then dominate. However, with Madison's concept of an additional and larger national government (where more people create a larger running race) you would have the opportunity to place him in the race of five thousand. This would limit his chances of success and help to secure liberty for the others. "The influence of factious leaders," Madison wrote in his now-famous Federalist No.10, "may kindle a flame within their particular states [the race of five], but will be unable to spread a general conflagration through the other states [the race of five thousand]."

> A religious sect [for example] may degenerate into a political faction in part of the Confederacy but the variety of sects dispersed over the entire face of it, must secure the national Councils against any danger from that source... [and thus], improper or wicked project[s] will be less apt to pervade the whole body of the Union.[17]

We readily observe this principle played out in places like Saddam Hussein's Iraq. Here was a street thug from the streets of Tikrit who became a bodyguard to the then dictator. He convinced his boss to make him a general over the military. Then he just started threatening or killing people above him, including the officials who had promoted him. He eventually became the evil tyrant. There was no process that required the voice of the people, no strong *national councils* to keep such evil in check, and no divine constitutional order that would have held such evil at bay. Saddam represented a faction unto himself with few, if any, serious competing or warring factions to rebuff him. He ran in the race of five, and simply won the race by killing or exiling his few fellow racers. Because of this, Satan has, until recently, been ruling that country for decades—thwarting moral agency and prohibiting gospel principles and ordinances.

Now that we understand Madison's general intention, how do we connect his plan specifically to the Lord's purposes? Or, in other words, if this political theory is in furtherance of God's work, how might we theoretically apply it to gospel restoration, stability, and growth?

Let us suppose, hypothetically, that within the fifty United States, there exists one state which is highly biased against the relatively large population of red-haired individuals, which, notwithstanding their numbers, make up a minority of the citizenry of that state. The laws in this particular state go so far as to persecute the red-head, prohibiting his ability to freely pursue his righteous desires and goals. Though they have relentlessly appealed to their local governments for help, it is all in vain—for nobody in that state likes the red-head. But what if there were another source of power that could come and liberate the red-heads, even a source which included people from outside this particular state. What if there were a national venue—an all-encompassing "voice of the people"— that included every individual from the other forty-nine states. Certainly among so many added participants in this new forum, there would exist other red-haired individuals and/or sympathizers of the red-head cause who would be willing to act in behalf of their oppressed countrymen. These rescuers would have the *national* legislative, executive and judicial branches from which to launch their campaign to secure liberty and justice for all.

Let's pause for a moment, jump back into the real world, and ask ourselves, *Where, after all, did black Americans in the South find* *their defenders? Was it from the state and local governments in South Carolina? Mississippi? Tennessee? Georgia?* No, in every case—from Civil War on through the Civil Rights Act—the reprieve and redress came from the federal or national level, just as Madison might have predicted. As will be detailed in the next chapters, there is no clearer or dramatic validation of Madison's inspired theory than the heaven-induced progress made in black America's fight for equal rights.*

Now, returning to the hypothetical example, let us suppose now that the red-headed people we are talking about throughout the United States happen to be God-seekers, even truth-seekers searching for eternal life. Suppose they are chosen disciples and prophets of God, who were raised in the latter-days to receive, organize, and carry Christ's restored gospel to all the world. Thanks to Mr. Madison's Constitution, standing at last in their midst, waving the sword of truth and justice over their local oppressors, is

---

* In spite of this constitutional theory and tool which would one day help free black Americans, several criticisms have been launched over the years at the Constitution's seemingly reprehensible compromises over slavery and blacks in general. For example, some argue that the Northern non-slave states should never have confederated with the Southern states unless they gave up slavery. Others love to argue that the original Constitution is clearly racist because it only counts blacks as three-fifths of a person. However, there is another side to both these stories. First, the Northern states knew that constitutionally abolishing slavery meant that the Southern states would not join the Union. If this had happened, blacks in the South would have lost a constitutional and societal connection to the Northern factions, who would eventually intervene and help them gain freedom. Keeping the South connected to the North, even at the cost of compromise, was absolutely essential for eventual black liberation. Furthermore, the Northern states at least were able to get the South to agree to constitutionally halt the slave trade after twenty years—not wholly effective, but it lit a dim light at the end of a dark tunnel. And second, it was the abolitionists in Congress who promoted counting slaves as three-fifths of a person (and they would have counted them as less than that if it had been possible). Why? Because members of the lower house of Congress are determined by proportional representation, which means that the more people that were counted in the South, the more representation (or the more delegates) the South would have had in Congress. Had the black man been counted as a "whole" person, there would have been even more racist delegates who would do all they could to maintain slavery. Simply put, the Three-Fifths clause in the Constitution actually assisted efforts toward abolition.

this new national government. It is a new government armed with the God-given laws pertaining to our inalienable rights, ensured by the protections of checks and balances, and tempered by the reasonable and enlightened voice of *all* the people of the land. Now we see, through even more finely focused lenses, why the Lord inspired a federal/national government under the Constitution. It was, after all, His work and His glory that hung in the balance.

A New Promise of Protection

Another American Covenant promise discussed throughout this book is that of *protection*. In Volume I, we saw how the Lord established and reestablished this blessing. We saw the covenant promise to the Nephites when the Lord declared that they "shall never be brought down into captivity" (2 Nephi 1:7) and that He would "fortify this land against all other nations" (2 Nephi 10:12). We further established that these blessings were equally applicable to latter-day Americans under their own national covenant. Additionally, we outlined how ancient Israel enjoyed this *protection* from its enemies while under the covenant, and we detailed how Abraham's grandson, Jacob, prophesied that this blessing would be bestowed upon his heirs of latter-day America—that their "bow [would] ab[i]de in strength, and the arms of his hands [would be] made strong by the hands of the mighty God of Jacob" (Genesis 49:24). Such scriptural references demonstrate that the American Covenant blessing of *protection* existed anciently and was foreordained for, and offered to, latter-day America so that wicked oppressors under the adversary could not rock the political foundations that supported God's kingdom on earth.[18]

If such a blessing is truly part of the American Covenant, and if the Constitution is a reflection of this covenant, then it follows that the Constitution should offer this very *protection* required to support God's kingdom.

The most direct demonstration of this constitutionally-derived *protection* is found in Article I, Sections 8 and 10 of the document, which charge Congress to raise and support armies, to deal with foreign nations, to declare war, to raise funds, to coin money, and to regulate foreign commerce. Article II, Section 2 charges the president to run the military and foreign policy apparatus (among other things). Before these governing principles existed, the individual states were alone, for the most part, in dealing with any economic or physical threat from overseas. Even if one state decided to place its militias at its borders to stop such threats, all the enemy had to do was approach the land through a neighboring state, which had no such militia. The borders of the United States were thus completely porous to whatever or whoever might do the nation harm. Such weak defenses would make the nation vulnerable to a vast array of threats.

Imagine, for example, if foreign invaders entered the nation in droves and took over the many small state governments and changed the laws to limit personal or religious freedom. Or imagine if these invaders entered the land and posed a constant threat to our infrastructure and physical safety, thus driving us to a constant state of survival. This would severely limit our time, resources, and wherewithal to develop and maintain our individual pursuits of happiness, to include our ability to worship God and build His kingdom on the earth. Satan, knowing what America would mean for the gospel in the latter-days, would certainly make America a target and thus influence such invaders. How would the United States, then, ever become the promised land that the Lord designed it to be, complete with freedom unto eternal salvation? Fortunately, the Lord would preemptively attack such wickedness by creating the Constitution, which offered the *protection* required for His work and glory in the latter-days.

For example, the constitutional principles listed above encouraged the creation of a new national military, which set the stage for what would become the largest and most powerful physical force on the planet—a force which would fight and defeat the enemies of freedom and liberty both at home and abroad. Without the Constitution, we would be limited to individual state militias, which could never have resembled the massive national military presence we see today and could never have stopped evil in its tracks as the U.S. military has done. It is certainly no coincidence that the very land where God restored His gospel is also the very land whose military budget (as a percentage of its GDP) is more than double that of any other nation in the industrial world. Furthermore, the military budget of the United States in real numbers is greater than all the other major powers combined, and represents approximately half of what the entire rest of the world spends on defense.[19]

Another one of the very first applications of the Constitution was the creation of the United States Customs Service (1789), which protected the nation and its borders, and set the stage for other law enforcement entities. In fact, the modern day Department of Homeland Security (DHS)—to include its many agencies and offices like Homeland Security Investigations, Customs and Border Protection (of which the Border Patrol is a part) and the Coast Guard —is directly derived from this constitutional mandate. Today, DHS directly targets those people and things that could threaten our indispensable freedoms.

And finally, these constitutional principles direct that the national government maintain a foreign policy, which has allowed the nation to secure its interests overseas and preemptively identify foreign threats. We see the application of these principles through the creation and maintenance of powerful intelligence agencies (like the CIA) and effective diplomatic machines, to include embassies around the world dedicated to protecting the United States and influencing freedom everywhere.

It is easy to see that without these protections of the Constitution, our most cherished institutions and ideals, to include freedom of thought and religion, would be threatened by those who, under the influence of the Evil One, would attack and oppress man and thus separate him from gospel principles and ordinances. The

Constitution indeed does much to provide the *protection* of the American Covenant, thus fulfilling the ancient prophecies of this covenant and making the United States a safe-haven for the gospel.

A New Promise of Prosperity

If a nation is to serve God under a national covenant, prosperity and wealth are necessary blessings. They provide the strong military, law enforcement, diplomatic, and other resources necessary to maintain those freedoms that allow God's children to access His restored gospel. Furthermore, economic prosperity brings wealth to tithe payers, which directly increases the Church's financial resources, thus allowing—among other things—churches and temples to be built throughout the world.

This is why (as explained in Volume I) God blessed His earlier national covenant-makers in ancient Israel with such *prosperity*—even with a land "flowing with milk and honey" (Exodus 3:8). It similarly explains why He did the same for His ancient American Covenant-makers, repeatedly expressing to them that "Inasmuch as ye shall keep my commandments, ye shall prosper in the land" (2 Nephi 1:20). We further proved in these earlier chapters how such *prosperity* was to include economic success and was also intended for the latter-day American nation. We even showed how the ancient prophet, Jacob, prophesied that his latter-day American heirs through Joseph would, under the latter-day American Covenant, enjoy the "blessings of the deep that lieth under, blessings of the breasts and of the womb" (Genesis 45:25), and how Moses blessed this same posterity with the blessings of "precious fruits brought forth of the sun," and for "the chief things of the ancient mountains" (Deuteronomy 33:14-16). Indeed, through these and other scriptural examples, we have established that such blessings are clearly associated with the American Covenant and are intended for latter-day Americans, that God's purposes might be realized.[20]

And once again, if these are blessings of the American Covenant, and if this covenant is represented by the Constitution, then it follows that the Constitution would serve as a support and enabler for the realization of such blessings. And it does just that.

For example, Article I, Section 8 of the Constitution allows for the national government to tax and control money, which secures and maintains the capital market. This constitutional mandate further calls on the national government to foster growth through regulating trade. The Constitution also defines the rights to private property and includes specific protections of those rights. Finally, one of the greatest prosperity-inducing principles of the Constitution is its lack of overbearing regulations and controls. The document's relatively hands-off approach represents what history has proven to be the only true wealth-sustaining economic practice —free markets and capitalism. Indeed, one of America's greatest economic assets has less to do with what the Constitution says, and more to do with what it does *not* say. The Fifth Amendment even maintains protections against the temptation to reign in capitalism in exchange for schemes or policies involving radical redistribution of wealth.[21]

One of the earliest examples of how the application of these constitutional principles provided much needed wealth occurred shortly after the Constitution was implemented. With a national financial crises on the horizon (interest from Revolutionary War loans was piling up uncontrollably, and the states were unequipped to cobble together a financial solution), George Washington, the first president, pooled all the national resources available to him and assigned his Secretary of the Treasury, the brilliant Alexander Hamilton, to develop a plan. The plan, signed off by Washington himself, included the formation of a national bank, which fostered both domestic investment and growth. Perhaps more importantly, with domestic investments in the bank, the nation was able to service its foreign debt (which debt Hamilton wisely consolidated under the federal government). Hamilton utilized federal powers implied in the Constitution, as described above, to aid all the states and all the people.[22]*

Hamilton's plan not only enabled payments on national loans through the new banking system, but also federalized and standardized tariff schedules. He then created the U.S. Customs Service to collect those tariffs. In addition to resurrecting America's good credit, the monies produced under these constitutional programs allowed the country to conduct defense explorations of the West (such as the Lewis and Clark Expedition); to acquire lands (such as those obtained via the Louisiana Territory Purchase, which brought sacred lands like Jackson County and Adam-Ondi-Ahman in under America and her covenant); to facilitate infrastructure growth (like the Transcontinental Railroad); and to grow the military.[23]

The nation, complete with these new federally-based tools and a flourishing economy, continued to grow from that early point in American history. The economic success achieved by the U.S. system is obvious enough as to not require statistical proof. Notwithstanding, we will mention one interesting indicator here. Recently published data lists the wealthiest people that ever lived, beginning from our earliest recorded history. In order to level the playing field, the net worth of the many individuals is calculated and adapted relative to the historical value of commodities at the time in which they lived. The list goes as far back as kings and

---

* Many people interpreted (and still interpret) the Constitution in a way that would have prevented Hamilton from creating a national banking system among the many states. Critics of Hamilton cited the Tenth Amendment, and argued that since the Amendment states that unless the Constitution specifically charges the federal government with a responsibility, then the federal government must defer to the states. And, as the critics pointed out, nowhere in the Constitution does it specifically state that the national government can create a national bank. The issue was resolved in the case of *McCulloch vs. Maryland* (1819). The Supreme Court pointed out that Article I, Section 8 of the Constitution states that Congress may do whatever is "necessary and proper" in carrying out its responsibilities. In that one of these federal responsibilities was to secure economic stability in the nation, the Court ruled that the national bank was constitutional. Thanks to this decision, the bank stayed, which arguably saved the nation from becoming bankrupt.

pharaoh's who lived centuries ago. And yet, of the top seventy-five names listed, an astonishing forty-five were Americans who made their wealth in the United States of America.[24] Americans represent fully sixty-percent of the names on the list! And of course, the wealth made by these individuals reflects the vast amount of jobs created and further wealth generated by the entire nation under national capitalism. Indeed, among nations and history, America has been calculably blessed with *prosperity.*

Further proof that this national wealth was connected to God and his plan for the Restoration of the gospel is found in a study of economic prosperity conducted by economist Angus Madison. Madison concluded that the modern prosperity we see today in the world, to include everything from base wealth to advances in science, electronics, and transportation, began in one single year. That year was 1820. Commenting on the study, economist William Bernstein stated that "before that date [1820], growth was essentially nonexistent, and after, sustained and vigorous."[25] Is it just a coincidence that wealth drastically picked up in the middle of a pivotal year for the Restoration? Or was it all a part of God's plan to begin prospering His children in preparation for greater things on the horizon?

Again, that such *prosperity* directly fulfills ancient prophecies of the American Covenant, and that it does so through the Constitution, is abundantly clear. And that this covenant-based blessing of *prosperity*—along with its sister-blessings related above—has served and continues to serve the gospel purposes of the Lord, by supporting and sustaining His kingdom on the earth, is unquestionable.

Covenant Obligations of the Constitution

The American Covenant requires the American citizenry to "serve the God of the land" (Ether 2:12), and to "keep [His] commandments" (2 Nephi 1:20).[26] Only then will the blessings detailed above be delivered. If the Constitution is truly a reflection of the American Covenant, then it should promote these American Covenant obligations. And it does. Much has already been said in Volume I (and much more will be said throughout this volume) regarding our obligations under the American Covenant, in general. For now, however, we will simply verify and corroborate the idea that the *Constitution* incorporates these obligations.

The idea that the Constitution incorporates obligations should not be taken lightly. It should compel us to reexamine what the Constitution is. Instead of always asking what the Constitution is doing for us, it prompts us to ask what we are doing for it—what we are doing for the God who offered it to us. It helps us see it for the covenant it is, and it calls us to action.

One reason to believe the Constitution has been delivered to the people with covenant obligations attached to it, has to do with the fact that God Himself implied the notion. It was God who told us that He influenced the language of the Constitution (D&C 101: 78-80); and we know that God's communications to us are almost always issued as covenants, particularly when so many promised blessings—as with the Constitution—are involved. For, "I, the Lord am bound when ye do what I say; but when ye do not what I say, ye have no promise" (D&C 82:10). Could we possibly expect God to release those most profound blessings of the Constitution, to include *liberty, protection,* and *prosperity,* if we do not live worthily as a nation to receive them?

But, in addition to applying our understanding of how God generally releases such blessings through a covenant relationship, there are even more specific reasons to believe the Constitution has been given as a covenant with real obligations. We will now discuss some of them.

God Commands Adherence to the Constitution

Why does God command that we read and study the scriptures? Because His law and covenant are found therein. He wants us to know the law and covenant, that we might live it and gain eternal life. Him asking us to study the scriptures, then, is a manifestation of our covenant relationship with Him. It is Him telling us that action is required—that His instructions must be learned and applied—for the blessings to be received. If the Constitution is covenant, than we should expect to see the same pattern. We should expect to see God commanding that we read and study it. If He does, then this commandment, likewise, would manifest a covenant relationship between Him and the nation, whose Constitution it is. It would mean that He requires us to know something about what this document sets out to do, that we might apply the instructions therein and thus activate the blessings He wants to give us. Indeed, it would imply that the Constitution's covenant blessings are not free, but are contingent upon us, as a nation, to do something—to act on it. In other words, it reflects a clear covenant relationship.

So, does God command us to read the Constitution, thus confirming that document as a covenant? He *does*. The First Presidency and other modern apostles have repeatedly asked us and all Americans to study the Constitution and adhere to—and oppose infringements of—its principles.[27] The First Presidency even issued a booklet about the importance of the Constitution. According to the First Presidency, they did this so that families might teach the Constitution in their homes, that "family members may feel the divine significance of the Constitution in their minds and hearts."[28]

Additionally, the scriptures tell us the "law of the land which is constitutional, supporting that principle of freedom...is justifiable before me." Therefore, says the Lord, "concerning the laws of the land, it is my will that my people should observe to do all things whatsoever I command them" (D&C 98:4-5). Further, the Lord commands us to "obtain a knowledge of history, and of countries, and of kingdoms, of laws of God and man, and all this for the salvation of Zion" (D&C 93:53). Thus saith the Lord, "Let no man break the laws of the land" (D&C 58:21). And finally, He asks us to elect "honest men and wise men" into government positions (D&C 98:10).

Why would God thus command us if He required no action relative to the law and the Constitution? And remember, the Lord is not asking us to study and adhere to just any document, but it is a document that He Himself claimed to have "established" (see D&C 101:80). This certainly makes His instruction for our adherence to it all the more credible.

God's words and instructions relative to the Constitution certainly help substantiate the Constitution as a covenant. We can easily envision how this covenant relationship might play out. For instance, as we follow God's command and learn what the First Amendment is, and what rules have been provided to ensure it is maintained, then we, as a citizenry, will elect officials who we know understand these constitutional principles and rules. These leaders will, in turn, act in a manner that secures these promised blessings to our benefit. It is almost a self-fulfilling blessing of the covenant. But it is contingent upon our willingness to listen to the Lord, and *know* the Constitution. It is contingent upon us seeing the Constitution for what it is—a covenant, whose blessings become activated upon our willingness to adhere to God's counsel.

The Constitution Maintains Natural Covenant Obligations

The political formula on which the Constitution is based naturally requires obligations to God. For, in light of how the Constitution lays out the governmental system, the only way for the people to access the constitutional blessings listed above, is for the people to live righteously. We see this idea manifested in at least two different ways.

First, as the Constitution allows vast freedoms to the people, it becomes incumbent upon people to apply virtue to their own lives, thus keeping their passions and desires in check. Only then can the government trust the citizenry to take care of itself, without having to apply oppressive controls to keep order. But if the people fail to keep themselves in check, the government is pressed to intervene, which might help to temporarily bridle the wicked, but ultimately represents a general decline in the ability to acquire the blessings of the Constitution, particularly the blessings of *liberty* and *prosperity*. For once governments begin to grow in influence, too often they grow so large that they begin to impede and stomp out individual and economic freedoms.

We see real world examples of how this works today. For example, almost twenty years ago the Soviet Union fell. Consequently, Russia began introducing principles of democracy, which led to the restored gospel entering that land for the first time. With the U.S. Constitution as its model, the Russian people sought to gain the same constitutional blessings Americans enjoy. However, after more than a century of virtual godlessness in that region (true freedom of religion was no hallmark of the Soviet Union), the people were ill-equipped to keep themselves in check. With the blessings of freedom came the opportunity to choose good or evil. Sadly, without moral and religious traditions, too many citizens chose the latter. Widespread organized crime, government corruption, and the most immoral acts against the innocent have thrived in that country since that time. (I have personally been involved in combating some of these most wicked elements.)

With the inability of the Russian people, in the aggregate, to apply morality and religion to their daily lives, the Russian government could not trust the people. Consequently, the government felt compelled to crack down on their freedoms. By 2005, President Vladimir Putin had taken over private industries, rolled back the free elections of Russia's regional governors, and nationalized the media.[29] The gospel still remains, but the country is on the slippery slope that threatens *liberty, protection,* and *prosperity*

—even those supports for gospel nourishment. However, had the people adopted national morality, such may not have been the case.

America has struggled with the same problem. The economic hardships we see today have undoubtedly been produced by years of selfishness and greed in the aggregate. Such national immorality has led to national panic, which has led to an increase in governmental control of private affairs. (For example, the government has recently sought to take over more private enterprises and to start making more healthcare decisions for us.) We are witnessing the beginning of that slippery slope that threatens our own constitutional blessings of the American Covenant. Had we stayed spiritually worthy, and bridled our passions and appetites, we would not currently be wondering if our most cherished rights are under attack from within.

We would do well to adhere to the advice of the 18th Century British statesmen—and one of the aforementioned recipients of the St. George Temple miracle—Edmund Burke, who warned, "Men are qualified for civil liberty in exact proportion to their disposition to put moral chains on their appetites."[30] Our own Benjamin Franklin echoed the same warning, declaring: "Only a virtuous people are capable of freedom. As nations become corrupt and vicious, they have more need for masters." This is precisely why Franklin promoted the idea that "nothing is more important for the public weal, than to form and train up youth in wisdom and virtue."[31] Finally, a latter-day apostle of the Lord, D. Todd Christofferson, recently added his own testimony of the same, warning us that national disobedience will compel the government to enforce more rules, which "leads to diminished freedom for everyone." Elder Christofferson continued, "In the memorable phrase of Bishop Fulton J. Sheen, 'We would not accept the yoke of Christ; so we now must tremble at the yoke of Caesar.'"[32]

Considering how much the Lord values covenants, and considering that the Lord inspired the Constitution, this system, based on a built-in covenant relationship, is certainly no coincidence. The Lord designed the Constitution to require national worthiness in order for His children to access and maintain the constitutional/covenant blessings.

The second natural, or built-in, covenant system we see in the Constitution is connected to the idea that in order for us, the people, to administer the government in a way that allows us to access the covenant blessings, we must first be worthy to receive proper inspiration from on high. In that the Constitution mandates that the people create their own government and decide how to manage and maintain it, the people are naturally placed in a position of great trust; for the constitutional blessings of the covenant will only be activated to the extent that the people appropriately apply the constitutional principles found within the Constitution. The Constitution allows much wiggle room for proper and righteous interpretation or, conversely, for inappropriate and wicked misinterpretation. The Constitution, as noted above, may even be amended (for good or evil). As such, a sound understanding of what the Constitution says (which, as noted above, God has commanded us to gain), while necessary, is not always enough. In an ever-changing world, with new problems and issues arising daily, we must be able to appropriately apply the Constitution to things it has never been applied to before—things the Founders did not necessarily foresee. In this quest, we the people, in whom all political power lies, need divine inspiration. For, a healthy dosage of divine inspiration is the only sure way to properly apply and amend the Constitution and thereby activate and preserve the covenant blessings.

The only way to receive such inspiration, of course, is to live righteously as individuals, that as a nation we might be clean and worthy receptacles of this needed inspiration. And so we see, once again, how the design of the Constitution promotes a natural covenant relationship with the Almighty. Indeed, the covenant pattern again applies—blessings come only as we live righteously under God.

An example of this naturally built-in covenant may be illustrated as follows. Though we read about the mandated principles of free markets in the Constitution, suppose we lose inspiration and begin to misapply the Constitution by allowing the government to dominate commerce or other basic sectors of the economy. We would risk losing our American Covenant blessings. For not only could this lead to a loss of *prosperity*, but it could also set a bad precedent that places the government on a path to power, thus threatening individual and national *liberty*. Other constitutional rules that need to be followed for the same reasons include those regulating taxation, foreign policy, federalism, and most importantly, the freedom of religion.

On the other hand, if we maintain our righteousness, and thus continue to merit inspiration, we will correctly apply the grand constitutional principles and put them into righteous practice. Then, the Restoration will not fail. So prophesied Thomas Jefferson in one of the most astonishing statements of any Founding Father. In the sacred year of 1820, Jefferson declared: "If the freedom of religion, guaranteed us by the law in *theory*, can ever rise in *practice* under overbearing inquisition of public opinion, truth will prevail...and the genuine doctrines of Jesus, so long perverted by his pseudo-priests, will again be *restored* to their original purity."[33] And so we see how important it is under the American Covenant to righteously adhere to constitutional principles by applying and interpreting these principles under the inspiration of Heaven. Only then will righteous *theories* be put into *practice*, thus fulfilling the purposes of God.

Let us ever remember that the Spirit, which reveals the truth of all things, cannot dwell in unclean places. Therefore, disobedience among the American citizenry will limit the Spirit and will eventually breed faulty political notions about how things should be. If such notions become accepted by the majority and find their way into policy, the covenant blessings will be diminished.

Thankfully, the Constitution was formulated in such a way that if the majority of us adhere to the Light of Christ, which is given to all men, then we will have the necessary cumulative inspiration to ensure that constitutional *theories* are put into *practice*. Also, the

Constitution's checks and balances protect us from any given executive who has lost his spiritual grip, or from any handful of unenlightened congressmen or judges. But if the majority of the citizenry loses its spirituality and virtue, the American Covenant (the Constitution) is breached, and the entire divinely mandated American mission is jeopardized. Simply put, it is a covenant relationship that needs to be respected.

Again, considering how much the Lord values covenants, and considering that the Lord inspired the Constitution, this system of natural, built-in covenants was no accident. We must do His will to receive His blessings.

The Founders Taught of Constitutional Obligations Under God

Based on the above analysis, it is clear that national worthiness is a requirement for the covenant blessings of the Constitution to be activated. The Founders understood this and, as such, taught and admonished the people to live worthily.

James Madison, who was closer to the Constitution than anyone, seemed to comprehend the importance of having a virtuous citizenry in order to reap the blessings of the Constitution. Madison said that there had to be "sufficient virtue among men for self government," and that "republican government presupposes the existence of these qualities in a higher degree than any other."[34] Madison once asked rhetorically: "Is there no virtue among us? If there be not, we are in a wretched situation. No theoretical checks, no form of government, can render us secure. To suppose that any form of government will secure liberty or happiness without the virtue of the people, is a chimerical idea."[35]

John Adams also understood and promoted this concept, declaring, "We have no government armed with power capable of contending with human passions and unbridled by morality and religion...*Our Constitution was made only for a moral and religious people*. It is wholly inadequate to the government of any other."[36]

Adams further noted that "Statesmen...may plan and speculate for liberty, but it is religion and morality alone, which can establish the principles upon which freedom can securely stand....Religion and virtue are the only foundations...of all free governments."[37] Adams was resolute in his belief that, as he himself stated, "the highest story of the American Revolution is this: It connected in one indissoluble bond the principles of civil government with the principles of Christianity."[38]

Speaking on the same theme, Samuel Adams added his own testimony, declaring:

> A general dissolution of principles and manners [meaning standards of morality] will more surely overthrow the liberties of America then the whole force of the common enemy. While the people are virtuous, they cannot be subdued; but once they lose their virtue, they will be ready to surrender their liberties to the first external or internal invader....[But] if virtue and knowledge are diffused among the people, they will never be enslaved. This will be their great security.[39]

In short, without good people in America who adhere to God's commandments, the Constitution, and the covenant blessings it guarantees, will naturally suffer. This divinely designed program built into the Constitution, and the words of the prominent Founders, certainly lend support to the idea that the Constitution is a covenant whose strength lies in righteous adherence to God.

Of course, those inspired leaders quoted above were not the only Founders who believed there was a covenant relationship connected to the Constitution. After all, if it is true that the Constitution was given as part of the national covenant, complete with obligations necessary to access its blessings under God, then surely we would expect that the other Founders who created the document might have known something about it as well. And they did.

In a 1989 *Ensign* article entitled, "Seeing the Constitution as Covenant," law professor Lynn Wardle explains that the "U.S. Constitution arose largely from beliefs about the importance of making covenants with God and one another....For colonial Americans, the concept of covenant was not limited just to religious doctrines; it was central to their view of the world and God's workings in it."[40] Historians have commented that these early settlers knew that "God had always dealt with his children by covenant...It was not only individual, between each man and God; it was also public, respecting the formation of churches and civil government."[41] As Wardle points out, it was due to this "covenant theology" abounding in America that the delegates "incorporated their belief in covenant-making into the Constitution of the United States."[42]

To confirm that the Founders truly understood the importance of seeing the new government as a covenant with God, we need only turn to the Northwest Ordinance. This law and ordinance was not only written and issued by the same Congress that created and signed the Constitution, but it was written and issued in 1787—the same year of the Constitution. Article III of the document states, "Religion, morality and knowledge being necessary to good government and the happiness of mankind, schools and the means of education shall forever be encouraged."[43] In that the Congress felt compelled to write this law in the year it issued the Constitution, shows how clear their understanding was that their new Constitution would be best served by a righteous, God fearing citizenry.

Additionally, many of the state constitutions, which had already been created, or which were in the process of being created or amended, also included a healthy dosage of this same covenant theology.[44]

But why should such an idea surprise us? After all, we have seen (in Volume I) how this same concept was reflected in the words and deeds of America's first settlers, who clearly came to this land under what they understood to be a covenant with God. They set up governing documents, such as the Mayflower Compact, which codified this belief. We further saw this covenant theology expressed and acted out among the revolutionary generation, which called on God in the halls of Congress and which invoked His name upon the battlefields of war. That generation truly expressed an understanding that God would make them victorious if they but lived worthy of their national covenant. If we have learned anything from this study, it is that Americans have historically understood that "righteousness exalteth a nation; but sin is a reproach to any people" (Proverbs 14:34). Why would the Founders have applied the covenant theology to all aspects of their national life and not to their first national compact?

The most pressing evidence that they did incorporate covenant theology into the Constitution is that, from the day the Constitution was activated, the Founders and leaders of the new nation could not express enough how its success would be contingent upon righteous adherence to God's commands. We have already quoted many of these Founders, who believed and taught this principle. However, above all the rest, there was one who led this call to the covenant under the Constitution—George Washington. We have already seen Washington's relentless invocations of the national covenant throughout the days of the Revolution (see Volume I). Then, as first president of the nation, we see how he continued right where he left off. In his first address to the nation as president, and the first since the Constitution came into force, Washington directly appealed to the American Covenant, calling upon his fellow citizens to live in righteousness so as to merit the constitutional blessings. Toward the beginning of his message, given April 30, 1798, Washington stated:

> It would be peculiarly improper to omit in this first official act my fervent supplications to that Almighty Being who rules over the universe, who presides in the councils of nations, and whose providential aids can supply every

human defect, that His benediction may consecrate to the liberties and happiness of the people of the United States.

He then expounded upon the covenant relationship between the American people and the Lord, paying special attention to the people's covenant obligations:

> No people can be bound to acknowledge and adore the Invisible Hand, which conducts the affairs of men more than those of the United States. Every step by which they have advanced to the character of an independent nation, seems to have been distinguished by some token of providential agency. And in the important revolution just accomplished in the system of their United Government, the tranquil deliberations and voluntary consent of so many distinct communities, from which the event has resulted, cannot be compared with the means by which most Governments have been established, without some return of pious gratitude along with an humble anticipation of the future blessings which the past seem to presage. These reflections, arising out of the present crisis, have forced themselves too strongly on my mind to be suppressed.

Washington then applied the covenant more directly to "the great constitutional charter under which [we] are assembled" by stating that "the foundation of our national policy will be laid in the pure and immutable principles of private morality..."

> I dwell on this prospect with every satisfaction which an ardent love for my country can inspire, since there is no truth more thoroughly established than that there exists in the economy and course of nature an indissoluble union between virtue and happiness; between duty and advantage; between genuine maxims of an honest and magnanimous policy and the solid rewards of public prosperity and felicity; since we ought to be no less

persuaded that the propitious smiles of Heaven, can never be expected on a nation that disregards the eternal rules of order and right, which Heaven itself has ordained."[45]

Washington ended this first presidential inaugural speech with one final reminder that the Constitution is a covenant with God, declaring that

the benign Parent of the Human Race...has been pleased to favor the American people with...dispositions for deciding with unparalleled unanimity on a form of government for the security of their union and the advancement of their happiness, so His divine blessing may be equally conspicuous in the enlarged views, the temperate consultations, and the wise measures on which the success of this Government must depend.[46]

Months later, Washington (reflecting over the entire American Revolution, which had recently culminated with the Constitution), reaffirmed his position on the American Covenant when he expressed his belief that "[t]he man must be bad indeed who can look upon the events of the American Revolution without feeling the warmest gratitude towards the great Author of the Universe. And it is my earnest prayer that we may so conduct ourselves as to merit a continuance of those blessings with which we have hitherto been favored."[47]

Weeks later, and again reaffirming his position that this new government under the Constitution was firmly based on a covenant with God, Washington would deliver an even more detailed and powerful testimony of this concept. Upon comparing this speech against what we have learned, particularly from the scriptures, regarding the American Covenant, with its blessings and obligations, his chosen words are phenomenal. For, a close study of it reveals that Washington is telling the nation that it must obey God, be grateful to Him, repent, and implore His help; and in return it will receive the constitutional and covenant blessings of *liberty, protection,* and *prosperity*. Declared Washington:

> Whereas it is the duty of all nations to acknowledge the providence of Almighty God, to *obey His will*, to *be grateful* for His benefits, and *humbly implore His protection* and favor....Now therefore I do recommend and assign Thursday the 26th day of November next to be devoted by the People of these States to the Service of that great and glorious Being, who is the beneficent Author of all the good that was, that is, or that will be. That we may then all unite in rendering unto Him our sincere and humble thanks, for His kind care and *protection* of the People of this country previous to their becoming a Nation, for the single and manifold mercies, and the favorable interpositions of His providence, which we experienced in the course and conclusion of the late war, for the great degree of tranquility, union, *and plenty*, which we have enjoyed, for the peaceable and rational manner in which we have been enabled *to establish constitutions of government for our safety and happiness*, and particularly *the national One now lately instituted, for the civil and religious liberty with which we are blessed*, and the means we have of acquiring and diffusing useful knowledge and in general for all the great and various favors which He hath been pleased to confer upon us.

> And also that we may then unite in most humbly *offering our prayers* and supplications to the Great Lord and Ruler of Nations, and beseech Him *to pardon our national and other transgressions, to enable us all, whether in public or private stations, to render our national government a blessing to all people*, by constantly being a government of wise, just and constitutional laws, discreetly and faithfully executed and obeyed, *to protect* and guide...all Nations...and to bless them with good government, peace and accord. To *promote the knowledge and practice of true religion*...and generally to

grant unto all Mankind such a degree of *temporal prosperity* as he alone knows to be best.[48]

Washington knew what the nation needed to do in order to activate its blessings. He knew, as the scriptures declare, that "in nothing doth man offend God, or against none is his wrath kindled, save those who confess not his hand in all things, and obey not his commandment" (D&C 59:21). If that were not enough to confirm his invocation of the American Covenant in this speech, he specifically called out, by name, the American Covenant blessings we might gain through our national worthiness: *liberty, protection,* and *prosperity,* even those building blocks required for a fullness of agency unto eternal salvation. Furthermore, he clearly understood, and thus stated, that this covenant relationship was sealed up by the Constitution "now lately instituted, for the civil and religious liberty with which we are blessed." His understanding of the covenant ran so deep that he even declared that—in addition to religious liberty— the ultimate fruit of this constitutional endeavor would be "the knowledge and practice of true religion." It is simply astounding.

Eight years later, upon delivering his final address to the nation, before stepping down from the presidency, he would make one final plea for Americans to live up to the American Covenant. "Of all the dispositions and habits which lead to political prosperity," declared Washington, "religion and morality are indispensable supports. In vain would that man claim the tribute of patriotism who should labor to subvert these great pillars of happiness."[49]

Washington's repeated calls to the American Covenant— from the battlefields of war to the establishment and application of our Constitution—should not be lost on any one of us. We would do well as a nation to follow his council today. For, if we do not adhere to Him who Washington called "the Great Lord and Ruler of Nations," even Him who the Book of Mormon affirms is the "God of the Land [America]" (Ether 2:12), then we will—per the running theme of this book—fall into breach of covenant, lose the blessings of the Constitution, forfeit our liberties, and ultimately self-destruct. (See 1 Nephi. 14:6-7; 3 Nephi. 16:8-16; Mormon 5:19-24).

The Title of Liberty Supports U.S. Constitutional Obligations Under God

History does repeat itself; the United States Constitution was not the first contract under an American Covenant. Nor was Washington the first American general who acknowledged such a contract as being associated with God's covenant, and who thus called his people to adhere to it for the blessings of Heaven. "And now it came to pass that when Moroni, who was the chief commander of the armies of the Nephites, had heard of these dissensions [described, within the context of the scriptural narrative, as threats to liberty and free agency]...he rent his coat; and took a piece thereof, and wrote upon it—

> In memory of our God, our religion, and freedom, and our peace, our wives, and our children....And therefore at this time Moroni prayed that the cause of the Christians, and the freedom of the land might be favored....And he said: Surely God shall not suffer that we...shall be trodden down and destroyed, until we bring it upon our own transgressions. And when Moroni had said these words, he went forth among the people, waving the rent part of the garment in the air, that all might see the writing which he had written upon the rent part, and crying with a loud voice, saying: Behold whosoever will maintain this title upon the land, let them come forth in the strength of the Lord, and enter into a covenant that they will maintain their rights, and their religion, that the Lord God may bless them. And it came to pass that when Moroni had proclaimed these words, behold, the people came running together...rending their garments in token, or as a covenant, that they would not forsake the Lord their God;

or in other words, if they should transgress the commandments of God...the Lord should rend them even as they had rent their garment (Alma 46: 11-21).

The creation of the Title of Liberty was, in fact, a political document. It served as a call to the national covenant between God and the people, that their freedom, and thus their ability to worship God unto salvation, might be preserved. This was not a priesthood covenant—for it was open to all the people of the nation and was administered not by a prophet, but by a national leader. Indeed, the Title of Liberty was, like the Constitution, a written standard inspired of the Lord to preserve the promised national blessings necessary for God's ultimate work to flourish.

Moroni understood this so well that (as described a few verses after his above-cited call

Captain Moroni and the Title of Liberty

to the covenant) he reminded the people of the divine origin of this national covenant and Title of Liberty. Said Moroni, "Yea, let us preserve our liberty as a remnant of Joseph; yea, let us remember the words of Jacob before his death" (Alma 46: 24). These words of Jacob are those we have reviewed at length, particularly in Volume I of this book. They are the words of Jacob's blessing given to Joseph (and his posterity) just before Jacob's death. It was that blessing that promised *liberty, protection,* and *prosperity* under the American Covenant, as documented in Genesis 49. Moroni possessed these scriptures. He understood that as a Nephite descendant of Joseph, he had the authority to administer this covenant. He knew that his countrymen, of the same bloodline, were likewise authorized to enter this covenant. And so the covenant was rightfully and legitimately renewed through the Title of Liberty.

What does this have to do with the United States of America? Throughout this book, particularly in Volume I, we have shown how this foreseen and ancient American Covenant was to be restored in latter-day America. It only makes sense that just as Moroni had *his* Title of Liberty to represent this covenant and its obligations in ancient America, the founding leaders of modern America would have *their* Title of Liberty (the Constitution) to serve the same purpose. Furthermore, Washington, like Moroni, even made an indirect reference to the same Old Testament promises of the American Covenant and attached them to the Constitution and to the building of the modern American nation. For (as explained in Volume I, Chapter 2), as Washington expounded upon the American Covenant in his first inaugural address, he swore his oath and covenant to God and America by placing his hand on a Bible opened to Genesis 49—even the ancient American Covenant text as given by Jacob to Joseph of old.[50] Furthermore, we have seen how Washington repeatedly told his people the same thing that Moroni told the Nephites: that they must remember God, adore Him, thank Him, and keep His commandments in order to receive the national blessings promised of old and found within the Constitution—even the blessings of *liberty, protection,* and *prosperity.*

Indeed, we see that the Book of Mormon commands us under the American Covenant to "serve the God of the land" (Ether 2:12), and "keep my commandments...[that] ye shall prosper in the land" (2 Nephi 1:20), that the people might enjoy the blessings of *liberty, protection,* and *prosperity.** And so, when we add to this knowledge the fact that a Book of Mormon commander invoked

---

* These are but a sample of the many commandments given by the Lord in reference to living worthily of the national blessings of *liberty, protection* and *prosperity.* Refer to Volume I of this book. See also 1 Nephi 13:16, 2 Nephi 10:10-12, 1 Nephi 13:15, 1 Nephi 13:19, 1 Nephi 22:7, (and there are many others).

these blessings through a formal charge to live up to these obligations, and did so through a national written standard, and then when we see a modern American commander, who we know was "raised up" by God (D&C 101:80) invoke the same national covenant, detailing the same blessings and obligations to his people, and we see him do so under a similar written national standard, over which God placed His own stamp of approval (D&C 101:80), the parallel is obvious. The Constitution is a covenant, like unto the Title of Liberty, complete with national obligations and blessings.

Conclusion

In these last two chapters we have outlined how and why God and the inspired Founders of America chose to adopt what would become the U.S. Constitution. We have seen God's hand in the Constitution's creation, and we have seen His national covenant blessings and obligations embedded into the Constitution's content. Thus, we have confirmed yet again a powerful fulfillment of the ancient prophecies surrounding the American Covenant and the divine purposes this covenant represents.

With this historical foundation, perhaps we can more fully comprehend why it is that the Lord directly put His stamp of approval upon the Constitution, and revealed that He had raised up wise men specifically for its creation (D&C 101: 80; 98:6). Perhaps we see more clearly why covenant leaders like Washington took their public oaths, to protect and defend the Constitution, by placing their left hand upon the bible, their right arm being raised and forming a square. Perhaps now we can also more fully appreciate the fact that the Prophet Joseph Smith included, in the first temple dedicatory prayer offered in this dispensation, a plea to God that "those principles, which were so honorably and nobly defended, namely the Constitution of our land, be established forever" (D&C 109: 54). We have already detailed earlier the magnificent endorsements that Joseph gave the Constitution (calling it a "heavenly banner" and likening it to scripture). The fact that he included it once more in this first temple dedicatory prayer only reinforces his sensitivity to its importance. It was, after all, those constitutional principles that protected (and protect today) the very existence of temples.

This truth was not lost on Joseph's successor, Brigham Young, who issued his own powerful endorsement:

> We believe that the Lord has been preparing that when he should bring forth his work, that, when the set time should fully come, there might be a place upon his footstool where sufficient liberty of conscience should exist, that his Saints might dwell in peace under the broad panalopy of constitutional law and equal rights.[51]

But perhaps the apostle, Elder Bruce R. McConkie, summed it up most directly when he declared the following:

> In the providences of the Almighty, the constitution of the United States was established to serve an even greater purpose than that of setting up a stable government under which freedoms would prevail. It was designed to do far more than guarantee the preservation of natural and inalienable rights to the American people. The constitution came forth to prepare the way for the restoration of the gospel, *the fulfilling of the covenants God made with ancient Israel*, and the organization of the Church and Kingdom of God on earth in the last days.[52]

In addition to laying out the heavenly purposes of the Constitution, Elder McConkie's above statement connects the Constitution to the "covenants God made with ancient Israel." This corroborates our constant claim, particularly throughout this chapter, that these ancient national covenants, stemming from both Old Testament and Book of Mormon prophets, were fulfilled in latter-day America.

Our own national monuments in Washington D.C. also remind us constantly of this powerful connection. It is no coincidence that engraved in bronze upon the floor of the entrance to the U.S. National Archives, which houses the original Constitution and the Declaration of Independence (which, as we affirmed in Volume I, was also part of the covenant), are the words of that most famous national covenant of old. The engraved words are the Ten Commandments.[53] This is a fitting memorial to the final resting place of the original Constitution.

The symbolism continues. Along with other religious imagery decorating the U.S. Supreme Court building (which houses the guardians of the Constitution), we again see prominent symbolism of the great and ancient national covenant. In no less than four locations in and around the building are depictions of Moses and the Ten Commandments (this imagery is at the center of the sculpture over the east portico of the building, on the bronze doors of the building, inside the courtroom itself, and engraved over the chair of the Chief Justice).[54] Similarly, perched upon the wall of Congress, overlooking the interior of the House chamber (where the Constitution is applied through lawmaking) is a large image of the Prophet Moses. Other ancient law-makers are depicted around the chamber as well, but all have their heads turned to Moses, who is the only full figured image and the only one that hangs directly in the middle of the room.[55] This is no coincidence. With our national covenant perspective, the significance of it all shines radiantly.

Furthermore, as seen throughout this two-volume book (particularly in this chapter), ancient scriptures, namely the Old Testament, and especially the Book of Mormon, also shine forth as stunning reminders of the ancient Israelite prophecies of latter-day America that have been fulfilled through the Constitution. Though for years many have mused over the abundance of political instructions and governmental commentary laced throughout these ancient scriptures—especially the Book of Mormon—the purpose of their existence has become clear. For these are the scriptures not only of the priesthood covenants unto salvation, but also of the national covenant that support them—even the American Covenant. And as we have seen the application of these scriptural-political instructions in the Constitution, we have yet another witness of the Constitution's greatness and divine nature under the covenant.

One of the most powerful witnesses to the spiritual power behind the Constitution is President Ezra Taft Benson. The fact that President Benson maintains the unique distinction of having held the highest offices in both the Church and the United States government makes him a powerful witness indeed. In an October 1987 General Conference address, President Benson expounded on the deeper meaning of the Constitution, declaring, "Our Father in Heaven planned the coming forth of the Founding Fathers and their form of government as the necessary great prologue to the restoration of the gospel."

> Recall what our Savior Jesus Christ said nearly two thousand years ago when He visited this promised land: "For it is wisdom in the father that they should be established in this land, and be set up as a free people by the power of the Father, that these things might come forth"(3 Ne.21:4). America, the land of liberty, was to be the Lord's latter-day base of operations for His restored church.[56]

It is no wonder that President Benson, on another occasion, testified that the "Constitution of the United States is a sacred document...its words are akin to the revelations of God."[57] Indeed they are, for this document's words are a covenant given by God for His work and glory in the latter-days.

As a final witness and reminder of the Constitution's grand place in the eternal designs of God, we return to that founder, James Madison—even the Father of the Constitution, who, under God, initiated this building block of the American Covenant. It was Madison's personal testimony that there is no happiness without virtue.[58] He declared that in our many worldly endeavors, we should not "neglect to have our names enrolled in the Annals of Heaven," and that we should season our lives with "a little Divinity now and then," which he said would make us "more precious than fine gold." Madison expressed the importance of "always keep[ing] the Ministry obliquely in View whatever your profession be," that we might always be prepared to become "fervent Advocates in the cause of Christ."[59] This is exactly what Madison was, particularly while playing his indispensable role in the creation of the Constitution. Even as an old and frail man at the age of seventy, he reiterated this testimony, stating that Christianity was the "best and purest religion."[60] He had certainly done his part in ensuring its development through establishing the political foundations that would support and protect it.

When Madison's life at last expired, and he crossed through the veil, a greater knowledge and testimony of this "best and purest religion" would likely be his, along with a greater understanding of what his actions in mortality had done for the development of this religion. For it is recorded in Church records that—pursuant to the grand vision of the Founders, received by Wilford Woodruff in the St. George Temple—James Madison's temple work was done. The work was simultaneously done for his wife, Dolley. It appears that together, they received Priesthood covenants administered by an apostle of God.[61]*

Madison and his fellow Founders surely comprehended that their ability to stand in the House of the Lord had been facilitated by the very Constitution they had created. For without the Constitution, the existence of this House of the Lord might not have been realized. The fact that Madison and his colleagues built this Constitution, then received a special invitation to stand on its back in order to reach those sacred places of God, where exaltation is made possible, leaves us with perhaps our greatest witness and reminder of the power of the Constitution as a covenant from God.

---

* Upon accepting the gospel in the Spirit World, it must have been gratifying for Dolley Madison to have remembered that, while in mortality, she had assisted in raising money for the then struggling and beleaguered Latter-day Saints. Refer to Michael K. Winder, *Presidents and Prophets*, 28.

All these things, including the above-outlined history of the Constitution, from its creation to its content, have truly borne witness of the principal argument of these last two chapters: that God inspired the Constitution as a divine tool of the American Covenant so that the foundations of His kingdom on the earth might be fortified and that His work and glory might roll forth. Based on all the contributing evidence provided above, it becomes clear that the Constitution holds the distinction of being perhaps the only governmental document in the history of the world with so many endorsements, approvals, and interventions derived directly from the hand of God. Let us never forget this fact, and let us never forget what the Lord has given us through this heaven-sent document.

Indeed, we have now witnessed the details of how God, knowing that Satan's war plan was to "destroy the agency of man" (see Revelation 12:7-8 and Moses 4:3-4), created a powerful defense. This divine defense was the Constitution, which God Himself declared represented "holy principles" that would counter Satan's efforts by preserving "moral agency"(see D&C 101:77-80). More specifically, God provided this defense by lacing, throughout the Constitution, the American Covenant promises of *liberty, protection,* and *prosperity.* If we live up to our obligations, also put forth in association with the Constitution, then a fullness of these blessings, and thus, a fullness of *moral agency,* will be ours. Then, our ability to access the principles and ordinances of the gospel unto eternal life will forever be secured.

Let us see the Constitution in this gospel light—let us see it as the covenant it is—that we might better adhere to it, sustain it, and promote it. Let it be an ensign to all God's children, both at home and abroad.

On September 17, 1787, after the delegates at the Constitutional Convention had sufficiently prepared their sacred document, they signed it. But, as Article VII of the Constitution required, the states would have to consider it individually, and ratify it for themselves before it could become the "Supreme Law of the Land" (Article VI). The debates abounded in state legislative houses for months upon months. Finally, enough states approved it and ratification was achieved. In light of what we now know concerning the eternal blessings that would flow out of this Constitution, it is quite fitting that the prominent founder, Benjamin Rush, after hearing of its ratification, declared: "I am as perfectly satisfied that the union of the states, in its form and adoption, is as much the work of divine providence as any of the miracles recorded in the old and new testament were the effects of a divine power. 'Tis done! We have become a nation."[62]

That the ratification and implementation of the Constitution was a work of Providence was not lost on President Ezra Taft Benson, who explained that "on April 6, 1789...the Constitution of the United States went into operation as the basic law of the United States when the Electoral College unanimously elected George Washington as the first president of the nation. This date [April 6], I believe, was not accidental."[63] As revealed in D&C 20:1, April 6 was also the date in 1830, which the Lord revealed as the day His restored church was to be established. President Benson only recognized the Lord's hand in connecting the founding date of the U.S. government with that of the Church because the two institutions are spiritually connected. They are connected by the covenant.

This connection is readily observed upon considering the Church's divine placement in American history. With the discovery, the settlement, the war, and now the national constitutional standard all finally completed—all under the American Covenant— the stage was at last set for the ultimate return of the saving principles and ordinances of the everlasting gospel. Indeed, within the short span of thirty years after the Constitution went into force (in just enough time for it to begin to congeal) the boy-prophet Joseph entered a grove of trees to ask his Heavenly Father a question.

ENDNOTES

[1] Refer to Volume I, Part I (Chapters 1 and 2) of this book.

[2] Chris Stewart and Ted Stewart, *Seven Tipping Points That Saved the World* (Salt Lake City: Shadow Mountain, 2011), 12.

[3] Feiler, *America's Prophet*, 92-93.

[4] Bennett, *America: The Last Best Hope,* Vol I, 130.

[5] Dallin H. Oaks, "The Divinely Inspired Constitution," *Ensign*, February 1992," 70-71.

[6] See W. Cleon Skousen, *The Five Thousand Year Leap* (Washington D.C.: The National Center for Constitutional Studies, 1981), 15-17.

[7] Oaks, "The Divinely Inspired Constitution," 69.

[8] Thomas Jefferson, as quoted in Monk, 117.

[9] President Rueben J. Clark, as quoted in Oaks, "The Divinely Inspired Constitution," 71.

[10] From Gettysburg Address, as quoted in Bennett, *America: The Last Best Hope*, Vol. I, 368.

[11] Joseph Ellis makes this point in his audio lecture series, *Patriots, Brotherhood of the American Revolution*. Lectures recorded by Recorded Books, Inc, and Barnes and Noble Publishing: 2004. Study Guide lecture 7.

[12] See Cleon Skousen, *The Five Thousand Year Leap* (Washington D.C.: The National Center for Constitutional Studies, 1981), 17.

[13] Feiler, *America's Prophet*, 94.

[14] Feiler, *America's Prophet*, 94-95.

[15] Dallin H. Oaks, "The Divinely Inspired Constitution," *Ensign*, February 1992, 68.

[16] Refer to Volume I, Part I of this book for the details concerning how these promises and prophecies were part of the American Covenant and how they apply to latter-day America.

[17] James Madison, *Federalist No. 10*, as quoted in George C. Edwards III, et al, *Government in America* (New York: Pearson-Longman, 2004), 703.

[18] Refer to Volume I, Part I of this book for the details surrounding these prophetic claims and how they apply to latter-day America.

[19] Mark Steyn, "Helium Diplomacy," *National Review*, May 4, 2009, 56; study also quoted in Mark Hitchcock, *The Late Great United States* (New York, Multnomah Press, 2009), 75.

[20] Refer to Volume I, Part I of this book for the details surrounding these prophetic claims and how they apply to latter-day America.

[21] Refer to Linda Monk, *The Words We Live By, Your Annotated Guide to the Constitution* (New York: Hyperion, 2003), 171-172; See also *Foundations For Teaching Economics: The Constitution-An Economic Document*, available at www.fte.org/teachers/programs/history/lessons/lesson02.htm.

[22] Willard Sterne Randall, *Alexander Hamilton: A Life* (New York: Perennial, 2003), 396-401.

[23] Refer to *History of the U.S. Customs Service at the Port of New York,* available at www.oldnycustomshouse.gov/history/.

[24] A list of the wealthiest persons ranked in history is available at http://en.wikipedia.org/wiki/Wealthy_historical_figures_2008. Details concerning the data can also be found in Malcolm Gladwell, *Outliers, The Story of Success* (New York, Little, Brown and Co., 2008) 56-61.

[25] William J. Bernstein, *The Birth of Plenty* (New York: McGraw-Hill, 2004), vii-viii (preface).

[26] Refer to Volume I, Chapter 1 for the details surrounding these American Covenant obligations and how they apply to latter-day America for the purposes of God.

[27] From First Presidency letter of 15 January, 1987, as referenced and affirmed by Elder Dallin H. Oaks, "The Divinely Inspired Constitution," *Ensign*, February 1992, 68-9. President Ezra Taft Benson quoted a First Presidency statement from 1973, which reads: "We urge members of the Church and all Americans to begin now to reflect more intently on the meaning and importance of the Constitution, and of adherence to its principles," as quoted in Ezra Taft Benson, "The Constitution—A Glorious Standard," *Ensign*, May 1976, 91. As an apostle, President Benson personally asked us to read the Constitution so that we "can sustain it and the free institutions set up under it," as quoted in Ezra Taft Benson, "America at the Crossroads," *New Era*, July 1978, 36. This is but a sample of such official instruction given by the Church.

[28] *Family Home Evening Lessons for the Bicentennial of the Constitution* (Salt Lake City: The Church of Jesus Christ of Latter-day Saints, 1987). The quote is from the Introduction of the booklet.

[29] Joan DeBardeleben, "Russia," *Introduction to Comparative Politics*, ed. Mark Kesselman, et al (New York: Houghton Mifflin Co., 2007), 372-373; Thomas Remington, "Politics in Russia," *Comparative Politics Today*, ed. Gabriel A. Almond, et al (New York: Longman, 2010), 368.

[30] Edmund Burke, as quoted in Lynn D. Wardle, "The Constitution as Covenant," *BYU Studies* 27, no.3, 1987, 9.

[31] Franklin, as quoted in Skousen, *The Five Thousand Year Leap*, 49, 55.

[32] D. Todd Christofferson, "Moral Discipline," General Conference Address, October 2009, available at www.lds.org/conference/talk.

[33] Jefferson, as quoted in Callister, *The Inevitable Apostasy and the Promised Restoration* (Salt Lake City: Deseret Book, 2006), 105-106.

[34] Madison, as quoted in Dallin Oaks, "*The Divinely Inspired Constitution*," *Ensign*, Feb 1992, 68.

[35] Madison, as quoted in Skousen, *The Five Thousand Year Leap*, 54.

[36] John Adams, as quoted in Charles Frances Adams, *The Works of John Adams, Second President of the United States* (Boston: Little Brown and Company, 1854), Vol. IX, 229, to the officers of the First Brigade of the Third Division of the Militia of Massachusetts on October 11, 1798, emphasis added.

[37] Adams, as quoted in Peter Marshal and David Manuel, *The Light and the Glory* (Grand Rapids: Revell, 2009), 12.

[38] Adams, as quoted in Newt Gingrich, *Rediscovering God in America* (Nashville: Integrity House, 2006), 92.

[39] Sam Adams, as quoted in Marshal and Manuel, 11.

[40] Lynn D. Wardle, "Seeing the Constitution as Covenant," *Ensign*, September 1989, 7.

[41] Nelson Burr, et al, eds, *A Critical Biography of Religion in America*, Vol.4 (Princeton, N.J.: Princeton University Press, 1961), 4:969-70.

[42] Wardle, 9.

[43] Skousen, *The Five Thousand year Lea*, 75-76.

[44] Consider the words from one of the first state constitutions in America, Delaware: "Through Divine goodness, all men have by nature the rights of worshipping and serving their Creator according to the dictates of their conscience." Or consider the words from the most recent state constitution—that of Hawaii. This document recognizes God in its preamble, expressing how the people are "grateful for Divine guidance." The state of Washington similarly recognizes God in its constitution, stating that "We the people…[are] grateful to the Supreme Ruler of the Universe for our liberties." Kansas and Florida agree, both formally extending thanks in their respective constitutions to "Almighty God," and both recognizing that it is from Him that all blessings of freedom are derived. Such references in state constitutions are certainly not the exception, but the rule. For a complete list of what the many state constitutions say about God as their political foundation, refer to www.undergodthebook.com.

[45] George Washington, as quoted in Bennett, *The Spirit of America* (New York: Simon and Schuster, 1997), 382; also available at www.yale.edu/lawweb/avalon/presiden/inaug/wash1.htm.

[46] George Washington, as quoted in Bennett, *The Spirit of America,* 382.

[47] George Washington (September 1789), in a letter to Samuel Langdon, as quoted in Janice T. Connell, *The Spiritual Journey of George Washington* (New York: Hatherleigh Press, 2007), 105.

[48] George Washington (October 1789), as quoted in Novak and Novak, *Washington's God* (New York: Basic Books, 2006),144-145.

[49] George Washington, as quoted in *Address of George Washington, Preparatory to His Declination* (Baltimore: George and Henry S. Keating, 1796), 22-23; also quoted in Waldman, *Founding Faith*, 60.

[50] That Washington had his Bible opened to Genesis 49 during his swearing-in ceremony is documented in H. Paul Jeffers, *The Freemasons in America* (New York: Kensington Publishing Corp., 2006), 28.

[51] Brigham Young, as quoted in *Doctrine and Covenants Student Manual, Religion 324-325* (Salt Lake City: The Church of Jesus Christ of Latter-day Saints, 1981), 244.

[52] Bruce R. McConkie, *Mormon Doctrine* (Salt Lake City: Bookcraft, 1966), 160, emphasis added.

[53] Gingrich, *Rediscovering God in America*, 27.

[54] Gingrich, 87.

[55] Feiler, *America's Prophet,* 283.

[56] Ezra Taft Benson, Conference talk given in Saturday morning session, October 3, 1987, published as "Our Divine Constitution," *Ensign*, Nov. 1987, 4.

[57] Ezra Taft Benson, "The Constitution-A Glorious Standard" *Ensign*, May 1976, 91.

[58] Madison, as quoted in Skousen, *The Five Thousand Year Leap*, 54.

[59] Waldman, 98.

[60] Waldman, 99.

[61] Vicki-Jo Anderson, *The Other Eminent Men of Wilford Woodruff* (Cottonwood, Zichron Historical Institute, 1994), preface and 411-413.

[62] Benjamin Rush, as quoted in Meacham, *American Gospel*, 99.

[63] Ezra Taft Benson, "The Constitution—A Glorious Standard," *Ensign*, May 1976, 92.

Joseph in Liberty Jail, by Liz Lemon Swindle
Courtesy of Foundation Arts

CHAPTER 3

A BROKEN COVENANT
AND A GODLY SOLUTION

*And if the president heed them not, then will
the Lord arise and come forth out of his hiding
place, and in his fury vex the nation; and in his
hot displeasure, and his fierce anger, in his name
will cut off those wicked, unfaithful, and unjust stewards
.... That I may proceed to bring to pass my act, my
strange act, and to perform my work, my strange work.*

—Doctrine and Covenants 101:89-90, 95 (1833)

With the Constitution and its covenant foundations in place, the Lord was prepared to restore His gospel to the earth. As such, shortly after the Constitution went into effect, the Lord provided the Prophet Joseph Smith with the necessary keys and revelations to bring the Church into being once more. By the early 1840's, some ten years after the restored Church was officially organized, if one were to observe God's kingdom on the earth, it would at first appear the Constitution was fulfilling its divine purpose: a prophet of God lived in the city of Nauvoo, revelations and blessings through the restored priesthood flowed abundantly, and a temple was in the planning. And all these God-given, First Amendment-derived rights were defended by a state-approved city charter and a legal militia under the spirit of the Second Amendment.[1] Indeed, the Lord's Zion was being created, and the American political system—even the American Covenant—was shielding it according to the divine plan. Or was it?

Sadly, LDS history (beyond the mere snapshot provided above) reveals the tragic truth: the Constitution was failing; the American Covenant was failing. Though it is true the Restoration was occurring per the description above, America had failed to serve its purpose. Those familiar with Church history know how the Saints were persecuted, beaten, killed, and driven from city to city and state to state, by traitors and tyrants who thwarted their constitutionally "guaranteed" freedoms. Tragically, as the nation received the covenant blessings of *liberty, protection,* and *prosperity* unto a fullness of moral agency, it also seemed to do what it could to block the Latter-day Saints from receiving these blessings—a sad commentary when considering these blessings were divinely and specifically designed for the Saints in their efforts to build up the kingdom of God. Once again, we see how the adversary had inserted himself to do what he always has done since before the world was—thwart man's agency so he lacks the full opportunity to access, make available, and fully enjoy all the blessings of the gospel. It was Satan's attempt to rehash the War in Heaven all over again in Joseph Smith's America.

While such challenges positively strengthened the Saints, perhaps helping their cause in the end (see D&C 122),* the Lord would not forever permit the desecration of the Constitution, which He had inspired to protect His children's moral agency and promote His gospel for future generations.

As the nation violated the American Covenant in its utter disregard for the heaven-sent Constitution, and in its cruel and

---

* Not only did the Lord state that such challenges would "give thee experience and shall be for thy good" (D&C 122:7), but He also pointed out that the Saints' own slowness in obedience had perhaps stayed the Lord's hand and was thus responsible for some of the affliction (see D&C 101:2, 6-8).

92

torturous treatment of the innocent, the American Covenant fell further into breach. Something had to be done to strengthen the covenant and thus make America what God intended it to be—a safe-haven and support for His restored gospel. If such change was to occur it would only be through a national application of two basic principles, which we will refer to in the next several chapters as *national repentance* and *universal agency*. The nation would need to humble itself and employ this *national repentance* for its sins against the innocent, so as to be worthy enough for the Lord to trust and bless it with the promised blessings of the covenant and the divine mandate associated with this covenant. Furthermore, as part of its repentance, the nation would have to make restitution for its sins against the covenant by implementing a national policy that would reverse its persecution of the Saints and forever secure the blessings of the covenant, not just for some Americans, but for *all*. Only then could the *liberty, protection,* and *prosperity* responsible for securing a fullness of moral agency unto salvation reach out and touch all people—especially God's church and kingdom. With such a policy of *universal agency* supporting God's church and kingdom, then (and only then) could the gospel of eternal salvation flourish and reach all mankind.

Though the Lord provided America with ample opportunity to make these changes on its own, ultimately America chose to remain in breach of its covenant. As such, the Lord would unleash His fury and anger in a national vexation and scourge that would influence America to make the required changes—to once and for all humbly begin its *national repentance*. Then, with a restored spirit of purity and worthiness, the nation would, at last, feel compelled to apply the constitutional and covenant-based blessing of *universal agency*. It was the great solution, and a Godly solution, to save America by more fully converting it into that divinely appointed vessel and tool of the Lord.

While this chapter will provide the scriptural and prophetic background to God's dealings with America during this remarkable period, following chapters will offer a more detailed account of the actual historical happenings that validate such scripture and prophecy. Through exploring this most powerful era of American history, we will witness the nation's struggle to turn from sin, embrace the Lord, and return to the national covenant. We will further witness God's miraculous workings in facilitating national redemption under this covenant. In the end, as we explore this tragic, yet ultimately triumphant, relationship between God and His people—as we see the covenant in action—we will once again confirm certain powerful truths. Specifically, we will confirm that the American Covenant is real, that it comes with serious obligations that require adherence, and that God not only offered it to be received, but expected it to be righteously maintained. This He did in an effort to provide for the eternal salvation of His children.

The Prophet's National Plea

Sins Against the Covenant

James Madison was all too correct in his arguments surrounding the destructive power of local factions. Just as he might have predicted, the state of Missouri (not to mention the other states where the Saints resided) had been compromised by just such oppressive factions that controlled local governments. These factions pushed local authorities to disregard the constitutional principles which should have protected the early Church. Instead of protection, however, the Saints received brutality. They were oppressed, chased out, burnt-out, and killed. And all this occurred because, as the Prophet Joseph explained, "[We] wished to worship God according to the revelations of heaven, the constitution and the dictates of [our] own consciences. Oh liberty, how are thou fallen!"[2]

Many less informed historians attempt to consign anti-Mormon fever at the time to the strange practice of plural marriage. (Perhaps it can be understood, they argue, why their neighbors

94

wanted them out.) The truth is that polygamy was practiced at the time by a tiny percentage, and these marriages were both administered and lived under complete secrecy (the marriages were even recorded in code).[3] According to historian Richard Bushman, the practice was not made public until 1852, well after Joseph's death and not until the Saints had already been driven to Salt Lake.[4] Though rumors of its practice admittedly existed in Nauvoo, its manifestations were too well hidden to justify the overbearing hatred poured out over the Saints. Furthermore, the persecution of the Saints, and their inability to access constitutional protections, began long before the thought of plural marriage even existed in the budding church—indeed, the persecution began almost at the moment of Joseph's First Vision.

The same can be said of the many other allegations hurled at the Church and its prophet in order to justify the actions taken against them by the state. For example, modern-day critics—bent on painting Joseph as a scoundrel—will point out that he was continuously "in trouble" with the law. However, they are slower to point out that the Prophet was never found guilty of any wrongdoing.

The point is that there was no "comprehensible" explanation for the Saints' oppression, except that the adversary stirred the hearts of men against that one true gospel. One honest local observer of the Saints in Missouri summed it up best when he told a journalist that "the people of Jackson can stand any thing but men who profess to have seen angels, and to believe the book of Mormon."[5] As President Gordon B. Hinckley declared, quoting Wilford Woodruff, "When God has had a people on the earth, it matters not in what age, Lucifer...and the millions of fallen spirits that were cast out of heaven, have warred...against the people of God."[6] The Church's struggle was indeed connected to a much larger and expansive conflict. The Saints' persecution was nothing but an extension of the War in Heaven. Once again, Satan was attacking the one thing he knew would bring about eternal progression—he was attacking moral agency. The adversary knew that hampering such agency through local factions and oppressors would make it difficult for the Saints to worship freely, to build temples, and to access, share, and enjoy a fullness of the blessings of the kingdom.

That such evil intentions were truly at the center of the persecution is further evidenced by the fact that the Saints' oppressors cited another justification for their cruel actions against the Church. Enemies of the Church were openly upset that the Saints were friendly towards, and at times champions of, both African slaves and Native Americans.[7] The adversary's evil plan of oppression that hampered the agency of Church members incorporated attempts to obstruct the agency of anyone, including African Americans and Native Americans. This the adversary did for the same evil purpose of thwarting the progression of man. This was the adversary's work, which had not relented since before the world was. And this evil influence was everywhere, especially in those locales settled by the Saints.

Satan's influence in this grave injustice over God's kingdom is perhaps best illustrated by a series of oppressive maneuvers employed by the state of Missouri, which hampered the liberty and agency of the Saints. Beginning in 1833, a manifesto was issued by Jackson County which prohibited the Saints from voting, owning property, printing a newspaper, and even working in the county.[8] Then, when the Saints filed complaints against these injustices to the local judges (many of which had signed the manifesto), their appeals were not only ignored, but often times produced a reversal conviction on the Church-member filing the complaint. When the Saints appealed to the governor, Daniel Dunklin, he responded with a most perverse interpretation of American constitutionalism. He claimed that "public sentiment may become paramount law; and when one man or society of men become so obnoxious to that sentiment as to determine the people to be rid of him or them, it is useless to run counter to it...all I can say to you is that in this Republic the voice of the people is the voice of God."[9]

This twisted application was galvanized some five years later under the infamous *Mormon Extermination Order* of Governor Lilburn Boggs.[10] Such government-backed policies naturally led to some of the worst and most brutal abuses against the innocent that America has ever seen. And this terror over the Church in Missouri was not an isolated experience. It only reflected what had happened earlier in New York and Ohio, and that which would shortly come to pass in Illinois.

All of this leads us to a most tragic conclusion: though the Constitution of the United States seemed to have been prepared for this moment in history and for this specific people, it was failing. Madison's warning of the propensity and ability of brutal factions to take over the government had indeed hit too close to home for the Saints. As Bushman explained, echoing this Madisonian warning, "The Saints learned that the mobs were the people and the people were the government. No law officer or court would come to their defense."[11] Such occurred repeatedly, as Satan hunted down the Saints wherever they went, thus testing the Constitution against its divine purpose. Sadly, Satan won too many of the battles. As the people and government continued to violate the principles of the Constitution (by denying the guaranteed constitutional blessings to certain segments of society), and as they simultaneously continued to violate the basic laws of God (by persecuting, beating, and running out the innocent), the American Covenant fell further into breach.

But how could the adversary do this in America? Shouldn't such intolerance and persecution in the Promised Land be relegated forever to the pre-Constitution days? Did Madison not explain that the Constitution included built-in solutions to the oppressive faction problem? Did he not explain (as detailed in the last chapter) that a *federal* government existed to counter the unjust local factions, by bringing in the collective inspiration and reasoning of *all* Americans? He most certainly did. As it was the Lord who had inspired such a safety net, it should be of no surprise that He Himself repeated this same reaffirming message to His Saints in response to the great persecution—even the sins against covenant—that were plaguing them.

In 1833, as the persecution against the Saints began to grow ever more intense, the Lord invoked His constitutional system. He recognized what the state government was doing to His Saints, and so He laid out the solution. This divine solution is provided in Doctrine and Covenants, Section 101. In this section, the Lord professes His hand in the Constitution, declaring that this Constitution was established on "holy principles" and was intended to preserve "moral agency" for "all flesh" (verses 77-80). Then, in the verses that immediately follow this declaration, the Lord reminds the Saints, as Madison would have reminded America, of the constitutional process that must be applied to ensure the deliverance of these blessings: "Let them importune at the feet of the judge; and if he heed them not, let them importune at the feet of the governor; and if the governor heed them not, *let them importune at the feet of the president*" (D&C 101: 86-88, emphasis added). The Lord invoked the principle of *federalism*.

He was asking the Prophet to, if necessary, place the most pressing issue of protecting moral agency on the table of the federal government, even that sole venue that transcended state and local factions and where existed the safety of the voice of all the people. As quoted earlier, whereas "it is common for the lesser part of the people [e.g. the state of Missouri] to desire that which is not right...it is not common that the voice of the people [e.g. the federal government or all the states combined] desireth anything contrary to that which is right...therefore this shall ye observe and make it your law—to do your business by the voice of the people" (Mosiah 29:26).

A Plea for Help

Having received the above command, Joseph set out to follow it. As he had already "importuned" unsuccessfully to the state government (at the feet of the judge and governor), he would now obey the next step of God's command and make his final plea to the federal government. Within months of the revelation, an appeal had been made to President Andrew Jackson. But the Prophet was turned down, as the president did not see how any federal law had been violated.[12] A later appeal to President Martin Van Buren produced the same results (though the President agreed the Mormon cause was "just," he said his federal authority was too limited to intervene).[13] Joseph even secured an audience with very prominent members of Congress, but their response did not vary from that of the White House.[14]

The Constitution, Joseph was told, did not permit the federal government to intervene in protecting the suffering Saints—only state and local governments, as mandated by the Tenth Amendment, had jurisdiction over such matters.[15] The Tenth Amendment clearly reserves "[t]he powers not delegated to the United States by the Constitution...to the States respectively, or to the people." A strict interpretation of this amendment indeed might lead one to believe that unless a certain right is *specifically* given to the federal government by the Constitution, then the federal government should not intervene. And nowhere in the Constitution is it spelled out in detail where the federal government can create laws of intervention and enforcement to supersede state policies (like those of Missouri) on matters of religious freedom.

The Saints turned to the Constitution's First Amendment, which clearly forbids the government from persecuting its citizens based on their religious affiliations. This is precisely what was happening to them. Surely, they believed, the federal government, even the custodians of the First Amendment, would feel inclined to enforce these rights. For the spirit of the First Amendment clearly promises the *free exercise of religion* and clearly stands in testimony that such is the right of all Americans.

Unfortunately, the Saints' hope for such protection was dashed by a subjective constitutional interpretation by the Supreme Court. In the case of *Barron v. Baltimore* (1833), the Court implied that the individual states were exempt from having to consider or enforce the U.S. Constitution's Bill of Rights. The Court pointed out that the First Amendment does not include specific language that compels the states to adhere to it.[16] From our contemporary point of view, imagine an America where any given state could, for example, take away our freedom of the press, or our freedom of speech, and then maintain that its action is legal because states do not have to adhere to the Bill of Rights. As absurd as this sounds to us today, this was the reality of Joseph Smith's America. In fact, this tragic interpretation of the Constitution only encouraged the notion that states could (flying in the face of the First Amendment) maintain state-sponsored religions, even at the expense of minority religions. That is precisely what some states sadly chose to do.[17] The idea that "states' rights" were paramount to all else had been taken to an extreme and unhealthy level. For the "states' rights" ideology seemed to be trumping the most cherished constitutional protections.

In fairness to the Court, the *Barron* decision had nothing to do with the plight of American citizens (like the Mormons) who had been stripped of basic liberties. Instead, the case dealt with the federal government's right, or lack of right, to trump state law in matters dealing with eminent domain. In this particular case, Mr. Barron (of Baltimore) sued his city in federal court, claiming that his Fifth Amendment rights had been violated when the City of Baltimore unfairly tampered with his property. In the decision, the Court ruled against Mr. Barron, stating that, while the *federal* government was restrained by the Constitution from unfairly disturbing private property, the states were not. (The state of Maryland contended that they could tamper with Barron's property for the greater good of its society. Mr. Barron, thinking his property would be protected by the Constitution and the federal government, instead suffered the loss of his perceived property rights to the City of Baltimore.) Whether this difficult decision was ultimately right or wrong, it worked against the Saints. For, it gave fodder to cowards in the federal government who chose to duck behind *Barron* and stretch its meaning in order to justify why they could not, or would not, come to the aid of the suffering Saints.

And so, backed by its own legal interpretations of the Constitution (and of the *Barron* decision), the federal government coldly and cowardly accepted the notion that the Bill of Rights, including the First Amendment's promised freedom of religion, was something that only applied to or restrained the *federal* government, but did not apply to or restrain state governments. As it was the *state* governments that were guilty of administering (or allowing) the religious persecution of the Saints, not the *federal* government, the Constitution and the First Amendment were rendered absolutely useless to the Saints. In perhaps one of the cruelest ironies in American history, the Saints would have to read the Constitution's promise that the government will not persecute religious minorities and then simultaneously watch its own government smoke them out and shoot them dead.

While the interpretations of the Constitution (and the misuse of the *Barron* ruling) would eventually, and inspiringly, be overturned by the Fourteenth Amendment (which inspired action will be detailed later), up until this point in history, different theories regarding the issue of federal authority abounded. The Constitution was, after all, a bit murky on how far federal authority extended. However, one might be suspicious about the timing of *Barron*. It was handed down just three years after God's Church was organized, and precisely during the height of the Saints' persecution. Indeed, it arrived in just enough time for it to be misused in uninspired hands. Certainly the Court had no ill-intent in its ruling. But the adversary, perhaps, did not miss the opportunity to fuel the fire of haters. Interestingly, the *Barron* ruling, perhaps, came out of nowhere. According to the prominent legal scholar, Winslow Crosskey, "the fact is the [*Barron*] decision was contrary to the considered opinion of good lawyers before that time, and,...in the scope in which the court announced it, it was without any warrant at all."[18]

The Saints were thus compelled to ask in bewilderment: *How could the Constitution have been so badly applied? How could it have served as such an ineffective tool—even a dead tool—for the protection of the Church? Did Madison not teach that the Constitution, with its new federal government, possessed built-in protections against such tyranny over minority rights? Did God not deliver the Constitution for the protection of His kingdom?* Something was clearly being misapplied and mismanaged. As Brigham Young declared, it was not in the Constitution itself where we find the problem; instead, the failure lies in the fact that it is "too often administered in unrighteousness."[19] Joseph Smith and the Church would not accept such unrighteousness sitting down. There were, after all, several clear constitutional arguments that existed even in Joseph's America, which certainly justified and encouraged federal intervention on behalf of the suffering Saints.

To begin with, while the Founding Fathers intentionally included the Tenth Amendment, they themselves preempted its misapplication by including, within the body of the Constitution, certain provisions that would provide federal protection in such needed circumstances. This protection is represented most prominently in Article I, Section 8 of the Constitution. In this section, the document lists the many areas for which the federal government can and should create legislation, and specifically lists things like raising armies, declaring war, and coining money. The section concludes with a mandate to Congress to "make all laws which shall be *necessary and proper* for carrying into Execution the foregoing powers *and all other Powers* vested by this Constitution." And what are these "other powers vested by the Constitution" whereupon the federal government should act? Certainly they include the very basic ones found in the Constitution's Preamble—to "establish justice," "insure domestic tranquility," "provide for the common defense," "promote the general welfare" and "secure the blessings of liberty." (It should be noted here, as discussed last chapter, that these blessings directly reflect the American Covenant blessings of *liberty, protection,* and *prosperity.*) These constitutional directives, if administered as designed, were all the Church needed from its government. Yet the Church was unarguably being denied these rights. With such injustices occurring under its watch, the Congress —and federal government in general—certainly had every right and responsibility to intervene per Article I, Section 8. This alone provides all the justification needed for federal intervention.

But there were even more reasons for the Church to expect the protection of the federal government. Some ten years before the Church was organized, the Supreme Court ruled in the case of *McCulloch v. Maryland* (1819) that the federal government does, in fact, enjoy implied powers from the Constitution's Article I, Section 8, that allow it to intervene in important situations. In the case of *McCulloch*, the Court considered the constitutionality of Alexander Hamilton's much needed federal/national banking system. The Court ruled that even though there was no specific mandate in the Constitution for the federal government to establish a national bank, Article I, Section 8 *implied* the federal government had the power to do so. In its decision, the Court pointed out that the Tenth Amendment phrase, "The powers not delegated to the United States by the Constitution...are reserved to the States" did not include the word *expressly* before the word *delegated*, as it had been written in the Articles of Confederation. This obvious omission from the Constitution, according to the Court, was the Founders' way to deliberately leave wiggle room for Congress to apply this principle in Article I, Section 8, and thereby do whatever is *necessary and proper* in fulfilling constitutional mandates.[20]

The *McCulloch* decision certainly gave the Church even more reason to expect federal intervention. After all, if the federal government could justifiably create legislation for national banks, and then insert these banks into the many states, even though there is no mention of national banks in the Constitution, then the federal government most certainly should have been able to intervene on an issue regarding religious freedom. In fact, even more than its right to intervene on financial matters, the federal government should have known it had the power to intervene on matters of religious freedom. After all, there exists a specified amendment in the Constitution—the First Amendment—that defends and supports the principle of religious freedom. This is not to say the First Amendment alone easily justified federal action on behalf of the

Saints (as the *Barron* decision pointed out). But it does tell us that religious freedom has held a special place in America from the beginning—a special place that should have been especially honored by the federal government. This should have given the federal government even more reason than it already had to utilize Article I, Section 8 and the *McCulloch* decision to restore religious freedom to the Saints.

There was even further justification for federal intervention. For even in Joseph Smith's time, a constitutional precedent had been set for federal action in the states, particularly where insurrection and domestic violence were in play, as they were in Missouri. The Prophet Joseph was astute enough to point these precedents out, citing, for example, Washington's action as president to physically quash the Whisky Rebellion in Pennsylvania in 1794 and President Andrew Jackson's efforts to do the same in South Carolina in 1832-33. Even the "states' rights" proponent, Thomas Jefferson, recognized his authority as president to intervene in the states to prevent the unruly mobocracy rising in response to the Embargo Act.[21]

But tragically, in spite of the many reasons to do the right thing, the federal government did nothing other than turn a blind eye to the many constitutional justifications for action. It upheld that the constitutional promises of religious freedom were not really promised at all to the people, so as long as the individual states (like Missouri, for example) chose not to adhere to them. Admittedly, as pointed out above, there was a legal justification (albeit a weak one) given to support federal inaction, making the federal government feel justified that it had done its duty. However, the result of inaction clearly resulted in the suffering and death of innocent men, women, and children, because of their desire to practice their religion freely. Therefore, for the federal government to do nothing, when the Constitution justified action and opened a clear door for action, represents a clear violation of law—not only constitutional law, but the basic law of God. For how could God be pleased with the federal government's cold hearted and cowardly response to the Mormon persecution, especially when it was given to this federal government to render such service to the innocent and abused? How soon it seems the government had forgotten what the Founders had taught them: that adherence to God's law was essential for national blessings. The American Covenant was in breach.

Perhaps if that first generation of inspired Founders had been around for the Church, then the persecution would have been thwarted as it should have been. Throughout this book (including Volume I), we have witnessed the passionate belief these early Founders had that the government of America, particularly after the U.S. Constitution was in place, should protect and support the right to freedom of religion. They were the ones, after all, who declared boldly that "all men are created equal" and that their "inalienable rights" to "life, liberty and the pursuit of happiness" are the responsibility of governments to "secure." After writing these words, would Thomas Jefferson have argued that he was referring only to local governments, and that if these local governments refused to act, then any other governing body over such afflicted minorities were free to negate responsibility to enforce these inspired principles? It was, after all, Jefferson who, in defining what he called a "sacred principle," stated that "though the will of the majority is in all cases to prevail, that will, to be rightful, must be reasonable; that the minority possess their equal rights, which equal laws must protect, and to violate would be oppression."[22] Another absolute principle from Jefferson, which also shames those who refused to respond to the Church's plight, is found in his declaration that "all men shall be free to profess, and by argument to maintain, their opinions in matter of religion, and that the same shall in nowise diminish, enlarge, or affect their civil capacities."[23]

George Washington had also made it clear that the purpose of America was to provide the means whereby the religious minority might "sit in safety under his own vine and fig tree, and there shall be none to make him afraid. May the father of all mercies scatter light and not darkness in our paths, and make us all in our several vocations useful here, and in his own due time and way everlastingly happy."[24] Washington also had stated that the "bosom of America is open to receive, the oppressed and persecuted of all Nations and Religions, whom we shall welcome to a participation of all our rights and privileges."[25] This is but a sample of his many declarations (which have been detailed throughout both volumes of this book) concerning the purpose of the America he had created.

Then there was Madison, the Father of the Constitution, who was just as open and powerful about his conviction of the government's duty to protect freedom of religion. In past chapters we have detailed Madison's relentless work in creating a government that stood for religious rights.[26] It was Madison who promised to make a government that included "the most satisfactory provisions for all essential rights, particularly the rights of Conscience in the fullest latitude."[27]

Madison was so clearly in favor of the federal government's right to impose itself upon the states in matters of "equal rights of conscience," that he called for such a federal mandate to be specifically included within a constitutional amendment. This amendment, he declared, "was the most valuable amendment on the whole list."[28] That Madison proposed such an amendment should be of little surprise. It was, after all, Madison who taught that the federal government would serve to temper states' oppressive actions against minorities (see previous chapter). In *The Federalist*, Madison upheld the implied powers given to the federal government: "Wherever the end is required, the means are authorized."[29] Madison's founding brother, Alexander Hamilton (one of the most influential Founders in creating the Constitution and securing its passage), would have agreed. Hamilton declared that "the general [federal] government will at all times stand ready to check the usurpations of the state governments."[30]

Unfortunately, Madison's teachings on the matter were largely ignored, and his proposed amendment was denied. The other delegates did not want to appear overbearing upon the states. Furthermore, they believed there was enough in the Constitution to ensure that future lawmakers would do the right thing—a severe miscalculation. If Madison had seen his proposals met, the Church might not have suffered as it did.

These original Founders were among the first to run the federal government. Based on their stated testimonies, and the testimonies of other likeminded Founders quoted throughout this two-volume book, it is unfathomable to believe they would have stood by and done nothing for the suffering Church. Lest they be hypocrites against their own testimonies and actions, the slightest constitutional justification would have compelled them to save the Saints—and they certainly would have had ample constitutional justification for action on behalf of the Saints (as proven above). However, they were not there to opine on the issue. But perhaps we might feel their testimonies through one of their greatest sons who was there. John Quincy Adams, son of the great Founder John Adams (and a recipient, along with his father, in the St. George Temple miracle) stated that the persecution of the Latter-day Saints represented "one of the most disgraceful chapters in the history of the United States."[31]

The Founders' influence went unfelt on most of their successors. These early Founders, through word and deed, created the political infrastructure that could have been utilized by later generations to righteously interpret the Constitution. But these influences were ignored, as was Madison's warning that, upon interpreting the Constitution, future Americans should "not separate text from historical background. If you do, you will have perverted and subverted the Constitution, which can only end in a distorted, bastardized form of illegitimate government."[32] Joseph knew this had, in fact, happened. "Were the venerable fathers of our independence permitted to revisit the earth," wrote the Prophet, "how would they frown with indignation at the disgrace of their country."[33]

Looking at this issue in its totality—based on *all* the arguments listed above—there is ample evidence to conclude that even during Joseph's day, the proactive protection of religious rights was indeed "delegated" by the Constitution to Congress and the federal government in general. This, backed by the true spirit and meaning of the First Amendment, and backed by the Light of Christ which teaches man to stand up against brutality over the innocent, makes futile any argument that "states' rights" justified federal inaction.

Again, the state governments' atrocities committed against men, women, and children of the Church were completely intolerable and put these states in breach of the national covenant. For not only were these states blocking the constitutional and covenant blessings of *liberty, protection,* and *prosperity* that rightly belonged to the Saints as American citizens, but these states were also involved in (or at best tolerated) the beating, burning out, and killing of the innocent. Furthermore, the unwillingness of the federal government to render assistance when it was both justified and responsible to do so, also placed the federal government in direct violation of these most basic laws of God and man. We would do well to remember that these were not violations of high and lofty commandments that require adherence to any particular faith. These were basic laws, which all men (regardless of their personal religions) should recognize as sinful. Their violation and toleration by the nation, then, represented a clear breach of the American Covenant. And when the federal government, represented by *all* the people, even the last bastion of constitutional hope, refused to act, the entire nation at last fell under condemnation.

We might imagine the pain and frustration suffered by the Prophet Joseph and the Saints in the face of such unjust denial. For they knew, as Joseph declared, that God had inspired the Constitution, which provided that "Mormons, as well as those of every other class and description, have equal rights to partake of the fruits of the great tree of our national liberty."[34]

After realizing that the current federal government would not fight for these God-ordained rights, a frustrated and disillusioned Joseph wrote a stinging letter to a leading "states' righter," Senator John C. Calhoun, who was running for president at the time and who had defended federal inaction in the case of the

Saints. "If the General Government [federal government] has no power, to re-instate expelled citizens to their rights, there is a monstrous hypocrite fed and fostered from the hard earnings of the people!" Joseph marveled at the irony in the fact that the federal government professed the constitutional power to "protect the nation against foreign invasion and internal broil," and yet his Saints —who were being hounded, robbed, raped and killed by raging mobs that were supported and enabled by the state—were not protected by the same power.[35] The Prophet laid out his feelings plainly to Calhoun, declaring that "all men who say the Congress has no power to…defend the rights of her citizens have not the love of truth in them."[36] In his final assessment of the issue, Joseph declared the following: "The States' rights doctrine are what feed mobs. They are a dead carcass, a stink and they shall ascend up as a stink offering in the nose of the Almighty."[37]

A Plea for the Provision

Assuming the Prophet had secured the serious attention of the federal government, what exactly did he want of it? Or better yet, what did he believe the Lord specifically wanted him to "importune" or demand of the federal government? What specific policy should be implemented to bring the Church under the protection of the national covenant? As the nation approached its 1844 presidential election, the Prophet had begun to internalize and solidify his answers to these questions. As he did so, he interviewed the candidates to see which would best carry out his vision. Unfortunately, as had always been the case with the Saints, no candidate was willing to implement any adequate solution.[38]

But the Prophet understood the American Covenant and, more importantly, he understood it had been breached. As such, he refused to relinquish his responsibility, not only as prophet over priesthood covenants, but as prophet over the American Covenant. Therefore, if no candidate would even attempt to solve the national covenant crisis, the Prophet himself would. Indeed, he would publicly identify the problems and provide the solutions. In short, he would offer a proposal that would bring the nation into compliance with the American Covenant, thereby saving the country and restoring the integrity of its God-given mission. So important and urgent was his message to the nation that he sought the highest, most visible venue from which to broadcast it—he declared himself a candidate in the 1844 United States presidential election.

The Prophet touched the core of the national plight and offered his solution to it in the following declaration given a few months before publicly declaring his candidacy:

> It is one of the first principles of my life, and one that I have cultivated from my childhood, having been taught it by my father, to allow every one the liberty of conscience. I am the greatest advocate of the Constitution of the United States there is on earth. In my feelings I am always ready to die for the protection of the weak and oppressed in their just rights. The only fault I find with the Constitution is, it is not broad enough to cover the whole ground.
>
> Although it provides that all men shall enjoy religious freedom, yet it does not provide the manner by which that freedom can be preserved, nor for the punishment of Government officers who refuse to protect the people in their religious rights, or punish the mobs, states, or communities who interfere with the rights of the people on account of their religion. Its sentiments are good, but it provides no means of enforcing them. It has but this one fault. Under its provision, a man or a people who are able to protect themselves can get along well enough; but those who have the misfortune to be weak or unpopular are left to the merciless rage of popular fury.
>
> The Constitution should contain a provision that every officer of the Government who should neglect or refuse to

extend the protection guaranteed in the Constitution should be subject to capital punishment; and then the president of the United States would not say, *Your cause is just, but I can do nothing for you*, a governor issue exterminating orders, or judges say, *The men ought to have the protection of law, but it wont please the mob; the men must die, anyhow, to satisfy the clamor of the rabble; they must be hung, or Missouri be damned to all eternity*. Executive writs could be issued when they ought to be, and not be made instruments of cruelty to oppress the innocent, and persecute men whose religion is unpopular.[39]

The Doctrine and Covenants supports the Prophet's plea, declaring that, instead of taking a passive role in the principles of religious and civil liberties (like the federal government was doing), "governments require civil officers and magistrates to enforce the laws...[of] free exercise of conscience, the right and control of property, and the protection of life." (D&C 134:2-3). In his published document defining his political platform, Joseph emphasized that constitutional blessings should be the right of all men and that, in order to guarantee these rights, the president of the United States should have "full power to send an army to suppress mobs," without requiring the invitation of the state.[40]

The Prophet recognized that even though God had inspired the Constitution with the tools necessary to fulfill its divine purpose, the adversary's influence over men had caused them to so poorly apply these tools, that the inspired protections became useless. (We can see here why the Lord commands us in D&C 98:10 to elect "honest men and wise men...and good men" to public office.) What was needed, according to the Prophet, was a clarifying provision that embodied and bolstered these constitutional principles so as to indefinitely prevent such erroneous interpretations. What Joseph was describing was what he so lacked in his time, but what we as Americans now enjoy—the federal Civil Rights Act of 1964. Under this provision—derived directly from the constitutional rights above, and completed after an acknowledgement that the

Constitution encourages its existence—the federal government is clearly mandated to enforce the prohibition of "discrimination because of race, *religion* or national origin." The act cuts through the misinterpretations of the Constitution and specifically calls on the *federal* government to prohibit such discrimination in places of "public accommodations," by "employers or labor unions," and by "voting registrars" (to name a few). It also sets up specific enforcement entities and clear punishments for any and all violators.[41]

This was what Joseph had called for; it would have elevated the Church to its rightful place, even into the protecting arms of the American Covenant. If the Church were severely persecuted today, as it was in the past, its most powerful political weapon of defense would be the Civil Rights Act. Joseph knew this and so he sought it out.

It would seem that the Prophet's proposal for religious freedom, backed by the Constitution and the federal government, if adopted and applied, would be enough to fix the problems of the past, bring the nation into compliance under its national covenant, and thus make America worthy of its covenant blessings and divine mandate. And yet, it still would not have been enough. For there was another national sin just as damaging to the nation as was the religious persecution suffered by the Saints. It was a national sin whose existence would make the nation unworthy of its covenant blessings and divine mandate—a sin which would independently obstruct the covenant. It was the elephant in the room that the most inspired Founders—including Washington, Adams, Jefferson, Franklin, and many others—recognized as an evil cancer that had to be eradicated. And though the Lord perhaps tolerated its existence for a season while His America was passing through the growing pains of first generation nation-building, He would not tolerate it any longer as the nation entered its second generation. The evil was slavery.

Slavery was one of the basic strategies utilized by the adversary to lure a nation into sin, making it an unworthy vessel for the purposes of God. As America, even modern Israel, would carry a divine mandate under a national covenant with the Almighty, the adversary would be sure to infect it with this poisonous influence. The Evil One, after all, had done the same to God's earlier national covenant people in ancient Israel—and for the same reason. It is documented in the Old Testament how the Lord rebuked the ancient Israelites for practicing slavery—an act which also placed them in breach of their national covenant (see Leviticus 25:10, Jeremiah 34:17). The words of God to ancient Israel include the refrain: "Proclaim liberty throughout all the land unto all the inhabitants thereof." America naturally adopted these words of the ancient covenant, and applied them to their own covenant by placing these very words on that sacred relic known today as the Liberty Bell. [42]

Some have tried to interpret parts of the Old Testament to justify slavery. (Misinterpretations of scripture, along with a misunderstanding of historical and cultural context might contribute to such erroneous conclusions). However, the Lord made it clear, in the cited scripture above, where He ultimately stands on the issue. Furthermore, the Light of Christ given to all men reveals to all men where God stands on the issue of enslavement and oppression of the human soul. The evil practice of slavery was, in fact, a sin in America and anywhere else it was practiced. Americans knew this in their hearts and minds. They knew the covenant. And their utter disregard for it had indeed made them unworthy to represent the Lord's base of operations. Therefore, even if religious persecution had come to a screeching halt, this other prevalent sin would have independently kept the nation in breach of its covenant.

In light of this, it should be of little surprise that when the Prophet Joseph announced his candidacy for the presidency, he included more than a proposal to redeem religious minorities. His official presidential platform also called for the freedom and elevation of African Americans. He seemed to know that unless slavery could be eradicated together with religious persecution, then the nation and her covenant would remain in jeopardy.

In his official declared political platform, the candidate Joseph Smith quoted the Declaration of Independence, stating that "all men are created equal" and are "endowed by their Creator... with life, liberty and the pursuit of happiness." Upon reading his message, it might at first appear he was quoting the Declaration in favor of his pet cause: religious freedom. But he did not use it this way in his foundation document for his presidential platform. Instead, he pointed out the great American irony of the Declaration: that it preached these words and promises even while "at the same time some two or three millions of people are held as slaves for life, because the spirit in them is covered with darker skin."[43] On an earlier occasion, the Prophet decried: "Break off the shackles from the poor black man and hire them to labor like other human beings." He demanded, "Set them free, educate them and give them their equal rights." He explained, "They come into the world slaves, mentally and physically. Change their situation... they have souls and are subject to salvation."[44]*

As part of his presidential platform, Joseph even offered a clever solution to freeing the slaves. He suggested that their freedom be purchased through the sale of public lands and through deductions of pay from members of Congress.[45] Indeed, the nation as a whole, and particularly its representatives who had failed God and country by encouraging or at least tolerating this sin, should have led the way. They should have sacrificed in their repentance and restitution.

---

* According to Joseph Smith Biographer Richard Bushman, the exclusion of black men from the Priesthood was not a church policy until after the death of the Prophet. Furthermore, blacks were permitted to participate in temple worship under Joseph's administration. Also, we know of at least one black member and friend of Joseph, Elijah Abel, who had been ordained an Elder under Joseph's administration. In 1836, Joseph Smith Sr. gave Abel a patriarchal blessing and declared him "ordained an Elder and anointed to secure thee against the power of the destroyer." See Richard Lyman Bushman, *Joseph Smith, Rough Stone Rolling* (New York: Alfred A. Knopf, 2005), 289, 617.

That it was the Lord's will that Joseph include the eradication of slavery in his petition to the government and people is perhaps expressed in His scriptural mandate to the Prophet. For in His Doctrine and Covenants Section 101 instructions to the Prophet—"to importune at the feet of the judge...governor...[and] president" (verses 86-88)—the Lord was clear that the solution to the national problem had to do with the proper application of constitutional principles. These were principles that, according to the Lord, were "holy principles" that should have been providing "moral agency," not just for the Saints, but for "all flesh." "It is not right," declared the Lord (in these very verses), "that any man should be in bondage one to another" (see verses 76-79).

And so, as mandated by God, the prophet-candidate had publicly addressed the twin-evils of racial and religious persecution that hampered America and jeopardized her covenant. In Volume I, Chapter 4, we discussed how the adversary had influenced the placement of these two sins early on in the settlement phase of the nation. The Evil One knew exactly what he was doing. For, by the time of the Restoration, these sins had festered in the land and had cankered the purposes of God. We cannot emphasize enough the crisis that America faced at this time —a crisis Joseph seemed to comprehend. America's entire purpose had been so badly jeopardized by the decisions of its people that it was on the verge of losing its divine mandate. It was on the verge of losing its national covenant. Neither of these evils could co-exist with the restored gospel in the Promised Land.

Consider again the scripturally documented obligations of the American Covenant. In order to be worthy as a nation of the covenant blessings, we must "keep [His] commandments" (2 Nephi 1:20) and "serve the God of the land" (Ether 2:12).[46] The twin-sins of racial and religious persecution were clearly violating the first covenant obligation to *keep His commandments*. The national covenant does not oblige its recipients to live higher laws, such as those issued in temple worship. However, we are not speaking here of higher laws. No matter the conditions under which one is born, or the culture or religion one is raised in, all have the Light of Christ, and as such can identify clear violations of God's basic laws. Enjoying the constitutional rights of *liberty*, *protection,* and *prosperity*, while selfishly denying these rights to others because of their race or religion is a violation of God's basic laws. Furthermore, persecuting, beating, torturing, killing, yoking, and enslaving fellow human beings on the basis of their race or religion most certainly is a violation of God's basic laws. God cannot and will not bless a nation that participates in and tolerates such evil: for "righteousness exalteth a nation: but sin is a reproach to any people" (Proverbs 14:34); and "I the Lord am bound when ye do what I say; but when ye do not what I say, ye have no promise" (D&C 82:10).

As pointed out in the previous chapter, there exists an inherent covenant in the Constitution, which would only further condemn America and facilitate its disintegration as it tolerated these basic sins. For the mere toleration of such sins against humanity would make it increasingly difficult for the people to be worthy of the inspiration required to apply the Constitution in righteousness. Without such national inspiration (born only though national worthiness), constitutional laws and principles were bound to be misconstrued and misapplied, thus hampering even more the ability of all Americans to appropriately access the promised constitutional blessings.

The second obligation of the American Covenant, to *serve the God of the land*, was also in clear violation. At the very least, the nation should have been serving God by maintaining the rights and principles He provided for the country in its founding documents. In the Declaration of Independence, the Founders had mutually recognized that these "unalienable rights" were for "all men" who they knew were "created equal." They also professed in the Declaration that these rights were "endowed by their Creator." The Constitution, also recognized as being of God, then further defined these rights designed for *all flesh*, which rights included the blessings of the covenant: *liberty, protection,* and *prosperity* in support of moral agency unto salvation. We have analyzed these concepts at length and certain conclusions are now definite: the nation knew this law, it knew God had delivered this law, and it had pledged to keep this law in exchange for specific blessings. The blood of the revolutionaries, along with the inspired words and deeds of the Founders, sealed this covenant relationship. Now, by blocking racial and religious minorities from accessing these blessings, the nation was failing to keep the law and covenant.

The sins of racial and religious persecution represented Satan's attack on God's purposes. Just as Satan knew in the pre-mortal existence that hampering man's agency would thwart his eternal progression, so he knew it in Joseph's day. Naturally then, just as Satan worked to oppress man in an attempt to stunt his eternal progression in the pre-existent War in Heaven, so he would do the same in Joseph's day. Indeed, Joseph Smith's America had turned into a battleground in an extension of that War in Heaven, with African Americans and Mormon Americans standing squarely in the adversary's crosshairs. And as the nation continued to adhere to the influence of the Evil One (in breaking basic commandments and not serving Him), the covenant was severely breached.

As we recognize the grave circumstances under which the nation found itself, Joseph Smith's proposed constitutional provision becomes increasingly more significant. We need make no mistake about what he was attempting to do. He really was, in no uncertain terms, proposing in his day, in almost every detail, what America would eventually achieve well over one hundred years after he proposed it. It was a prescient articulation of the Civil Rights Act. For as detailed above, the Prophet had proposed that the nation elevate the status of *all* races and religions to their rightful positions as equals under the Constitution (just as the Civil Rights Act eventually did), and he proposed that the federal government be given the power to intervene in any state or in any affair that violated such promises (just as the Civil Rights Act eventually did).[47] In short, Joseph Smith sought—through his Civil

Rights Act-like provision—to make good on the covenant promises of the Constitution: promises of *liberty, protection,* and *prosperity,* not just for the privileged and socially accepted portions of the populace, but for *all* of it.

Martin Luther King famously declared in his *I Have a Dream* speech, which helped secure the Civil Rights Act, that when the Founders signed the Declaration of Independence and the Constitution, "they were signing a promissory note to which every American was to fall heir. This note was a promise that all men would be guaranteed the unalienable rights of life, liberty and the pursuit of happiness"—even the promises of the American Covenant. Sadly, Dr. King pointed out the same problem the Prophet Joseph had seen, felt, and fought against in his day: "America has defaulted on this promissory note."[48] But Joseph put forth the solution—a solution that would ultimately be realized through the Civil Rights Act and echoed in Dr. King's words over one hundred years later. Dr. King declared, "Now is the time to open the doors of opportunity to all of God's children."[49] If the nation had only adhered to the Prophet's political platform, the American Covenant would have been secured, along with America's divine mandate, much sooner and less painfully than it was.

As God directed His efforts to fix this national problem, the prophet-candidate demonstrated that he was serious about accomplishing God's will for the nation. He was clear on his intentions. "I feel it to be my right & my privilege," declared Joseph, "to obtain what influence & power I can lawfully in the United States for the protection of injured innocence."[50] If given the opportunity, Joseph would have expanded the powers of government to do its job, as the Constitution intended. Speaking in the year before his campaign, the Prophet passionately declared: "[W]hen we have petitioned those in power for assistance, they have always told us they had no power to help us. Damn such traitors! When they give me the power to protect the innocent, I will never say I can do nothing for their good; I will exercise that power, so help me God."[51]

In closing his peroration of his presidential platform, Joseph declared: "I would, as the universal friend of man, open the prisons, open the eyes, open the ears, and open the hearts of all people to behold and enjoy freedom, unadulterated freedom; and God...should be supplicated by me for the good of all people."[52] If the government was not willing to do its job as God intended, particularly the federal government, even the ultimate guardian of the Constitution, then Joseph would do all in his power to become part of the federal government himself, and then govern justly before God. He was certainly exhausting all his resources to follow the command from God to importune at the feet of the federal government (see D&C 101: 86-88).

If the Prophet could have only convinced the nation of his national plan, whether through persuasion, or even through his own election, if possible, then the provision known today as the Civil Rights Act, or something very similar to it, would have blessed the nation when the nation needed it most. We should not fail to recognize what a powerful tool such a constitutional provision would have been. Its implementation would have signaled that the nation had forsaken the sins of racial and religious persecution and replaced its wicked acts with a policy of righteousness. The nation would have found favor before God as it elevated all minorities to their rightful place—as it elevated God's kingdom to a place where it might carry forth His work and glory. This single act and provision would have largely fulfilled the national obligations to keep the commandments and serve the God of the land. Through forsaking sin, the needed *national repentance* would have commenced. And as the nation then provided this constitutional provision, the restitution phase of its repentance would have also commenced, as the heaven-prescribed principle of *universal agency* took root in the land.

What Joseph had proposed here was nothing less than a powerful response to the adversary's war against the agency and salvation of mankind, through the rehabilitation, augmentation, and fulfillment of the national covenant.* His vision would be that of a silent partnership between racial minorities (represented most prevalently by African American slaves), and religious minorities (represented most prevalently by Latter-day Saints). For these targeted groups in this particular American battle—in this portion of the greater war commenced in heaven—were ultimately seeking the same thing: *national repentance* and *universal agency*. It was the only hope for America to fill the measure of its creation. Joseph Smith, the prophet and presidential candidate, seemed to know all this, and therefore proposed that the secret weapon would be such a provision equal to the Civil Rights Act. It would be the redemption of the American Covenant; the redemption of *liberty*, *protection*, and *prosperity*; the redemption of moral agency unto eternal salvation.

---

*That Joseph's political platform was focused on empowering the national covenant is further evidenced by the fact that he proposed a national bank and supported the extension of America "from the east to the west sea." See Arnold Garr, "Joseph Smith's Campaign for President of the United States," *Ensign*, Feb. 2009, 51. Such a move would not only have increased the power of what was a weak federal government, giving it the ability to raise new revenues, but it would have also brought more inhabitants under the *liberty* of the land, offered increased *protection* by limiting the possibility of dangerous neighbors to the west, and provided further *prosperity* through increased land and through access to a new ocean for trade. As Joseph himself said concerning his proposals, they would permit America to "extend her influence" and "inspire the nations with the spirit of freedom." With this expanding influence, America could, according to the Prophet, "suppress mobs" and spread "equity, liberty, justice, humanity and benevolence; to break down tyranny and oppression and exalt the standard of universal peace," as more people would naturally be "protected in those rights...which constitutionally belong to every citizen of this republic..." (See Richard Vetterli, *Mormonism, Americanism and Politics*, 254-55). In short, the Prophet's policies would have allowed for the speedy distribution of the national covenant blessings that were to support the restored gospel. It would have also brought the territory of what would one day be Utah under the American Covenant—even that territory, seen in vision by the Prophet, which would serve one day as the temporary capital of God's kingdom.

The Prophet's National Warning
And God's Fulfillment

Prophetic Warnings

The Prophet Joseph's pleas for the constitutional provisions listed above were delivered more boldly and more powerfully than many perhaps realize. Not only did he run for the presidency of the United States in an effort to implement his provisions (something many consider a bit rash, if not irrational), but he also openly expressed powerful warnings to the nation if his provisions were not adhered to. For example, in 1843 he told Congress that if they failed to "hear our petition and grant us protection, they shall be broken up as a government."[53] Furthermore, he announced publicly that his 1844 presidential run would be the "last effort which is enjoined upon us by our Heavenly Father before the whole nation may be left without excuse and He [God] can send forth the power of His mighty arm."[54]

As arresting as the Prophet Joseph's words and actions proved to be over this issue, there is something that might have rationalized this seemingly overbearing behavior. Indeed, there is strong evidence to believe that Joseph was not only trying to restore the integrity of the American Covenant, but was also trying to spare the nation a terrible fate in the process. It seems Joseph understood that, one way or another, the Lord would have the Constitution He had designed for His purposes. After the many miracles and interventions administered by the Lord in building America, He certainly would not give up so easily. His gospel would not be sidelined by man's feeble attempt to take the Constitution out of context. For God had brought America the Constitution; yet, His foreordained children were not receiving the constitutional blessings, as per the prophecies. His Restoration, and the exaltation of souls, was at stake.

Therefore, it is quite possible Joseph believed that if the people and government refused to heed his prophetic call—if America refused to humble itself, repent, and make the change on its own—then the Lord would intervene and purge the nation of its iniquity until such repentance and restitution had occurred. And the purging would not be pleasant. Joseph's national plea, then, was perhaps delivered so strongly because he understood that, more than providing wise counsel, he was issuing one of the most significant prophetic warnings ever given to America. He was pushing so hard for national change not only to spare his people unjust persecution, but to spare the nation a divinely mandated consequence.

But what corroborating evidence is there to suggest the Prophet was aware of such consequences to the struggling nation? What proof do we have that his words and actions of warning were thus justified? The most powerful piece of evidence that speaks to this issue stems from the Lord's very own declaration. Returning to Doctrine and Covenants, Section 101, after the Lord claims His hand in the Constitution (verse 80), and after He instructs Joseph to plea for its proper application, first to the judge (verse 86), then to the governor (verse 87), and then to the president (verse 88), the Lord then—beginning in the very next verse— unveils His final contingency and warning:

> And if the president heed them not, then will the Lord arise and come forth out of his hiding place, and in his fury vex the nation; and in his hot displeasure, and his fierce anger, in his name, will cut off those wicked, unfaithful, and unjust stewards and appoint them their portion among hypocrites and unbelievers (D&C 101: 89-90).*

This is nothing less than a forewarning to the nation that if it continued to deny God's church access to the covenant and

---

* Some may question the meaning behind the Lord's use of the phrase "vex the nation." According to some definitions of the verb *to vex*, it merely means *to annoy* or *to bother*. However, prominent dictionaries also include the following, more arresting, definitions: *to stir up; to toss about; to bring distress or suffering; to plague or afflict*. See *Random House Webster's College Dictionary* (2000) and/or *American Heritage Dictionary*, available at www.dictionary.com.

constitutional blessings created for its support, especially at the federal level wherein rested the final hope for a fullness of agency unto salvation, then God Himself would intervene. He would intervene through hurling upon America a vexation that would at last humble the nation sufficiently enough to inspire in it the required change. And that vexation would come in the form of the American Civil War.

This Civil War connection is most prominently reflected in the verses that immediately follow this "vex the nation" prophecy—verses that reveal *why* this national vexation is necessary for God's purposes:

> What I have said unto you must needs be, that all men may be left without excuse; That wise men and rulers may hear and know that which they have never considered; That I may proceed to bring to pass my act, my strange act, and to perform my work, my strange work, that men may discern between the righteous and the wicked, saith your God (D&C 101:93-95).

Upon considering these D&C 101 verses—revealed some thirty years before the Civil War—it becomes clear that they were, in fact, made in reference to the Civil War. In order to comprehend this connection we must revisit and reemphasize what the Lord told the Prophet leading up to this prophetic warning. The Lord was specifically addressing the U.S. Constitution and its divine intention to serve God's kingdom on the earth through protecting "all flesh," ensuring that man was not "in bondage one to another," and through supporting Heaven's gift of "moral agency" (See D&C 101: 77-80). Since the Constitution was clearly not benefitting the Saints or other beleaguered minorities as it should have, the Lord revealed to the Prophet (in verse 88) that he should importune at the feet of the federal government. As noted above, the Prophet did so by presenting the solution to the American Covenant crisis—a solution which would halt the national sin of oppression over racial and religious minorities (indicating the advent of *national repentance*), and replace the sin with a policy of liberty to all people, including, most specifically, African Americans and Mormon Americans (indicating the advent of the desired *universal agency*). His proposals, as we detailed above, if accepted would have looked very similar to what we know today as the Civil Rights Act.

The D&C 101 prophecy then stated clearly that if the Prophet's efforts were rejected (and they were) then God would intervene and accomplish the intended goal (see verses 89-90). In other words, God's vexation would include some heavenly act that ultimately produced the Civil Rights Act. Furthermore, in this warning, God described His pending intervention as something to be delivered in "fury" and "fierce anger" (see verses 89-90). Finally, the intervention would create something that would allow that "wise men and rulers may hear and know that which they have never considered." As the prophecy explains, it would ultimately end in the allowance for the "strange act" and "strange work" of the Restoration to bless the world (see verses 93-95).*

If there ever was an event that incorporated all these elements of the prophecy, the Civil War fits the bill like nothing else. For not only was the war hurled upon the same generation that rejected the Prophet and his proposals, and not only was it "furious" and delivered in "fierce anger," but it produced the very results the Prophet had proposed. Or, more importantly, it produced the very results the Lord promised in the prophecy that He would deliver after the nation rejected His prophet.

These heavenly-induced results are most readily viewed through tracking the progress made by black Americans, who evolved through the Civil War from lowly slaves to full-fledged citizens. This occurred as the Civil War's emancipation of slavery led to constitutional amendments outlawing slavery forever (Thirteenth Amendment), providing citizenship to all Americans regardless of

---

* That the Lord's reference to His "strange act" and "strange work" is synonymous with the fullness of His gospel is corroborated by similar declarations found in Isaiah 28:21, D&C 95:4, and comments made by Joseph Smith, as documented in *Times and Seasons* 3.22 (Sept. 15, 1842): 3:922.

race (Fourteenth Amendment), and providing voting rights to all men (Fifteenth amendment). These amendments arrived as a direct result of the Civil War and the Union's victory of the war. The war literally humbled the nation so deeply that it caused the nation to forsake its most profound national sin of enslaving an entire race, which in turn made the nation worthy of its divine mission under its divine covenant.

Though many may fail to see beyond this single fruit of the conflict, there was much more to it. As discussed above, the Civil War—if it was, in fact, God's solution to what Joseph sought for, but failed to receive on his own—would not only elevate black Americans, but would also elevate the status of God's church and kingdom. And it did so profoundly. Of all the Civil War amendments listed above, the Fourteenth Amendment is perhaps the most underappreciated. Though it has gone largely unnoticed, it was this amendment which—for the first time—definitively incorporated the Bill of Rights, to include a fullness of religion freedom, into every state of the Union. The United States government finally came to recognize that all citizens in the Union, regardless of which state they lived in, were citizens of the United States. Therefore, all citizens had claim on the divine blessings of the Constitution.

As the guardian of the Constitution, and as the protector of its rights, the federal government, at last, decided it was time to intervene in those states that violated the God-given constitutional rights of its people. This is what the Fourteenth Amendment mandated. The lost promise of the Constitution had been restored. No longer could Missouri (or any other state) deny the blessings of the Constitution, even the blessings of the covenant, to any citizen or group of citizens by claiming the Bill of Rights does not apply to the states. For, if a state were to attempt such a stunt again, this time the federal government would have *no excuse* to ignore the violation. Note, again, that the prophecy declared that the vexation would cause that "all men may be left without excuse; that wise men and rulers may hear and know that which they have never considered" (D&C 101:93-94). Indeed, the rulers would learn that which they had "never considered" before (e.g. the Fourteenth Amendment), and then they would be left "without excuse."

Joseph despised the excuses from the federal government. Now, they would not be able to refuse the pleas of the innocent. They would, by constitutional mandate, come to the aid of the suffering, and deliver the promised blessings of the covenant. Yes, the federal government would intervene, as Joseph had desired. Thanks to the Civil War, the misapplication of the *states' rights doctrine* was at last cast aside. Indeed, the great misapplication of the Constitution had been ripped away, just as Madison had originally planned and just as the Prophet Joseph had called for years earlier.

And so we see how the Civil War represented a victory not only for black Americans, but for all minorities, including the Saints. It brought the beginnings of *national repentance*, making America worthier of its calling, and it brought the beginnings of *universal agency*, which would facilitate man's eternal progression. In short, it brought the American Covenant back to life and hope back to God's children.

The Fourteenth Amendment, in turn, led to the social movements which brought us the specific provision pled for by the Prophet, even that provision which sealed America's *national repentance* and *universal agency* and restored the integrity of the American Covenant. Indeed, out of all this was born—largely through the spirit of the Civil War's Fourteenth Amendment—the inspired Civil Rights Act. With this additional provision, if state or local oppressors had been able to sneak in persecution against minority races or religions, even after the Fourteenth Amendment (which they had done, in violation of this amendment), then the federal government would, through the Civil Rights Act, finally be able to close out the last oppressive loopholes. The federal government would (by force, if necessary) secure moral agency; and it would secure moral agency *anywhere* it was threatened in the Union.

The provision Joseph had relentlessly pushed the nation to accept had finally been accepted. The federal government would at last take a constitutional stand; the voice of all the people would at last come together to seal up the covenant principles within the now properly applied Constitution. The states would eventually comply, making sure they secured, for all their citizens, full constitutional rights. Indeed, today we rarely have to depend on the federal government to intervene to restore basic rights—like freedom of religion. But it was the federal influence and threat over wicked state policy that caused state compliance—that caused a powerful protection for the rights of God's children.

In his book *America's Hope,* BYU professor Douglas Brinley recognized this most powerful fruit born of the prophecy. Stated Brinley, "The Church suffered severe persecution in the past. Hopefully, those days are now past as the Civil Rights Movement in the United States has also benefited the Saints in that our missionaries are free to proselyte and they are not imprisoned or threatened with legal action for preaching the gospel in public."[55] The Civil War was indeed God's prophetic answer to America's sinful demise; for it had brought His "strange act" and His "strange work" into the light for all to access.

If the Civil War and its subsequent fruits really are that significant to the American Covenant and to the kingdom of God on the earth, then should we not expect to find additional scriptural and prophetic references to it? We will now explore what additional prophetic and scriptural substantiation exists.

One corroborating piece of evidence comes from the commentary of the Prophet Joseph Fielding Smith—arguably the greatest historian-prophet of the latter-days. While commenting on the above-mentioned warning in D&C 101, President Smith declared that "the Saints were also to carry their grievances to the proper tribunals and seek for redress of their wrongs."

> This was a very necessary step, and when the Saints did this and were denied their civil and religious rights, those officials were left without excuse, and the judgments of the Almighty which later came upon them during the Civil War, were justified....Since there is a just law of retribution, as fixed and eternal as are other laws of the Almighty [D&C 6:33; 2 Corinthians 9:6], the day must come when there shall be *adjustments* made before a Just Magistrate, who will not be cowed by the threats of mobs.[56]

Furthermore, when President Smith made this comment, he himself was standing on additional scriptural proof, beyond what we have discussed, that independently supports the claim. For example, as early as 1831 the Lord revealed that such a vexation would occur and gave instructions to the Church on the issue. In this revelation, the Lord appears to indicate that such a tragedy would occur within the same generation to which the first-generation Church belonged: "And when the times of the Gentiles is come in, a light shall break forth among them that sit in darkness, and it shall be the fullness of my gospel; But they receive it not; for they perceive not the light, and they turn their hearts from me because of the precepts of men...And there shall be men standing in that generation, that shall not pass until they see an overwhelming scourge; for a desolating sickness shall cover the land." The Lord then describes this scourge in part, leaving little room to imagine what He is referring to: "...and they will take up the sword, one against another, and they will kill one another" (D&C 45:28-33). Considering the time frame and description of this imminent scourge, and considering it was given in response to a general disobedience of the people, perhaps the Civil War fulfills this prophecy.

The prophecy continues on some verses later, as the Lord instructs the Church on what to do in preparation for this scourge:

"Ye hear of wars in foreign lands; but behold, I say unto you, they are nigh, even at your doors, and not many years hence ye shall hear of wars in your own lands. Wherefore, I, the Lord have said, gather ye out from the eastern lands...go ye forth into the western countries" (D&C 45:63-64; see also D&C 38:29). Though many correctly point to Missouri being the place referred to as "western countries," it should be remembered that the Saints did not find safety from war there—nor, for that matter, did common Missourians find safety from war there. Perhaps this scripture *also* refers to lands even further west, which provided complete safe-haven from the national calamity of civil war.

In 1832, and in much more specific terms, the Lord revealed to the Prophet Joseph the coming of the Civil War over thirty years before it began, even revealing the very state where it would commence:

> Verily, thus saith the Lord concerning the wars that will shortly come to pass, beginning with the rebellion in South Carolina, which will eventually terminate in the death and misery of many souls....for behold, the Southern States shall be divided against the Northern States...And it shall come to pass, after many days, slaves shall rise up against their masters, who shall be marshaled and disciplined for war. And it shall come to pass also that the remnants who are left of the land will marshal themselves, and shall become exceedingly angry, and shall vex the Gentiles with a sore vexation (D&C 87:1-5).[*]

---

[*] This prophecy was fulfilled, as the first shots fired in the Civil War were at the Southern invasion of Fort Sumter, South Carolina in April 1861. This D&C prophecy also states that the "Southern States will call on...Great Britain" (verse 3). This part of the prophecy was certainly fulfilled when, at the beginning of the conflict, a Southern delegation was dispatched to Great Britain in hopes of obtaining recognition and aid for the new Southern Confederacy. See William J. Bennett, *America: The Last Great Hope*, Vol. I, 323, 330-332, 350.

The Church later emphasized the importance of this particular revelation by including it a second time in the scriptural record. As read in D&C 130: 12-13, in 1843 the Prophet Joseph expounded upon the revelation and, after again naming South Carolina as the place of war's outbreak, declared that the war would "arise through the slave question" and that "This a voice declared to me while I was praying earnestly on the subject" (D&C 130:12-13). Why was the Lord so adamant that this prophecy be included in His scripture—not once, but twice—unless it held some gospel significance, such as that outlined above? Furthermore, the fact that the Lord here called the Civil War a "vexation," and that He utilized this same language in His D&C 101 warning and prophecy is perhaps no coincidence.

Speaking of that D&C 101 prophecy, there is perhaps further corroborating evidence found within this section of scripture. As pointed out, this particular revelation was given in response to the heavy persecutions hurled upon the Saints in Missouri in the year 1833. But before expounding upon the constitutional issues at stake and the national vexation which was to serve as a remedy (the part of the revelation we have already detailed), the introductory verses hint at the same idea. For, after recognizing the national crisis, the Lord declares, "I have sworn...that I would let fall the sword of mine indignation in behalf of my people; and even as I have said, it shall come to pass" (verse 10). Then in the verses immediately following, the Lord explains that His "indignation is soon to be poured out without measure upon all nations" in order that "all mine Israel shall be saved." The Lord promises that His actions will allow Israel to be gathered, comforted, and crowned. He promises: "Zion shall not be moved out of her place." Instead, His scattered ones "shall return, and come to their inheritances, they and their children, with songs of everlasting joy, to build up the waste places of Zion—And all these things that the prophets might be fulfilled" (see verses 11-19). If the Lord truly meant what He said in 1833—that His sword would soon fall upon the nation in order to allow the Restoration to break through oppressive obstacles and go forth—what but the Civil War fulfills the prophecy?

On yet another occasion, as the Prophet Joseph was unjustly imprisoned at Liberty Jail in the spring of 1839, he pled with the Lord to understand the terrible persecutions being suffered by the Saints. In response, the Lord again echoed the above national warning in a prophecy found in Doctrine and Covenants Section 121. God revealed to the Prophet that the enemies of the Church "shall melt away as the hoar frost melteth before the burning rays of the rising sun," that "their hopes may be cut off," that in "not many years hence...they and their posterity shall be swept from under heaven," that these "children of disobedience" who "swear falsely against my servants, that they might bring them into bondage and death" will surely suffer and "their basket shall not be full," and "their houses and their barns shall perish." The revelation continues, "Wo unto all those that discomfort my people, and drive, and murder, and testify against them, saith the Lord of Hosts; a generation of vipers shall not escape the damnation of Hell." And finally, the Lord assured the Prophet that, "I have in reserve a swift judgment in the season thereof, for all of them" (see D&C 121:11-24).

Some may argue that these verses apply to broader events and that confining them to a Civil War prophecy is overly presumptuous. However, this Liberty Jail prophecy, like other proposed civil war prophecies cited above, is directed at the very generation that attacked the Church, and the punishments refer directly to mortal events like the burning of houses and barns. When else, if not during the Civil War, could these prophecies have been fulfilled?

We especially see their fulfillment in the devastations hurled upon the state of Missouri during the Civil War. The Lord, in this and other revelations, specifically points out that the recipients of this national punishment would include the enemies of the Church. Since a large portion of these enemies of the Church resided in Missouri—and if these prophecies were, in fact, referring to the Civil War—then we should expect that Missouri would have been hit particularly hard by this war. The Prophet Joseph, after all, was never shy about expressing his prophecy that Missouri would one day "witness scenes of blood and sorrow."[57] And indeed it did.

As the nation became contentious over the issue of slavery's expansion to the West, even years before the Civil War, Missouri proved to be a violent enemy of the anti-slavery efforts. As its neighbors—particularly those in Kansas—fought passionately against slavery, Missourians ended up launching and receiving violent attacks. According to David McCullough, the Civil War in Missouri began some seven years before it began in the rest of the country: "It was a war of plunder, ambush and unceasing revenge. Nobody was safe. Defenseless towns were burned...Neither then nor later did the rest of the country realize the extent of the horrors." According to one eye-witness, "The Devil came to the border [state], liked it, and stayed awhile."[58]

Particularly brutal was the Union's General Order No. 11, which in 1863, forced the residents of Jackson County—even those who were the most brutal to the Saints—to evacuate their cities, after which their houses and barns were burnt to the ground.[59] (Let us not forget the above-quoted D&C 121:12 prophecy of 1839, which stated that "their houses and barns shall perish." We will discuss the details of this particular prophecy, and its proposed fulfillment, in a later chapter.) Perhaps the Lord had been especially slow to calm such horrors in this region of the country. Perhaps He had good reason.

Furthermore, in the middle of this D&C 121 warning, the Lord stated that, during the execution of this punishment, He would "blind their minds, that they may not understand his marvelous workings" (D&C 121:12). This becomes significant in the days of the Civil War when Abraham Lincoln points out on several occasions, as will be detailed in the next chapters, that the nation did not know what spiritual meaning and overall purpose was *really* behind the Civil War.

Perhaps the most significant part of this D&C 121 revelation is when the Lord indicated His ultimate intent behind this vexation, scourge, and punishment. The Lord declared that these marvelous workings would allow Him to "set his hand and seal to change the times and seasons" (D&C 121:12). Reference to such powerful change is completely consistent with the ultimate fruits of the Civil War, as discussed above and as defined in D&C 101:93-95; that is, the result of the calamity would be a national change that would powerfully amend the Constitution to protect God's kingdom on the earth.

As the Civil War and its divine fruits seemed to play such a large role in the prophecies and promises surrounding the establishment of God's latter-day kingdom, perhaps the Book of Mormon—even that most prominent American Covenant book of scripture—has something to say about it as well. When the resurrected Christ was with the Nephites, He expounded upon the American Covenant, declaring that latter-day America would "be set up as a free land by the power of the Father...that the covenant of the Father may be fulfilled," after which God could "work a marvelous work among them" (3 Nephi 21:4-9). But shortly after this declaration, Christ also added a warning that perhaps reflects the Civil War prophecies above. For Christ warned that "at that day whosoever [indicating that the following applies to anyone and everyone in the land] will not repent and come unto [me], them will I cut off from among my people...And I will execute vengeance and fury upon them, even as upon the heathen, such as they have not heard (3 Nephi 21: 20-21)."

It seems odd that Christ would be saying here that such furious vengeance would be reserved for "whosoever" in latter-day America does not accept the restored gospel. But if He was referring to the national sins against His national covenant (i.e. basic sins against man and sins against God's plan for the Promised Land), then perhaps such vengeance is understood. For such vengeance, in this case, would be an absolutely necessary step in delivering His gospel to the earth.

This interpretation is further substantiated by what Christ told the Nephites next. Explaining the fruit of this vengeance in the very next verses, Christ declared: "But if they will repent and harden not their hearts, I will establish my church among them, and they shall come in unto the covenant....And they will assist my people that they may be gathered in....And then shall the power of Heaven come down among them....And then shall the work of the Father commence at that day, even when his gospel shall be preached" (3 Nephi 21:22-26). In that the Lord made these warnings shortly after outlining the American Covenant in the latter-days, might these prophecies have reference to the American Covenant in breach? Might the Lord have been referring to the furious vengeance of war that would humble the nation, bring them "in unto the [national] covenant," and thus allow the gospel to be "established among them" (the American people) who would then "assist my people," so that the gospel might flourish upon divine American political foundations?

Another fascinating, albeit obscure, prophecy dealing with this topic came at the time of the American founding. While the Founders were creating the Constitution, one of the delegates at the convention, George Mason, warned his countrymen of what God would do if America continued to permit the sin of slavery to persist in the land. Such national sin, he prophesied, would "bring the judgments of heaven on a Country. As nations can not be rewarded or punished in the next world they must be in this. By an inevitable chain of cause & effect providence punishes national sins, by national calamities."[60]

Thomas Jefferson had also uttered such a prophecy a few years earlier, warning that "[t]here must doubtless be an unhappy influence on the manners of our people produced by the existence of slavery among us...Indeed, I tremble for my country when I reflect that God is just: that his justice can not sleep forever." He then described "a revolution" over the conflict as being "among possible events." He also stated that such an event would be administered by "supernatural interference!" "The Almighty," he concluded, "has no attribute which can take side with us in such a contest."[61] They understood the national covenant; and they understood the consequences should that covenant be broken by the people.

Another relevant prophecy was uttered by the Prophet Joseph Smith in 1843:

> I prophesy in the name of the Lord God of Israel, unless the United States redress the wrongs committed upon the Saints in the state of Missouri and punish the crimes committed by her officers, that in a few years the government will be utterly overthrown and wasted, and there will not be so much as a potsherd left for their wickedness in permitting the murder of men, women and children, and the wholesale plunder and extermination of thousands of her citizens to go unpunished, thereby perpetuating a foul and corroding blot upon the fair fame of this great republic, the very thought of which would have caused the high-minded and patriotic framers of the Constitution of the United States to hide their faces with shame. [62]

(This prophecy perhaps sheds light on why Joseph Smith included the following description of God in his presidential platform publication: "God, who once cleansed the violence of the earth with flood.")[63]

When Joseph's political provision was rejected, the fulfillment of this prophecy was soon to follow. For the Civil War not only physically destroyed America—especially Missouri, as described above—but the old government was in fact "overthrown and wasted" in a way that at last made it unconstitutional for the "murder of men, women and children" and the "wholesale plunder and extermination" of the Saints. Indeed, the advent of the Fourteenth Amendment—even that direct fruit of Civil War—*drastically* changed the government forever.

Perhaps all of this might even be a partial validation of another oft-referenced prophecy of Joseph, in which he declared that "when the constitution is on the brink of ruin, this people [the

Church] will be the staff up[on] which the Nation shall lean and they shall bear the constitution away from the very verge of destruction."[64] Before the Civil War, and especially during the Civil War, the Constitution had been brought to near ruin (the only time since the prophecy that the Constitution had come so close to complete failure), and yet the Lord saved it in the end by influencing a Union victory, which led to provisions like the Fourteenth Amendment and the Civil Rights Act. He did this that His church and kingdom might have soil for its roots. In this sense, the Church *was* the reason the Constitution was not left on "the brink of ruin." Indeed, the Church's presence in the Promised Land, and its need to survive and thrive, was what motivated the divine power that would "bear the constitution away from the very verge of destruction."

The Point of No Return

The above-cited prophetic warnings were obviously in the forefront of Joseph Smith's mind and heart. He, therefore, did all in his power to express these warnings to the nation he loved. One political scholar noted that the Prophet had exhausted all his resources in carrying out "his duty as a prophet of God to warn his nation, even as Isaiah of old had warned the nation of Israelites, of impending doom and destruction."[65] "Oh that I could snatch them [the people of the United States] from the vortex of misery, into which I behold them plunging themselves…," cried the prophet-candidate, "that I might be enabled by the warning voice, to be an instrument of bringing them to unfeigned repentance."[66]

In his final attempt to change the nation as a public figure, even as a presidential candidate, the nation still could have listened and changed. Instead it did the opposite, and by so doing passed the point of no return—even that point when the prophecies, promises, and warnings to the nation would, by necessity, be fulfilled. This fateful point of no return was passed on June 27, 1844, at five o'clock p.m., when the Constitution's application failed so greatly as to permit the cold-blooded murder of the Prophet Joseph and his faithful brother Hyrum at Carthage, Illinois. Even though the governor, Thomas Ford, had guaranteed their constitutional rights and protection, his promise was made—as would be expected—so half-heartedly and in vain, that it not only failed completely but also "cost the best blood of the nineteenth century" (D&C 135:6). This was followed by the burning of God's temple, even that portal into eternity required for a fullness of salvation.

So, what happens when the people kill the prophets and burn the temples? "The anger of the Lord is kindled, and his sword is bathed in heaven, and it shall fall on the inhabitants of the earth. And the arm of the Lord shall be revealed; and the day cometh that they who will not hear the voice of the Lord, neither the voice of his servants...shall be cut off" (D&C 1:14). In the very year of the Prophet's attempt for the presidency—of his attempt to restore the national covenant—the nation not only failed to hear the voice of the Lord, but watched idly by as His prophet was murdered. Later, the nation watched-on, uninterested, as God's temple was burnt to the ground.

The judges, the governors, the president, and the people had officially failed God and His efforts. And so, as the prophecy declared, "if [they] heed them not, then will the Lord arise and come forth out of his hiding place, and in his fury vex the nation" (see D&C 101: 86-89). The point of no return had at last arrived, even that point foreseen by the Prophet, who had, before his death, ultimately conceded that the final appeal would be directed "to the Courts of Heaven, believing that the Great Jehovah...will undoubtedly redress our wrongs."[67]

Though Joseph might have taken comfort in the idea that God would ultimately make things right, the prophecies pained him deeply. He wrote in his journal, upon returning from the nation's capital (after having been rejected once again), that "my heart faints within me when I see, by the visions of the Almighty, the end of this action, if [America] continues to disregard the cries and petitions."[68]

He saw his fellow Americans "plunging themselves" into "the vortex of misery."[69] He saw the vexation. He saw the Civil War. And indeed it would be enough to faint the heart: with over 600,000 deaths (not a family in the nation went unaffected), it was by far the most deadly and tragic calamity America has ever seen or felt.

The Lord did not desire this outcome. The Lord Himself told Joseph and the Church—in the midst of His D&C 101 prophetic warning of the looming national vexation—to "pray ye, therefore, that their ears may be opened unto your cries, that I may be merciful unto them, that these things may not come upon them" (D&C 101:92). But God is just and His purposes must prevail. The American Covenant, after all, has been clear from the beginning: "And now, we can behold the decrees of God concerning this land, that it is a land of promise; and whatsoever nation shall possess it shall serve God, or they shall be swept off when the fullness of his wrath shall come upon them...it is the everlasting decree of God" (Ether 2: 9-10).

While such vengeance might be difficult to understand, it has (nevertheless) always been God's way. He gave such warnings and carried out such actions to His ancient peoples of the Old World (see Leviticus 26) and to His ancient peoples of the New World (see Alma 50:21; Helaman 12:3). He further allowed death and suffering for His purposes even in the modern New World, placing Himself at the forefront of the American Revolutionary War (1 Ne. 13:17-19; D&C 101:80). Now He would do it again.

Fighting Satan's efforts to oppress mankind is difficult business. Satan, after all, has successfully denied a fullness of freedom to over ninety-five percent of all God's children who have ever walked the earth.[70] This explains why *so much* goes into creating a covenant land to provide freedom. Consider the prophecies of the American Covenant. This latter-day land of promise was foreseen by ancient prophets of the Old World (e.g. Genesis 49) and by ancient prophets of the New World (e.g. 1 Nephi 13). Indeed, it was designed and planned thousands of years before its advent. And when the promised land and nation finally materialized, it did so *only* because of God's unceasing miracles during the discovery, settlement, and revolution phases of the nation. God does all this because his work and glory is to bring to pass the eternal life of man—nothing is more important. So when His children disobey and hear Him not—and thus frustrate His plans for freedom unto eternal salvation—He will do *whatever* needs to be done. It is for their own wellbeing and salvation. As Elder Dallin Oaks explained, "God's anger and His wrath are not a *contradiction* of His love but an *evidence* of His love."[71]

Oh, but if only they had listened to the Prophet and changed on their own! How much sadness and devastation might the nation have eluded! As the Mormon leader and politician George Q. Cannon wrote: "Certain it is that had Joseph Smith been elected President of the United States and had been sustained by Congress in his policies, this land would have been spared the desolating war which filled its hamlets and fields with carnage and its homes with sobbing widows and orphans."[72]

It was not only Mormons who recognized this truth. Years after the war, the one-time mayor of Boston, Josiah Quincy, recognized how things might have been different had the nation heeded the Prophet. Quincy had visited the Prophet during the Prophet's 1844 run for the presidency, and therefore knew something about his politics. Based on this knowledge, Quincy made a most astonishing statement about Joseph Smith and the Civil War. While discussing the merits of a certain Christian scholar, who had developed a plan in 1855 that, if implemented, might have spared the nation any civil war, Quincy said this in the 1880's:

> We, who can look back upon the terrible cost of fratricidal war which put an end to slavery, now we say that such a solution of the difficult would have been worthy a Christian statesmen. But if the retired scholar was in advance of his time when he advocated his disposition...in 1855, what shall I say of the political and religious leader [Joseph Smith] who had committed himself in print, as well as in conversation, to the same course in 1844?[73]

Even the late historian Don Seitz reflected upon the same, asking the following rhetorical question in reference to the Prophet Joseph: "What other voice in all the madness was so sane?"[74]

All these admissions and concessions, though inspired indeed, were far too few and far too late. And so the war came.

The tragic acts of murdering the Prophet and destroying God's temple, not only brought to light the prophecies concerning the need of Civil War, but caused additional prophecies to be revealed. For example, immediately after the assassinations, the senior apostle, Brigham Young, knew the time of the foretold national vexation was very close at hand. In a revelation received by Brigham, the Lord declared:

> Thy brethren have rejected you and your testimony, even *the nation* that has driven you out; And now cometh the day of their calamity, even the days of sorrow, like a woman that is taken in travail; and their sorrow shall be great unless they speedily repent, yea, very speedily. For they killed the prophets, and them that were sent unto them; and they have shed innocent blood, which crieth from the ground against them (D&C 136:34-36, emphasis added).

Commenting upon this "sorrow" that was to shortly be the nation's, Brigham declared that, because they "reject the servants of God, they reject the gospel of salvation, turn away from the principles of truth and righteousness...[and] are sinking in their own sins and corruptions....

> The nation that gave me and many of you birth is very nigh to the hours of sorrow....What will be their condition

when the Spirit of the Lord is withdrawn? They will whet the knife to cut each other's throats and...will try to make Mason and Dixon's the dividing line [Mason and Dixon's was the name given to the border between Northern and Southern states]; but they will not remain, for they will cross it to destroy each other, and the sword and fire will be prevalent in the land.[75]

Though the nation continued to pay no heed to such prophetic warnings, they were certainly not lost on the Saints. According to a Church publication, when the Civil War finally arrived, the Saints were immediately convinced that it was nothing less than "a judgment upon the nation for the murders of Joseph and Hyrum Smith, for not keeping the commandments of God [one of these violated commandments was certainly the atrocities of slavery], and for injustices inflicted upon the Saints in Missouri and Illinois."[76]

Another part of the prophecy that was not lost on the Saints —though perhaps largely forgotten today—was the connection between the Saints westward migration and the Civil War prophecies. We have already discussed the prophetic statement that explains how, in order for the Saints to avoid war, they must move to the lands westward (see D&C 45:64-65). But there were further prophetic utterances related to this. In 1833, for example, the Lord revealed a prophecy related specifically to the land which hosted His Zion in America. The Lord declared: "For behold, and lo, vengeance cometh speedily upon the ungodly as the whirlwind. And who shall escape it? The Lord's scourge shall pass over by night and by day, and the report thereof shall vex all people.... Nevertheless, Zion shall escape if she observes to do all things" (D&C 97:1, 22-25).

A follow-up commentary to this notion came years later by the Prophet Brigham Young, as he addressed the Saints in their new

The End of Parley's Street, by Glen Hopkinson
Courtesy of Glen Hopkinson

home in Salt Lake, even as the Civil War raged in the East. Had the Saints not been led out of the United States, commented Brigham, "we would now be in the midst of the wars and bloodshed that are desolating the nation, instead of where we are, comfortably located in our peaceful dwellings in these silent, far off mountains and valleys."

> Instead of seeing my brethren comfortably seated around me to-day, many of them would be found in the front ranks on the battlefield. I realize the blessings of God in our present safety. We are greatly blessed, greatly favored and greatly exalted, while our enemies, who sought to destroy us, are being humbled"[77]

Shortly after the Civil War had begun, Brigham Young further commented on the issue, stating, "We are not now mingling in the turmoils of strife, warring and contention that we would have been obliged to mingle in had not the Lord suffered us to have been driven to these mountains." Brigham concluded that "it had been designated, for many generations, to hide up the Saints in the last days, until the indignation of the Almighty be over..."[78] Such an idea, particularly with its connections to the Civil War, perhaps adds additional significance to the Prophet Joseph's oft-quoted prophecy that the Saints would eventually settle in the Rocky Mountains.[79]

The Lord's plan, then, comes into sharp focus. At that point of no return, He would quite literally pick up his kingdom—physically removing it—and place it outside of the country (the Utah territory was not a part of the United States at the time of the Saints' exodus). Then, with His gospel and its carriers safely tucked away, the Lord would work His powerful and devastating work, that the nation might be made worthy of the divine kingdom it had been foreordained to support and protect. Only after that refining process could the kingdom return to its rightful place under God's reconstructed national covenant.

Conclusion

Let us never lose sight of the fact that the Prophet Joseph Smith had been sent to the earth to accomplish the impossible. He summed up his life purpose, declaring that God had sent him to "so firmly [establish His kingdom on the earth] that all the powers of earth and hell can never prevail against it."[80] Joseph clearly knew of, and witnessed, such evil powers as they continually attacked him and God's kingdom. And so he did what he could to combat these evil powers in furthering his efforts to build God's kingdom on the earth. Specifically, he tried with all his might to prop-up and establish, or reestablish, the American Covenant. And when the nation adhered not, the terrible warnings became a reality. For in the end (and to again quote the aforementioned scriptural warnings), God took His Saints out of the United States and into the "western countries," where "Zion shall escape" and "the Lord's scourge shall pass over [them] by night and by day." Then, with the Saints safely tucked away, "with hot displeasure and fierce anger" the Lord could work His constitutional corrections, "com[ing] forth out of his hiding place and in his fury vex the nation," through civil war and thus humble the "children of disobedience" to the point that He might "seal to change" the nation until He had the nation He originally intended. Only then might His gospel—even His "strange act" and "strange work"—safely return and flourish under the divine principles of good government.

That these promises and prophecies were fulfilled through the Civil War, and through the war's ultimate gospel fruits (e.g. the Fourteenth Amendment and the Civil Rights Act), seems convincing enough. However, the most compelling evidence of these scriptural interpretations should be found in the annals of American history. For, if what we have claimed above is true, American history should validate our claims. As we enter the next wave of chapters, we will dive into this history and will clearly achieve such validation. We will explore the prophetic and spiritual nature of the Civil War and the Civil Rights Movement—a prophetic and spiritual nature which has, for years, been hiding in plain sight.

We will begin our journey at the commencement of the war, and will see how it indeed represented the Godly vexation of the scriptures, which was to humble the nation and cause it to turn to the Lord—cause it to turn to the covenant. As the federal government (represented largely by the North, or what we call the Union) was the group called upon by the Prophet to protect the people, we will see how it was the Union who made the first turn toward repentance and restitution.* As the Union began applying *national repentance* and *universal agency*, we will witness how the American Covenant became active and led to Union victory. We will also be introduced to a wicked ideology and system proposed by the South—an ideology and system which represented Satan's plan. And we will see how God eradicated this evil plan in America through the power of a righteous war fought under the power of the American Covenant. It was an extension of the War in Heaven, for it was fought over the same principles. We will be surprised to see how this entire experience played out like a series of scenes from the Old Testament or the Book of Mormon. For it was, in many ways, the same story. A chosen, yet sinful, people were humbled by the Almighty, that they might be made tools in the hands of Heaven. In the end, good prevailed over evil, and the covenant was thus redeemed in furtherance of God's work and glory.

The fruit of God's victory and the evidence of the covenant thus redeemed, would eventually become overwhelmingly apparent. As we will witness in the coming chapters, it was this victory and renewal of covenant that allowed the elevation of black Americans, who went from slaves to full participants in society, even

---

* That it was the *federal* government that would come to enforce the Constitution, just as Joseph had called for, becomes all the more significant when we consider that the root word for *federal*—the Latin *foedus*—directly translates into the English word "covenant." See Bruce Feiler, *America's Prophet* (New York: Harper Collins, 2009), 28.

reaching the presidency of the United States. (This is not to say that this particular president's policies are necessarily in line with the covenant, only that his ability to ascend to the presidency as a black man represents America's redemption from sins past.)

The Latter-day Saints would also follow an enlightened path of elevation. We will see a great national transition, from a time when state governments beat, killed, and exiled the Saints, to a time when these same governments formally and officially apologized for their sins, and allowed the Saints to rejoin the Union;* from a time when the federal government sat idly by, to a time when the federal government honored the prophet of God with the highest honor given to civilians; from a time when members of the Church were denied all civil rights, to a time when Church members hold the most prominent positions in Congress, and are considered strong candidates for the presidency of the United States; and from a time when God's temples were allowed to be burned to the ground, to a time when the government called on special police forces to protect the temple from the threat of mobs. And thus we shall see how the gospel of Jesus Christ has been made *so* accessible to mankind in these the latter-days.

The Civil War and the righteous movement toward progression that followed in its wake truly represent the covenant in action. As we now analyze this great and terrible era of American history, we will gain further testimony of the reality, the functionality, and the eternal significance of the American Covenant.

---

* U.S. President Polk's request for Mormon Pioneers to join the U.S. Military as the Mormon Battalion, even as the Saints were on their trek into exile, was perhaps an inspired move to keep the estranged Church connected in some small way to the government—a reminder to the Church that it did belong, and would one day return, to the providential and covenant-based care of the United States of America. Furthermore, not long after the Saints' exile, the United States acquired the foreign territory that included the Salt Lake Valley. Perhaps this was, yet another, inspired reminder to the Church about where it belonged.

ENDNOTES

[1] Richard Lyman Bushman, *Joseph Smith, Rough Stone Rolling* (New York: Alfred A. Knopf, 2005), 423-424. Also note that the First Amendment includes the right of free exercise of religion and the Second Amendment includes the right to bear arms, particularly as given to militias, such as the one in Nauvoo.

[2] Joseph Smith, as quoted in Bushman, *Rough Stone Rolling*, 226-227.

[3] Bushman, *Rough Stone Rolling*, 491.

[4] Bushman, *Rough Stone Rolling*, 491.

[5] Terryl Givens, *By The Hand of Mormon* (New York: Oxford University Press, 2002), 68.

[6] Gordon B. Hinckley, "An unending Conflict, a Victory Assured," *Ensign*, June 2007, 7.

[7] Givens, 68; Bushman, *Rough Stone Rolling*, 289.

[8] Bushman, *Rough Stone Rolling*, 224.

[9] Letter from Governor Dunklin to the Church, as quoted in *Church History in the Fulness of Times* (Salt Lake City: Church of Jesus Christ of Latter-day Saints, 2000), 182.

[10] *Church History in the Fulness of Times*, 201.

[11] Bushman, *Rough Stone Rolling*, 230.

[12] Bushman, *Rough Stone Rolling*, 236.

[13] Bushman, *Rough Stone Rolling*, 393, 396.

[14] Bushman, *Rough Stone Rolling*, 397, 512.

[15] Bushman, *Rough Stone Rolling* 396; Gerald Lund, *The Coming of the Lord* (Salt Lake: Deseret Book, 1971), 53.

[16] Monk, *The Words We Live By*, 128, 215.

[17] Waldman, 52, 136, 173.

[18] Winslow Crosskey, as quoted in Richard Vetterli, *Mormonism, Americanism and Politics* (Salt Lake City: Ensign Publishing Company, 1961), 121. Crosskey, it should be noted, served as Professor of Law at the University of Chicago. He also clerked under Chief Justice William H. Taft of the Supreme Court.

[19] Brigham Young, as quoted in John A. Widstoe, ed., *Discourses of Brigham Young* (Salt Lake City: Deseret Book Co., 1954), 361-362.

[20] Monk, *The Words We Live By,* 194-195.

[21] See Richard Vetterli, *Mormonism, Americanism and Politics*, 110-114.

[22] Jefferson, as quoted in Skousen, *The Five Thousand Year Leap*, 232.

[23] Jefferson, as quoted in John J. Stewart, *Thomas Jefferson and the Restoration of the Gospel of Jesus Christ* (U.S.: Mercury Publishing, 1959), 28.

[24] Washington, in a letter to the Touro Synagogue in Newport, Rhode Island, August 17, 1790, as quoted in Waldman, *Founding Faith*, 164.

[25] Waldman, 63.

[26] See Chapters 1 and 2 of this volume.

[27] Novak, *On Two Wings: Humble Faith and Common Sense at the American Founding* (San Francisco: Encounter Books, 2002), 53.

[28] Monk, 215.

[29] Willard Sterne Randall, *Alexander Hamilton*, 398.

[30] Hamilton, as quoted in Skousen, *The Five Thousand Year Leap,* 226.

[31] John Quincy Adams, as quoted in Michael Winder, *Presidents and Prophets* (American Fork: Covenant Communications, 2007), 38.

[32] Madison, available at www.quotes-museum.com/quote/56704.

[33] Joseph Smith, as quoted in Richard Vetterli, *Mormonism, Americanism and Politics*, 202.

[34] Joseph Smith, as quoted in Richard Vetterli, *Mormonism, Americanism and Politics*, 107.

[35] Bushman, *Rough Stone Rolling,* 514.

[36] Joseph Smith, as quoted in Richard Vetterli, *Mormonism, Americanism and Politics*, 107.

[37] Bushman, *Rough Stone Rolling,* 514.

[38] Donna Hill, *Joseph Smith, The First Mormon* (Midvale: Signature Books, 1977), 375.

[39] Joseph Smith (October 1843), as quoted in Joseph Fielding Smith, ed, *Teachings of the Prophet Joseph Smith* (Salt Lake City: Deseret Book Company, 1976), 326-327.

[40] Arnold Garr, "Joseph Smith's Campaign for President of the United States," *Ensign*, February 2009, 50; *History of the Church*, 6:206.

[41] Milton C. Cummings, Jr. and David Wise, *Democracy Under Pressure*, 10th ed. (Toronto: Thomson-Wadsworth, 2005), 163-164.

[42] Skousen, *The Five Thousand Year Leap*, 15.

[43] Garr, *Ensign* Feb, 2009, 50.

[44] Bushman, *Rough Stone Rolling,* 514-516.

[45] Garr, *Ensign*, Feb. 2009, 50.

[46] See Volume I, Chapter 1, of this book for a more detailed explanation of the national obligations of the American Covenant.

[47] That the Civil Rights Act of 1964 calls for such provisions is documented in Milton C. Cummings, Jr. and David Wise, *Democracy Under Pressure*, 10th ed. (Toronto: Thomson-Wadsworth, 2005), 163-164; and in Linda Monk, *Words We Live By*, 49, 228.

[48] Martin Luther King, as quoted in *Let Freedom Ring* (New York: Sterling Publishing Co., 2001), 150.

[49] Martin Luther King, as quoted in *Let Freedom Ring*, 15.

[50] Bushman, *Rough Stone Rolling*, 515.

[51] Joseph Smith Jr., *History of the Church of Jesus Christ of Latter-day Saints* (Salt Lake City: Deseret Book, 1973), Volume 5, 384; also quoted in J. Michael Hunter, *Mormon Myth-ellaneous* (American Fork: Covenant Communications, 2008), 77.

[52] Joseph Smith, as quoted in Richard Bushman, speech given at the Pew Forum on Religion and Public Life, May 14, 2007, available at http://Pewforum.org/events/? Event ID=148.

[53] Joseph Smith, as quoted in Lund, *The Coming of the Lord* (Salt Lake City: Deseret Book, 1971), 54.

[54] Joseph Smith, as quoted in Vetterli, *Mormonism, Americanism and Politics*, 173.

[55] Douglas Brinley, *America's Hope* (Salt Lake City: Deseret Book, 2005), 28.

[56] Joseph Fielding Smith, as quoted in *Doctrine and Covenants Student Manual, Religion 324-325* (Salt Lake City: The Church of Jesus Christ of Latter-day Saints, 1981), 245. emphasis added.

[57] Richard Vetterli, *Mormonism, Americanism and Politics*, 297.

[58] David McCullough, *Truman* (New York: Simon and Schuster, 1992), 26-28.

[59] For more information on General Order No.11, see http://en.wikipedia.org/wiki/Missouri_in_the_American_Civil_War#General_Order_No._11.

[60] George Mason, as documented in Robert A. Rutland, *The Papers of George Mason* (Chapel Hill, NC: University of North Carolina Press, 1970), 1:159.

[61] Thomas Jefferson, 1743-1826, *Notes on the State of Virginia, 1780* (Electronic Text Center, University of Virginia Library), 289, available at http://etext.virginia.edu/etcbin/toccer-new2?id=JefVirg.

[62] Joseph Smith, as quoted in *History of The Church of Jesus Christ of Latter-day Saints,* 7 volumes, edited by Brigham H. Roberts (Salt Lake City: Deseret Book, 1957), 5:394.

[63] Joseph Smith, as quoted in Richard Bushman, Speech given at the Pew Forum on Religion and Public Life, May 14, 2007, available at http://Pewforum.org/events/?Event ID=148.

[64] Bushman, *Rough Stone Rolling*, 404.

[65] Richard Vetterli, *Mormonism, Americanism and Politics,* 230.

[66] Joseph Smith, as quoted in Richard Vetterli, *Mormonism, Americanism and Politics*, 173.

[67] Bushman, *Rough Stone Rolling*, 404.

[68] Joseph Smith, as quoted in Lund, *The Coming of the Lord*, 53.

[69] Joseph Smith, as quoted in Richard Vetterli, *Mormonism, Americanism and Politics*, 173.

[70] Chris Stewart and Ted Stewart, *Seven Tipping Points That Saved the World* (Salt Lake City: Shadow Mountain, 2011), 12.

[71] Dallin H. Oaks, "Love and Law," General Conference Address, October 2009, as quoted from *Ensign*, November 2009, 27.

[72] George Q. Cannon, as quoted in Richard Vetterli, *Mormonism, Americanism and Politics* (Salt Lake City: Ensign Publishing Company, 1961), 197.

[73] Josiah Quincy, as quoted in Richard Bushman, *The Pew Forum of Religion and Public Life*, May 14, 2007, available at http://PewForum.org/events/?EventID=148.

[74] Don Seitz, *Uncommon Americans* (the Bobbs-Merrill Company, 1925), 13, as quoted in Richard Vetterli, 230.

[75] Brigham Young, as quoted in *Discourses of Brigham Young,* John Widtsoe, ed. (Salt Lake: Deseret Book, 1954), 365.

[76] *Church History in the Fullness of Times*, 381.

[77] *Church History in Fullness of Times*, 382.

[78] Brigham Young, as quoted in Lund, *The Coming of the Lord*, 90.

[79] Lund, *The Coming of the Lord*, 89.

[80] Joseph Smith, as quoted in *Presidents of the Church: Joseph Smith* (Salt Lake: Church of Jesus Christ of Latter-day Saints, 2007), 531.

Battle of Antietam--Army of the Potomac, by B. McClellan
Courtesy of the Library of Congress

CHAPTER 4

A WAR-TORN NATION
TURNS TOWARD THE COVENANT

[I]t is quite possible that God's purpose [for this war] is something different from the purpose of either party...I am almost ready to say this is probably true—that God wills this contest, and wills that it shall not end yet.

—Abraham Lincoln, 1862

If the Civil War truly was the national vexation and scourge prophesied of in the scriptures, then the historical account should reflect it. Specifically, we should see historical evidence that the Civil War began a process that humbled the people—that it caused them to repent, compelled them to recognize the breach of their sacred covenant, and pushed them to apply the vision of liberty put forth by the Prophet Joseph.

Considering these divine machinations at the core of the war's ultimate purpose, we might expect that the Lord would call a special servant to lead the difficult endeavor. As God always calls a prophet to restore His *priesthood* covenant, so we might expect Him to call a president to restore His *national* covenant. Even as the Saints were moving out of the United States, God's prophet, Brigham Young, clearly recognized this idea. For the covenant to come back into play, and thus to restore the status of God's Church, a chosen one must be sent. Declared the Prophet Brigham, "The government of the United States has remained silent, or refused us, when appealed to for redress of grievances."

> She has permitted us to be driven from our own lands... She has calmly looked on and permitted one of the fundamental and dearest provisions of the Constitution to be broken; she has permitted us to be driven and trampled under foot with impunity. Under these circumstances, what course is left for us to pursue? I answer that, instead of seeking to destroy the very best Government in the world, as seems to be the fears of some, we, like other good citizens, should seek to place those men in power, who will feel the obligations and responsibilities they are under to a mighty people; who would feel and realize the important trusts reposed in them by the voice of the people who call them to administer law under the solemn sanction of an oath of fidelity to that heaven inspired instrument.[1]

That Brigham was referring here to the American Covenant ("the solemn sanction of an oath of fidelity to that heaven inspired instrument"), and that he was referring to the need and hope for a leader within the government to stand up and preserve it, is clear. And that the Lord eventually acted on these hopes and prayers and did, in fact, raise up such a leader is even clearer.

Enter Abraham Lincoln

Abraham Lincoln was born on February 12, 1809 (some three years after the Prophet Joseph), to a barely educated and professionally failing farm family in an undersized log cabin in Nardin, Kentucky.

Abraham Lincoln
Courtesy of the Library of Congress

This biographical sketch alone perhaps exemplifies best the first dose of divine intervention Lincoln would experience throughout his life in preparation for his calling. For it was this challenging environment (like that experienced by so many of the Lord's anointed) that taught him hard and fast the virtues of humility and dependence on the Lord.

Lincoln eventually moved to Illinois and pulled himself out of obscurity. He trained himself in law, passed the bar, and began a successful career as a circuit-riding lawyer. Though he found success in his career, his humility and inspired nature prompted him to always keep his fees low and to never attempt to greedily amass a large fortune.[2] By the time he was forty-years-old he had also managed to serve for several years as an Illinois state legislator and had enjoyed a brief taste of national politics, serving a two-year (and largely uneventful) term in the United States House of Representatives. This sums up his professional experience prior to landing the presidency in 1860—hardly an impressive resume for a president-elect.

The son of John Quincy Adams—and grandson of the great founder John Adams—said of Lincoln that "I must...affirm, without hesitation that, in the history of our government down to this hour, no experiment so rash has ever been made as that of elevating to the head of affairs a man with so little previous preparation for his task as Mr. Lincoln."[3] But it was Lincoln's lack of pedigree that provided God what he needed at this crucial moment. For his lack of worldly credentials kept Lincoln humble and dependent upon the Lord. This made him a perfect would-be national savior.

Lincoln's humility was abundantly obvious. For example, he had the great humility to occupy the most powerful position in the land, yet still maintain the most accessible executive branch in American history, even receiving uninvited visits from the lowliest and commonest of solicitors. He did so that he might remember that it was "that great popular assemblage out of which I sprung."[4] It was this same humble soul who readily and characteristically apologized to General Grant, after a disagreement over military strategy, simply writing him, "I now wish to make the personal acknowledgement that you were right and I was wrong."[5] And it was Lincoln who, after reading a biographical sketch of his life, published to the nation, commented that there was not much to it because "there is not much to me."[6]

This humility naturally led him to a sense of reliance and dependence upon God—a relationship he would lean on during the national crises he presided over.

Though not affiliated with any particular religious denomination, Lincoln was most certainly a religionist. On one occasion before his presidency, he visited a woman on her deathbed, in his capacity as her lawyer, in order to help draft a final will. As he sat with her, he became filled with the Spirit and began reciting scripture and bearing testimony of Jesus Christ. The woman became enthralled with "Pastor" Lincoln, her countenance filling with light. Moments after Lincoln finished, and while he was still with the woman, she closed her eyes in peaceful contentment and passed away. As Lincoln left the house, he told a friend, "God, and Eternity, and Heaven were very near to me today."[7]

Lincoln's powerful relationship with God is further evidenced by the fact that he prayed regularly. In the midst of the war Lincoln declared: "I have been driven many times upon my knees by the overwhelming conviction that I had nowhere else to go. My own wisdom, and that of all about me, seemed insufficient for that day."[8] He openly declared, "I talk to God," and admitted the following to General Dan Sickles: "When I could not see any other resort, I would place my whole reliance in God, knowing that all would be well, and that He would decide for the right."[9]

Lincoln often connected his personal religion to the Bible. He once declared, "All the good Savior gave to the world was communicated through this book [the Bible]...all things most desirable for man's welfare, here and hereafter, are to be found portrayed in it."[10] And there is no doubt Lincoln applied righteous, Biblical principles to his personal life, which made him a more pure vessel for God. For instance, Lincoln maintains the rare distinction of being one of the few presidents in history to disdain and refrain from both tobacco and alcohol.[11]*

Lincoln's humility and reliance on God was complemented and reinforced by his ever-famous sense of absolute honesty. He certainly deserved his popular nickname "Honest Abe," as not a soul could point out any legitimate instance in which he sold out his moral integrity for avarice, greed, or some other personal gain (a remarkable commentary considering his chosen professions were lawyer and politician).[12] Lincoln's step-mother (who raised him through his adolescence) said "he was the best boy I ever saw. He never told me a lie in his life, never evaded, never quarreled, never dodged nor turned a corner to avoid any chastisement or other responsibility."[13] One influential contemporary of Lincoln said of him that "every beat of 'honest Abe's' heart was a throb of sincerity and truth." The *Chicago Press and Tribune* asserted that he was "above all, religiously honest," while the *Ohio State Journal* concluded that he has had "no crooked turns, no evasion, no duplicity in his past life, official or private."[14]

---

* Upon winning the Republican nomination for president in 1860, Lincoln was told that a delegation from the party was on its way to officially provide him the good news. His wife, Mary, insisted that they serve alcohol to the delegation. She became irate when Lincoln refused. "Having kept house for sixteen years, and having never held the 'cup' to the lips of my friends," explained Lincoln, "my judgment was that I should not, in my new position, change my habit in this respect." He served them water. See Ron L. Andersen, *Lincoln: God's Humble Instrument*, 127.

Another of his heavenly traits was his ever-abounding charity and forgiveness. At the annoyance of his military advisors, he would, for example, mercifully exaggerate any justification so that he might grant pardons to those Union-soldier deserters who legally should have hung for their acts of abandonment.[15] Not only was he tenderhearted toward those disobedient ones in his care, but (most remarkably) acted similarly towards his bitterest enemies in the South, even those who scorned him publicly and wished for his death. In an almost unprecedented gesture, particularly in time of war, Lincoln refused to demean or demonize the enemy.[16]

But perhaps his most famous act of kindness, charity, and forgiveness is memorialized in his Second Inaugural Address. After witnessing the bloodiest carnage ever to befall the nation (even to this date), and in an act of total mercy on the enemy, he charged the nation in this address to immediately forgive the South, instructing all to carry on "[w]ith malice toward none; with charity for all, with firmness in right, as God gives us to see right...to bind up the nation's wounds; to care for him who shall have born the battle, and for his widow and for his orphan."[17] The French sculptor Daniel Chester immortalized these traits in his famous statue of Lincoln, which today adorns the Lincoln Memorial. While he made one of Lincoln's hands clenched tightly, demonstrative of his firmness and resolve, Chester explained that he made the other hand opened and relaxed, emphasizing the great forgiveness and compassion the president so readily offered the enemy.[18]

Such benevolence was only bolstered by his kindness, his love of people, his story telling, his endless humor, and (strangely) his awkward, plain, or even odd physical appearance (his tall gangly body, it was said, mismatched most of his wardrobe and made him a funny spectacle on foot and horseback). All of this endeared people to him and made them feel at ease in his presence.[19]

Lincoln was also the first in American history to invite black Americans as honored guests to the White House (called the Executive Mansion at the time). This, among other gestures, inspired black abolitionist Frederick Douglas to point out Lincoln's "freedom from popular prejudice," calling him "the black man's president" and praising him as a great man "who in no single instance reminded me of the difference between himself and myself, of the difference of color."[20] Lincoln's propensity to believe in the equality of man, regardless of race or situation, would be especially significant to the Lord in that Lincoln's mission on the earth would be to propel such underdogs (including God's Church) to their rightful place under the Constitution. His deep belief in such equality had been born in him years before his presidency, as illustrated by his following statements:

- "This declared indifference...for the spread of slavery, I cannot but hate. I hate it because of the monstrous injustice of slavery itself....What I do say is that no man is good enough to govern another man without that other's consent" (October 1954).[21]

- "[T]he Negro is a man [and] his bondage is cruelly wrong" (August 1855).[22]

- "....but in [the black woman's] right to eat the bread she earns with her own hands without asking leave of anyone else, she is my equal, and the equal of all others" (June 1857).[23]

- "[The Declaration of Independence was the Founders'] majestic interpretation of the Universe. This was their lofty, and wise, and noble understanding of the justice of the Creator to His creatures. Yes, gentlemen, to all his creatures, to the whole great family of man. In their enlightened belief, nothing stamped with the Divine image and likeness was sent into the world to be trodden on, and degraded, and imbruted by its fellows (August 1858)."[24]

- "I think slavery is wrong, morally and politically. I desire that it should be no further spread in these United States, and I should not object if it should gradually terminate in the whole Union" (September 1859).[25]

The quotes go on and on. And these, of course, only reflect his pre-war thoughts. His fuller conversion, even passion, for slavery's emancipation did not surface until his presidency.

These examples of Lincoln's humility, reliance on God, honesty, kindness, charity, forgiveness, and his righteous sense of equality under the law would prove to be indispensable traits in the man who would lead the people through their darkest days and into the protection of the American Covenant. And though most good people in America recognized these strengths in Lincoln as being vital to the cause, other more apprehensive and shortsighted critics skimmed over his attributes and instead focused in on his relatively weak resume. For example, as he was appearing on the national stage just in time for the great conflict, the *New York Herald* presented his humble past by stating that "the conduct of the republican party in this nomination is a remarkable indication of small intellect...they pass over...statesmen and able men, and they take up a fourth rate lecturer."[26]

Still others recognized that it was this raw and untainted background that was responsible for the novice Republican candidate's ability to have "always held up the doctrines of the Bible, and the truths and examples of the Christian religion, as the foundation of all good."[27] A Connecticut paper saw him as one who "always conducts his arguments on high moral ground. Is this right or wrong, is the first, last, and only question he asks."[28] It is no wonder, then, that those inspired individuals who foresaw the imminent national catastrophe would uphold this man as the Lord's instrument in what many esteemed at that early time to be (in George Washington Julian's words) "a fight...between God and the Devil—between heaven and hell!"[29] Lincoln was a Christian soldier, unafraid to stand for right. "Let us have faith that right makes might" he declared in his famous 1860 Cooper Union speech, after charging slavery as "an evil not to be extended."[30]

Lincoln's attributes in this fight would serve to produce precisely what the Lord desired. For not only would these character traits allow him to lead by righteous example in this Godly cause of national redemption, but they made him worthy of whatever revelation the Lord needed to send him. It was this revelation that caused him to influence the nation to repent and return to God and covenant. It was also this revelation which led to some of the most brilliant political and military maneuverings in history (military historians point out that, though he had no military experience, somehow he strategically outsmarted top generals).[31] Altogether, Lincoln's divine attributes make it clear that he was the foreordained leader to guide the nation to its *national repentance* and to secure *universal agency.* Indeed, he led America in the reestablishment of the national covenant.

Though Lincoln would have little inclination or reason to understand, at the time, that the obscure and peculiar religious group called "Mormons" was, in fact, somewhere in the crux of this national conflict, he would nonetheless be chosen by God to be a savior to the Mormon cause. He never needed to know every detail. He walked by faith, which faith he often expressed by saying, "Whatever shall appear to be God's will, I will do."[32]

Such powerful characteristics in Lincoln went largely untapped and unrecognized until a couple of years before the Civil War. As such, before he could apply these traits in the service of God and country, he first had to be given the chance to come out of obscurity. This opportunity came in 1858 when he ran for the United States Senate. His goal was to oust the popular incumbent Stephen Douglas, who four years earlier had gained passage of the Kansas-Nebraska Act, which allowed the spread of slavery into new U.S. territories. Lincoln's abhorrence for such immoral legislation was the basis of his campaign platform. "A house divided against itself cannot stand," he would famously declare while stumping for the election. He prophetically continued, "I believe this government cannot endure permanently half slave and half free...It will become all one thing, or all the other." [33]

Though he lost the senate race, he gained much attention and applause from the anti-slavery movement, which continued to seek out his wisdom and oratory skills well after his defeat. He would continue to grow in popularity as he filled his audiences with both reverence and energy whenever he expounded on the moral sin of slavery that was plaguing the country.

His newfound popularity propelled him—even as an underdog Republican candidate—to the presidency in 1860 (the Democratic Party split and lost its potency). Considering what this single act accomplished for the purposes of God, perhaps it is no coincidence that Abraham Lincoln's ascendency to the presidency was attached to a prophecy delivered by the Prophet Joseph Smith. On May 18, 1843, the Prophet Joseph had dinner with Illinois Supreme Court Justice Stephen Douglas. Joseph, turning to Douglas, prophesied to him, saying, "Judge, you will aspire to the presidency of the United States; and if you ever turn your hand against me or the Latter-day Saints, you will feel the weight of the hand of the Almighty upon you; and you will live to see and know that I have testified the truth to you."

Thirteen years later, Douglas turned against the Saints, declaring in a speech delivered in June of 1857 that "the knife must be applied to this pestiferous, disgusting cancer [referring to Mormonism] which is gnawing into the very vitals of the body politic." Months later, the *Deseret News* published Joseph's prophecy regarding Douglas and addressed the column directly to Douglas—a most powerful reminder. Three years later Douglas had indeed aspired to the presidency and was expected by many to win it. Notwithstanding such expectations, however, Douglas felt the *weight of the hand of the Almighty.* And he felt it when his political nemesis, even the lowly Abraham Lincoln, was chosen to be president instead.[34] During the same year he lost the presidency to Lincoln, the forty-eight-year-old Stephen Douglas died, "a broken hearted man." [35]

The reaction to Lincoln's election was mostly positive in the North and almost entirely negative in the South. Because of his anti-slavery rhetoric, the South viewed his election as its cue to dissolve its connection with the United States.*

Why would Southerners want to stay in the Union with a man who openly hated the very thing that sustained their wealth and lifestyle? Though he promised not to touch their precious slavery in the South, how could they possibly trust this little-known man who represented the brand new party—the Republicans—whose platform was founded on anti-slavery ideals. Furthermore, Lincoln's firm position to prevent slavery from spreading to new states, if made into policy, would bring even more free-soil senators and representatives into the halls of Congress. This would, of course, make things all the more difficult for Southern politicians in Congress, who would eventually dwindle into a decided minority. With pro-slavery politicians being a minority in Washington, the slave states' lifeblood—the subjugation of men, women, and children—would be further threatened.

And so, even before the president-elect could take his oath of office, the Southern states had begun to secede. They would vie for independence at all costs.

This little-known and under-experienced man then packed his bags for Washington and stared into the most unbearably and overwhelmingly difficult challenge ever known, then or now, to a president-elect. What would he do? Whatever was going through Lincoln's mind at this time, a gospel perspective informs us that the Lord knew exactly what Lincoln would do and how he would do it. After all, as will be explained later, Southern secession had much deeper and more serious consequences in a gospel context than anyone could have understood at the time. The Lord, therefore,

---

* There were certainly other considerations that may explain why Southerners chose to leave the Union (like unfair federal tariffs that affected the Southern economy, cultural issues, principles of states' rights, etc). However, as will be *proven* later, the fear of losing their slavery (their economic lifeblood) is what drove both their decision to secede and sustained their energy to stay in the fight.

would not stand idly by. To be sure, now was the Lord's opportunity to unleash the promised vexation and scourge that would restore American worthiness and fix its covenant, all in furtherance of His work and glory. And the Lord would reveal much of this to Lincoln in His own due time.

Lincoln sensed early on that God's will would be revealed to him. As he was boarding the train for Washington D.C., a very emotional president-elect Lincoln declared the following to a crowd of well-wishers, many of whom had tear-filled eyes:

> I now leave, not knowing when or whether ever I may return, with a task before me greater than that which rested upon Washington. Without the assistance of that Divine Being who ever attended him, I cannot succeed. With that assistance I cannot fail. Trusting in Him who can go with me, and remain with you, and be everywhere for good, let us confidently hope that all will yet be well. To His care commending you, as I hope in your prayers you will commend me, I bid you an affectionate farewell.[36]

He had invoked the American Covenant. That this invocation was more than just rhetoric, but instead a reflection of Lincoln's truest desire and intent, is evidenced by the stream of similar speeches he gave in the days that followed while on his train route to Washington. At every stop he declared his dependence upon (in sequential order) "Divine Providence," "God," "the Providence of God," "that God who has never forsaken this people," "the Divine Power, without whose aid we can do nothing," "that Supreme Being who has never forsaken this favored land," "the Maker of the Universe," and "Almighty God."[37]

Days before his election to the presidency, Lincoln tearfully confided the following to a friend:

> I know there is a God and that he hates injustice and slavery. I see the storm coming and I know that his hand is in it. If he has a place and a work for me, and I think he

164

has, I believe I am ready. I am nothing, but truth is everything. I know I am right because I know that liberty is right, for Christ teaches it and Christ is God.[38]

Now, as the president-elect made his way to the capital, he expounded upon what he was "ready" to do. Stopping at Trenton, New Jersey, near where Washington had famously crossed the Delaware, Lincoln connected his mission to that of the Founding Fathers before him:

> I recollect thinking then, boy even though I was, that there must have been something more than common that those men were struggling for. I am exceedingly anxious that that thing which they struggled for; that something even more than National Independence; that something that held out a great promise to all the people of the world to all time to come; I am exceedingly anxious that this Union, the Constitution, and the liberties of the people shall be perpetuated in accordance with the original idea for which that struggle was made, and I shall be most happy indeed if I shall be an humble instrument in the hands of the Almighty, and of this, his almost chosen people, for perpetuating the object of that great struggle.[39]

Lincoln's thoughts here are profound. Even before entering his presidency, Lincoln was obviously clear about certain truths. He knew there was a divine plan for America and he knew this plan had to do with liberty under Jesus Christ. He knew America's creation was meant for something "more than common," something more important than just "National Independence," something that "held out a great promise to all the people of the world." He then connected this great promise to the Constitution—even that document which reflects the national covenant. Lincoln clearly had a testimony of the basic principles behind the American Covenant— something he received by God and through the inspired attributes he possessed.

Furthermore, Lincoln sealed his testimony regarding these principles by acknowledging that God had called him to "perpetuate" these lofty American goals, and that he would now become a "humble instrument in the hands of the Almighty." Lincoln further connected America's destiny to the national covenant by implying that America had taken the torch from the chosen people of the Old Testament. He called Americans "[God's] almost chosen people."

During the Civil War, Lincoln would confirm his testimony of God's plan for America when expressing that "God's purpose [for the war] is something different" than anyone could have imagined and that "God wills this contest."[40] He would also declare, "Surely [God] intends some great good to follow this mighty convulsion."[41] Admittedly, Lincoln made these comments after going through the spiritually purifying fire of war, which produced an even deeper comprehension for him concerning God's will for the nation. But his propensity to believe in America's deep connection to God's plan—something indispensable to the success of the war—can clearly be seen even before he officially entered his presidency.

On the day after his Trenton Speech, Lincoln made a stop in Philadelphia where he made another speech at Independence Hall—the signing place of the Declaration of Independence. Whereas in Trenton, Lincoln referenced the covenant blessings as associated with the Constitution, in Philadelphia he connected the covenant principles to the Declaration. After once again pointing out that America represented something bigger than just "the separation of the colonies from the Motherland," he once again reiterated that the nation would bring "hope to the world for all future time." He then further invoked national covenant principles when he affirmed the power of the Declaration of Independence. It was the Declaration, concluded Lincoln, that represented "the promise that in due time the weights should be lifted from the shoulders of men, and that all should have an equal chance."[42] Lincoln was describing *agency* versus *oppression*, *God's plan* versus *Satan's*; he was describing the principles fought over in the War in Heaven. And he was concluding, in no uncertain terms, that America was to be the great solution to ensure agency's victory—to ensure God's victory. The American Covenant was written in Lincoln's heart.

Lincoln's early intimations of national covenant principles should not be taken for granted. Though in retrospect we know today what the Civil War would mean for God and His kingdom, president-elect Lincoln could hardly have comprehended all that. In fact, when he gave these speeches, Lincoln had not even as-of-yet imagined the awful war that awaited him. And yet, his testimony of these things would prove to be indispensable for the war's success. For, once the Lord was ready to reveal His true intentions, Lincoln's preconceived and inspired notions of what America really was all about would facilitate his conversion to the national cause of God.

Another reason Lincoln should not be taken for granted has to do with the fact that so many of our national leaders—even today —have proven that they do not share Lincoln's vision of American exceptionalism under God. So many leaders were not and have not been so easily converted to the covenant. That Lincoln *was* converted to these principles early on is but further proof that he was the chosen one for this critical task.

Shortly after giving these profound speeches, Lincoln entered the capital, raised his right arm to the square, and took his oath of office, after which he (not insignificantly) bowed his head and kissed the Bible.[43] In true fashion of an American Covenant-maker, Lincoln declared, after making the oath, that it was a "solemn" oath "registered in Heaven" and that it was now incumbent upon him to "preserve, protect and defend" the United States.[44]

Lincoln was truly inspired and prepared for what the Lord was about to have him do. His entrance onto the national scene at this crucial point for America and its eternal destiny was no coincidence. Rather, it was evidence that God was watching over America and that He was concerned about the success of its national covenant. Whether or not Lincoln fully understood what he was about to do, the spiritual preparation he had received and the divine attributes and testimony he possessed, would make it easier for the Lord to work through him.

Illumination towards Emancipation

As Lincoln was entering the national scene, slavery—and its oppressive influence—was as strongly embedded into the country as ever before. In just two generations the number of slaves in America had jumped from 800,000 to 4,000,000.[45] Not only had slavery flourished and grown under the constitutional errors that legally encouraged its existence, but less than four years before Lincoln took office, slavery had received further bolstering from the Supreme Court. In the infamous *Dred Scott Case* (1857), the Court handed down perhaps the most despicable decision in its history. Black Americans, even free ones, "are not included, and were not intended to be included, under the word 'citizen' in the Constitution."[46] The decision further desecrated blacks by classifying them into "an inferior order" which "had no rights which the white man was bound to respect."[47] The decision also did much to open the way for slavery's insertion into the new U.S. territories.[48] This decision—significantly reminiscent of similar state court decisions and state executive orders against the Saints—not only underscored Lincoln's eventual challenge, but also emphasized the need for the mighty vexation and shake-up promised by the Lord.

Slavery was nowhere near being gently "phased out" as some have argued, but instead was a rapidly growing cancer that needed fast, hard, drastic, and painful treatment. As long as the evil act persisted, the unworthy nation would remain in breach of its national covenant, and the purposes of God would be frustrated. As was prophetically declared by John Jay (one of the most inspired Founding Fathers of the Revolution, and one of the most important proponents of the Constitution), "We have the highest reason to believe that the Almighty will not suffer slavery and the Gospel to go hand in hand. It cannot, it will not be."[49]

God's first step in rectifying the breach of covenant would be to move the nation toward the eradication of slavery. As history has taught us, the great Emancipation Proclamation, born of the Civil War, would serve as the key that opened the door toward slavery's ultimate eradication. But viewing it through a gospel perspective, the Proclamation would mean much more than that. For it represented the first official act toward *national repentance* and *universal agency*—toward restoring the American Covenant. It represented admission of guilt and the beginning of a process that would bring forth American liberty to the downtrodden and oppressed. It elevated the worthiness and readiness of the nation to fulfill its divine mission. It was the first step to achieving exactly what the Prophet Joseph pled for and what God had promised to fulfill. For as the covenant blessings began to flow, beginning with the issuance of the Proclamation, so would the safety and elevation of all minorities, to include Latter-day Saints, be more secure. The Proclamation was a crucial part of rebuilding the American Covenant and assisting in the salvation of mankind.

Though the Proclamation was not the final answer (it did not free all the slaves and was designed as a temporary solution), it laid a moral foundation and set the stage for further, more permanent acts toward *national repentance* and *universal agency*. These additional amendments and policies would include the Thirteenth and Fourteenth Amendments and the Civil Rights Act—changes that fixed the problems of minority races (e.g. the slaves) and minority religions (e.g. the Church of Jesus Christ of Latter-day Saints). As pointed out earlier, any effort to elevate black Americans—as the Proclamation clearly did—was bound to produce policies that would elevate all minority groups. As we consider this idea, the miracles surrounding the Proclamation's development and issuance should take on an even fuller meaning for us today. The Proclamation was most definitely imperative to the success of the American Covenant and the Restoration.

However, many may be surprised to know that as the Civil War got under way, the Proclamation was by no means a foregone conclusion. To be sure, Lincoln and the North did not come upon such high-minded goals overnight. It was a difficult process. In fact, the

North's decision, led by the federal government, to engage in war had nothing at all to do with freeing slaves, elevating minorities, or reinterpreting the misinterpreted Constitution. Logically, if the North could have so easily been convinced to fight for these purposes, then the Prophet Joseph would have had a much easier time getting his political solutions recognized and adopted; for Joseph had already called for just such a policy. The truth is that the nation—even the North—did not care much about elevating minorities of any kind. They chose to remain in breach of covenant.

If God could only convince Lincoln and the North to begin down the path of national redemption, by adopting the Proclamation, then He would have begun to fulfill His promise that He would intervene and influence the nation to do that which the Prophet Joseph had called upon it to do for the building up of the kingdom. Tragically, the only way to accomplish this was to bring the nation to its knees. Americans were, as Lincoln pointed out, the chosen people of God. They were latter-day Israel. As Ezra Taft Benson taught, "God will have a humble people. Either we can choose to be humble or we can be compelled to be humble"[50] (see Alma 32). As it was with ancient Israel and their Nephite cousins, so it would be with latter-day America.

We will now explore the beginnings of our national redemption —even God's efforts to humble the nation and convert it to His cause. We will travel the historic road toward the Emancipation Proclamation and beyond. We will witness how this miracle of repentance and conversion came about. And we will witness the Lord's great interest and involvement in America and the redemption of her covenant.

Lincoln's Illumination

As Lincoln entered his presidency, he was already a virtuous and God-fearing man. Furthermore, he was no stranger to the principles pertaining to the American Covenant (as illustrated above). However, he still needed to learn how deeply connected the national covenant was to God's purpose for the Civil War. Indeed, if Lincoln was to preside over a national calamity that would lead to the *national repentance* of sins like slavery and to *universal agency* for oppressed minorities, then he was in need of illumination he had not yet received. Lincoln would eventually receive this illumination and align his will and purpose with God's. His eventual issuance of the Emancipation Proclamation would be the initial signal that he had become *fully* converted to the cause of God and the American Covenant, particularly as this cause was connected to the terrible war. But his road to conversion, and his issuance of the Proclamation, was not simple and not immediate.

The most obvious sign that Lincoln needed a conversion to "the cause" is found in his First Inaugural Address as president, in which he stated clearly that he had "no purpose, directly or indirectly, to interfere with the institution of slavery in the States where it exists."[51] His early position on slavery was further confirmed when, even as the Civil War began, he made it clear that he "had no intention of making emancipation the war aim, nor is it likely he could have persuaded his troops to fight to free blacks."[52] Lincoln also made it clear at the onset that if the South would just return to the Union, it could keep its precious slavery intact.[53] Former slave and famed abolitionist Frederick Douglas recognized Lincoln's position during 1861 and through much of 1862, and lamented it greatly.[54]

Naturally then, when (in Lincoln's second month as president) the South opened fire on the federal Fort Sumter in South Carolina,* at once sealing Southern secession and forcing war upon the Union, Lincoln responded militarily, not in defense of abolitionist desires, but on a strict goal to defend the United States from this domestic enemy. Just prior to Fort Sumter, the South had seized other federal properties, including forts and ports, which struck a financial blow to the Union, as customs duties out of Southern ports were a major source of national revenue. The Northern military response was initially for the purpose of protecting and taking back federal

---

* Joseph Smith prophesied some thirty years earlier that the Civil War would begin in South Carolina (D&C 87:1-5; 130:12-13).

property and thus preserving the Union. The issue of slavery and national morality had been completely marginalized.

Lincoln's initial rejection of the idea of fighting to free the slaves, or fighting to revise the Constitution to elevate minorities, was no indication of his personal desires on the matter. As pointed out above, Lincoln knew slavery was wrong and wanted to see it eradicated. What Lincoln lacked initially, however, was the clarity and courage of the Lord to lead the nation to emancipation. What he lacked was definitive knowledge that God was opening the doors for such change.

In his defense, Lincoln was in a very difficult situation. America (in general) simply did not care enough about the status of minorities and certainly was not willing to fight a war to elevate them. Indeed, the people had interpreted the Constitution in a way that made it difficult for Lincoln to find an easy way to bring about significant change. As the war broke out, the nation believed the war was about nothing more than Lincoln had stated—a fight to preserve the Union. Lincoln needed to learn that God wanted him to assist in the terrible vexation—that God wanted him to see the war as a tool for drastic change, and then influence the people to support such change. The war would eventually create the needed change within the hearts and minds of the people, as God humbled them. And when the change came, Lincoln would need to comprehend, even before the masses did, that God was behind this scourge of war —that God had a purpose for it. Only then would Lincoln have the clarity and courage to bring the people—once God had prepared them—through the doorway of emancipation and beyond. Lincoln was in need of a deeper conversion (than he already had) to God and covenant.

While critics then, and now, reprimand Lincoln for being too slow and hesitant over emancipation (and perhaps he was too slow), they do so at the cost of overlooking one of the greatest gems in American history and one of the greatest acts surrounding the American Covenant. They overlook the deeply spiritual conversion of Abraham Lincoln to God's purposes for the war (in particular) and for America (in general).

It is impossible to know exactly when Lincoln began this conversion process. However, as a thoughtful man, and one who despised slavery, it is difficult to believe he did not, even early on, entertain the thought that perhaps the Lord was providing a solution to the national problem of slavery. The federal government was the only force powerful enough to bring about such an attack on evil. Lincoln knew he had become, in effect, the federal government and thus represented the only viable saving influence for this noble cause. Lincoln himself had declared years earlier that the evil problem of slavery "is too mighty for me—may God, in his mercy, superintend the solution."[55] Surely he recognized early on that his new and unique national position, together with this new and unique national tragedy forming, might create this heavenly solution he had been seeking long before.

That Lincoln did feel such promptings early on in his presidency, even if he did not articulate it immediately, is perhaps reflected in his continued effort to push for a policy to contain and phase out slavery. As early as 1861 he even proposed a policy—similar to that proposed by the Prophet Joseph—of "compensated emancipation." This solution suggested that Congress buy slaves then set them free, so that, as Lincoln put it, emancipation would come "gently as the dews of heaven, not rending or wrecking anything."[56] What Lincoln wanted was exactly what the Prophet Joseph wanted: the fruits of God's foretold vexation without the vexation. But just as the nation rejected Joseph's attempt at this national policy, it did the same to Lincoln's. Both men had to eventually learn that hundreds of years of sin would not be overcome with requests, pleas, and policy proposals. A peaceful solution was not going to be an option, which only emphasizes how badly the president needed to learn for himself that it was war—and war alone—that had the power to change hearts and minds on this matter. It was a lesson that perhaps would only hit him through personal revelation from on high.

In the meantime, Lincoln's hesitant approach on the issue of slavery was supported by his once political rival, now his secretary of state and dear friend, William Seward (who, as will be detailed later, played a critical role in the divine advancement of God's plan). But in spite of their initial approach, Lincoln and Seward could not forever hide from the Lord and His plans for emancipation. They would both fully realize, in short order, that the Civil War and their place in it went way beyond reuniting the Union and was, more importantly, about eradicating slavery and securing the blessings *national repentance* and *universal agency*. Once they realized this, they would have to come out and say it, live it, and fight for it in the open.

One of their first clues that such would be the case came fast and sharp from Seward's inspired, and very religious, wife Frances. After Seward gave an 1861 speech in which he placated the South and, compromising his moral anti-slavery position, expressed a desire that the South return to the Union with slavery intact, Frances responded with a stinging rebuke:

> Eloquent as your speech was it fails to meet the entire approval of those who love you best...Compromises based on the idea that the preservation of the Union is more important than the liberty of nearly 4,000,000 human beings cannot be right. The alteration of the Constitution to perpetuate slavery—the enforcement of a law to recapture a poor, suffering, fugitive...these compromises cannot be approved by God or supported by good men....No one can dread war more than I do. For 16 years I have prayed earnestly that our own son might be spared the misfortune of raising his hand against his fellow man—yet I could not today assent to the perpetuation or extension of slavery to prevent war. I say this in no spirit of unkindness...but I must obey the admonitions of conscience which impel me to warn you of your dangers. [57]

Frances' position proved that she had possessed an advanced understanding of God's purposes—advanced for the American populace and advanced for her own dear spouse. While Seward was contemplating his wife's rebuke, Lincoln was passing through his own process of purification of purpose, which heated up through the months of 1862—the year of Lincoln's crucial conversion. As documented above, Lincoln was already predisposed to seeking God's will concerning the nation's plight. That propensity was only energized by humbling events surrounding his presidency and personal life—events that would force the president to his knees in search of answers. The most obvious of these humbling events was a war that had not shaped up to be the minor skirmish many had predicted. By 1862, there was no end in sight, as death, depression, and humiliation surrounded the president from all sides. As commander-in-chief, he could not avoid the haunting fact that it was ultimately his decision to stay in the war—a war many believed to be unnecessary—that was responsible for the continuation of the terrible affliction.

Such anguish was especially burdensome for a gentle man like Lincoln, who hated violence and suffering so much that he could not even tolerate being in the presence of dying animals. Indeed, this was a man who had declared early in life that he could never even bring himself to participate in the commonly accepted practice of hunting for food.[58] Presiding over this war of immense human death and suffering was destroying him from the inside out.

If that were not enough, in February 1862, in the midst of the nation's darkest days, Lincoln's beloved eleven-year-old son, Willie, died of typhoid fever. During the boy's illness, Lincoln was already overburdened beyond human capacity. He was managing a failed war *and* running a country. Yet, in spite of these already overwhelmingly weighty matters, he was now forced to deal with the ultimate parental nightmare. According to Lincoln's secretary, John Nicolay, in the days leading up to Willie's death, the president—already spent to capacity with no spare time on his hands—gave "pretty much all his attention" to the child.[59]

That it was his dear boy Willie that was forced to suffer and die (while Lincoln watched on, completely helpless) made it all the more unbearable for Lincoln. For Willie, above all others, was Lincoln's most cherished friend. His other children were a bit more distant. (His oldest boy, Robert, was very independent, while his youngest son, Tad, was attached to his mother, with whom he shared so many characteristics.) But Willie was his *father's* little boy. He looked like his father (tall and thin), he thought like his father (intellectual and analytical). He reminded Lincoln of himself. Lincoln indulged Willie, allowing him to ride his pony on the White House lawn. Lincoln also enjoyed getting down on the floor and playfully wrestling with his son. Willie would accompany his father often—his true companion in the White house. According to one Lincoln scholar, "Lincoln loved no one more."[60]

Willie Lincoln, photo taken before he died tragically in 1862.
Courtesy of the Library of Congress.

On February 20, after Willie passed away, Lincoln marched into Nicolay's office and declared, "My boy is gone—he is actually gone!" He then began to sob. According to one witness, when he later entered the room, after Willie's lifeless little body had been washed and dressed, Lincoln stopped and looked at his boy. He then "buried his head in his hands, and his tall frame was convulsed with emotion."[61] To make matters worse, after the boy's death, Mary Lincoln became inconsolable and would never recover.[62] The Lincoln's had already lost their three-year-old Eddie a few years earlier. To ask them to also give up their Willie was unbearable. Upon looking at his Willie's lifeless body, Lincoln exclaimed, "He was too good for this earth...but we loved him so."[63]

For weeks after the boy's death, Lincoln would hide away every Thursday (the day Willie had died) where he would grieve and weep in solitude.[64] Lincoln found some comfort in Shakespeare's *King John*, particularly in Constance's lamentation over her lost boy. Lincoln's aide commented on how the president would recite the lines from the lamentation from memory, with tears always forming in his eyes:

> *And, father cardinal, I have heard you say*
> *That we shall see and know our friends in heaven*
> *If that true, I shall see my boy again.*[65]

During his darkest hours, Lincoln was described by an eyewitness as a tormented soul, sleepless and pacing the halls of the White House, "his hands behind him, great black rings under his eyes, his head bent forward upon his breast,—altogether such a picture of the effects of sorrow, care, and anxiety as would have melted the hearts of the worst of his adversaries."[66] Another close associate, Noah Brooks, was surprised to see how the once "happy-faced lawyer" had by 1862 become sad and stooped, with "a sunken deathly look about the large, cavernous eyes."[67] Lincoln would try, at times in vein, to self-medicate with his relentless storytelling and humor. But Lincoln admitted that "nothing could touch the tired spot within, which was all tired."[68] On one occasion during the difficult days of 1862, an intolerant senator rebuked Lincoln for attempting a little humor, to which the president replied, "I say to you now, that were it not for this occasional vent, I should die."[69]

As devastating as these days were to Lincoln, perhaps there was something of the divine therein. Perhaps the difficulties were a manifestation of the prophesied vexation which would create humility and thus facilitate conversion to the light and goodness of the American Covenant. It is no coincidence, after all, that it was precisely during these dismal days of 1862 that Lincoln peaked spiritually. It was at this time that he asked the difficult questions concerning the war. Should he stay the course? Should he let the

South go? It was precisely then that he began to feel the divine promptings leading him down a new path—a path which one Lincoln scholar described as something that "transformed the war's purpose from one with the single purpose of maintaining the Union to one that was also to free the slaves."[70] This was the path that led him to the conviction that God was behind the war, and that it must continue until God's purposes were fulfilled. It was the path that led him toward the reinstitution of the American Covenant. It was the path the president needed to forge for the nation. Indeed, the evidence is strong that 1862 was Lincoln's crucial year of conversion to the cause of the national covenant.

It is, for example, well documented that the vexing environment caused by the war, and by Willie's death, brought Lincoln closer to the Lord. According to the government printer, John DeFrees, Lincoln (though always a God-fearing man), became much more of a religionist "about the time of the death of his son Willie," which had provoked in Lincoln a desire to expound and converse "on the subject of religion."[71] Mary Lincoln implied that as the war became increasingly intense, so did the president's reading of the Scriptures. In fact, several witnesses during this time commented on how they had stumbled in upon the president— whether in his office or in an obscure corner of a steamboat transport —"reading a dog-eared pocket copy of the New Testament." Lincoln's longtime friend, Josiah Speed, noted that, though Lincoln had been somewhat of a religious skeptic in his more youthful days, he had now "sought to become a believer."[72]

The effects of it all were working. Lincoln began to recognize like never before that he was being called to commune with God over the plight of the nation. "It has pleased Almighty God to put me in my present position," Lincoln told one friend in the spring of 1862, "and looking up to him for divine guidance, I must work out my destiny as best I can." Similarly, he told another group that "it is my earnest desire to know the will of Providence in this matter [of emancipation]. And if I can learn what it is I will do it."[73] In September 1862, after being pressed by those seeking clarification of his intention over emancipation, he would only say that the subject was "on my mind, by day and by night, more than any other. Whatever shall appear to be God's will, I will do."[74]

The God-fearing in America began rallying around their president. During these dark and confusing months of 1862, a friend and Baptist minister, Noyes Miner, told Lincoln that "Christian people all over the country are praying for you as they never prayed for a mortal man before," to which Lincoln responded: "This is an encouraging thought to me. If I were not sustained by the prayers of God's people I could not endure this constant pressure."[75]

The events leading up and through 1862 ultimately provided what Lincoln sought. Revelations began arriving, his conversion began solidifying. Lincoln described it as "a process of crystallization" during which he "constantly prayed."[76] It is impossible to know exactly when, during this spiritual "process of crystallization," Lincoln learned what the war was really all about. However, we do know that on July 22, 1862, he submitted his first draft of the Emancipation Proclamation to a very stunned cabinet. We also know that on September 22, 1862, he issued the official preliminary Emancipation Proclamation, and on January 1, 1863, it became national policy.[77] Referring to Lincoln's change of heart—to his new belief that emancipation was the real purpose of the war— one prominent historian stated, "Truly, it was a 'Damascus Road' experience for the president."[78]

To further confirm that these changes in Lincoln's understanding of the war were, in fact, born of God and revelation, we turn to Lincoln's own words. Within days of issuing his official preliminary Proclamation, Lincoln openly recognized what the Doctrine and Covenant's prophecies suggested he should recognize. "[I]t is quite possible," stated Lincoln, "that God's purpose [for this war] is something different from the purpose of either party...I am almost ready to say this is probably true—that *God wills this contest, and wills that it shall not end yet.*"[79] Lincoln's thought that both sides might be wrong, and that God was bringing this scourge and vexation upon the nation, most certainly reflected the prophecies.

Lincoln would eventually gain further clarity on the matter when he began shouting to the nation that God had brought the war in order to bring the nation to repentance and to affect "our national reformation as a whole people."[80]

Lest one accuse Lincoln of making these initial statements (about God bringing the war down upon both sides) only to pander to his religious constituency, it should be noted that he wrote this declaration in a private memo to himself, which was later titled "Meditation of the Divine Will." According to his secretaries, Nicolay and Hay (not necessarily religious men themselves), the memo was "not written to be seen of men. It was penned in the awful sincerity of a perfectly honest soul trying to bring itself into closer communion with its maker."[81]

Just days after writing his "Meditation of the Divine Will," he met with his cabinet. The date was September 22, 1862. He stood before them and, while issuing his official preliminary Proclamation, he boldly declared to them that "it was his duty to move forward in the cause of emancipation" because "God had decided this question in favor of the slaves."[82] This decision, based on personal revelation, provided both joy and sorrow for the president. Joy, because the Almighty had weighed in. And sorrow, because Lincoln now knew that he must follow through with God's will. He must continue the war until God's purposes for full liberty had been met. He must pursue a course of action that would bring continual and seemingly endless bloodshed.

Once, while riding through the capital, past medical camps and ambulances, Lincoln became overwhelmingly emotional. Turning to his companion, he lamented, "look yonder at those poor fellows. I cannot bear it. This suffering, this loss of life is dreadful."[83] He once sadly confessed to a congressman: "Doesn't it seem strange to you that I should be here? Doesn't it strike you as queer that I, who couldn't cut the head off a chicken, and who was sick at the sight of blood, should be cast into the middle of a great war, with blood flowing all about me?"[84]

Many attempted (and still do) to put the blame on Lincoln for allowing the carnage of war to continue for so long. As hard as these misjudgments were to the ears the gentle leader (who *hated* war), he knew, as the gospel prophecies affirm, that it *was* God's will to move forward at all costs. And Lincoln would obey, notwithstanding the hurtful misjudgments that would be directed at him (then and now).

One other stunning thing occurred during Lincoln's year of conversion and illumination. Months after the North's first devastating defeat (First Battle of Bull Run), and just weeks before his darkest days of 1862, Lincoln checked out a book from the Library of Congress. Lincoln definitively had this book in his possession during his days of purification of purpose—during his "process of crystallization" or his "Damascus Road experience." That this book might have played some role in his conversion to the covenant ideals is based on the following facts. First, he was given permission by the library to check it out for one week, yet he kept it for eight months. Second, he returned the book (after those eight months) to the Library of Congress on July 29, 1862—*seven days* after he submitted his first draft of the Proclamation to his cabinet; *seven days* after our *first* indication that his conversion had finally congealed (as if to say, *I've used it and now I am finally done with it*). And third, the book contained the most detailed and reliable account of the truth and power behind the American Covenant. It described and illustrated the covenant Lincoln had come to understand and act on under God's direction. According to records held by the Library of Congress, the president had checked out the Book of Mormon.[85]

What caused Lincoln to check out the Book of Mormon? Was it a desire to learn about the Saints in order to devise policy for the Utah territory? Was it connected to some spiritual prompting? Whatever the motive, the book ended up in his possession *precisely* when he needed it most. Indeed, during those specific weeks and months, Lincoln found himself a humbled, sleepless, restless soul—searching for something. Anything. Searching for God. And there was this book. (That he read it is almost certain. Among U.S. presidents, Lincoln was one of our most voracious readers. It is hard to imagine that he would check out a book for eight months and not read it.)

Close up photo images of the Library of Congress ledger Lincoln signed to check out the Book of Mormon and other books related to the Church. He kept the Book of Mormon for eight months. Photos provided courtesy of the Library of Congress.

So he picks this book up and learns of a people, an ancient nation, which lived upon the very land he now occupies. He learns that this nation was bound by a covenant, a covenant which was clearly projected for the United States*—even that government Lincoln now presided over. He learns that this nation was characterized by several civil wars. The book describes these wars, even detailing military tactics (which Lincoln was, at the time, also studying voraciously). At the core of these wars was God's purposes for the land and His children. At the core of these wars was often a fight between good and evil, between oppression and freedom. At the core of these wars was a divine intention to humble the nations, that they might carry out God's plans. At the core was the promise of American Covenant.

It might seem strange to some that Lincoln had begun to outwardly place the Civil War in the context of a holy war—a war that God had hurled upon the land in order to humble His people. It might seem odd that Lincoln began describing the war as a conflict whose end game would be "our national reformation as a whole people."[86] However, in light of the notion that Lincoln had been inspired by the Book of Mormon, his conclusions make perfect sense. Lincoln would have read the profound doctrines of the American Covenant. He would have internalized the principle that "except the Lord chasten his people with many afflictions, yea, except he doth visit them with death and with terror…they will not remember him" (Helaman 12:3). He would have learned that God will cause civil wars to this inspired end (see Alma 9:18). Perhaps it was no coincidence that Lincoln wrote his private memo, "Meditation of the Divine Will" (in which he initially espoused these ideas), just weeks after having returned the Book of Mormon to the Library of Congress.

No, we do not have definitive proof that Lincoln read or internalized Book of Mormon principles. But the circumstances

---

* The details concerning how Book of Mormon prophecies clearly project the American Covenant for latter-day America can be found in Volume I, Chapter 1, of this work.

surrounding it make it difficult to believe it was just a coincidence. Furthermore, we will see (in the chapters that follow) how Lincoln applied the national covenant principles of the Book of Mormon as though he understood them, believed them, and loved them to the extent that Captain Moroni did. (There is one very specific, and astonishing, event, detailed next chapter, which lends even more credibility to the notion that Lincoln had taken this scripture of the Restoration to heart.)

But whatever particulars led to his conversion under God, the evidence is clear that this conversion happened. And it happened through a process of national humbling, as prophesied by the Lord. The award-winning Lincoln biographer, Richard Carwardine, concluded:

> Lincoln's private understanding of his moral obligations, and the meaning of the conflict itself, evolved under the grueling burden of leadership, the wider suffering of wartime and personal grief....His understanding of providential intervention both shaped the thinking by which he reached the most profound of his decisions, for emancipation, and—even more powerfully—steeled his nerve to stand by the implications of that decision once made. [87]

As detailed above, before arriving in Washington to take the presidential oath, Lincoln stated plainly that he knew America had a divine purpose. Within two years he had built upon that testimony and had come to know that this terrible war he presided over was part of that purpose. And while God would continue to teach Lincoln more as the war went on— revealing to him what would be required for His kingdom—he knew by 1862 that God's purpose would at least *begin* with emancipation. The mending of the American Covenant was well under way. The prophesied vexation was fulfilling its divine mandate.

The Nation's Illumination

One of the greatest leaders of the ancient American Covenant, the general and prophet called Mormon, provided a very powerful lesson. Though he, as the covenant leader, had become converted to the cause of God, it would do little for the covenant's success if the people did not repent and follow him in righteousness. Though he had retired as commander-in-chief of his people's army, due to their wickedness, he reluctantly returned, but in doing so he lamented, "I was without hope, for I knew the judgments of the Lord which should come upon them; for they repented not of their iniquities" (Mormon 5:2). Mormon was not speaking of a temple covenant dealing with priesthood holders; he was speaking of a national covenant dealing with the Nephite nation and its army. As it was with Mormon and the Nephites, so it would be with Lincoln and America. The people also—and especially—needed to repent and turn to the covenant lest the entire cause be wasted.

In the case of America, the people did repent. They passed through a miraculous illumination toward emancipation. This general conversion, some of which was inspired by their president's example and encouragement, was mostly inspired by a much higher power. The story of this heavenly influence over the nation is found in answering the following questions, which naturally emerge at this point in our narrative: How would the people make the change unto repentance, which would allow Lincoln to realize emancipation, and which would eventually lead to equal rights to all minorities, racial and religious? How would America finally make the change that the Prophet Joseph so desperately sought to bring to pass in his lifetime?

The answer takes us back to the thesis of the preceding chapter and calls upon the aforementioned prophecies in Doctrine and Covenants, Sections 101 and 121 (as well as the other similar prophecies previously outlined). That is, the answer was the prophesied vexation we call the Civil War. It was the final contingency to compel humility, righteousness, and a return to the covenant. "And thus we see," declared the ancient prophet, "that except the Lord doth chasten his people with many afflictions, yea except he doth visit them with death and with terror...they will not remember him" (Helaman 12:3).

This message was not lost on the more inspired minds of those Americans living in the years leading up to the great vexation of the Civil War. Author and abolitionist, Harriett Beecher Stowe, for example, published her most important work, *Uncle Tom's Cabin* in 1852 (some eight years before the war). Not only would this book serve the Lord's cause, in that it began to open American minds and hearts to a recognition of slavery's sin, but it also warned the nation as the Prophet Joseph had. The last lines of the book read as follows:

> Both North and South have been guilty before God....Not by combining together, to protect injustice and cruelty...is this Union to be saved,—but by repentance, justice and mercy; for, not surer is the eternal law by which the millstone sinks into the ocean, than that stronger law by which injustice and cruelty shall bring on nations the wrath of Almighty God![88]

Perhaps it was the great Frederick Douglas who understood it best. Addressing a large audience in 1852, Douglas presaged the need for God's vexation, stating:

> It is not light that is needed, but fire; it is not the gentle shower, but thunder. We need the storm, the whirlwind, and the earthquake. The feeling of the nation must be quickened; the conscience of the nation must be roused; the propriety of the nation must be startled; the hypocrisy of the nation must be exposed; and its crimes against God and man must be proclaimed and denounced.[89]

Douglas' inspiration ran so deep that he even understood that the final answer he sought under God was not just for the slave, but for all the oppressed. "All great reforms go to together," he declared.[90] (We bring up these prophetic visions of Stowe and Douglas due to the proximity of time between their visions and the fulfillment of their visions. However, let us not forget the equally powerful prophecies of the same, quoted in the previous chapter, from the Founders Thomas Jefferson and George Mason and from the Prophets Joseph Smith and Brigham Young.)

Interestingly (and perhaps counter-intuitively) the American faction that *first* needed the purging, wrath, scourge, and vexation was not the South, but the North. After all, it was the North who would ultimately be fighting for, developing, and implementing a policy of emancipation and other needed constitutional changes (e.g. the Thirteenth and Fourteenth Amendments). Yet at the onset of war, most Northerners were not converted to the cause of liberating minorities but were instead fighting for other reasons. Like Lincoln, their initial goal was reunification with the South, even if that meant slavery remained.[91] Lincoln's own leading general, George McClellan, took it a step further, suggesting a proactive policy that allowed the South to leave peacefully with slavery intact.[92] But perhaps the most accurate example of Northern sentiment at the beginning of the conflict is witnessed in an 1861 resolution of Congress, even that representative body of all the people. Declared Congress: "...this war is not waged...for any purpose of... overthrowing or interfering with the rights of established institutions of those states [referring to slavery], but... to preserve the Union."[93] The North was in need of a deep shift—a deep conversion.

The Lord did not need the Union army to set out only to restore the Union. He needed them to fight for something deeper and more profound. He needed a revised and corrected interpretation of the Constitution that would signal a road toward *national repentance*. He needed an empowered Constitution that reestablished and protected the eternal and saving principle of *universal agency*. Ultimately, God needed them to understand and fight for the American Covenant.

Imagine, for example, what would have happened if the South had been allowed to peacefully leave the Union, as many Northerners desired. Not only would evil have remained unchecked in the new Southern Confederacy, but the Northern government—what remained of the United States—would have retained the constitutional status quo. It would have maintained its old interpretation of the Constitution, one that did little to apply the covenant blessings to God's people, particularly to His church. And so, a Northern conversion was imperative first and foremost. The North might have thought that the only problem needing fixing was in the South. But as the prophecies imply, and as history later confirmed, the North needed fixing first. For it was the Northern conversion that not only kept the North in the fight but also provided the North a vision as to why. It was this vision that enabled the North to eventually redeem itself, reestablish the Constitution, redeem the American Covenant, and thus make America what God had always intended it to be—a footstool for His kingdom.

Though some in the North had already received this vision on their own before the war (even before Lincoln had), the general public would need the scourge of war to gain a similar conviction. As inspired black soldiers pointed out years into the war, the North was guilty of "forgetting God," which is why "defeat followed defeat." And such defeat would continue until, as one historian explained, "the Union purged itself of the evils of slavery."[94] The South, too, would eventually begin to be positively affected by the vexation, though it would take longer (well past the Civil War) and would come at the hands of an already mostly converted North.

The earliest signs that God's vexation was beginning to have the prophetic effect over the American public (particularly the North) is perhaps reflected in the events surrounding the war's first major battle, the Battle of Bull Run, which occurred in Manassas,

Virginia (some 26 miles south-west of D.C.). In a shocking defeat, the Union troops were routed and sent running back to Washington. Lincoln, who had only barely been sworn in as president some four months prior, was overwhelmed at the implications. As he watched from the White House as the bloodied soldiers staggered through the city in retreat, military advisors prompted the Lincolns to evacuate the city in fear of Southern invasion. Lincoln, along with his brave wife, responded, "Most assuredly I will not leave."[95]

Instead he would stay and begin drafting a message to the nation, declaring—in the spirit of George Washington—his first presidential call for national fasting and prayer. In this act he invoked the national covenant by imploring the nation to "acknowledge and revere the supreme Government of God, to bow in humble submission to his chastisement, to confess and deplore their sins and transgressions." In it he fully acknowledged "the hand of God in this terrible visitation" and said it is being done that America might achieve "sorrowful remembrance of our own faults and crimes as a nation and as individuals." Most remarkably, and in echoing the national covenant, Lincoln stated that such should drive us to "humble ourselves before him, and to pray for his mercy[.]"

> —[T]o pray that we may be spared further punishment, though most justly deserved; that our arms may be blessed and made effectual for the re-establishment of law, order, and peace...and that the inestimable boon of civil and *religious* liberty, earned under his guidance and blessing, by the labors and sufferings of our fathers, may be restored in all its original excellence.[96]

Such sentiments surely opened the hearts of his countrymen and caused them to at least begin to implore the God of Heaven and begin the process of repentance. Lincoln was literally calling the country to repentance and publicly recognizing, for the first time, that a purpose of this war was to bring to pass a humbling punishment and change for God's ultimate purposes. Remarkably, he recognized that a fruit of this change would include civil and religious liberty, as per the American Covenant.

Admittedly, when Lincoln issued these inspired words, he still had not fully converted to the covenant. To be sure, there is no reason to think that (at this early time in the war) his initial offer to the South—to return to the Union with slavery intact—did not still stand. However, his words were indeed a foreshadowing of where he and his nation were headed.

Lincoln's audience may have initially found this notion, put forth by his call to the covenant, difficult to grasp at the time. Americans on both sides were fighting over differing goals surrounding Southern secession and not for civil or religious liberty per se. However, this new idea grew further into focus for the nation as the battles continued to rage, and as the body-count continued spinning out of control. Lincoln and the nation, like any group under severe vexation, naturally grew closer to the Lord and seemed to learn from Him that this war was about something greater. As would be expected from true prophecy, it was finally being fulfilled. God's true purpose for the war was finally being realized. After almost two years of devastating war, there began to emerge palpable indications that hearts in America were turning to the Lord in humility. Indeed, America began to clearly recognize the great sin slavery was. And miraculously, America began calling for its eradication as a defining purpose of the war!

The first group to experience the change of heart was made up of the Union soldiers. Though at first there was little, if any, indication that soldiers were enlisting to free the enslaved and fix the Constitution,[97] it did not take long for the effects of God's scourge to hit them hard. As these boys from the North penetrated the Southern states, they began witnessing things they had scarcely heard about before—things that went beyond war's obvious trauma of death and terror. They witnessed firsthand the severe and brutal physical and sexual abuse of the African slave. Most heart wrenching was the plight of the slave family and slave children. About one third of slave marriages ended in a greedy business decision by the master, and over one half of all slave children lost at least one of their parents (and many times both of their parents) for the same reason.[98] "I have been so saddened by the miseries I have seen that I can hardly enjoy my own blessings," noted one Union soldier after witnessing such obscenities.[99]

By the fall of 1861—over a year before emancipation—the hearts of the Union soldiers fighting in the South had changed enough so as to ignite a general call for freedom. The Union was experiencing a clear transformation of its purpose for fighting. In October 1861, a member of the Third Wisconsin reported to a newspaper that "the rebellion is abolitionizing the whole army." He further explained that being in the South has forced the Union soldier to "face the sum of all evils...You have no idea," he concluded, "of the changes that have taken place in the minds of the soldiers in the last two months...men of all parties seem unanimous in the belief that to permanently establish the Union, is to first wipe the institution [of slavery]." Another soldier agreed that to win the war would require "the eternal overthrow of slavery."[100]

In addition to being forced to witness the overwhelming plight of the slaves, it should be noted that the Union soldiers' change of heart was also encouraged by their own sense of mortality. With death following them about, how could they not turn to the Lord and try to choose the right?

Many Union soldiers did choose the right and turned words into action. This is reflected in their efforts to assist runaway slaves, even though their own military directives prohibited the practice. Many soldiers declared that the North's hesitancy to involve itself in such service to the innocent was nothing but "disgraceful." "They can court martial me and be -------", proclaimed one soldier.[101] Such sentiment encouraged the idea among the ranks to allow free black Americans to fight for the North. Union soldier Leigh Webber noted that, while the idea was not unanimously accepted by the army, soldiers who "less than a year ago would threaten to desert if the Government ever enlisted negroes are now among the most earnest in the new policy."[102] (The final draft of the Emancipation

Proclamation included the allowance for the formation of black regiments, which policy gained continuous support as black troops proved themselves time and again on the battlefield.)[103]

In 2007, Georgetown University history professor Chandra Manning conducted a study to determine the Union soldiers' motives for fighting in the Civil War. Professor Manning analyzed hundreds of letters, diaries, and army camp newspapers from Union soldiers during the war.[104] Her conclusions are consistent with a central theme in this book: that the war brought on a change of heart, beginning with the soldier, that led to a change in American policy, which ultimately elevated and protected minority rights. While this study will be referenced throughout the next few chapters, her excerpt below summarizes her conclusions, particularly as applied to events leading up to emancipation:

> Few white Northerners initially joined the Union rank and file specifically to stamp out slavery, and most shared the anti-black prejudices common to their day, especially when the war began. Yet the shock of war itself and soldiers' interactions with slaves, who in many cases were the first black people northern men had ever met, changed Union troops' minds fast....
>
> [E]nlisted men in the Union army forged the crucial link between slaves and policy makers....[I]n 1861 and 1862, [Union soldiers] developed into emancipation advocates who expected their views to influence the prosecution of the war....The men of the rank and file used letters, camp newspapers, and their own actions to influence the opinions of civilians, and leaders who, lacking soldiers' direct contact with slaves, the South, and the experience of living on the front lines in a war that most people wanted over, lagged behind soldiers in their stance for emancipation.[105]

By the end of the second year of war, the American North certainly felt the message emanating from their fathers and sons on the battlefields. As Carwardine commented, "Those who withstood unmoved the buffeting of war were rare indeed." He further explained that "[a]cross the Union, including the conservative lower North and border, even those who wanted 'nothing to do with abolition in the common sense of the term' bombarded Lincoln with calls for bold and decisive measures against 'the monster' slavery, 'the real cause of the war.'" [106]

One Virginia-born loyalist, who had expressed his pre-war apathy toward slavery in general, told Lincoln, "You will be forced before long to proclaim universal liberty—the people are ripe for it and the politicians are coming to it."[107] Another Wisconsin correspondent wrote Lincoln that "I am only one of thousands who have changed views."[108] Even the Democrat George Bancroft, whose party had obstructed Republican attempts in the past to contain slavery, declared now that eradicating slavery was "the universal expectation and hope of men of all parties." Lincoln's assistant John Hay observed in bewilderment how Lincoln was being so pressed to emancipate by "those who so bitterly denounced his radicalism [anti-slavery position] a few years ago."[109] When Lincoln checked the pulse on the few slave states loyal to the Union, his response from a local office-holder there was, "Do not believe half traitors who will tell you that others will rebel in these Border States in consequence of such an act [of emancipation]....On the contrary men all beg for this policy!"[110]

Spurred by such realignment and conversion of the Northern soldiers, and now of Northern society in general, Congress began legislating certain changes, such as freeing the slaves in the one place they had total jurisdiction—the District of Columbia. Additionally, Congress moved in other ways that would have meant political suicide before the war, even by Northern standards. It had outlawed the return of fugitive slaves, outlawed slavery in the Western territories, and ratified a treaty with Britain that choked the slave trade.[111] And though it may be true that some of this altered public view was derived from a strategic desire to win a war rather than a spiritual desire to remedy a national sin, at least preliminary steps had been made. The North was growing to see that, as Carwardine so appropriately put it, "Emancipation alone would free the Union from the sin of covenant breaking, of reneging on the pledge of freedom in the Declaration of Independence."[112]

The prophecies were being fulfilled. The required changes in the hearts of Americans were infectiously being passed from soldier to citizen to legislator, with Lincoln guiding the process with a wise and God-fearing hand. The vexation was working! Standing thousands of miles from the scene of war, the Prophet Brigham Young declared (during the war's second year), "[O]ur enemies, who sought to destroy us, are being humbled."[113] The American Covenant was reemerging. The future of the Restoration was looking brighter.

Not only had the war made the Union ready for this inspired change, but it had also facilitated a legal means by which such a policy could come about. Honest Abe desired to act within the framework of the Constitution, which was a problem in that slavery was technically legal at the time. However, the Constitution allowed Lincoln, in time of war, to defend against "all enemies foreign and domestic" by means of destroying the enemy's war production capabilities. Since slaves were producing material in support of the Southern war effort, and since the South considered their slaves "property" or "tools of production," Lincoln could constitutionally seize—in reality "free"—the South's "property" and "tools."

As if following some prophetic script, Lincoln (sensing this miraculous societal transformation and constitutional escape clause) marched into his cabinet meeting on July 22, 1862 with a draft of an executive order that would change the world forever. It read: "All persons held as slaves within any state or states, wherein the constitutional authority of the United States shall not then be practically recognized...shall then, thenceforth, and forever, be free."[114]

The Proclamation Comes Forth

After almost eighteen months of war, emancipation had yet to materialize. Critics (then and now) berated Lincoln for his hesitancy on the matter. But the critic should be slow to judge Lincoln too harshly on this issue. For, even after his conversion to the cause, Lincoln had to be careful about his timing in issuing the Proclamation. He presided over a nation that legally and socially accepted slavery, and swimming against the popular current could have had devastating results. Indeed, as detailed above, while most Northerners were willing to fight for unification, few would have initially been willing to lay down their lives for black freedom. Furthermore, there were slave states (like Maryland and Kentucky) that were allied to the North. Had Lincoln issued the Proclamation at the beginning of his presidency, he would have lost many Northern recruits and might have pushed such indispensable Northern allies, such as Maryland and Kentucky, toward the Southern cause. This might have condemned the North to defeat, which, in turn, would have pushed the slaves into endless hopelessness.

But, ironically, instead of viewing his hesitation to emancipate as a wise step toward ultimate and lasting emancipation, many misinterpret it as a sign of his passiveness towards blacks. Lincoln is, for example, condemned by some because, early in the conflict, he had reversed local emancipation orders by two of his generals in the field—John C. Fremont and David Hunter.[115] But, asserting that these were signs of his opposition to black freedom is like saying Moses, by hesitating on the Hebrew liberation and subsequent occupation of Israel, was revealing his true desire not to inherit the Promise Land. The truth of the matter is that Lincoln, like Moses, needed to first receive that steeled resolve, from God Almighty, to do the difficult thing. He needed to be fully converted to the covenant. Also, like Moses' decision to stall his people's possession of the Promised Land (for what would be forty years), Lincoln, too, was inspired in his decision to exercise patience in fulfilling God's will on emancipation. The timing had to be just right. The people, in general, had to be ready so that once the Proclamation arrived, it would stick and not be rejected.

As Carwardine explains, "Lincoln's great—possibly greatest —achievement was to take a stethoscope to Union opinion and read it with such skill that he times to perfection his redefinition of national purpose."[116] "Lincoln is the most truly progressive man of the age," declared one contemporary reporter of Lincoln, "because he always moves in conjunction with the propitious circumstances, not waiting to be dragged by the force of events or wasting strength in premature struggles with them."[117]

Even Frederick Douglas, some years after Lincoln's death, penitently declared:

> I have said that President Lincoln was a white man, and shared the prejudices common to his countrymen towards the colored race. Looking back to his times and to the condition of his country, we are compelled to admit that this unfriendly feeling on his part may be safely set down as one element of his wonderful success in organizing the American people for the tremendous conflict before them....His great mission was to accomplish two things: first, to save his country from dismemberment and ruin; and second, to free his country from the great crime of slavery. To do one or the other, or both, he must have the earnest sympathy and the powerful co-operation of his loyal fellow countrymen. Without this primary and essential condition to success, his efforts must have been vain and utterly fruitless. Had he put the abolition of slavery before the salvation of the Union, he would have inevitably driven from him a powerful class of American people and rendered resistance to rebellion impossible. Viewed from the genuine abolition ground, Mr. Lincoln seemed tardy, cold, dull, and indifferent; measuring him by

the sentiment of his country, a sentiment he was bound as
a statesmen to consult, he was swift, zealous, radical and
determined.[118]

As much as he may have wanted to, Lincoln could not issue
the order of emancipation until the people themselves arrived at his
general level of moral clarity. Only then could he act under
democratic consent to issue the Proclamation. Lincoln might have
constitutionally justified the Proclamation—but did the people?
Without them, the order might not have lasted very long. And so,
Lincoln would stand in watch for the moment to arrive. While he
delegated many presidential responsibilities to cabinet members, he
"resolutely kept in his own hands all decisions bearing upon slavery,
emancipation and race," causing one of his contemporary observers
to define him as "that great, wonderful, mysterious, inexplicable
man: who holds in his single hands the reins of the Republic: who
keeps his own counsels: who does his own purpose in his own
way."[119] As his purpose for the nation became aligned with God's,
we get an even fuller sense of how his hesitation was all a part of a
greater plan. Perhaps we see why he so jealously guarded his right
and calling to be lone shot-caller on emancipation. When it came to
timing, perhaps he was waiting for the divine inspiration only he
was entitled to receive.

Though there is clear proof of Lincoln's intentional and
inspired period of waiting, we must avoid the temptation to believe
that Lincoln was always converted to the cause, and was only hiding
it until the nation arrived at his level. We have already proven that
Lincoln most assuredly passed through a very real conversion
himself, which occurred *after* many of his own countrymen. We
certainly do not want to belittle this conversion, for it manifests
some of the greatest evidence of God's influence in supporting His
covenant with latter-day America. The evidence suggests that the
delay in emancipation was derived from a combination of Lincoln's
personal conversion *and* his inspired hesitation in taking the next
step.

While Lincoln maintained strict control over the final decision to issue the Proclamation, there was one very inspirational moment when he allowed his most important colleague, advisor, and friend to influence him. This person was his secretary of state, William Seward.*

Seward had maintained a much more impressive resume than that of Lincoln. As state senator of New York, governor of New York, and U.S. senator from New York, he had gained the trust and love of the people he had served and had become a household name nationally. "He is beloved by all classes," observed the *New York Herald.* "As a landlord he is kind and lenient; as an advisor he is frank and reliable; as a citizen he is enterprising and patriotic; and as a champion of what he considers to be right he is dauntless and intrepid."[120] As such, it came as a shock to many when—in an unusual twist of fate—the much less popular Lincoln won the Republican nomination for president in 1860, even when most people had already considered it rightfully Seward's. Even stranger than this is the fact that Lincoln, after winning the general election, called his political rival to serve in the most important position in his cabinet. Seward accepted.

And what an inspired move it was! Seward often spoke of "higher laws" than those of man, which laws dictated his moral objection to slavery. Stating that we cannot "be either true Christians or real freemen" and still "impose on another a chain," he resolved that "there is a higher law than the Constitution, which regulates our authority over the domain," and which "is bestowed upon [us] by the Creator of the universe. We are his stewards."[121] This was a man who understood the covenant. He knew that there was a law—even the law of the covenant—that trumped all other law. Naturally, he eventually came to agree with his wife Frances over the true

---

* Considering how Seward's ultimate service assisted in creating the government God designed for His Restoration, it is interesting to note that years before Brigham Young had been introduced to the Church, he had worked for Seward as a carpenter. See Goodwin, *Team of Rivals,* 13.

purpose of the Civil War—to eradicate slavery—and he fought valiantly for it.[122]

Beyond this, Seward was responsible for the master diplomacy which kept Great Britain from siding with and aiding the Southern cause—an act which may have saved the Union.[123*] After Lincoln's untimely death, it was Seward who would stay onboard under the Andrew Johnson administration to make sure his former president's plan for reconstruction was implemented correctly. His support of the plan offended the radicals in his own party (they thought the plan too charitable to the South), and they eventually pushed him out of politics forever.[124] But he knew it was the right thing to do, so he did it.

According to White House insiders, Seward had grown to feel "a sincere and devoted personal attachment to Lincoln,"[125] which compelled him to stay loyal to Lincoln, even after Lincoln's death. And though Seward had originally joined Lincoln in 1860 hesitatingly, if not a bit jealously, he would truly become Lincoln's best advisor and friend during the dark and dreary days of civil war. He described the president as being, in some ways, "superhuman" and conceded that Lincoln is "the best of us."[126] The two had created such a lasting bond, that Mary Lincoln often scolded her husband for spending too much time at the Seward residence, where the president and Seward would stay up late into the night, laughing, joking, and discussing a wide variety of topics.[127]

With such a man and friend in the cabinet, it should come as no surprise that Seward supported Lincoln's plan for emancipation. He called it "justifiable" and showed more loyalty to the unpopular decision to free the slaves than other cabinet members did. But beyond just his approval, Seward also offered a most inspired addition to the plan. During that fateful July 22, 1862 cabinet

---

[*] As a Southern delegation arrived in Great Britain seeking its support, they were at that very moment fulfilling Joseph Smith's 1832 prophecy about the Civil War, which declared that shortly after the onset of the war, "the Southern States will call on...the nation of Great Britain" (D&C 87:3).

meeting (in which the president informed his team of his plan), Seward reminded Lincoln that the Union troops had suffered a series of tragic defeats. Issuing the Proclamation at that moment would, according to Seward, look like a "last measure of an exhausted government,…our last shriek, on the retreat."[128] Seward knew it would pose a credibility problem for the Proclamation, particularly as the North attempted to implement the bold policy. He knew also that it might create increased anger in the South, which would influence a strong rallying cry for an already over-confident enemy. Seward's solution was to wait on issuing the Emancipation Proclamation until after a solid Union military victory was accomplished. Seward's suggestion may appear obvious and non-eventful on the surface. However, upon analyzing what heavenly intervention occurred when Lincoln acted on his friend's advice, the divine inspiration from whence Seward's simple suggestion had sprung comes sharply into focus.

Remember, the Proclamation would serve as the first major turning point in achieving the nation's status as the great protector of, and base of operations for, God's kingdom on the earth. It would ignite the flame which would gloriously spread and illuminate the covenant. It placed America on the path of redemption. It opened the doors for the Thirteenth and Fourteenth Amendment, which were the divine solutions the Prophet Joseph had proposed, and which God had promised to make happen. As such, any act to further the Proclamation's effectiveness most certainly reflected God's influence.

Lincoln would have agreed. He fully expected to see God's hand in the event that would deliver the policy. And he did. Soon after Seward provided his inspired and prophetic counsel, Lincoln saw its fulfillment approaching in what would become one of the bloodiest battles of the Civil War: the Battle of Antietam. As the opposing sides were converging upon each other, Lincoln knew something significant pertaining to God's plan was about to happen. He later testified to his advisors that, just prior to the battle, "he had made a vow, a covenant, that if God gave us victory in the approaching battle, he would consider it an indication of the Divine Will, and that it was his duty to move forward in the cause of emancipation."[129] If the Battle of Antietam really manifested God's influence and power, as Lincoln implied, then the facts surrounding the battle do not disappoint.

The premise of this battle might be described as a gamble by the South's revered general, Robert E. Lee, in taking his army into the North to score a victory. With the South already on a roll, Lee believed a sound victory within Northern territory would bring French and British recognition of the Confederacy and thus mark the beginning of the end for Lincoln and the Union. However, as the Southern army entered Maryland in September 1862, Lee had not planned on a single, small, yet highly miraculous, incident that would stymie his plans.[130]

Though Lee, knowing his army would be marching through enemy territory, took enormous precautions to secure all military documents revealing his top secret plan of attack, somehow, someway, a copy of these plans (wrapped around three cigars) was left unattended in an empty field near Frederick, Maryland. And somehow, someway, two Union soldiers, walking past that very spot in that very field, happened upon the document, known ever-after as "Lee's Special Order No. 191." The plans rapidly made their way into the hands of Lee's opponent, Union General George McClellan.

Then, in a second miracle, McClellan was able to immediately verify the order's authenticity only because his aide had been close friends in the pre-war U.S. Army with Lee's adjutant, Robert Chilton. The Union aide quickly recognized his old Southern friend's handwriting. "Here is a paper," McClellan then declared, "with which if I cannot whip 'Bobbie Lee,' I will be willing to go home."[131] Without the discovery of Lee's plans, military historians agree that the battle would have probably terminated in certain Union defeat, which might have been all France and Britain needed to lend support to the Confederacy. Once this happened, the Northern cause most likely would have collapsed entirely.[132] Thus, the restoration of God's Constitution and His plans for America and her divine mission would have been deeply frustrated right then and there. *With* the plans, however, McClellan's army was able to respond in such a way that secured the Union a narrow victory,* thus saving America and providing Lincoln a platform from which to launch the Proclamation to the world.

The Pulitzer Prize-winning historian, and renowned expert of Antietam, James McPherson, concluded that "the odds against the sequence of events that led to the loss and finding and verification of these orders must have been a million to one."[133] Considering what was at stake here—either Union surrender and the reign of American oppression or Union victory and the start to *universal agency*—the odds of "a million to one" cannot be taken lightly. Indeed, considering what was at stake, these events can scarcely be seen as coincidence; for the events responsible for Union victory were so incredibly unlikely, yet so important to God's plan, that the only explanation for what happened is God. He was, once again, in the battlefields of America.

Furthermore, the miraculous events surrounding this indispensable Union victory were proof that the North had begun to change and repent. God's hand in the victory is evidence that the North's humility had reactivated the covenant, thus enabling the American Covenant blessing of *protection*. As it had been offered in earlier days to Washington and his revolutionaries, so it would again be offered to Lincoln and his Union soldiers—and for the same gospel cause.

Such thoughts of divine intervention were not lost on Lincoln. Within days after the battle, on September 22, 1862, Lincoln called a special cabinet meeting—a cabinet meeting that would go down in history. It was at that meeting that Lincoln issued the official preliminary Proclamation. The Union victory under God had sealed it. As recently noted, before the battle, Lincoln had floated the

---

* Though the Union defeated Lee, sending him fleeing in retreat back south, the Battle of Antietam's combined losses were counted at 22,719, making it (then and now), the bloodiest single day in American history. See Bennett, *America, The Last Best Hope,* Vol. I, 346.

Lincoln at Antietam, by Alexander Gardner.
Courtesy of the Library of Congress.

idea that the whole ordeal was a "covenant." By battle's end, he *knew* it was a covenant—it was the American Covenant, and Lincoln was about to fulfill his end of the sacred agreement. Lincoln boldly told his cabinet that "his mind was fixed, his decision made." He made it clear that he needed no advice about "the main matter—for I have determined for myself." According to a witness, Lincoln stated unequivocally that "God had decided this question in favor of the slaves." The president declared: "[I will keep] the promise to myself, and [he paused here for emphasis] to my maker."[134] The head of the Navy, who was there present, was so moved by the experience that he wrote in his journal that Lincoln's act was indeed a "covenant" with the Almighty.[135]

Lincoln had set things in motion that would culminate in the historic moment on January 1, 1863, when he stood in the White House as William Seward handed him the official and engrossed copy of the Emancipation Proclamation, ready for his signature. As if reviewing some sacramental prayer, Lincoln scrutinized the text one last time and identified a minor error, after which he sent it back to be corrected. This had to be perfect. With the correction remedied, and the refreshed document placed before him, Lincoln signed the Proclamation, which concluded with the following words: "And upon this act, sincerely believed to be an act of justice, warranted by the Constitution, upon military necessity, I invoke the considerate judgment of mankind, and the gracious favor of Almighty God."[136]

In a remarkable side note to this historical event, as Lincoln placed his pen over the document to sign it, his hand began to tremble uncontrollably. He had to stand back for a moment, flex his arm, and battle off whatever was causing this last-minute obstruction. One might attribute the strange distraction to his nerves or lack of personal resolution. However, as he explained to the witnesses there, "I never, in my life, felt more certain that I was doing right than I do in signing this paper."[137] In light of a restored gospel perspective, and in considering what policies the Proclamation would inspire in the future for the protection of moral agency for all minorities (including for the Lord's church), might this have been the adversary making a last-ditch effort to halt the progress? Might this have been a similar adversarial attempt as that which had occurred to the Prophet Joseph some forty-three years prior in the sacred grove? If it was, it would have been carried out by the adversary for the same reason. Lincoln did, fortunately, gain his strength and make his immortal mark (though it was a shaky one) squarely on the document. Knowing that his signature would be forever examined, he smilingly commented, "They will say, 'he had some compunctions.'"[138]

As a fitting epilogue to this story of the Proclamation, the original document was eventually placed, and rests today, on display in the National Archive, directly adjacent to the original Declaration of Independence and the original Constitution. As the Proclamation represents a powerful symbol of the national covenant, it is altogether fitting that it has been laid to rest alongside those other most prominent representations of the America Covenant. It is equally fitting that engraved upon the floor, welcoming visitors to the divine documents, is the Ten Commandments—that very first symbol of the national covenant.[139]

Before concluding this great American Covenant story surrounding the Emancipation Proclamation, there is an important issue that deserves further attention. This issue has to do with the severe criticism launched at the Proclamation's true intent. Even if the critics can be calmed on the issue of Lincoln's apparent hesitation to issue the document (that he was, in fact, passing through a personal conversion and was waiting for the people to be readied for such a policy), they still maintain that, even once issued, it was no moral triumph as many believe. Lincoln's true intention for the Proclamation, claim the critics, had little to do with a moral or lasting solution, but instead had everything to do with tactical advantage in the war: free the slaves and stop the South's most powerful war making resource—the slaves. Critics claim it was nothing more than the modern equivalent of bombing the enemy's military industrial machine. Furthermore, and along the same lines, emancipation was naturally accompanied by freed slaves joining the Union army—further evidence that the Proclamation was mere military strategy.[140]

The evidence to support the critics' claim is bolstered by a statement Lincoln made in August 1862 (after he was supposedly already "converted" to the cause of God). "My paramount object in this struggle is to save the Union, and is not either to save or to destroy slavery" wrote Lincoln in a letter for publication. "If I could save the Union without freeing any slaves I would do it, and if I could save it by freeing all the slaves I would do it."[141] Lincoln's comments here do make him appear rather apathetic toward the moral crusade to emancipate. Seen in context, however, this argument can be explained away by the fact that we do not know how much had been revealed to Lincoln at that point (it was not until the Battle of Antietam that he declared unequivocally that he *knew* what God wanted him to do).

However, our evidence above does suggest that Lincoln most likely had already been converted at this point, which compels us to seek another explanation for his comments. And another explanation indeed exists. We must remember that the idea of emancipation was new to the nation. It is possible, then, that Lincoln was merely testing the waters—testing his plan against the very opinionated public. He was boldly throwing out the idea of freeing the slaves, but diplomatically couching his statement in the idea that it was purely tactical and only to support his goal of restoring the Union. This was, after all, the only real legal justification he had at the time for freeing the slaves, and so he used it to the maximum. But whatever his intentions, this much is certain: by saying what he did, Lincoln was the first president in American history to introduce the idea that the president had the authority to free slaves at all. This was actually a positive and promising thought for the abolitionist cause, which made many abolitionists at the time hopeful that Lincoln's comments meant he was "preparing for a dramatic step" toward freeing slaves.[142] Though critics today would have us believe that the president's comments should have made abolitionists despair, his comments had actually had the opposite effect.

Furthermore (and this part the critics fail to emphasize), in this same statement Lincoln clearly signaled to the people where he stood morally on the issue and where he was perhaps going to take the nation. For he concluded his above remarks, stating that "I intend no modification of my oft-expressed personal wish that all men everywhere could be free."[143]

Disregarding this response, however, the critics assert that the Proclamation itself supports their position, as it is self-described as a war tactic. Furthermore, it only freed the slaves in rebel states, leaving the slaves in Union-friendly states in chains. (If it really had been a moral issue for Lincoln, and not merely a tactical one, would he not have freed *all* the slaves?) The critic might then add the seemingly deflating notion that because the Proclamation liberated only Southern slaves, it really liberated no slaves. For, the North had no legitimate control over Southern slavery, only Northern slavery. Lincoln, then, was freeing those slaves he could *not* free and leaving alone those slaves he *could* free.[144]

However, these arguments—while technically backed with correct facts—do nothing to take away from Lincoln's powerful and godly intent for the Proclamation. Once again, Lincoln desired only to go as far as the Constitution (and the people in general) would allow him to go. The Proclamation was a legal document and therefore had to be *legal* per the constitutional thought of the day. However, whereas the Constitution (at least the interpretation of the Constitution at the time) did not permit Lincoln to free the slaves, it did permit him to destroy the war machines of the enemy. As the slaves were producing the Southern means for war, Lincoln could at least temporarily emancipate the Southern slaves. He did what he could. He was, after all, not a king. He was the president of a constitutional democracy that recognized slavery as a legal institution. Had he tried to be more than a constitutionally-bound president by freeing the slaves in the Union border-states, he could have lost those states to the South, perhaps securing Southern victory. Then what hope would the slaves have had?

That he stayed within his limits initially, however, does not indicate that he did not plan on expanding those freedoms once God opened the doors that would allow him to do so. All we have to do to defeat the critics' argument in this case is to consider Lincoln's efforts surrounding the Proclamation in the aftermath of its issuance. Indeed, had it really only been a war tactic, then Lincoln surely would have revoked the Proclamation upon the termination of the war, as he promised to do when he temporarily repealed the right to habeas corpus (which is the right for an arrestee to appeal his detention by the government). As in the case of slavery, Lincoln believed his decision to temporarily suspend habeas corpus was a justified war tactic. Therefore, if military advantage was the real reason behind suspending slavery and habeas corpus, then they both should have been restored at war's end. Unlike habeas corpus (which *was* eventually restored), Lincoln vowed in 1864, in a message to Congress, that, "while I remain in my present position, I shall not attempt to retract or modify the Emancipation Proclamation, nor shall I return to slavery any person that is free by the terms of that proclamation."[145] Does this not show Lincoln's true intent over slavery?

Not only would Lincoln refuse to reinstate slavery at war's end, he did just the opposite. He pushed for the Thirteenth Amendment, which would constitutionally prohibit slavery in all the United States, including the slave states loyal to the Union. He even laid the groundwork for eventual black citizenship and suffrage (what would become the Fourteenth and Fifteenth Amendments). As we will see later, he knew, and pronounced, that this course of action would provide refuge, not only for black Americans, but for *all* suffering Americans. (He knew he was working, under God, on something truly magnificent. It was as though he held, in his hand, the prophecies of Joseph Smith.)

Far from revoking the Proclamation, Lincoln wanted to replace it with something that would make African Americans (and all Americans) "forever free."[146] An amendment, unlike the Proclamation (which, as an executive order could be blotted out by a Supreme Court decision), would be almost untouchable and permanently binding. If he had framed the Proclamation as a mere war tactic, or if his Proclamation had failed to free the slaves in all the border-states, it was to maintain the legality and general acceptability of his first steps—in this still very sensitive time—toward full *national repentance* and *universal agency* in the future.

And so, not only does our response to the critics illuminate Lincoln's moral intent, it also answers the shortsighted assertion that the Proclamation freed nobody. "The old cliché," wrote McPherson, "that the proclamation did not free a single slave because it applied only to the Confederate states where Lincoln had no power, completely misses the point. The proclamation announced a revolutionary new war aim—the overthrow of slavery by force of arms if and when Union forces conquered the South."[147] Without the Proclamation, Union soldiers might have continued occupying Southern states, but they would have left slavery alone in those states. For example, we already mentioned how, early in the conflict, local emancipation orders by Union Generals Fremont and Hunter were rescinded. They had been commanded to continue to re-take the South, but to free no slaves. And so, yes, the Proclamation was necessary. Slavery was going nowhere without it.

With the Proclamation, however, once the South *was* conquered, the slaves *were* freed; and thus, the Proclamation *did* accomplish much. For critics to say (as they do) that the Proclamation did nothing, is like saying the U.S. declarations of war against Imperial Japan and Nazi Germany did nothing. For, initially, they were just declarations. Upon their issuance, Imperial Japan and Nazi Germany remained a force largely undeterred and untouched by America. If we had to add the obvious fact that these declarations eventually led the U.S. to defeat these foreign enemies, it would be embarrassing. So it is with the Proclamation. The critics' argument on this issue is amazingly short-sighted.

Then (to further frustrate those who call the Proclamation *useless*), when the Proclamation grew into the Thirteenth and Fourteenth Amendments, freedom for *all* the oppressed began to ring loud and clear for the first time in our history. Indeed, history has proven that the Proclamation was a clarion call that led to the greatest of freedoms for all Americans.

Perhaps most importantly, for critics to take one statement out of context, or to misapply the meaning of the Proclamation so badly (so as it strip Lincoln of his moral intent) is to absolutely ignore the overwhelming evidence that independently clarifies the truth of the matter. For, the countless declarations made by Lincoln and witnesses during this time about how he had been converted by God, about how it was God's will to free the slaves, and about how it had all been given under covenant, surely flies in the face of the critics' commentary. (And we can add to the argument the fact that all of these declarations and actions are corroborated by scriptural prophecies, as detailed in the previous chapter.) Furthermore, we have seen how the nation passed through a similar conversion. Indeed, despite what critics say, emancipation did not flow from Lincoln and the North in a casual, haphazard, or temporary fashion; nor was emancipation based solely in military necessity. This is not to say the tactical benefits of emancipation were not a factor, for they were. But after reviewing all the evidence, we must agree with renowned historians Larry Schweikart and Michael Allen, who, after admitting Lincoln understood the military advantages of emancipation, concluded, nevertheless, that Lincoln's Proclamation was "first and foremost...a moral and legal issue, not a military or political one."[148]

Ultimately, Lincoln's actions (as will be further detailed in the next chapters) speak much louder than any of his misunderstood words. The evidence is indeed strong that what inspired the Proclamation was a deeply spiritual conversion based in covenant and induced by God's prophesied and miraculous vexation. It certainly is not by coincidence that Lincoln, in sealing his decision, concluded the Proclamation in the style of a true American Covenant-maker, declaring: "I invoke...the gracious favor of Almighty God."[149]

A Note on the Anti-Lincoln Movement

Thus far, we have only scratched the surface of the evidence that Lincoln and the North had been converted by God to the covenant—all in fulfillment of prophecies related to God's latter-day kingdom. But before delving into the more profound evidence of this powerful conversion, and how it was put to use, we will first discuss why it is so important for us to recognize the significance of this conversion. Too many do not recognize it and, therefore, fall into strange and inaccurate perceptions of the Civil War and Lincoln's place in it.

Among this group, there even exists today a small (but dedicated and growing) faction of Latter-day Saint students of the Constitution (who we will refer to as theorists or Mormon theorists) who reject that Lincoln was a man of God, sent to preserve the rights of God's children. In fact, these theorists suggest just the opposite is true.

The theorists' argument is based on the notion that Lincoln fought the Civil War for the purpose of "saving the Union;" that is, he "authorized" the death of over 600,000 Americans because of his subjective (and wrong) interpretation of what the "Union" meant under the Constitution. Lincoln believed the South had no right to secede, and *that* (according to the theorists) was his justification for war. The theorists, on the other hand, believe the South had every right to leave. And so, they are outraged that Lincoln instructed Union soldiers "to begin killing the people and destroying the property of the separatists" simply because of the separatists' (the South's) "desire to withdraw from the Union." The theorists claim Lincoln's intent was based in "love of money and dominion." Further, they deny history and evidence (such as that recently presented), and claim the Emancipation Proclamation did *nothing* to free the slaves.[150]

It is absolutely true that Lincoln believed the South had no right to leave the Union. The theorists do their best to convince us that Lincoln was way off base in this argument. The theorists, for example, ask us to read the rather vague words James Madison once used to describe how the Union was composed. They then ask us to conclude that Madison believed in the right for states to secede.[151] What the theorists *don't* ask us to read are James Madison's words when he *specifically* addressed, not broad brush concepts of constitutional law, but the actual issue of *secession*. For, Madison was alive to witness South Carolina's *first* effort (in 1832) to leave the Union. (This secessionist movement grew out of Southerners' outrage over unfair tariffs being forced upon them by the federal government.) Madison's response was as follows: "It is high time that the claim to secede at will should be put down by the public opinion." He declared that a state's proposed twin rights to nullify federal law ("nullification") and leave the Union ("secession") are the "twin heresies" that "ought to be buried in the same grave."[152] If Lincoln was off base, he was in good company with the "Father of the Constitution."

Andrew Jackson was the president during this time of possible secession between 1832-1833. As a staunch defender of states' rights over the federal government, he has long been a hero to the theorists' cause. Jackson also weighed-in heavily on the issue of the right of Southern secession; though the theorists (ironically) would not like what he had to say. "Our Union," he declared, "It must be preserved." He stated that "to call [the right to secede from the Union] a constitutional right, is confounding the meaning of terms, and can only be done through gross error." Jackson then passed the Force Act in January 1833, which gave him his sought-after congressional authority to send the federal military into the rebellious state to collect the duties *by force*, if necessary.[153] (The South then backed down). The theorists do not encourage their students to read this account either.

These same theorists also try to convince us of a state's right to secede using colonial-era descriptions that define the states' very weak relationship with the national government. Indeed, the descriptions do suggest that that states' collective bond under the Union might easily and lawfully be cracked. The problem is that the only convincing descriptions the theorists offer as proof were made *prior* to the Union created by the Constitution. They cite the relationship forged under the weak Articles of Confederation, and pretend that this standard of "Union" was the same as the standard set later by the Constitution. This is like a doctor trying to diagnose a health problem, not using the patient's data from the current illness, but using data from a previous illness years ago. Similarly, they point us to the words Madison recorded during the Constitutional Convention—words used by the bickering delegates. During the hotly contested debates, the delegates used words like "voluntary," "sovereignty," and "compact."[154] They used these words to draw vague conclusions. Furthermore, these words are taken from arguments made *prior* to the final product. They represent differing opinions, not a conclusive voice that can offer any conclusive definition of the Union or the right to secede from it. These tactics by the theorists are both deceptive and misleading.

Though the theorists make weak arguments (pretending they are strong), the truth is, we could spend all day debating a state's right to secede and never come to an easy conclusion. For the Constitution is quiet on this issue. (Unlike the Constitution, the commentators, from the founding to the present, have been loud. But they have also been widely diverse in their opinions). And so, as there were never definitive lines drawn about a state's right to secede, nobody knew what to do when it started happening at the end of 1860. Then, when the South began seizing and attacking federal property (like forts and ports) in the South, thus consummating its decision to leave, Lincoln (understandably) responded militarily. The federal government was under attack! By the spring of 1861, the war had begun.

But this is where the theorists get thoroughly confused. They want to believe that Lincoln continued his fight—his endless push for death and bloodshed—over the constitutionally murky argument regarding the right to secede. They *completely* miss the central theme of the conflict. This is what happens when we fail to see the conflict through the clarity of the American Covenant, when we fail to recognize the latter-day prophecies pertaining to the covenant (as detailed last chapter), and when we close our eyes to Lincoln's and the North's great conversion to this covenant.

The war may have begun over issues related to rights of secession, but Lincoln and his people learned that it was actually about something very different. As Lincoln wrote in a memo to himself (not intended to be made public), "God's purpose [for this war] is something different from the purpose of either party...I am almost ready to say this is probably true—that *God wills this contest, and wills that it shall not end yet.*"[155] We have seen proof in this chapter (and we will see even more proof in later chapters) that Lincoln learned, in no uncertain terms, that God was administering this war as a punishment, to purge the nation (both North and South) of sin. Lincoln's understanding of this was the result of his heaven-induced conversion. He knew, and thus stated, that the war was "a punishment inflicted upon us for our presumptuous sins, to the needful end of our national reformation as a whole people..."[156]

Lincoln had caught Joseph Smith's vision that God would bring down hell on the nation so that *national repentance* and *universal agency* might reign. He worked as God's instrument in fulfilling the prophecy. (As will be seen in a later chapter, Lincoln put his words into action when he rejected the South's proposal to finally agree to his original offer and return to the Union with slavery intact. Once converted to the real cause, Lincoln took that option off the table, even though it meant the war must go on. Indeed, the war was now about freedom for the oppressed, not just unification. Though the theorists do not acknowledge this fact of history, it is clear that the war meant much more to Lincoln than mere unification.)

Seen in this light, the argument over "right of secession" becomes completely irrelevant. We are talking about higher laws here. We are talking about the national covenant God had placed the Promised Land under—both North and South. Neither side was going to duck out of this one—not even by the best constitutional argument that it is a right to secede, and thereby maintain, an iniquitous system of governance (which system of governance was clearly responsible for keeping the covenant/constitutional blessings out of the hands of the Saints, the slaves, and many others). God would not have it—for it was this very iniquity (in both the North and the South) that God was, just then, trying to strip the nation of in preparation for the restoration of His Kingdom. And so, the theorist may continue to blame Lincoln for administering this scourge and vexation. But the prophecies are clear: *it was God*. Lincoln had become, as he claimed himself to be, nothing but "a humble instrument in the hands of our Heavenly Father."[157]

But the theories of the theorists become stranger still. They claim that the liberty they love was lost because of the war. "What the people lost during the Civil War (the Great War of Coercion), we have yet to get back." So argue the theorists. The theorists encourage us to believe that "Lincoln himself became the principal instigator of America's suicide" and that his Civil War "ended the Founders' dream in America."[158] What the theorists are referring to is the fact that state sovereignty—or states' rights—had been damaged by the advent of the Civil War fruit: an empowered federal government. More particularly, this fruit of war was largely represented by the Fourteenth Amendment, which mandated the federal government to intervene in the states to restore basic civil rights to the innocent and suffering. The theorists seem to turn a blind eye to the fact that this Amendment restored liberty to all, and instead focus upon the fact that it allowed the federal government to grow (which is something the theorists despise). The theorists claim that the Amendment was "foist[ed] upon the states."[159] (Definition of *foist*: "to force upon or impose fraudulently or unjustifiably.")[160]

Do the theorists *really* believe things were better in America before the Fourteenth Amendment—before the federal government had a mandate to intervene in states that sucked away the promised blessings of the Constitution? Do we really need to revisit, again, the plight of the Latter-day Saints before the war? Oppression. Exile. Extermination. Dead Saints. Dead prophets. Burnt and seized temples. All this was carried out by *state* governments—not the federal government. These atrocities are the *real* things we lost because of the war. Is this what we want back? And what about the plight of African Americans? (More on this issue later.) Is this the Constitution we want? Do we really want to return to the pre-war interpretation of it? What "the people lost" pursuant to the war was not liberty, but the opposite of liberty. The only thing we *really* lost was wicked oppressors who utilized state governments to work the most ungodly works ever known to our nation.

The theorists may believe the original intent of the Constitution was to have *states* preserve and promote the great blessings of liberty. But, to argue that the states were doing a fine job of this is to absolutely deny history. If the states had done their job, the war and the Fourteenth Amendment would not have been needed. God will correct His children. If He has to influence an amendment to the Constitution for the sake of preserving liberty, and for the sake of securing His church, of course He will do it. This is not a difficult concept to internalize. There are a few groups in American society that should especially understand this concept: Mormons are one of them.

It would be interesting to see the Mormon theorists ask the Prophet Joseph Smith about his feelings on the subject. How would the Mormon theorists respond to what we know the Prophet believed? For, what the theorists portray as a *wonderful* liberty-bearing concept (the doctrine of "states' rights")—even that great thing they claim "the people lost" during "the Great War of Coercion"—was *not* wonderful to the Prophet. Let us, again, consider the following words of the Prophet, who was *actually there* to witness this system of government that the theorists seems to pine for: "The States' rights doctrine are what feed mobs. They are a dead carcass, a stink and they shall ascend up as a stink offering in the nose of the Almighty." [161]

Fortunately, the Lord had an inspired plan and response to the iniquitous nation. (And this is where things get especially tricky for the Mormon theorists.) As explained in detail in the last chapter, God sent forth His prophet and specifically told him to "importune" to the federal government, as per D&C 101: 88. (*Yes*, God commanded His prophet to seek federal intervention. Why would the Lord do that if the federal government was not meant to intervene?) Joseph, of course, responded. He went to the federal government and told it loud and clear that it needed to eradicate slavery and it needed to intervene in the states and restore the constitutional promises—restore civil rights. The Prophet ran his presidential campaign on this idea.

The federal government (using the same political arguments as those used by the theorists) told the Prophet that it had no right to step on the states' toes and that it would not intervene. Joseph then told the federal government, in writing, that "If the General

Government [federal government] has no power, to re-instate expelled citizens to their rights, there is a monstrous hypocrite fed and fostered from the hard earnings of the people!" [162] He continued, "all men who say the Congress [referring to the *federal* Congress] has no power to...defend the rights of her citizens have not the love of truth in them." [163] Declared the Prophet: "[W]hen we have petitioned those in power for assistance, they have always told us they had no power to help us. Damn such traitors! When they give me the power to protect the innocent, I will never say I can do nothing for their good; I will exercise that power, so help me God!" [164]

The theorists are apparently blind to their own religion's history. Ironically, they love to quote D&C 101:80, about how God inspired the Constitution. And yet, they seem to ignore the entire context in which that *very* revelation was given. The revelation came as an answer to the Prophet Joseph, who had been pleading with the Lord to know what to do about the gut-churning violations of constitutional law that were befalling him and the Saints. Indeed, Joseph had identified the wicked system of government produced by the politics that the Mormon theorists seemed to applaud—a system that disallows federal intervention and thus permits states do what they want to the suffering minority. The irony thickens for the Mormon theorists when the Lord then tells the Prophet to seek *federal intervention*, and then the Prophet goes and does just that.

In obeying God's command on the matter, Joseph dutifully called for what he termed a "provision," to be added to the Constitution. As it was, said Joseph, "the Constitution is...not broad enough to cover the whole ground." Though the theorists claim the Constitution was pretty much perfect on the first go-around (what they call the "First Founding"), Joseph seemed to disagree. As wonderful as it was, its misapplication was so severe that it required something more. Joseph said something was *missing* in the Constitution. The Constitution, stated the Prophet, needed a "manner by which that freedom can be preserved." He called for a "provision" that would, when wicked state governments oppressed the Saints and others, "punish the mobs, *states*, or communities who interfere with the rights of the people..."[165] In his published document defining his political platform, Joseph emphasized that constitutional blessings should be the right of all men and that, in order to guarantee these rights, the president of the United States should have "full power to send an army to suppress mobs," without requiring the invitation of the state.[166]

Let us make no mistake: Joseph was calling for the Fourteenth Amendment. This is precisely what the Fourteenth Amendment provided. It recognized, for the first time, that Americans are U.S. citizens that are entitled to all the rights of the Constitution. If the states decided that certain citizens were not so entitled (as they did), the Fourteenth Amendment contested them. It gave power to the federal government to intervene in the states and restore the rights of the covenant. It produced exactly what Joseph sought. (And let us not forget, the "Father of the Constitution," James Madison, had originally called for such a provision to be added to the Constitution, calling it "the most valuable" of the amendments. Madison's amendment, which would have compelled the states to respect "equal rights of conscience," and other basic civil rights, was, unfortunately, rejected by jealous state rights' advocates.[167] It should also be remembered that Madison's amendment was part of a larger political theory he put forth in promoting the need for the Constitution. The inspired idea, which we discussed at length in Chapter 2, was that of "warring factions," which is found in Madison's Federalist No.10.[168] It placed the federal government in a position to stand as a check against state governments that would oppress.)

Then came the warning (detailed at length in the previous chapter). According to the *many* prophecies—including, but not limited to, those cited from D&C 101 and 121—if and when the Prophet-candidate was rejected (which, of course he was, even by the murderous hands of the state), God would bring a furious scourge and vexation to deliver the "provision" put forth by the Prophet. Joseph had told the nation, as detailed last chapter, that if it did not heed his warning, such a disaster would occur.[169] We would also do well to remember that other prophets, like Brigham Young, and some of the great Founders before him, like George Mason and Thomas Jefferson, made similar prophecies for their nation (also cited last chapter).

Furthermore, as will be detailed in a later chapter, Brigham Young sided squarely and proactively with Lincoln and the Union. We will see how Brigham offered moral support, provided monetary support, and even ordered manpower support to Lincoln. (He could have sided with the South, and yet he did not.) We will also see how other prophets and apostles praised Lincoln as God's servant—the first U.S. president presiding over the Saints ever to receive such praise from the Saints. If Lincoln was so wrongheaded in what he was doing, as the Mormon theorists declare, how do they explain away the actions of the Church? If Lincoln's presidency was based in wicked politics and an unrighteous war, why would the prophet of God assist Lincoln in such unrighteousness? Before shouting out from the rooftops our subjective interpretations of the Civil War, we would do well to first consult the actions and words of the prophets of God—including Joseph and Brigham—who actually walked the earth during this crisis and during the events leading up to this crisis.

All of this leads us back to Lincoln. As the chosen one to carry out God's will in this matter, he did just that. Not only did he do it, but the manner in which he did it only confirms his divine mission. As we have seen, and will further see, Lincoln carried out this mission through his conversion and through his prophetic and spiritually moving words and actions. But, as is the fate of almost any prophet of God, when Lincoln's words and actions are divorced from the scriptural and spiritual context in which they come forth, Lincoln (like the prophets) is written off, by many, as a tyrant, a dictator, a madman, or worse. (One prominent Mormon theorist claims not to know whether Lincoln was a good man or a bad man, only that he made a series of foolish and wrongheaded decisions based on bad advice.[170] The same theorist, however, also claims that

Lincoln was the "principal instigator of America's suicide" and that "the fundamentals" of his "national policy" included the "love of money and dominion." This begs the question: how could Lincoln be both a good man *and* maintain such sinister intentions, even "authorizing" the death of over 600,000 people just to realize these sinister intentions?)[171] Indeed, such false, mean, confused, and gurgled labels have always—and will always—be laid upon the servants of God by those who do not understand.

The Mormon theorists claim Lincoln led us into a "Second Founding," which they describe as wicked. Perhaps it was a "Second Founding," but it is anything but wicked. For, the "First Founding" was great on paper, but not in practice. We should thank God for the "Second Founding." It is but another name for the "provision," backed by scripture and called for by the Prophet of the Restoration. And Lincoln *did* bring it.

Sadly, the very man who brought the Mormon Church (and other minorities) out of the darkness caused by states' rights, and into the protective light of the Constitution, is cast aside, debased, and thrown out. And, in painful irony, he is cast aside, debased, and thrown out by those (including the Mormon theorists) who now bask in the light he brought. He gave them, "under God...a new birth of freedom."* He brought them their Prophet's "provision." Where their temples once burned, now they stand! This cost him everything he held dear, including his own life. Now, they happily thrive under this freedom, while coldly turning their backs to the bearer. (I do not claim the people who maintain this anti-Lincoln position are bad, or that they are doing these things intentionally or with malice. But, notwithstanding, they *are* doing these things.)

The irony continues. For all of this puts the Mormon theorists into another, similar, predicament. What would have happened had Joseph obtained what he sought in mortality. What if he had won the presidency? What if he had then brought forth his "provision"? To be academically honest, and consistent, had this

---

* From the Gettysburg Address

scenario played out, the theorists would have to hurl some of the same allegations on the Prophet as they do on Lincoln. Would the theorists claim that Joseph, too, had "foisted" the amendment upon the states? Would they allege that he had "forced or imposed fraudulently" his "provision" upon them? (Incidentally, the Mormon theorists who claim the idea of a national bank is so clearly wrongheaded and unconstitutional, must also contend with the fact that their Prophet had called for a national bank when running for the presidency.)[172]

In the face of obvious evidence, the theorists may, in desperation, claim Joseph did not seek the Fourteenth Amendment. True. He actually sought something stronger. For, the Fourteenth Amendment, though it had set a standard, was mostly a dead promise until the federal Civil Rights Act came along some one hundred years later. Still others may argue that Joseph, though he was a prophet, was not a politician. His political thought, they say, was a matter of personal opinion. To make this already difficult and problematic argument, however, the critic must get around the fact that what Joseph did was profoundly based in revelations from God —revelations that were fulfilled in every particular by Lincoln and the Civil War. (I have yet to hear the argument that, perhaps, all this was just *God's* opinion.)

The theorists might also argue that *states* protect civil rights today, not the federal government. This is also mostly true (though the Federal Government still does much to enforce civil rights). However, this relatively recent trend (since the Civil Rights Movement) only occurred because the Fourteenth Amendment and the Civil Rights Act stood as a powerful force of influence upon the states—a force to ensure the states adopted a policy of full moral agency. Today, as God designed, the states have adhered. But the federal government still stands as the late originator and as the current check and backup.

The theorists interpret Lincoln's efforts as a scheme to create a "domestic empire under control of an all powerful central government."[173] Not so. Lincoln simply brought the federal government to the level where God, the Prophet, (and Madison) had directed it to be. He brought it to a point where it could serve as a check against iniquitous states—states that abused the Saints, African Americans, Jews, Catholics, and others. But has the federal government not grown in power beyond its constitutional bounds? And was the federal government not afforded the opportunity to thus grow because Lincoln gave it its first significant dose of power? The answer to these questions is *yes*. But to blame Lincoln for that is akin to saying that because God gave us the Internet to do genealogy, He is also responsible for the pornography that came with it. It's ridiculous. Furthermore, whatever federal increases and abuses of power have come about since the Civil War (and while we must be aware of them and always push back), they do not even approximate the sins derived of "states' rights" that prevailed before the war. They do not even hint at enslaving races, exiling and murdering the Saints and their prophets, or burning temples of God. Let us keep some perspective.

What about the fact that Lincoln did stretch the limits of the Constitution during the war? For example, it is a fact that he suspended the right of habeas corpus and did other things that pushed the limits (or even violated) the strictest interpretations of the Constitution. It is true that presumably innocent people lost their rights due to these war-time policies. It is easy to argue that Lincoln was wrong to do this. Perhaps he *was* wrong. But remember, he was the president in a capital city that was embedded geographically in the middle of the South. He laid his head on a pillow each night in a residence that was less than one hundred miles away from the Confederate capital.[174] In the bloodiest war America has ever been involved in, the commander-in-chief was completely surrounded and inundated with rebels and traitors to his cause. They severely threatened the godly vision he sought to bring the world. Perhaps his strong hand saved the very Constitution he was accused of violating. It was a difficult decision he had to make. Said Lincoln:

It became necessary for me to choose whether, using only the existing means, agencies, and processes which Congress had provided, I should let the government fall at once into ruin, or whether, availing myself of the broader powers conferred by the Constitution in cases of insurrection, I would make an effort to save it with all its blessings for the present age and for posterity.[175]

Specifically addressing his decision to suspend the right of habeas corpus, Lincoln explained that, as president, it was his job to ensure "that the laws be faithfully executed." In that a major portion of the states had subverted the "whole of the laws" (to include God's laws), Lincoln wondered aloud what the nation would gain by him maintaining one law (habeas corpus) at the expense of allowing traitors to subvert all the others and destroy the government. Asked Lincoln, "Are all the laws, but one, to go unexecuted, and the government itself go to pieces, lest that one be violated?"[176]

Whatever questionable (or even wrong) war-time powers Lincoln assumed during this war over moral agency, they are a drop in the bucket relative to what God was doing here for the Promised Land. Not only were these drastic measures very temporary, but, we must remember, they were in furtherance of a foreordained war whose purpose was to provide the fertile ground for God's Kingdom on the earth.

In 1820, Thomas Jefferson declared that "if the freedom of religion, guaranteed us by the law in *theory* can ever rise in *practice*... truth will prevail...and the genuine doctrines of Jesus, so long perverted by his pseudo-priests, will again be *restored* to their original purity."[177] Jefferson knew what the Prophet Joseph would soon learn —even that thing that the theorists cannot, to this day, seem to grasp. Jefferson knew that, even in his twilight years, at the very end of the revolutionary generation, the glorious Constitution was yet but a *theory*. The "First Founding" was awesome and wonderful, but sadly, it had not, as-of-yet, risen from *theory* to *practice*. Unfortunately, wicked men had hijacked its original divine intent, which required

God to step in. His intervention is clearly reflected in history and scripture. Indeed, history and scripture fulfilled Jefferson's prophecy. For Lincoln did take this *theory* and, at the direction of God Almighty, brought it into *practice*. What the theorists lament so much, what they call "the Second Founding," actually brought the blessings of the Constitution—for the *first* time—into *practice*. And *the genuine doctrines of Jesus...have again been restored to their original purity.* They have taken root in the land, and gone forth more boldly than ever, because of that liberty won by Lincoln and the Civil War.

Having addressed these issues, what might we learn here about blinding ourselves to God's designs for America and her covenant? What the theorists have done, in this case, and what they are striving to do still, is to put forth a principle—a principle which they, themselves, have largely devised. They believe they have tapped into the unified voice and singular intent of the Founders. The problem, for anyone who has studied the Founders, is that there was seldom a unified voice. Yes, they *all* believed in liberty unto salvation, and they believed God was behind it, but they had very different ideas about how to achieve this liberty. This is why the Constitution, as inspired as it was, is often vague and open to much interpretation (the bickering colonists could not get too specific in the document, so as to not offend each other's opinions, thus causing a state to walk away from the table, and thus failing to design "a more perfect Union.") Even two of our greatest revolutionaries, Jefferson and Adams, who were once best friends, did not speak to each other for years on end because of disagreements pertaining to how the Constitution should be applied. For the theorists to claim there was a solid, unitary voice (what they call the "First Founding"),[178] and that they have, today, figured out precisely what that voice was, is highly presumptuous (if not a bit arrogant).

The result of such presumption is that the theorists draw a nice little box and fill it with notions of how things were always meant to be. In this case, the notions include that states have a right to secede from the Union and that the federal government does not have the right to grow. There are few, if any, exceptions to these rules. (Though, we have seen that many Founders—sustained by God—did *not* maintain these same notions.) When the theorists identify violations of their notions, they begin accusing so many people of being traitorous followers of Satan. Innocent bodies fall everywhere in their wake, and conspiracy theories abound. This is what they have done to Lincoln. This is not to say we should not be mindful of evil lurking (because it is), but we need to see things in full perspective. We need to read history with *all* the facts, not just the ones that fit into our little box. We need to read history with the scriptures in our hands. We need to read it with the American Covenant always in the forefront of our minds. God and covenant created the Constitution; our subjective interpretations of the Constitution, therefore, must be subservient to our God and to our covenant.

We might draw an analogy here to what has happened to Father Adam—even God's noble son, Michael the Archangel. It saddens Mormons to hear their Christian brethren write Adam off as a sinful man who brought God's children down through his evil decision in the garden. With the light of the gospel, Mormons know that Adam was anything but evil, and that he, in actuality, was only furthering God's plan. A restored gospel perspective on things *completely changes* our perceptions and knowledge of who Adam was. Sadly, what happened to Adam, has (without a full gospel perspective) happened to Lincoln and others.

Let us heed the counsel of James Madison: As we interpret the Constitution in history, we should "not separate text from historical background. If you do, you will have perverted and subverted the Constitution, which can only end in a distorted, bastardized form of illegitimate government."[179] By separating Lincoln from historical and scriptural background, the theorists have offered up a *distorted, bastardized* and *illegitimate* interpretation of Lincoln and history.

When all we are willing to see is what we have placed into our little box, we fall into a trap. It is trap that can lead us to call good evil and evil good. Indeed, we yelp for liberty with so much fire that the very thing that brings our liberty ends up burnt. It is a trap that the great French philosopher and politician, Victor Hugo, identified in his classic, *Les Miserables*. He called it being "ultra."

> To be ultra is to go beyond. It is to attack the scepter in the name of the throne, and the miter in the name of the altar; it is to mistreat the thing you support...it is to insult through an excess of respect; it is to find too little papistry in the pope, in the king too little royalty, and too much light in the night; it is to be dissatisfied with the albatross, with snow, with the swan, and the lily for not being white enough; it is to champion things to the point of becoming their enemy; it is to be so pro you become con.[180]*

As I have met with groups of Saints to present the research found in this book, I have often been approached by people who had been exposed to the theorists' conclusions about Lincoln. And on every occasion, Saints (often with tears in their eyes), have expressed gratitude for this pro-Lincoln material. "It has restored my faith in Lincoln," I hear them say again and again. They have

---

* These words were published in the spring of 1862, even as the Civil War raged. More specifically, they were published during the exact months Lincoln was passing through his deep conversion to the covenant. A few short years after the Civil War and Union victory, the inspired Victor Hugo stood in Paris, rallying a massive group of freedom-lovers to stand on true principles related to God and country. Hugo noticed that the U.S. embassy was in view of the crowd. He pointed to the U.S. flag flying high and noble. He then declared the following: "That banner of stars speaks today to Paris and France proclaiming miracles of power which are easy to a great people, contending for great principle, the liberty of every race and the fraternity of all." See Stewart and Stewart, *Seven Miracles That Saved America*, 195. Incidentally, the same Library of Congress ledger which shows that Lincoln checked out a Book of Mormon, also shows that he checked out a book by Victor Hugo.

often told me that something deep inside them whispered that the allegations hurled against him were not true. In spite of what the theorist claimed, Lincoln was, in fact, the servant of God they had always believed him to be. Of course they felt this truth! After Joseph had been killed, and the rest of the prophets and Saints exiled from the Promised Land, Lincoln was it! He had to carry the burden to bring the national covenant back, that God's words might be fulfilled—that His "strange act" and "strange work" of the Restoration might flourish as designed. He was like a prophet!

It is for those Saints I have come in contact with, and others like them, that I have written this note on the Anti-Lincoln Movement. It is for them that we have included all this research on the true Lincoln—that they might be empowered with the history and scripture that validate and confirm their spiritual manifestations about that great man and his mission. He was not just *one* of many Founders. For the mission he was called to do, and for laying his own life upon the altar to do it, he was perhaps the *greatest* Founder. It is time we defend him with the gospel truth.

As stated, the issuance of the Emancipation Proclamation was only the beginning. It merely represented one of the first of many manifestations to follow—manifestations of the great conversion that would bring about God's plan for America and her covenant. And so, we now continue the story.

ENDNOTES

[1] Brigham Young, as quoted in John A. Widtsoe, *Discourses of Brigham Young* (Salt Lake City: Deseret Book Inc., 1954), 362.

[2] Richard Carwardine, *Lincoln: A Life of Purpose and Power* (New York: Alfred A. Knopf, 2003), 7.

[3] Charles Francis Adams, as quoted in William Lee Miller, *President Lincoln, The Duty of a Statesman* (New York: Alfred A. Knopf, 2008), 37.

[4] Carwardine, 197.

[5] Abraham Lincoln, as quoted in Doris Kearns Goodwin, *Team of Rivals* (New York: Simon and Schuster, 2005), 534.

[6] Carwardine, *Lincoln, A Life of Purpose and Power* (Audio Book Version), Chapter: Power of Party, Sec: The 1860 Presidential Campaign: The Power of a Righteous Party.

[7] Ron L. Andersen, *Lincoln: God's Humble Instrument* (Salt Lake City: Millennial Mind Publishing, 2010) 70-72.

[8] Lincoln, as quoted in Toby Mac and Michael Tait, *Under God* (Minneapolis: Bethany House, 2004), 165.

[9] Lincoln, as quoted in Ron L. Andersen, *Lincoln: God's Humble Instrument* (Salt Lake City: Millennial Mind Publishing, 2010), 6.

[10] Lincoln, as quoted in Newt Gingrich, *Rediscovering God in America* (Nashville: Integrity House, 2006), 55.

[11] Carwardine, 7, 223, 311.

[12] Carwardine, 51.

[13] Ron L. Andersen, *Lincoln: God's Humble Instrument*, 18.

[14] Carwardine, 126.

[15] Goodwin, 385, 539, 670-671.

[16] William Lee Miller, *President Lincoln, The Duty of a Statesman* (New York: Alfred A. Knopf, 2008), 365-367.

[17] Lincoln, as quoted in Leidner, 114.

[18] Newt Gingrich, *Rediscovering God in America* (Nashville: Integrity House, 2006), 51.

[19] Carwardine, 284-5.

[20] Allen T. Rice, *Reminiscences of Abraham Lincoln by Distinguished Men of His Time* (New York: North American Review, 1888), 193-195.

[21] Leidner, 72.

[22] Leidner, 76.

[23] Leidner, 76.

[24] Lincoln, as quoted in Miller, 43-44.

[25] Leidner, 83; Carwardine, 123.

[26] Goodwin, preface.

[27] Carwardine, 123.

[28] Carwardine, 126.

[29] Carwardine, 122.

[30] Carwardine, 98.

[31] Carwardine, 252.

[32] Leidner, 18.

[33] Lincoln, as quoted in Carwardine, 76.

[34] The prophecy and related fulfillment is documented in Tad Callister, *The Inevitable Apostasy*, 361-362.

[35] Richard Vetterli, *Mormonism, Americanism and Politics*, 149.

[36] Lincoln, as quoted in Gordon Leidner, *Lincoln on God and Country* (Shippensburg: White Mane Books, 2000), 88; Ron L. Andersen, 132-133.

[37] Carwardine, 146.

[38] Lincoln, as quoted in Ron L Andersen, *Lincoln: God's Humble Instrument, 98.* A variation of Lincoln's words are quoted by William J. Bennett, *America, the Last Great Hope, Volume II, From a World at War to the Triumph of Freedom* (Nashville, Thomas Nelson, 2007), 364.

[39] Lincoln, as quoted in Chris and Ted Stewart, *Seven Miracles That Saved America* (U.S.A.: Shadow Mountain, 2009), 179; Carwardine, 146-7.

[40] Lincoln, as quoted in Carwardine, 227; Roy P. Basler et al., eds. *The Collected Works of Abraham Lincoln,* 9 vols. (New Brunswick, NJ: Rutgers University Press, 1953-55), 5:278-279, 403-404.

[41] Carwardine, 234; Leidner 110, emphasis added.

[42] Miller, 44.

[43] Leidner, 23.

[44] Miller, 25.

[45] Chandra Manning, *What This Cruel War was Over* (New York: Alfred A. Knopf, 2007), 14.

[46] Dred Scott v Sandford, 19 Howard 393 (1857).

[47] Linda Monk, *The Words We Live By, Your Annotated Guide to the Constitution* (New York, Hyperion, 2003), 207.

[48] Manning, 17.

[49] John Jay, as quoted in Mac and Tait, *Under God*, 287.

[50] Ezra Taft Benson, "Beware of Pride," *Ensign* , May 1989, 4.

[51] Goodwin, 328.

[52] Larry Schweikart and Michael Allen, *A Patriot's History of the United States* (New York: Sentinel/Penguin Books, 2004), 313.

[53] Schweikart and Allen, 315.

[54] Schweikart and Allen, 328.

[55] Leidner, 74.

[56] Lincoln, as quoted in Carwardine, 202.

[57] Frances Seward, as quoted in Goodwin, 303.

[58] Ron L Andersen, *Lincoln: God's Humble Instrument*, 13-14.

[59] Goodwin, 419.

[60] James Swanson, *Bloody Crimes* (New York: HarperCollins, 2010), 168-169. Bill O'Reilly and Martin Dugard: *Killing Lincoln* (New York: Henry Holt and Company, 2011), 112.

[61] Goodwin, 419.

[62] Goodwin, 419-420.

[63] Ron Andersen, *Lincoln: God's Humble Instrument*, 196.

[64] Ron Andersen, *Lincoln: God's Humble Instrument*, 196.

[65] Ron Andersen, *Lincoln: God's Humble Instrument*, 197.

[66] Francis Carpenter, as quoted in Carwardine, 314.

[67] Carwardine, 223.

[68] Carwardine, 223.

[69] Carwardine, 314.

[70] Leidner, 28.

[71] Carwardine, 223.

[72] Carwardine, 223.

[73] Carwardine, 227-228.

[74] Carwardine, 210.

[75] Carwardine, 235.

[76] Carwardine, 223.

[77] Carwardine, 363.

[78] Schweikart and Allen, *A Patriot's History of the United States, 328.*

[79] Lincoln, as quoted in Carwardine, 227, emphasis added; Roy P. Basler et al., eds. *The Collected Works of Abraham Lincoln,* 9 vols. (New Brunswick, NJ: Rutgers University Press, 1953-55), 5:278-279, 403-404.

[80] Lincoln, as quoted in Leidner, 107-108; full speech available from Richardson ed, "A Proclamation by the President of the United States of America (March 30, 1863)," *Messages and Papers of the Presidents* (Washington DC: United States Congress, 1897), 164-165; also available at www.showcase.letin.net/web/creative/lincoln.speeches/fast.htm.

[81] Matthew S. Holland, *Bonds of Affection* (Washington D.C.: Georgetown University Press, 2007), 209.

[82] Carwardine, 228.

[83] Ron Anderson, *Lincoln: God's Humble Instrument*, 277.

[84] Ron Anderson, *Lincoln: God's Humble Instrument*, 277.

[85] Michael K. Winder, *Presidents and Prophets* (American Fork: Covenant Communications, 2007), 107; see also Cyril D. Pearson, "Abraham Lincoln and Joseph Smith," *Improvement Era* 48, no.2 (February 1945).

[86] Lincoln, as quoted in Leidner, 107-108; full speech available from Richardson ed, "A Proclamation by the President of the United States of America (March 30, 1863)," *Messages and Papers of the Presidents* (Washington DC: United States Congress, 1897), 164-165; also available at www.showcase.letin.net/web/creative/lincoln.speeches/fast.htm.

[87] Carwardine, 193.

[88] Stowe, as quoted in Holland, *Bonds of Affection*, 166.

[89] Mac and Tait, *Under God*, 266-267.

[90] Mac and Tait, *Under God*, 264.

[91] Schweikart and Allen, 313.

[92] Schweikart and Allen, 307.

[93] Quoted from Howard Zinn, *The People's History of the United States of America* (New York: Harper Collins, 1999), 190.

[94] Manning, 128.

[95] Goodwin, 373.

[96] Lincoln, as quoted in Leidner, 104-105, emphasis added.

[97] Manning, 4.

[98] Manning, 49.

[99] Manning, 77.

[100] Manning, 45.

[101] Manning, 77, 73.

[102] Manning, 95.

[103] Manning, 96.

[104] Manning, 8.

[105] Manning, 12-13.

[106] Carwardine, 193, 199.

[107] Carwardine, 198-199.

[108] Carwardine, 199.

[109] Carwardine, 199.

[110] Carwardine, 205.

[111] Carwardine, 202, 205.

[112] Carwardine, 225.

[113] Brigham Young, as quoted in *Church History in the Fulness of Times* (Salt Lake City: Church of Jesus Christ of Latter-day Saints, 2000), 382.

[114] Carwardine, 207; Basler, et al, eds., 5:336-7; Note: The word "forever" was taken out in the final Proclamation, perhaps because, as William Lee Miller suggested, "it promised something [Lincoln] was not quite sure at that point he could deliver." See Miller, 266.

[115] Carwardine, 180, 203.

[116] Carwardine, 193.

[117] Michael Burlington and John R. Turner Ettlinger, eds., *Inside Lincoln's White House: The Complete Civil War Diary of John Hay* (Carbondale: South Illinois University Press, 1997), 135.

[118] Frederick Douglas, as quoted in Leidner, 122.

[119] Carwardine, 192.

[120] From *New York Herald*, August 27, 1860, as quoted in Goodwin, 12.

[121] Seward, as quoted in Goodwin, 146.

[122] Evert A. Duyckinck, *Portrait Gallery of Eminent Men and Women* (New York: Henry Johnson, 1873), 463.

[123] Goodwin, 364.

[124] Ron Anderson, 346.

[125] Goodwin, 365.

[126] Goodwin, 364.

[127] Goodwin, 387-388.

[128] Carwardine, 207; Goodwin, 463-468.

[129] Carwardine, 210.

[130] Bennett, *America: The Last Best Hope,* Vol. I, 344.

[131] James M. McPherson, "If The Lost Order Hadn't Been Lost," from Robert Cowley, ed., *What If? The World's Foremost Military Historians Imagine What Might Have Been* (New York: Penguin Putnam Inc, 1999), 231-232.

[132] McPherson, 237-238.

[133] McPherson, 232.

[134] Carwardine, 210, 228.

[135] Bruce Feiler, *America's Prophet: Moses and the American Story* (New York: HarperCollins, 2009), 162.

[136] Emancipation Proclamation, Online Source: http://www.archives.gov/exhibit_hall/featured_documents/emancipation_proclamation/transcript.html.

[137] Bennett, *America*, Vol. I, 349.

[138] Bennett, *America*, Vol. I, 349.

[139] Gingrich, *Resdiscovering God in America*, 27.

[140] For a more detailed account of such criticisms, see Howard Zinn, *A People's History of the United States*, Chapter 9: "Slavery Without Submission, Emancipation Without Freedom," particularly pages 187, 191.

[141] Carwardine, 209.

[142] Carwardine, 209.

[143] Lincoln, as quoted in Carwardine, 209.

[144] For more on these criticisms, see Zinn, 191-192.

[145] Lincoln, as quoted in Leidner, 100.

[146] Carwardine, 231, 242.

[147] Monk, 208.

[148] Schweikart and Allen, 328.

[149] Emancipation Proclamation, Online Source: http://www.archives.gov/ exhibit_hall/featured_documents/emancipation_proclamation/transcript.html.

[150] See the research of Stephen Pratt at http://www.libertyandlearning.com/downloads/ an-heuristic-exploration-of-the-union. See also Stephen Pratt, "The Three Foundings" (video presentation), available at www.libertyandlearning.com/videos; and Stephen Pratt, "The Second Founding," video available at www.libertyandlearning.com. I encourage all to read Brother Pratt's conclusions on Lincoln and compare them with the research in this book. Other prominent sources which use similar allegations to paint Lincoln in a very negative light include Thomas J. DiLorenzo, *Lincoln Unmasked: What You're Not Suppose to Know About Dishonest Abe* (New York: Three Rivers Press, 2006); Jeffrey Rogers Hummel, *Emancipating Slaves, Enslaving Free Men: A History of the American Civil War* (Chicago: Open Court, 1996); Allen Buchanan, *Secession: The Morality of Political Divorce from Fort Sumter to Lithuania and Quebec* (Boulder, CO: West view Press, 1991); Robert Higgs, *Crises and Leviathan: Critical Episodes in the Growth of American Government* (New York: Oxford University Press, 1987). These authors/presenters represent some of the sources I refer to as "the theorists."

[151] See Stephen Pratt, http://www.libertyandlearning.com/downloads/an-heuristic-exploration-of-the-union/.

[152] Sidney Howard Gay, *American Statesman: James Madison* (New York: Houghton Mifflin Co., 1898), 237-238; *The Writings of James Madison,* The Online Library of Liberty, A Project of Liberty Fund, Inc, available at http://oll.libertyfund.org/title/ 1940/119377.

[153] Schweikart and Allen, *A Patriot's History of the United States,* 212-213; see also "President Jackson's Proclamation Regarding Nullification," (December 1832), *The Avalon Project,* Yale Law School, available at http://avalon.law.yale.edu/ 19th_century/jack01.asp.

[154] See Stephen Pratt, http://www.libertyandlearning.com/downloads/an-heuristic-exploration-of-the-union/.

[155] Lincoln, as quoted in Carwardine, 227, emphasis added; Roy P. Basler et al., eds. *The Collected Works of Abraham Lincoln,* 9 vols. (New Brunswick, NJ: Rutgers University Press, 1953-55), 5:278-279, 403-404.

[156] Lincoln, as quoted in Leidner, 107-108; full speech available from Richardson ed, "A Proclamation by the President of the United States of America (March 30, 1863)," *Messages and Papers of the Presidents* (Washington DC: United States Congress, 1897), 164-165; also available at www.showcase.letin.net/web/creative/lincoln.speeches/fast.htm.

[157] Lincoln, as quoted in Carwardine, 227.

[158] John Denson, *A Century of War*, 22, as quoted and supported by Stephen Pratt, "Empire of Debt," DVD available at www.libertyandlearning.com; See Pratt's research on the subject, also available at http://www.libertyandlearning.com/downloads/that-troublesome-word-sovereignty/.

[159] See Stephen Pratt, http://www.libertyandlearning.com/downloads/that-troublesome-word-sovereignty/.

[160] Random House Webster's College Dictionary (New York: Random House, 1999).

[161] Bushman, *Rough Stone Rolling*, 514.

[162] Bushman, *Rough Stone Rolling*, 514.

[163] Joseph Smith, as quoted in Richard Vetterli, *Mormonism, Americanism and Politics*, 107.

[164] Joseph Smith Jr., *History of the Church of Jesus Christ of Latter-day Saints* (Salt Lake City: Deseret Book, 1973), Volume 5, 384; also quoted in J. Michael Hunter, *Mormon Myth-ellaneous* (American Fork: Covenant Communications, 2008), 77.

[165] Joseph Smith (October 1843), as quoted in Joseph Fielding Smith, ed, *Teachings of the Prophet Joseph Smith* (Salt Lake City: Deseret Book Company, 1976), 326-327.

[166] Arnold Garr, "Joseph Smith's Campaign for President of the United States," *Ensign*, February 2009, 50; *History of the Church*, 6:206.

[167] As explained last chapter and detailed in Monk, 215.

[168] See Chapter 2 of this book, under the subheading *A New Promise of Liberty.*

[169] See Chapter 3 for the details of these prophecies and how they were so clearly fulfilled.

[170] Stephen Pratt, "The Second Founding," video available at www.libertyandlearning.com.

[171] See the research of Stephen Pratt at http://www.libertyandlearning.com/downloads/an-heuristic-exploration-of-the-union. See also Stephen Pratt, "The Three Foundings" (video presentation), available at www.libertyandlearning.com/videos; Stephen Pratt, "The Second Founding," video available at www.libertyandlearning.com; and Stephen Pratt, "Empire of Debt," DVD available at www.libertyandlearning.com.

[172] Arnold Garr, "Joseph Smith Campaign for President of the United States," *Ensign*, Feb. 2009, 51.

[173] Stephen Pratt, "The Second Founding" and "The Third Founding" video presentations, available at www.libertyandlearning.com.

[174] Swanson, *Bloody Crimes*, 62.

[175] Miller, *President Lincoln: The Duty of a Statesman*, 101.

[176] Kearns-Goodwin, *Team of Rivals*, 355.

[177] Jefferson, as quoted in Callister, *The Inevitable Apostasy and the Promised Restoration* (Salt Lake City: Deseret Book, 2006), 105-106. Emphasis added.

[178] See Stephen Pratt, "The Three Foundings" (video presentation), available at www.libertyandlearning.com/videos.

[179] Madison, available at www.quotes-museum.com/quote/56704.

[180] Victor Hugo, *Les Miserables* (New York: Penguin Books, 1987), 621-622. (Originally published in 1862).

To Save a Nation, by Larry C. Winborg, copyright 2011
Courtesy of Larry C. Winborg

CHAPTER 5

A HUMBLED NATION
CONVERTS TO THE COVENANT

*And insomuch as we know that by [God's] divine law,
nations, like individuals, are subjected to punishments and
chastisements in this world, may we not justly fear that the
awful calamity of civil war which now desolates the land
may be but a punishment inflicted upon us for our
presumptuous sins, to the needful end of our national
reformation as a whole people?*

—Abraham Lincoln on *national repentance*

*[This Civil War is]an important crises which involves...not only
the civil and religious liberties of our own dear land, but in a large
degree the civil and religious liberties of mankind in many
countries and through many ages.*

—Abraham Lincoln on *universal agency*

Emancipation was a profound first step, but it was, nonetheless, a
first step. Many still remained unconverted to the idea behind

emancipation; and many of those who agreed with it, had yet to comprehend that much more was still needed to redeem the covenant and bring God's moral agency to *all*.

We have documented in previous chapters how the Prophet Joseph sought to redeem the American Covenant through *national repentance* and *universal agency*—ideals which, if applied, would have made the nation worthy of its covenant blessings and would have elevated the status of all minorities, to include God's kingdom on the earth. We further documented how, according to the prophecies, upon the nation's rejection of the Prophet, the Lord would unleash a national vexation which would ensure the Prophet's inspired proposals were accepted and applied, thus saving the nation and her covenant. That said, if the Civil War truly was the fulfillment of these prophecies, then we should expect to find historical evidence that Lincoln and the North grew in their knowledge of the covenant and came to adopt the Prophet's proposals—or better said, God's proposals—as a result of the vexation/war. In other words, we should be able to find clear evidence that Lincoln and the North came to understand and declare that the Civil War's ultimate purpose under God was, not only emancipation, but *national repentance* and *universal agency*.

Such historical evidence, if it exists, would certainly corroborate the Civil War prophecies. It would also help explain how Lincoln and the North possessed the knowledge and inspiration necessary to set the nation on a divine course that would result in securing the Kingdom of God on earth. We have already seen this national vision begin to unfold between 1861-1862, culminating in the conversion to, and issuance of, the Emancipation Proclamation. However, the issuance of the Proclamation did not necessarily signify that the national purging and purification process was complete. Though it manifested certain elements of *national repentance* and *universal agency*, it did not signify that these covenant ideals had sufficiently penetrated the national heart. In fact, this greater change of heart would not be greatly manifested until war's end, when the Union's conversion ran so deep that it took and applied the newfound principles of *national repentance* and *universal agency* to specific legislation (namely, the Thirteenth, Fourteenth, and Fifteenth Amendments).

We will now explore how, in the post-emancipation years of war (1863-1865), God further influenced Lincoln and the North to become even more converted to the cause of the American Covenant by helping them recognize and apply the deeper gospel purposes of the war. Only then might He secure His church and kingdom.

A Fuller Conversion: Seeking and Finding The Great Good of the War

"If any man will do his will, he shall know of the doctrine" (John 7:17). How true this scriptural principle became for Lincoln and the North. They had indeed done the Lord's will through emancipation, for which the Lord blessed them with further light and knowledge concerning the cause for which they were fighting. If before emancipation Lincoln had ever expressed doubt about whether God had some powerful design for the war, those days were forever gone.

In the days leading up to his presidency, Lincoln made it clear that he believed America had been established for "more than common" purposes, which were in the "hands of the Almighty," and which were connected to His American "almost chosen people."[1] But now, in post-emancipation America, Lincoln's understanding of God's purposes grew even deeper. "[W]e find [the war] still continues," wrote Lincoln, shortly after deciding conclusively upon emancipation, "and we must believe that He permits it for some *wise purpose* of His own, mysterious and unknown to us; and though with our limited understanding, we may not be able to comprehend it, yet we cannot but believe, that He who made the world still governs it."[2]

During this same time Lincoln admitted, "I have talked with God. It is His cause, and the Union is His. As He willeth, so it will be."[3] In 1864 he made it plain that the true purpose of the war was not what "either party, or any man devised, or expected," for "God alone can claim it."[4] As quoted last chapter, Lincoln made a similar comment in 1862, but prefaced it by saying that such was "possible" or "probable."[5] Now he was determined it was so. Even as late as 1865, he declared in his Second Inaugural Address that "the Almighty has his own purposes" for the war.[6] From that fateful moment in September 1862, when Lincoln crossed the threshold of emancipation, testifying that "God wills this contest, and wills that it shall not yet end,"[7] he only grew bolder and more confident in his knowledge of God's covenant and plan.

But there is something else to be said of these declarations and testimonies. It seems Lincoln may have believed that freeing the slaves was only a part of God's design for the war. The war continued under God "for some *wise purpose* of His own, mysterious and unknown to us." Lincoln made this comment *after* he had already learned that freeing the slaves was in fact a profound purpose of the war. Did he sense there was something even bigger at stake? Did he sense there was something God was working on that nobody could, as of that moment, fully comprehend? If Lincoln was thinking such thoughts, we now know that he was not too far off the mark. For the prophecies declared that the war would do more than free slaves. It would also—in the process of freeing the slaves— redeem the national covenant and help to more fully and securely usher in the fullness of the gospel.

We cannot, after all, ignore one very important part of the prophecy which is directly fulfilled by Lincoln's testimony. As quoted earlier, the Lord revealed to the Prophet Joseph, while imprisoned at Liberty Jail, that when the Lord administers the scourge and vexation, He will "blind their minds, that they may not understand his marvelous workings; that he may prove them also..." (D&C 121:12). This clearly implies that the war's *full* purpose was a mystery to all but God, just as Lincoln declared. This prophecy becomes further fulfilled in that the Civil War had, in fact, become a way for the Lord to "prove them" (or test them) to see if they would make the necessary changes to align their will with His.

Notwithstanding the notion that the war's *full* purposes seemed to have been wrapped in divine mystery, Lincoln's insights on the matter do beg the question: How much did Lincoln know? Beyond the now obvious goals of restoring the Union and freeing the slaves, what additional details (if any) were revealed to him about God's ultimate intentions? In September 1864, Lincoln expounded, once again, upon the subject. In a letter to Eliza Gurney, he stated:

> The purposes of the Almighty are perfect, and must prevail, though we erring mortals may fail to accurately perceive them in advance. We hoped for a happy termination of this terrible war long before this; but God knows best, and has ruled otherwise. We shall yet acknowledge His wisdom and our own error therein. Meanwhile we must work earnestly in the best light He gives us, trusting that so working still conduces to the great end He ordains. *Surely He intends some great good to follow this mighty convulsion,* which no mortal could make, and no mortal could stay. [8]

He then concluded the letter, asking Ms. Gurney for her "earnest prayers to our Father in heaven." [9]

Whatever Lincoln's knowledge, he certainly knew at least enough to serve God's purposes. It was enough to know that God had a will for the war and that it was Lincoln's job, along with the nation, to (just as Lincoln said), "work earnestly in the best light He gives us, trusting that so working still conduces to the great end He ordains." And yet there was more. For Lincoln made it clear in his above testimony that God had some "great good" planned. Once again, he made this comment well over a year after confirming that the eradication of slavery was a central purpose of the war. In light of this, we might ask what other (as-of-yet unnamed) "great good"

Lincoln was referring to. What Godly purpose still remained, of which Lincoln said, "we erring mortals may fail to accurately perceive...in advance"? Did he see or feel some deeper gospel connection?

Another incident may shed further light on the testimony and revelations of Lincoln. After a congressional delegation visited Lincoln during the war and pressed him to make sure slavery would be cast away forever, Lincoln made a most astonishing comment. First, he echoed the principles behind the American Covenant—that national salvation is dependent upon doing right, and so slavery's eradication would be paramount. Then he went further, testifying that perhaps there was even more to it. Lincoln's words were powerful enough for Congressmen James Wilson to record them. Wilson noted that as the president spoke these words with his right arm outstretched, "his face [was] aglow like the face of a prophet."[10] Lincoln's full response was as follows:

> My faith is greater than yours. I not only believe that Providence is not unmindful of the struggle in which this nation is engaged; that if we do not do right, God will let us go our own way to ruin; and that if we do right, He will lead us safely out of this wilderness, crown our arms with victory, and restore our dissevered union, as you expressed your belief....

After expounding upon his belief in the covenant relationship, Lincoln explained why his "faith is greater." He declared:

> ....But I also believe that He will compel us to do right in order that He may do these things, not so much because we desire them as that they accord with His plans of dealing with this nation, in the midst of which He means to establish justice. *I think He means that we shall do more than we have yet done in furtherance of His plans,* and He will open the way for doing it. I have felt His hand upon me in great trials and submitted to His guidance, and I trust that as He

shall further open the way I will be ready to walk therein, relying on His help and trusting in His goodness and wisdom.[11]

Perhaps Lincoln *had* received a deeper, gospel-based understanding. And the evidence that he had received such light goes way beyond the fascinating (though admittedly vague) comments he made, as cited above. Remarkably, and in fulfillment of the prophecies, there is ample evidence that Lincoln and the North had come to see that the war was to produce more than emancipation. Though the war's full purpose—the elevation of God's Kingdom on the earth—would be largely hidden (as the prophecy implies), the tools to create such fruit would be powerfully revealed. Indeed, Lincoln and the North would learn that the war was to produce those two indispensable things—those things God would need to restore His covenant and kingdom, even those very things the Prophet Joseph had called for: *national repentance* and *universal agency*. Through the recognition and application of these ideals, Lincoln and the North would help fulfill the prophecies of God's vexation—to "set his hand and seal to change the times and seasons," that His "strange act" and "strange work" might come to light (D&C 121:12; D&C 101:93-95).

With emancipation behind them, the nation would now seek even greater light and knowledge and would indeed find Lincoln's "Great Good." The nation would prepare the fertile soil for God's kingdom and gospel restoration by completing the repentance process and amending the Constitution to ensure a fullness of agency for *all* God's children.

The First Great Good: National Repentance

The Civil War was designed to bring about *national repentance*. Without repentance, the nation would remain in deep sin, unworthy of the covenant blessings and unworthy of the divine mandate to be the Lord's base of operations in the latter-days. "Righteousness," so the scripture says, "exalteth a nation: but sin is a reproach to any people" (Proverbs 14:34). The Prophet Joseph was acutely aware of this national principle, and so he declared his intention "to be an instrument of bringing [America] to unfeigned repentance."[12]

During the first years of war, Lincoln and the North became converted to the idea that God wanted slavery eradicated. It was a change of heart that compelled the North to righteously fix evils in the South. However, it was not until after emancipation became policy that the North really began to see the extent of God's will. Far from merely fixing the problems in the South, it became clear to the North that it too had problems—that it too needed to repent further. Emancipation would not be enough. A more permanent and universal solution to America's sins had yet to be discovered and applied. And too many people—including many Northerners—had yet to catch the vision.

This self-realization struck hard upon the Northerners as they recognized that the vexation was not only affecting the South, but was pouring down upon them as well. Even after emancipation, the North began to see that more self-change was needed. That God meant for this to happen became clear to the North when they considered the otherwise inexplicable reason for their lack of military success. They did, after all, maintain a stunning advantage from the beginning of the conflict. For example, Union troops numbered 2.1 million while Southern troops topped off at 800,000 (the desertion rate was also significantly higher among Southern troops). Additionally, the North had twenty thousand miles of railroad track (much of which ran north-south, facilitating supplies to the battlefront), while the South had perhaps ten thousand miles of track (much of which went east-west, unable to supply the frontlines). Furthermore, the North dominated the South in other areas: 32 to 1 in firearm production, 14 to 1 in merchant shipping, 3 to 1 in agricultural acreage, and 412 to 1 in wheat. The North also controlled over ninety percent of the cotton cloth industry and the boot and shoe industry, and maintained almost all of the iron furnaces needed for arms manufacturing.[13]

As the war produced Union defeat after Union defeat (even after emancipation), what else could be said except, as Lincoln repeatedly pointed out, "the North as well as...the South, shall pay fairly for our complicity in that wrong [the national sin]."[14] The North and the federal government had watched and done nothing as the sins of oppression hit innocent minorities—from black slaves to Mormon settlers (not to mention many other minority groups). It became every day clearer that the North also needed fixing. For if the war had ended early—either with Southern subjugation (a quick Union victory) or Southern independence (a quick Southern victory) —the North would have remained unchanged. The United States would have remained unchanged. The Kingdom of God would have been left to contend with the same weak application of the Constitution, which weak application was responsible for the Church's frustrated growth and ultimate exile.

And so, God would make sure that—notwithstanding Northern advantage—the war would go on until the vexation ran its course, until North as well as South repented and mended the national covenant by adding the constitutional provisions called for by the Prophet. It is here where Lincoln's and the North's conversion to the idea of *national repentance* comes strongly into play. For if *national repentance* was God's purpose, then He would be sure Lincoln and the North eventually got the message.

Lincoln on National Repentance

As *national repentance* was God's purpose for the war, it is no wonder the inspired Lincoln made it a running theme, particularly after his post-emancipation conversion to the cause. Lincoln had first intimated such an idea to the nation after its first defeat at Bull Run, when he suggested that the North "humble ourselves before him, and to pray for his mercy."[15] But his exhortation took on a whole new meaning after his deeper conversion. In March 1863, for example, just months after the Proclamation was issued, Lincoln called for a "day of national humiliation, fasting and prayer." This official announcement, calling for the national fast, represents perhaps the most profound call to the American Covenant that the nation (then or now) ever witnessed. It is reminiscent of a Nephite prophet calling to his people who are in the depths of the pride cycle. Lincoln's speech clearly identifies the covenant blessings, and it warns that national sin most assuredly threatens the perpetuation of these blessings. Declared Lincoln:

> [I]t is the duty of nations as well as of man to own their dependence upon the overruling power of God; to confess their sins and transgressions in humble sorrow, yet with assured hope that genuine repentance will lead to mercy and pardon; and to recognize the sublime truth, announced in the Holy Scriptures and proven by all history, that those nations only are blessed whose God is the Lord.

> And insomuch as we know that by his divine law nations, like individuals, are subjected to punishments and chastisements in this world, may we not justly fear that the awful calamity of civil war which now desolates the land may be but a punishment inflicted upon us for our presumptuous sins, to the needful end of our national reformation as a whole people?

> We have been the recipients of the choicest bounties of Heaven; we have been preserved these many years in peace and prosperity. We have grown in numbers, wealth, and power as no other nation has ever grown. But we have forgotten God. We have forgotten the gracious hand which preserved us in peace and multiplied and enriched and strengthened us, and we have vainly imagined, in the deceitfulness of our hearts, that all these blessings were

produced by some superior wisdom and virtue of our own. Intoxicated with unbroken success, we have become too self-sufficient to feel the necessity of redeeming and preserving grace, too proud to pray to that God that made us.

It behooves us, then, to humble ourselves before the offended Power, to confess our national sins, and to pray for clemency and forgiveness. Now, therefore...I do by this my proclamation designate and set apart Thursday, the 30th of April, 1863, as a day of national humiliation, fasting and prayer. And I do hereby request all the people to abstain, on that day, from their ordinary secular pursuits, and to unite at their several places of public worship and their homes in keeping the day holy to the Lord...[L]et us then rest humbly in the hope authorized by the Divine teachings, that the united cry of the nation will be heard on high, and answered with blessings no less than the pardon of our national sins, and the restoration of our now divided and suffering country...[16]

Then again in 1865, as the war was at last winding down, Lincoln again made it clear to the nation that God expected *national repentance* to follow His vexation. In his Second Inaugural Address, given on March 4, 1865, the newly re-elected president stood to address his fellow-Americans. The single sheet of paper in his hand —typeset and printed in double columns—included the contents of the great speech. Though only 701 words in length (one of the shortest inaugural speeches in history), it invoked God fourteen times, referred to prayer three times, and quoted or paraphrased the Bible four times.[17]

The entire inaugural celebration that morning, leading up to the president's address, had been plagued by terrible winds and thunderstorms, prompting a general advisory to women and children to stay indoors for their protection. But at the very moment that Lincoln approached the podium (as reported by the prominent journalist Noah Brooks, who was there present), something strange occurred. "Just at that moment," recalled Brooks, "the sun, which had been obscured all day, burst forth in its unclouded meridian splendor, and flooded the spectacle with glory and light. Every heart beat quicker at the unexpected omen...so might the darkness which had obscured the past four years be now dissipated."[18] Lincoln later said to a friend who had been present, "Did you notice the sunburst? It made my heart jump."[19] Chief Justice Chase called it "an auspicious omen of the dispersion of the clouds of war and the restoration of the clear sun light of prosperous peace."[20]

With the audience in full emotion and in full attention, Lincoln bellowed, "The Almighty has his own purposes."

> "Woe unto the world because of offenses! for it must needs be that offenses come; but woe to that man by whom the offense cometh." If we shall suppose that American slavery is one of those offenses which, in the providence of God, must needs come, but which, having continued through his appointed time, he now wills to remove, and that he gives to both North and South this terrible war, as the woe due to those by whom the offense came, shall we discern therein any departure from those divine attributes which the believers in a living God always ascribe to him? Fondly do we hope—fervently do we pray—that this mighty scourge of war may speedily pass away. Yet, if God wills that it continue until all the wealth piled by the bondman's two hundred and fifty years of unrequited toil shall be sunk, and until every drop of blood drawn with the lash shall be paid by another drawn with the sword, as was said three thousand years ago, so still it must be said, "The judgments of the Lord are true and righteous altogether."[21]

Amazingly, as if in possession of the Doctrine and Covenants' Civil War prophecies (and the other prophetic statements concerning the divine purposes behind the war), Lincoln was essentially repeating these scriptural concepts. (Though we have no evidence that Lincoln had ever heard of such prophecies as those found in the Doctrine and Covenants, he might have been acquainted with the similar aforementioned prophecies from Jefferson, Mason, Stowe, and Douglas.) In that his speech recognized the fulfillment of all these prophecies, perhaps we see why Frederick Douglas told Lincoln that his speech was "a sacred effort."[22] It was indeed sacred in that it screamed aloud that the American Covenant was in breach for sinful behavior, and the nation was reaping the consequences. Like Washington and the other American Covenant leaders before him, Lincoln knew that humility and repentance represented the keys to national salvation. As Lincoln stated, "If we do right God will be with us, and if God is with us we cannot fail."[23]

While Lincoln was, in this Second Inaugural Address, certainly referring to the most glaring American victims, the African Americans, he also recognized (as we will discuss later) that persecution of blacks had inevitably led to persecution of other minority groups, and that it was slavery "out of which all our other national evils and dangers have come."[24] Therefore, it would be fully fitting to concede that Lincoln could have included, as additional reasons for this punishment, any persecution that had been leveled against any other minority, including the Latter-day Saints. (And, as detailed earlier, we have modern revelation which confirms that the war was, in fact, also a response to the Saint's treatment and a solution to their major obstructions.)

Lincoln's understanding of the war in relation to the gospel and the covenant becomes even more profound upon considering the scripture he chose to lay his hand upon while taking (for the second and final time) the sacred oath of office. He chose the fifth chapter of Isaiah. His choice was indeed profound due to the fact that this scripture makes direct reference to America in the latter-days. In fact, during his prophetic statements about latter-day America, the Prophet Nephi quotes this Isaiah chapter. In the second book of Nephi, Nephi spends a significant amount of time commenting on latter-day America and her national covenant. He quotes his father Lehi, declaring that latter-day America will be a land of liberty (2 Nephi 1); He foresees the coming of the Prophet Joseph Smith (2 Nephi 3); He quotes Isaiah about the gathering of latter-day Israel (2 Nephi 8); He quotes his brother, Jacob, who speaks directly about the latter-day American covenant, to include its blessings of *liberty, protection,* and *prosperity* (2 Nephi 10); And then he again quotes Isaiah's prophecy—found in Isaiah 2— about the latter-day gathering of Israel and the building of latter-day temples (2 Nephi 12). It is within this latter-day American context that we get to Nephi's recitation of Isaiah 5 (found in 2 Nephi 15), even the words Lincoln chose during his inaugural ceremony. Most astonishingly, these ancient words seem to directly reflect the American Civil War and how the war humbled the people (causing them to repent), thus producing the necessary fruits for the perpetuation of the Restoration.

The fifth chapter of Isaiah speaks of God's people falling into wickedness. The LDS Church Education System's *Old Testament Student Manuel* asserts (interpreting verse 8) that "they built up great estates through wickedness."[25] Isaiah further identifies how the unrighteous people call "evil good and good evil" (verse 20). And finally, the people "justify wickedness for reward" (verse 23), which, according to the LDS manual, means that "those who were guilty of crimes were declared innocent by bribed judges and other officials, whereas the innocent were found guilty so that they could be silenced or their property exploited."[26] These crimes against man and God, which Isaiah saw among the people of his day, were clearly being projected for latter-day America. And sure enough, these sins describe the very thing that brought America under condemnation—they describe in detail what the nation did to both black Americans and Mormon Americans.

The prophesied consequences from the Lord for these sins further match what occurred in the Civil War. We are told that "therefore hell hath enlarged herself and opened her mouth without measure: and their glory, and their multitude, and their pomp...shall descend into it" (verse 14). Isaiah experts interpret the Hebrew word for *hell* (sheol) used in this verse to mean *Spirit World* (not necessarily eternal punishment), which indicates that God's vexation, in this case, would result in countless deaths.[27] Isaiah further declares that after "hell hath enlarged herself" then "the mean man shall be brought down, and the mighty man shall be humbled, and the eyes of the lofty shall be humbled: But the Lord of hosts shall be exalted in judgment, and God that is holy shall be sanctified in righteousness" (Isaiah 5:15-16).

After Lincoln completed his oath of office, he bent down to kiss the Bible. Chief Justice Salmon Chase, who had administered the oath, later commented that Lincoln seemed to intentionally kiss two particular verses from Isaiah chapter 5—verses 25 and 26.[28] These verses read as follows:

> Because they have cast away the law of the Lord of hosts, and despised the word of the Holy One of Israel. Therefore is the anger of the Lord kindled against his people, and he hath stretched forth his hand against them, and hath smitten them: and the hills did tremble, and their carcases were torn in the midst of the streets. For all this his anger is not turned away, but his hand is outstretched still.

Consider what the revelation provides as the reason for the Lord's anger: they had "cast away the law" and had "despised the word of the Holy One of Israel." Is this not a perfect fulfillment of the Civil War prophecies? Isaiah had just barely (in Isaiah Chapter 2) declared that, in the latter-days, "out of Zion shall go forth *the law*" (See Isaiah 2:2-5). President Harold B Lee declared that what Isaiah foresaw here as "Zion" was, in fact, America, and that what he called "the law" was, in actuality, the U.S. Constitution.[29] If "the law" in this Isaiah 5 prophecy was also in reference to the Constitution that had been "cast away," then indeed this prophecy was fittingly chosen by the President of the United States. Furthermore, after having cast away the law, Isaiah declared that they had "despised the word of the Holy One of Israel." Indeed, after having spit upon the Constitution, the wicked nation *despised the word* (and warnings) of the Holy One's prophet—even the Prophet Joseph. And so, the war came, as mandated by the prophecies detailed earlier, and as prophesied in Isaiah 5: for "the hills did tremble, and their carcasses were torn in the midst of the streets."

This clear description of war (found in verse 25) is then immediately followed by verse 26, which explains how the miraculous fruit of this war (i.e. national humbling, national repentance, and national change) would culminate in the perpetuation of God's latter-day gospel restoration. "And he will lift up an ensign to the nations from far, and will hiss unto them from the end of the earth; and, behold, they shall come with speed swiftly." That this *ensign* is referring to latter-day Zion is confirmed in Doctrine and Covenants 64:42 and 113:6.*

Furthermore, these verses are immediately followed by a description of what Isaiah saw as the great gathering of latter-day Israel. Isaiah described (in verses 27-30) great vehicles to assist in the work, to include vehicles that "roar like young lions" and "carry their prey [passengers] and carry it away safe." Other vehicles would have "wheels like a whirlwind." These vehicles would allow travelers to move without "slumber nor sleep; neither shall the girdle of their loins be loosed, nor the latchet of their shoes loosed [they would travel far distances without having to sleep or change clothes]." Elder LeGrand Richards explained that these words represent (in the best words Isaiah could find to describe them) visions of trains and airplanes supporting the work of LDS missionaries. "With this manner of transportation," said Elder Richards, "the Lord can really 'hiss [signal] unto them from the end of the earth,' that 'they shall come with speed swiftly.'"[30]

Altogether, Isaiah 5 is truly an astonishing parallel to the Civil War prophecies (cited earlier) in D&C 101. For it recognizes the great obstacles to American constitutional law, then provides the

---

* For further references connecting the term *Ensign* to latter-day Zion, refer to "Topical Guide," *Bible (KJV)* (Salt Lake City: The Church of Jesus Christ of Latter-day Saints, 1986), 122.

same divinely mandated vexation and scourge to fix the problem. Then, also paralleling D&C 101, Isaiah 5 places, as the fruit of the humbling of war, the advent of the Restoration and of God's Kingdom—even the advent of the great *ensign*, or what D&C 101 calls the "strange act" and "strange work" of the Lord (see verses 93-93).

Finally, we must not miss one very significant reference in all this to the American Covenant. As this latter-day gathering is occurring, we are told in verse 28 that their "arrows are sharp, and all their bows bent." We would do well to remember that Jacob's promise to Joseph's latter-day American posterity included *protection,* as symbolized in the "bow abode in strength, and the arms of his hands...made strong by the hands of the mighty God of Jacob" (Genesis 49:24). Isaiah scholars agree that verse 28 signifies that "the bows and arrows of the righteous who gather in Zion symbolize the protection that God will provide for them as they return. Similar imagery was used to describe how God brought Israel out of Egypt into the land of promise (Numbers 24:8)."[31]

The fifth chapter of Isaiah certainly makes a wonderful addition to the many other prophecies and promises (described in Chapter 3) that seem to reflect the Civil War and the ultimate gospel fruit of that war. That Lincoln saw something in these verses, and used them while placing his arm to the square to invoke the American Covenant, is beyond astounding. His actions are especially profound when we consider that the president had possessed (and most likely read) the Book of Mormon, which places these Isaiah verses in a latter-day American context. In fact, without seeing Isaiah's (Chapter 5) prophecy within a Book of Mormon context (as we do in 2 Nephi 15), it is difficult to see how Lincoln (or anyone) would have easily applied the prophecies to latter-day America and its civil war.

Whatever Lincoln knew about the deeper meaning of Isaiah's words, it is clear that his Second Inaugural Address had at least reflected this deeper meaning. Commenting later on his strong language in his Second Inaugural, particularly regarding his assertion that eternal punishments would continue as Heaven saw fit, Lincoln admitted that his speech would not be "immediately popular." As he explained, "Men are not flattered by being shown that there had been a difference of purpose between the Almighty and them. To deny it, however, in this case, is to deny that there is a God governing the world. It is a truth which I thought needed to be told...."[32]

Joseph Smith and other inspired prophets and patriots knew the nation needed to repent. They knew the national covenant needed repairing in order to fulfill the purposes of God's gospel plan. Therefore, they did what they could to inspire this change. Some twenty years after the Prophet's death—and in fulfillment of his prophecies, and in corroboration of the validity of the American Covenant—Abraham Lincoln worked diligently and boldly to accomplish the same sacred objective.

The Nation on National Repentance

Clearly, Lincoln had an overwhelming sense of God's intention to inspire *national repentance* through the vexation of war. But what of the people? For the fruits of God's works to come about, the people, too, would need to see this vision and follow their president in righteousness. During the last of the Nephite wars, which led to that peoples' ultimate destruction, their leader, Mormon, hoped beyond all hope that the humbling effects of war would lead them to *national repentance*. But, as Mormon lamented, "notwithstanding the great destruction which hung over my people, they did not repent of their evil doings" (Mormon 2:8). Would Lincoln be forced to conclude the same concerning his own American people of the covenant? Fortunately he would not.

In the previous chapter, we discussed how the war changed the national heart toward emancipation and the covenant during the first two years of war. We will now pick up where we left off and discuss how this national conversion to God's cause led the nation to an even deeper comprehension in the last years of the war. God's vexation would require a greater sacrifice than mere emancipation. The North would be pushed until it fully and openly recognized that God's true purpose for the war was to induce an even fuller application of *national repentance* unto national worthiness.

Once again, it was the Union soldier in the field, overcome by the effects of the vexation, who caught the vision early on. Some two years into the war, the message that slavery was, as one soldier put it, a "curse" that "hung like an incubus to tarnish" the very soul of America, began flowing out of Union camps.[33] One soldier newspaper declared that the ruined cities of the war were nothing less than divine fulfillment of the Biblical promise that "thy sin will find thee out." The newspaper further declared that the ash-heap of death and destruction, in the wake of battle, was proof-positive that "on their sin has the punishment fallen." Another soldier recognized that the "nation is passing through a terrible revolution, such a one as she doubtless needs to purge" her sins. Assistant Union Surgeon, John Moore, wrote to his wife that he was happy to report that Northerners were "beginning to see that slavery is and has been a national evil" and that "God will not bless a nation who are guilty of such gross evil."[34] "Any country that allows the curse of Slavery and Amalgamation as this has done should be cursed," according to another Illinois soldier, "and I believe in my soul that God allowed this war for the very purpose of cleaning out the evil and punishing us as a nation for allowing it."[35]

According to Private Orra Baily, removing this evil would (as the prophecy explained) require a powerful event to "shake the nation and our institutions to the very center."[36] Lt. Quincy Campbell agreed that the sin was so deeply rooted, that the Lord's purging would not be brief or easy. Even after the North had accepted and begun enforcing emancipation, and even after Union victories in Vicksburg and Gettysburg (in the summer of 1863) turned the tide in favor of the North, Campbell declared that "the chastisements of the Almighty are not yet ended...the Almighty has taken up the cause of the oppressed and...will deny us peace until we break every yoke and sweep every vestige of the cursed institution from our land."[37]

Shortly thereafter, Robert Winn, a foreign-born Union soldier, testified of an American Covenant-like connection to *national repentance*. He claimed: "American people are a sort of a chosen people, a people who will ultimately lead the nations in their forward march toward a kind of millennium." But he was rightly determined that such moral authority to lead this march would be stalled unless and until the vexation produced the desired result; that is, this war must "in the end emancipate the last slave."[38]

Even after Union victory was imminent, many Union soldiers had not yet forgiven themselves and the North (in general) for their sin of omission. Even though, as one Illinoisan soldier concluded, emancipation constituted "the salvation of our country and in a moral point the removal of an enormous sin,"[39] yet it was not enough. Many perceived the punishment of God through war as purging not only slavery, but as one soldier put it, "the enormity of [the nation's] crimes" to include bias and discrimination of all kinds. Until the nation repented of such crimes it could never "enjoy that peace which the nation has so long lost, and will never again have until made to know that God's image, of whatever hue, is worthy of respect, liberty and equality."[40]

The aforementioned historian, Chandra Manning (who conducted a long and systematic study of Civil War communications) concluded the following: By the summer of 1863, more than six months after the Emancipation Proclamation, the general conclusion among the Union rank and file was that the "North had some real soul-searching to do before it could meet God's demands. Many soldiers felt sure that destroying slavery was necessary to gain God's favor, but...emancipation was not, by itself, enough to appease the Almighty."[41] Such sentiments and conversions were precursors to the Northern movement that would result in the most prominent signs of *national repentance*: the Thirteenth, Fourteenth, and Fifteenth Amendments, which marked the unalterable eradication of minority oppression and the restitution of the American Covenant. Indeed, the soldiers grew to understand that this war was never intended to be a war like any other in history. They were in the middle of God's vexation unto *national repentance*, as foreseen and foretold by prophets and patriots—and they knew it!

And so we see how God's national scourge and vexation had produced precisely what the prophecies had implied it would produce. For, together with America's leaders, America's people also recognized the gospel need to repent and become worthy. Though the war might have been avoided had the nation adhered to the Prophet's call, ultimately God made the nation what it needed to be. "God will have a humble people. Either we can choose to be humble or we can be compelled to be humble."[42] In the end, and notwithstanding the easier path not taken, the prophecies and purposes of God's national scourge and vexation became further fulfilled. Thus, the American Covenant grew stronger in the heart of the nation.

The Second Great Good: Universal Agency

National repentance was only half of the story. We should recall, once again, why the need for the Civil War prophecies arose. The Prophet Joseph had called for special national provisions which would elevate black Americans and Mormon Americans (and any other oppressed minority). They were proposed provisions that would restore the covenant blessings of *liberty, protection,* and *prosperity* to *all*, per the covenant, thus ensuring a fullness of agency and an equal opportunity to access eternal life. They were provisions secured by things like the Fourteenth Amendment and the Civil Rights Act. Such a fullness of agency to *all* is what we call *universal agency*. And when Joseph's plea was rejected, the prophecies would be fulfilled; that is, the Lord would bring the scourge and vexation to influence the outcome Joseph had sought. As such, if the Civil War really fulfilled the prophecy, we should see evidence that the Civil War produced not only *national repentance*, but also the restitution phase of this repentance—a purpose and goal of *universal agency*. In short, *universal agency* should represent one of Lincoln's sought-after "great goods" of the war.

Indeed, as it would be Lincoln's (and the North's) God-given responsibility to shape the war's purposes—to lead the nation in accomplishing the Prophet's proposals (e.g. the Fourteenth Amendment and the Civil Rights Act)—we might expect that they came to a deep understanding of these purposes during the war. And they did.

Lincoln on Universal Agency

The principle of *universal agency* truly began to weigh heavily on Lincoln as the war progressed; and considering its eventual effect on the restored gospel, his recognition of this principle was eternally relevant. As Lincoln began to accept and apply these ideals as a purpose for the war, we once again see his divine role develop further under the covenant.

With a growing understanding of what America was to be, Lincoln naturally began parading his new war purpose. Lincoln told Congress: "In giving freedom to the *slave*, we assure freedom to the *free*." He went on to explain that in securing this larger freedom for all Americans, they would be enabling such freedom in all the world. In this necessary conflict, then, he prophesied, "We shall nobly save, or meanly lose, the last best hope on earth."[43]

During the very month that the Emancipation Proclamation was issued, Lincoln again commented on how the war's final outcome would not only bless the slave, but would—under God— bless all other suffering Americans:

> It is most cheering and encouraging for me to know that in the efforts which I have made and am making for the restoration of a righteous peace to our country, I am upheld and sustained by the good wishes and prayers of God's

people. No one is more deeply than myself aware that without His favor our highest wisdom is but as foolishness....I am conscious of no desire for my country's welfare that is not on consonance with His will, and of no plan upon which we may not ask His blessing. It seems to me that if there be one subject upon which all good men may unitedly agree, it is imploring the gracious favor of the God of Nations upon the struggles our people are making for the *preservation of their precious birth-right of civil and religious liberty.*[44]

Lincoln would revisit this theme of *universal agency* under God, some five months after issuing the Emancipation Proclamation, in a speech that would become perhaps the most famous ever given on American soil: the Gettysburg Address. In outlining this new purpose for the war, Lincoln—standing on the hallowed ground where more than 50,000 men had recently died in a Union victory—boldly invoked the core principles of the American Covenant. This speech would unequivocally declare that the war was about God's gift of *universal agency* (and it would do so in a way nothing had before). Considering the powerful gospel-based theme of the speech, and the powerful manner in which it was accepted, before analyzing its text we will first consider the environment in which it was given.

Lincoln had come to help dedicate the freshly dug gravesites at the new National Gettysburg Cemetery. The service was deeply religious. But, then again, the entire Gettysburg experience had been deeply religious for Lincoln. (As we will detail in the following chapter, during the battle itself, Lincoln had experienced something divine, something he recognized as the key to Union victory.) The chaplain opened the service in prayer: "Oh God, our Father, for the sake of Thy son, our Savior, inspire us with Thy Spirit." As he inspiringly spoke of the war as a fight related to "Liberty, Religion, and God," Lincoln was seen wiping tears from his face.[45]

At last it was Lincoln's turn to speak. And when he did, he kept the Spirit alive in Gettysburg. In one of the shortest, yet most powerful, speeches in history, Lincoln (appropriately) utilized the literary flare of the Bible.* According to one prominent Lincoln scholar, he spoke "the music of the ancient Hebrew."[46] But the connection with ancient Israel went way beyond literary devices. For it is the national covenant that binds America to Israel, and Lincoln's words brought that national covenant front and center.

Lincoln concluded with perhaps the most powerful statement of the address:

> It is rather for us to be here dedicated to the great task remaining before us—that from these honored dead we take increased devotion to that cause for which they gave the last full measure of devotion—that we here highly resolve that these dead shall not have died in vain, that this nation, under God, shall have a new birth of freedom, and that government of the people, by the people, for the people, shall not perish from the earth.[47]

Not once during the speech did Lincoln speak of North, South, re-unification, or even slavery. Though all of these elements led him to a personal understanding of his broader theme, it was to this broader theme that he spoke. And what was that theme? That one "nation under God" was fighting, and would continue to fight, for "a new birth of freedom" which would benefit all "the people" for whom the nation was divinely designed. After all, as Lincoln declared on a separate occasion, "The leading object" of American government should be "to elevate the condition of men—to lift artificial weights from all shoulders—to clear the paths of laudable pursuit for all—to afford all, an unfettered start, and a fair chance, in the race of life."[48] As the award-winning scholar and renowned

---

* "Four score and seven years ago" echoes Psalm 90. He also used other Biblical imagery in his speech, weaving the American story together with the ancient Hebrew account through the use of Old Testament themes and terminologies like "Fathers," "Brought Forth," "New Nation," "Conceive," "Perish," "Hallow" and "Devotion." See Boritt, *Gettysburg Gospel*, 120.

expert of Gettysburg, Gabor Boritt, said of the Address: "[It] reached beyond the American problem of slavery to the global problem of liberal democracy."[49]

The speech reached out and touched the root of the problems that had burdened the Kingdom of God on the earth. It echoed the American Covenant. It described what the Prophet Joseph had called for. It defined God's purpose behind the vexation. And now it was what Lincoln was trying to bring to the nation. It was *universal agency*. Lincoln was indeed invoking the national covenant, resurrecting the very principles which brought the ancient Israelites out of slavery and allowed them to access salvation. In that moment at Gettysburg, it became latter-day Israel's turn to invoke the covenant and reap the same gospel blessings.

It is altogether appropriate that the scholar Boritt would describe the Address as one that "weaved together the biblical story and the American story."[50] Award-winning author Bruce Feiler agreed that the Address spoke "on a deeper level." Lincoln, according to Feiler, "was presenting a vision of God's American Israel that reconnected it to God's original Israel."[51] One newspaper reporter on the scene even compared Lincoln to Moses, stating that the president "never stood higher, or grander, or more prophetic."[52]

Universal agency unto eternal progression for all Americans could at last be expected with Union victory. However, there would be a second set of beneficiaries, in addition to those in America; for *all* God's children worldwide would also benefit from this new vision of the Civil War. The fruit of political freedom, and thus the opportunity for gospel light, that would benefit this worldwide group was not solely dependent upon, or inherently connected to, the positive outcome of the traditional Civil War issues like slavery and equal rights. (Such issues were, on the other hand, directly connected to the Saints in America, as their religious freedom would be decided by the outcome of these issues.) Instead, the international hope of liberty and truth was connected to the more abstract idea surrounding the survival of the American experiment we call democratic republicanism. It is precisely this type of democratic and free-agency loving government that must exist in every land so as to secure eternal progress for all God's children. If America, as the forerunner of such a political experiment, failed to maintain it, what hope would others have to try it themselves? What hope, then (if men gave up on such a system of liberty) would the gospel restoration have in springing up throughout the world?

The critics of such a democratic system—which critics had existed since the Constitution rolled off the press—believed the American Civil War had brought them vindication. They had warned that America, in giving so much freedom to the people up front, had only encouraged a spirit of rebellion and entitlement. It was inevitable that one day there would be the sort of tragedy now being witnessed in the American Civil War. If any segment could secede at will in order to work whatever ungodly practice it saw fit, then a democratic republic, they argued, was bad government. They asserted that only a strong monarchical or patriarchal type government could keep the people in check, even if that meant civil and religious freedoms were somewhat curtailed. If Lincoln and the Union could prove them wrong, then the doorway to religious freedom, and thus to the gospel, would be open as a viable option for the world. If Lincoln and the Union failed, constitutional principles would be sidelined throughout the world; and the repercussions could mean dire consequences for the restored gospel's growth.

One might glean an inconsistency in this worldwide perspective of the vexation: if providence somehow permitted or encouraged this vexation, then it would seem that providence had put into jeopardy the very American system it had designed to be the standard among nations. One would be wrong, however, in this interpretation; for such an idea hangs on the premise that before Southern secession and Civil War, America was the pinnacle of good government. The truth is, up until the Civil War, the greatness of America was largely theoretical and as-of-yet unachieved. Consider, for example, the tragic plight of black Americans and Mormon Americans. Both experienced severe oppression at the hands of this very government. America had not as-of-yet become the shining city on a hill. In his Gettysburg Address, Lincoln even admitted that the glory of America was "dedicated to the *proposition* that all men are created equal," implying that such ideals were not yet fulfilled.

The challenge, then, was to show the worldwide critics of American democracy that a free government can bridle the generous freedoms given to early Americans (i.e. subdue the rebellious South) without strangling these freedoms (i.e. without becoming a European-like monarchy). Indeed, America would have to prove that, in spite of its great freedoms to the people, it could keep itself together. And Lincoln knew this could be done if the Union was victorious, demonstrating that even democracies have power to crack the whip on evil. Lincoln further knew this could be done if a newly reunited United States added *universal agency* to its constitutional application (through inspired amendments and provisions), further proving that, notwithstanding a sometimes tough posture, liberty could still reign like never before. If Lincoln and his faithful could do this, they would convince the world that democracies can work.

In the end, it was not the war that placed American hope or the American dream in peril. Instead, the war only emphasized the already existing problematic conditions that had always prevented America from being that hope and dream, then attempted to deal with these problematic conditions head on. It brought the American demons (that few in America wanted to acknowledge) out of hiding so they could be eradicated. This was the purpose of the prophecy— the purpose of the vexation. This was the divine intent of Lincoln and his faithful. If they were successful, then America could truly be the example and standard bearer of liberty. The American system of government would be emulated and the gospel would have ample fertile soil in which to grow worldwide.

Remarkably, Lincoln understood this general concept as part of his new and broader purpose in the war, as implied in the most famous portion of the Gettysburg Address:

> Fourscore and seven years ago, our fathers brought forth upon this continent a new nation, conceived in liberty and dedicated to the proposition that all men are created equal. Now we are engaged in a great civil war, testing whether that nation, *or any nation* so conceived and so dedicated, *can long endure* (emphasis added).*

The worldwide gospel implications are clear. No wonder Lincoln and the Gettysburg Address have been quoted by freedom fighters the world over—from Gandhi in India, to revolutionaries for democracy in Latin America, to Mandela in South Africa, and to liberty-loving student movements in Hungary (1956), Iran (1979), and China (1989).[53] No wonder Lincoln called America "the last best hope on earth."[54]

As Lincoln was concluding his famous address and laying out his new strategy, under God's direction, to realize *universal agency*, a wounded captain with an empty shirt sleeve buried his weeping and shaking face into his good arm. He then cried aloud, "God Almighty bless Abraham Lincoln," to which the crowd responded solemnly, "Amen."[55]

Lincoln would eloquently expound upon this general theme of *universal agency* on several other occasions throughout the war:

- "[T]his issue [of civil war] embraces more than the fate of these United States. It presents to the whole family of man the question whether a constitutional republic or a democracy—a government of the people by the same people—can or cannot maintain its territorial integrity...."[56]

---

* Interestingly, the two sections of the Gettysburg Address recited above are directly derived from our founding documents. First, Lincoln's reference to a government "of the people, by the people, and for the people" echoes the language "We the people," from the Constitution. Second, his recitation that "all men are created equal" is quoted directly out of the great promissory note of freedom, the Declaration of Independence. As both of these documents were directly inspired by God, and as they both lay the foundation for *universal agency*, the meaning behind Lincoln's words become all the more potent.

- "We already have an important principle to rally and unite the people in the fact that [in this war] constitutional government is at stake. This is a fundamental idea, going down about as deep as any thing."[57]

- "There is more involved in this contest than is realized by every one. There is involved in this struggle the question [of] whether your children and my children may enjoy the privileges we have enjoyed....It is not merely for to-day, but for all time to come, that we should perpetuate for our children's children that great and free government...."[58]

- "[This civil war is] an important crises which involves, in my judgment, not only the civil and religious liberties of our own dear land, but in a large degree the civil and *religious liberties of mankind in many countries and through many ages*...You may all recollect that in taking up the sword thus forced into our hands, this Government appealed to the prayers of the pious and the good, and declared that it placed its whole dependence upon the favor of God. I now humbly and reverently, in your presence, reiterate the acknowledgement of that dependence, not doubting that, if it shall please the Divine Being who determines the *destinies of nations* that this shall remain a united people, they will, humbly seeking the Divine guidance, make their prolonged national existence a source of new benefits to themselves and their successors, *and to all classes and conditions of mankind.*[59]

And so it was that Abraham Lincoln—in at least one sense —stood in the place of Joseph Smith, fought the Prophet's fight, and began to accomplish what the people refused to allow the Prophet to accomplish. The prophecies became further fulfilled, even as the American Covenant became further validated.

The Nation on Universal Agency

In addition to its leaders, the nation also had to arrive at an understanding of God's deeper purposes for the war. In order for God's required constitutional provisions to take hold at war's end, and in order to fulfill the prophecies, the nation, in aggregate, had to gain a testimony that the war was ultimately about *universal agency*.

Like we have seen before, the first Northern faction to receive this testimony, and then pass it on to the rest of society, consisted of the soldiers. After already having been converted to the cause of the Emancipation Proclamation and *national repentance*, the Union soldiers were ready to take it to the next level. According to one Union soldier, the new objective of the war would allow the flag of the United States to "triumphantly wave over a free land, which it has never done before."[60] An Indiana private expressed that he was fighting "to sustain a principle, to protect right, and secure the liberties of the oppressed."[61] A Kansas private declared that the Union soldier had to fight for the "Cause of Constitutional Liberty"—or what the Union faithful called "our political temple of liberty"—because "if we fail now, the hope of human rights is extinguished for ages."[62] One private fighting on the eastern front wrote his fiancé that the war was about "the defense of the rights of humanity, and the well-being of the unborn generations." Another private on the western front (and one who had recently lost many friends in a bloodbath of a battle), reaffirmed his belief that the blood of the fallen would "flow and mingle...to nourish and water the liberty, whose leaves are healing the nations."[63]

Consistent with such sentiments, Dr. Manning's aforementioned study concluded that, while Southern soldiers fought for an ideal that would benefit themselves (i.e. the materialism and status received through the institution of slavery), the Union soldiers' motivation (in general) was about an "American millennialist tradition" focused on the "rights of humanity."[64] The

Union soldier understood that freeing a race would, in fact, renew freedom for all oppressed Americans. This landed them squarely in line with God's scriptural purpose for the conflict: to not only free a race, but to free *everybody*, including those Saints He had planted in America; and this, that His truth unto salvation might be brought forth.

Like Lincoln, the Union soldier not only believed that Union victory would mean *universal agency* in America, but (for the same reasons Lincoln articulated) that it would also mean *universal agency* for the world. According to one Union army camp newspaper, the Northern cause was "to protect and perpetuate a Government which the oppressed in every land have looked upon for half a century as the beacon of liberty."[65] Union victory would serve as "a check to the tyranny of European monarchs" and would lead to "the establishment of free government throughout the earth."[66]

According to one Union soldier who had emigrated from Europe (and thus knew something of the heavy handedness of authoritarian regimes), understood that he was fighting for his oppressed family back home in Europe as much as he was fighting for the oppressed in America. Indeed, he stated that he was, ultimately, fighting for all "who would be free."[67] He understood, along with his fellow-soldiers, his president, and a growing number of Northern society, what the *New York Daily Tribune* captured early on in the conflict: that the United States was "engaged in trying a great experiment, involving not merely the future fate and welfare of this Western continent, but the hopes and prospects of the whole human race." Union victory would mean "the democratic principle of equal rights [and] general suffrage...[was] capable of being carried into practical operation," while its defeat would be seen by the world "as the first step toward the entire breakdown of our whole system of republican government."[68]

To show that these sentiments were not merely reflections of a few isolated comments, but, instead, were reflections of the general sentiment in the North, we refer to Manning's conclusions on the subject:

> The soldiers in this study show that they did feel a strong connection and duty to the United States government [or, as we might insinuate, to the American Covenant], which grew in part out of an ante-bellum millennialist understanding of the United States' unique mission in the world. In the main, Union soldiers cared about the United States not primarily because it served their families' interests, but because its survival mattered for the survival of ideals like liberty, equality, and self government for all humanity.[69]

Shortly after Lincoln delivered his Gettysburg Address (appropriately called by some, the "Gettysburg Gospel") it was transmitted across the North, "immersing the people," according to Boritt, "in one fastening ritual, creating community."[70] The divine principles of the Address were taking hold. The purposes of God were bursting forth. The Spirit born of a humbled nation's conversion was having a profound effect in America. Through its renewed purpose of *universal agency*—even through this national recognition of Lincoln's "great good"—the nation was fulfilling the prophecies surrounding the American Covenant. The covenant was beginning to more fully fill the measure of its creation. The restored gospel was everyday closer to finding its divinely ordained firmament. How comprehensible (though tragic) the furious vexation! How noble the Northern cause!

ENDNOTES

[1] Lincoln, as quoted in Chris and Ted Stewart, *Seven Miracles That Saved America* (U.S.A.: Shadow Mountain, 2009), 179; Carwardine, 146-7.

[2] Lincoln on October 16, 1862, as quoted in Newt Gingrich, *Rediscovering God in America* (Nashville, Integrity House, 2006), 53-54.

[3] Lincoln, as quoted in Ron Andersen, *Lincoln: God's Humble Instrument*, 121.

[4] Lincoln, in a letter to Albert Hodges, April 1864, Carwardine, 234.

[5] Quote from last chapter, as cited in Carwardine, 226-227.

[6] Gingrich, 52.

[7] Carwardine, 227.

[8] Carwardine, 234, emphasis added. Full letter available from Roy P. Basler, ed., *The Collected Works of Abraham Lincoln*, Vol. 7 (New Brunswick, N.J.: Rutgers University Press, 1955), 282, 535-36, available at http://quod.lib.umich.edu/lincoln/.

[9] Carwardine, 234, emphasis added. Full letter available from Roy P. Basler, ed., *The Collected Works of Abraham Lincoln*, Vol. 7 (New Brunswick, N.J.: Rutgers University Press, 1955), 282, 535-36, available at http://quod.lib.umich.edu/lincoln/.

[10] James F Wilson, Congressman, included this in his memoir *Some Memories of Lincoln* (1896), as quoted in Don and Virginia Fehrenbacher, ed. *Recollected Words of Abraham Lincoln* (Stanford: Stanford University Press, 1996), 499-500.

[11] James F Wilson, Congressman, included this in his memoir *Some Memories of Lincoln* (1896), as quoted in Don and Virginia Fehrenbacher, ed. *Recollected Words of Abraham Lincoln* (Stanford: Stanford University Press, 1996), 499-500; also quoted in Stewart and Stewart, *Seven Miracles That Saved America*, 180.

[12] Joseph Smith, as quoted in Vetterli, 173.

[13] Schweikart and Allen, *A Patriot's History, 307-308.*

[14] Carwardine, 234.

[15] Lincoln, as quoted in Leidner, 104-105.

[16] Lincoln, as quoted in Leidner, 107-108; full speech available from Richardson ed, "A Proclamation by the President of the United States of America (March 30, 1863)," *Messages and Papers of the Presidents* (Washington DC: United States Congress, 1897), 164-165; also available at www.showcase.letin.net/web/creative/lincoln.speeches/fast.htm.

[17] Gingrich, 52; Feiler, *America's Prophet*, 166.

[18] James Swanson, *Manhunt: The 12-Day Chase for Lincoln's Killer* (New York, HarperCollins Publishers, 2006), 2.

[19] Ron Andersen, *Lincoln: God's Humble Instrument*, 291.

[20] Matthew Holland, *Bonds of Affection*, 4.

[21] Abraham Lincoln, as quoted in Leidner, 113-114.

[22] Frederick Douglas, as quoted in William J. Bennett, *America, The Last Best Hope*, Volume I, 385.

[23]Lincoln, as quoted in Leidner, 110.

[24] Lincoln, as quoted in Carwardine, 143.

[25] *Old Testament Student Manuel: 1Kings-Malachi,* 2nd Edition, Religion 302 Student Manual (Salt Lake City: The Church of Jesus Christ of Latter-day Saints, 1982), 141.

[26] *Old Testament Student Manuel: 1Kings-Malachi,* 2nd Edition, Religion 302 Student Manual (Salt Lake City: The Church of Jesus Christ of Latter-day Saints, 1982), 142.

[27] Donald Perry, Jay Perry and Tina Peterson, *Understanding Isaiah* (Salt Lake City: Deseret Book, 2009), 57.

[28] Ron Andersen, *Lincoln: God's Humble Instrument*, 300.

[29] The Old Testament, LDS Student Manuel 1Kings-Malachi (Salt Lake City: The Church of Jesus Christ of Latter-day Saints, 1982), 138-9.

[30] *Old Testament Student Manuel: 1Kings-Malachi,* 2nd Edition, Religion 302 Student Manual (Salt Lake City: The Church of Jesus Christ of Latter-day Saints, 1982), 142.

[31] Donald Perry, Jay Perry and Tina Peterson, *Understanding Isaiah* (Salt Lake City: Deseret Book, 2009), 61.

[32] Meacham, 121.

[33] Letter from Private Levi Hines, as quoted in Manning, 119.

[34] Manning, 188-189.

[35] Manning, 85.

[36] Manning, 85.

[37] Manning, 113.

[38] Manning, 116.

[39] Manning, 119.

[40] Manning, 165.

[41] Manning, 118-119.

[42] Ezra Taft Benson, "Beware of Pride," *Ensign* , May 1989, 4.

[43] Lincoln, as quoted in Carwardine, 217.

[44] Lincoln, as quoted in Leidner, 107 (emphasis added).

[45] Gabor Boritt, *The Gettysburg Gospel, The Lincoln Speech That Nobody Knows* (New York: Simon and Schuster, 2006), 97.

[46] Boritt, 120.

[47] Lincoln, as quoted in Bennett, *America: The Last Best Hope*, Volume I, 368.

[48] Lincoln, as quoted in Carwardine, 240-41.

[49] Boritt, 117.

[50] Boritt, 120.

[51] Feiler, *America's Prophet*, 165.

[52] Feiler, *America's Prophet,* 165.

[53] Boritt, 202.

[54] Carwardine, 217.

[55] Boritt, 118.

[56] Lincoln, as quoted in John G. Nicolay and John Hays, eds, *Complete Works of Lincoln,* Vol. 6 (New York: Francis D. Tandy, 1905), 304.

[57] Lincoln, as quoted in Miller, 151.

[58] Lincoln, as quoted in Leidner, 117-18.

[59] Lincoln, as quoted in Roy P. Basler, ed., *The Collected Works of Abraham Lincoln,* Vol. 5 (New Brunswick, N.J.: Rutgers University Press, 1955), 212, emphasis added.

[60] Manning, 94.

[61] Manning, 94.

[62] Manning, 40-41.

[63] Manning, 70-71.

[64] Manning, 70.

[65] Manning, 39.

[66] Manning, 94.

[67] Manning, 151-152.

[68] Manning, 26.

[69] Manning, 6.

[70] Boritt, 122.

General Order No.11, by George Caleb Bingham
Courtesy of the State Historical Society of Missouri

CHAPTER 6

A Fight Between God and the Devil

[The Civil War is] a fight…between God and the Devil—
between Heaven and Hell.

—George Washington Julian, calling Union soldiers to arms

We have spent much time analyzing the North and its conversion under the prophesied vexation—and for good reason. The North, after all, had become converted to the covenant principles of *national repentance* and *universal agency,* and thus had become the agent for the great constitutional changes that would redeem the American Covenant. In light of this, one might wonder why the Lord did not direct the North, once it had been converted to the covenant, to simply forsake the endless fight with the South and begin to implement its newfound covenant principles under the banner of a new Northern United States government. The Kingdom of God, it seems, would have found the support it needed under such a renewed system of government. However, things were not so simple. It appears the Lord intended the national vexation to create something more than Northern conversion alone. He also needed the Southern rebellion to be crushed. This chapter will explore the

277

relationship and struggle between North and South and explain *why* the Southern Confederacy needed to be dissolved for the cause of the gospel. We will also see how the Lord miraculously influenced Northern victory over the South for this same divine purpose. Through it all, we will come to recognize the profound, spiritual, and eternal struggle that was the American Civil War. And at the center of it all, we will find the American Covenant—a key to salvation.

Satan in the South: An Attempt to Obstruct God's Plan

In order to understand why the Southern Confederacy had to be dissolved under God's plan, we must first understand the core principles that underlined the Southern cause and intent.

While we approvingly dwell upon our religious heritage stemming from the early religious settlements in the New England colonies, which set the covenant foundation between God and America, it should be remembered that this same light was not always experienced in every colonial settlement. Far from seeking God, early settlers in Jamestown, Virginia, for example, had the singular intent of gaining riches, first through gold mining (which failed) and then through the tobacco crop, which proved successful only after the employment of the evil practice of slavery.[1] This is not to say that seeking wealth is always bad, for often it is a blessing. But, wealth generated on the backs of kidnapped human-beings hardly sounds like the kind of wealth derived from heaven's hand. As the wicked cancer called "slavery" grew, becoming codified and tolerated, it would only make the entire nation unworthy before God to be that chosen land and host of the Restoration. It would also spread a culture of hate, persecution, and oppression that affected all minority groups in America, including God's restored church.

And so, in more than one way, slavery (particularly in the South) would be responsible for obstructing the Kingdom of God. The adversary was certainly strategizing early on. Satan knew that deep evil would flow from the introduction of slavery. We might even conclude that slavery was the adversary's strategic doing from the day it hit the beaches of Virginia in 1619. Interestingly, while slavery was going out of style, even being abolished in Europe (the British outlawed it by 1833), in America—even that land born of Christian men and women who should have comprehended freedom, love, and tolerance—slavery was only growing stronger. Taking a page from the playbook he used in the pre-mortal existence, Satan would again attempt to employ the same plan here in mortality: quash human freedom of choice and thus quash mankind's ability to achieve true salvation with the Father.

Just as he had fought a war over these principles in heaven, the adversary would defend his Southern stronghold and fight an extended version of this war here in mortality. Indeed, the American Civil War would represent yet another extended version of that great war in heaven. As the Lord's vexation was having the effect of converting the North to His cause and covenant, Satan had reason to fret. The adversary most certainly understood that Northern advancement in this cause meant power to God's covenant for America and therefore meant power to the Kingdom of God. Furthermore, as the North attempted to penetrate and defeat the South, Satan undoubtedly understood that this might lead to the end of slavery. He knew it might also lead to the dissemination of the covenant principles of *national repentance* and *universal agency* within the South. This threatened Satan's plan. He would not sit back and idly watch it happen. And so, whereas the adversary's influence had been seen and felt, particularly in the South, since the settlement of America, the Civil War brought this evil influence to the surface. It compelled the adversary to fight for his evil designs for America and thereby exposed these designs like nothing had before.

The War in Heaven—even a war of free agency unto eternal salvation versus oppression unto eternal stagnation—would truly be played out all over again on American soil. As such, should we not fully expect to find evidence that Satan was opposing God's efforts?

Satan had, after all, promised to buy up armies and navies and rule with blood, horror, and oppression on the earth. Would a war that threatened to empower the American Covenant unto the salvation of man not pique his interest then? Would he not use what influence he had over armies and navies? Would he not then use those armies and navies to take his usual position opposite the Father? Indeed he would. If the American Covenant prophecies truly are fulfilled in the Civil War, and if this conflict truly is the eternally significant event we claim it is, then we *must* see Satan in the middle of it. We *must* see Satan in the South. And as we dissect the evidence found in the pages that follow, we will most certainly find him there.

Admittedly, to suggest Satan drove the Southern cause in a war against God is to certainly offend Southern patriots, both past and present, who have a different perspective on the war. The purpose of this suggestion, however, is not to offend, but to introduce evidence that does, in fact, place the Southern cause in this category. But the evidence will *not* prove the South was plain evil. In fact, it is clear that Southerners, far from believing they were on some evil mission, believed God would justify and sustain their cause. Some even cited Biblical references to slavery as if it were an ordained practice.[2] Others maintained (and *truly* believed) that they were fighting for states' or personal rights. Others fought because it was their duty. Often they had been drafted into the fight. And so, as we sift through the evidence, let us not cast the entire South into the pits of hell. Let us, as Lincoln did, have mercy on the American Southerners, who were often unwitting pawns in a larger game.

At the same time, however, let us not neglect the fact that the Light of Christ testifies to *all men* that kidnapping, enslaving, persecuting, and raping the innocent is forever sinful. Indeed, it is sinful to destroy a family by ripping a child from her mother's arms because the deal was too good to pass up—and so mother was sold down the river. All those supporting the Confederacy knew they were supporting a government that allowed and encouraged this sin. And once Lincoln had issued the Emancipation Proclamation, thus making the war about freeing slaves, they knew they were fighting against him who would liberate the slaves and redeem the sinful land. If any man in the South ever fought against Lincoln with this knowledge in mind, then that man should have taken a long look in the mirror.

That said, let us now analyze the details surrounding the Southern cause in fighting the Civil War, that we might more fully comprehend why and how the Civil War truly was the scriptural, prophetic, and eternal conflict we claim it was.

Any analysis of the Southern cause must address what is known as the Lost Cause Theory: that the South was not fighting to preserve slavery, but was instead fighting for the noble cause of states' rights against an overbearing federal government. The theory (which many believe and promote even today) goes on to suggest that the South was on the road to emancipating the slaves on its own. Though it makes some Southerners feel more comfortable about their ancestry, and makes some modern-day states' rights advocates somehow feel more justified in their position, this theory denies history and is so far off the mark that it borders on the ridiculous. Southern secession began as a direct result of the election of a president who had spoken out boldly against the sin of slavery. Though the newly elected Lincoln initially promised, and truly intended, to leave slavery alone in the South, Southerners loved their slavery so much that they risked war instead of trusting Lincoln. And why would they trust this strange new political player, who represented the brand-new Republican Party, whose platform was so clearly anti-slavery?

Furthermore, the one thing Lincoln *was* always firm about (despite his promise to leave slavery alone in the South) was his intention to prohibit slavery from extending into new states and territories. This promise alone was enough to push the South out of the Union, for it meant an increase in free-soil representatives in Congress. This would leave the slaveholders with an ever-diminishing voice in Congress, and would perhaps even lead to slavery's eventual demise.[3]

But we do not need to rely on this obvious motive for Southern secession and aggression. All we really need to do is ask the South why it did what it did. The South was, after all, very clear on the matter. For example, the president and vice president of the Confederacy spoke frequently about the need for Southern victory in order to preserve slavery; they called slavery the "great truth," "the foundation," and the "cornerstone" of their new government.[4] Before the war, the would-be Confederate president, Jefferson Davis, "had frequently spoken to the United States Senate about the significance of slavery to the South and had threatened secession if what he perceived as Northern threats to the institution continued."[5]

In South Carolina's secession convention, the delegates discussed their fears that Lincoln would allow "black Republicans" who were "hostile to slavery," to take positions of leadership in the government.[6] The Confederate constitution made Southern intent clear: "Our new Government is founded...upon the great truth that the negro is not the equal of the white man. That slavery— subordination to the superior race, is his natural and normal condition." Confederate Vice President, Alexander H. Stephens, added that slavery was "the proper status of the negro in our form of civilization."[7]

During the war, Jefferson Davis sought to make slaves of all black persons, even those who were, at the time, free black-Americans. In response to the Emancipation Proclamation, Davis ordered the following: "On or after February 22, 1863, all free negroes within the limits of the Southern Confederacy shall be placed on slave status, and be deemed to be chattels, they and their issue forever." The order was not only issued for blacks in Confederate territory. Davis mandated that even those blacks "taken in any of the States in which slavery does not now exist...shall be adjudged...to occupy the slave status." Davis concluded (in a statement he made after the war had started), that blacks were "an inferior race, peaceful and contented laborers in their sphere."[8]

Furthermore, any fair and accurate reading of the history building up to and during Southern secession shows that all major proposals, negotiations, and pleas from both North and South to avoid war, hung on the fate of slavery. The issue was not states' rights (except where states' rights meant the right to own people) or any other excuse. When Lincoln stood and addressed the South during his First Inaugural address, the president was clearly scared of war and wanted to avoid it all costs. So he pled with the South, not on how both parties could negotiate an agreement on the tariff issue, or any other issue. He stood and addressed how they could work around *slavery*. That was *the* issue.[9]

Based on these powerful sentiments from Confederate leaders, it becomes readily apparent how ridiculous it is to promote the idea that the South was on the path to emancipating slaves on its own. We already discussed, in previous chapters, how slavery was nowhere near being phasing out, but was instead only growing immensely. The states in the Confederacy had even initiated the undoing of the one constitutional restraint against slavery: they sought to lift the constitutional ban on kidnapping and importing new slaves.[10]

In the end, we must conclude, as do the vast majority of trained American historians, that "it is not an exaggeration to say that the Civil War was about slavery and, in the long run, *only* about slavery."[11]

It was not only the leadership that knew it was fighting primarily for the preservation and growth of slavery. Dr. Manning's aforementioned study, which also analyzed Southern soldiers' letters, newspapers, and general motives for war, concluded that it is "patronizing and insulting to Confederate soldiers to pretend they did not understand the war as a battle for slavery when they so plainly described it as exactly that."[12]

At one point during the war, some in the South, who felt desperate, thought to recruit slaves into the army and induce them to fight by offering them some sort of emancipation. The Southern response was consistent with Manning's conclusions. One Mississippi newspaper declared that arming slaves represented "a total abandonment of the *chief object* of this war, and if the institution [of slavery] is already irretrievably undermined, the rights of the States are buried with it." We see, again, what "states' rights" *really* meant to the South. As late as 1865, a Confederate congressional report concurred: "The doctrine of emancipation as a reward for the service of slaves employed in the army, is antagonistic to the spirit of our institutions."[13]

The relevant question for us today is: *If the South did not try to hide its true intentions, why should we?* And yet, somehow, so many do. That anyone, especially today, would support a movement put forth upon these principles—that anyone would argue today that the South was actually *right*—is beyond stunning.

As tragic as the South's pursuit of sinful ambition was, a gospel perspective makes Southern intent even darker. Just as the emancipation of slavery was a platform for God to accomplish His eternal purposes, so was the preservation of slavery a platform for Satan to accomplish his. Not only would slavery keep the nation mired in sin, unable to perform its covenant obligations, but it would also provide the socio-political justification to oppress and deny agency to any and all minorities—to include the bearers of God's kingdom. It is here where we clearly see Satan's use of the Southern cause to gain those ends he sought from the beginning, even from the time of the War in Heaven.

But what proof do we have that the South really was hosting such eternally destructive politics, which grew out of slavery? Manning's in-depth study concludes that the Confederate soldiers, in fighting for slavery, were, in fact, fighting for much more than that. They were fighting for a socio-political system where they—by virtue of being white and male—maintained absolute dominance not only over blacks, but also over woman, children, and any others they deemed lesser than themselves. If their dominance over blacks was diminished, so too, they feared, would their dominance over all other segments of society be diminished as well.

According to Manning, "losing to the Union was unthinkable, according to Confederate soldiers, because it would mean abolition, and abolition would destroy the southern social order."[14] Manning continues, stating, "The loss of slavery would call white men's right to rule over blacks into question, and once right to rule in any sphere was weakened, its legitimacy became suspect in every sphere."[15] Manning further concludes that "black slavery constantly reminded white men that in a society where most residents (African Americans, women, and children) were disenfranchised and subordinate to them, the independence that white men enjoyed as adult white males, and the ability to command...set them apart and identified them as men."[16]

And so, the oft-repeated argument of the Lost Cause theorist that the South was not fighting for slavery, as evidenced by the fact that relatively few Southern soldiers actually owned slaves, loses potency. Slavery meant much more to Southerners than owning a person of African descent. As Manning concluded, "an entire social order was at stake, and it could be preserved only by isolating it from Northern influence."[17]

There is another powerfully obvious problem with the argument that because there were relatively few slave owners, the Southern people were not actually fighting for slavery. Slaves were the lifeblood of the economy, just like farm equipment and livestock are the lifeblood of an agricultural economy today. If all the equipment and livestock disappeared in such an economy, *all* would be affected, though relatively few actually own the equipment and livestock. Without these tools, the working folks would have nowhere to work, nothing to do. So it was with the Confederate working force—even those *without* slaves. They all wanted and needed their slavery. They understood what was at stake in the war, and so should we.

Altogether, then, whether seen through the eyes of the quintessential Southern plantation owner, or through the eyes of the lowly Southern white farm-hand, the social and economic order sustained by slavery was the very thing they would not let go of. It was their cause and intent for the fight. Sadly, this social order, this Southern cause and intent, was—any way you slice it—about maintaining a system where one group dominated at will any other group or groups it desired, to include minority religionists like the Latter-day Saints. It was a system most assuredly founded upon an ideal of oppression of the human spirit; and oppression of the human spirit obstructs eternal progression. Was this not Satan's plan being carried out in and by the South?

Lincoln seemed to recognize the Southern system as exactly that evil thing which perpetuates such oppression to all. "As a nation," he once wrote, "we began by declaring that 'all men are created equal.'"

> We now practically read it "all men are created equal, except Negroes." When the Know Nothings [anti-immigrant/ anti-minority party] get control, it will read "all men are created equal, except Negroes and foreigners and Catholics." When it comes to this, I shall prefer emigrating to some country where they make no pretense of loving liberty—to Russia for instance, where despotism can be taken pure, and without the base alloy of hypocrisy.[18]

Lincoln might have just as easily included "Mormons" to the list of "Negroes," "foreigners" and "Catholics." The socio-political problem for the blacks, once again, was also the socio-political problem for the Saints or any other minority group. Lincoln himself spoke again to this idea when he stated that "slavery is the evil out of which all our other national evils and dangers have come. It has deceived and led us to the brink of ruin, and it must be stopped."[19] If it could socially and politically be done to blacks, it could conceivably be done to anyone. This is perhaps why Frederick Douglas so poignantly declared that "the destiny of the colored man...is the destiny of America."[20] It is also why the Civil War witness and literary great, Ralph Waldo Emerson, stated, "I think we must get rid of slavery, or we must get rid of freedom."[21]

Naturally, any people that thought it was appropriate to enslave an entire race, would see the effects of such bigotry spill over into other areas of society as well. Indeed, the sinfulness of the South naturally led to a system that would forever threaten the covenant blessings required for God's kingdom. Consider, for example, how this culture of dominance and oppression was reflected in Confederate politics. Under the Confederate constitution, the powers of the president were nearly unlimited, as no judicial check against the executive was put into place. Furthermore, the South's constitution supported censorship, even that killer of democracy. Also, far more Confederate soldiers were drafted into the war than Union soldiers.[22]

In a study done by scholar Richard Bensel, he found that "the North had a less centralized government and was a much more open society than the South." In his study, he compared the North and South's handling of "property rights," "control of railroads," "destruction of property," and "confiscation." His conclusion: "the Confederacy [was] far more government centered and less market oriented." For example, seven-eighths of all freight moved on the Virginia Central Railroad was government owned and over ninety-two percent of some private industries were taken over by government employees. According to historians, "The Confederacy reached levels of government involvement unmatched until the totalitarian states of the twentieth century."[23]

As one author and federal judge pointed out, "The Confederacy was not a clone of the United States with the simple addition of humans being viewed as property. It rejected the American Constitution. It rejected the Bill of Rights. It rejected the very foundation of democracy."[24] (Ironically, the Lost Cause Theorists, who are largely libertarian in nature, and who are extremely anti-socialist, still want to side with the South. They want to side with a people who enslaved other human beings and were walking a fast and direct course to socialism).

Lincoln was particularly concerned about the fact that the Confederacy's founding documents erased any semblance of that American theme of "all men are created equal." Lincoln pointed out that, whereas the U.S. Constitution began with "We the People," the Confederate equivalent began with "We, the deputies of the sovereign and independent States." "Why?" asked Lincoln, "Why this deliberate pressing out of view, the rights of men, and the authority of the people."[25]

The answer: Satan, and his cause from before the world was, had landed squarely in the South. The South had left the covenant and attempted to place the Promised Land under an alternative purpose. Indeed, they buried the U.S. flag and gave themselves a new flag—a new mark.*

Based upon this entire study, it is clear how much Satan despised the U.S. Constitution, even that reflection of the American Covenant. Here was his chance to change it, destroy it, and turn it into something he could use to crush agency unto salvation. Under his evil influence, we may conclude from the evidences above that the South not only feared losing slavery, but all that slavery implied. The South wanted the Constitution left as it was (or made even worse), with all its flawed application that oppressed races, religions, and other minority groups. And when Lincoln came along threatening to change this system, the South fought to preserve it. But more than preserve it, they wanted this evil amended permanently into their new system. They wanted the promise that placed the white man (whether slave-owner or not) above all others

---

* According to the Book of Mormon, a group of Nephites, known as the Amlicites, decided to abandon the principles of democracy and freedom for all, and thus commenced a civil war against their brethren of the national covenant. They distinguished themselves, not only with a new set of rules and intentions, but with a new mark. Ultimately, though they grew in power, they stood on the opposing end of God and covenant. They were summarily destroyed. See Alma 2-3. Perhaps Lincoln gained profound insight from this story. Perhaps he gained resolve to follow in the footsteps of earlier American Covenant-makers.

in society—a system which fed a spirit of intolerance against all those who the majority of white men decided to shun and persecute.

The South had played right into Satan's hand. Do we need to be reminded again that it was this very flawed system of government the South desired (which system the North had only recently begun to abandon pursuant to heaven's vexation), even that flawed constitutional interpretation, which facilitated the driving out of the Church, the murder of God's prophet, and the burning of God's temple?

The examples do not stop there. Apostle Parley P. Pratt was murdered in the South, some three years prior to the Civil War, after converting a woman to the gospel. Her estranged husband disapproved of the conversion. And, in accordance with this accepted and intolerant society the South was fighting to preserve, even a world in which the white male controls all in his "dominion," the assailant caught up with Elder Pratt and killed him in cold blood, stabbing and shooting him in the back.[26] Elder B.H. Roberts recorded the deaths of other LDS missionaries and members in this same general time period: Elder Joseph Standing, killed in Georgia, Elders John Gibbs, William Berry and others killed in Tennessee, and up to four hundred additional Saints killed in the border state of Missouri.[27] The fact that few, if any, of these atrocities carried legal consequences to the offender, further shows the adversary's influence over an evil social order—a social order in need of eradication.

The high number of LDS casualties in Missouri certainly draws our attention to that state. We need make no mistake that, for all intents and purposes, Missouri most certainly embodied the evil, anti-gospel, political system the South was fighting to preserve. Though technically north of the Mason-Dixon line, the Missouri Compromise of 1820 legalized the already active practice of slavery in the state, which had unleashed the oppressive culture that hurt the restored gospel. As one political scholar pointed out, "the spirit of mobocracy loosed against the Mormon people, that ignoble spectre of hate, became characteristic of the controversy over slavery and political power and was to bathe in blood...Missouri...and eventually culminate in Civil War."[28] One Missourian summed it up accurately when he announced that Mormons should not have civil rights "no more than the negroes."[29] The Missouri mobocrats declared, "Mormonism, emancipation and abolitionism must be driven from the state."[30] This was the Southern cry. It was the opposite of God's designs for America. It countered Lincoln's new intention for the war. It directly challenged the American Covenant. This is why Northern victory was imperative: so that Lincoln's vision, backed by the Civil War Amendments, could put these evil designs to rest.

Elder Roberts stated that these murders of the Saints in the South were a direct fulfillment of the Book of Mormon prophecy, which declares that the Restoration would come forth "in a day when the blood of saints shall cry unto the Lord" (Mormon 8:27).[31] Indeed, the cries of the Saints would forever endure under the socio-political system the South was fighting for—that the adversary was fighting for. This system, above all else, which prevailed in the pre-humbled, pre-converted North, and especially in the South, was drowning the Church. With slavery on the rise, thus increasing the evil of all that slavery implied, hope grew dimmer. And as Satan bought his armies and navies in the South to enforce these evil designs, hope grew dimmer still.

The states' rights doctrine was allowing the states to get away with these atrocities, which is precisely why the Prophet Joseph's pleas, provisions, and prophecies took direct aim at states' rights. This is why Joseph called "the states' rights doctrine" a "stink offering in the nose of the Almighty."[32] It is why he called for the Fourteenth Amendment.

The North was getting the message. The South was not. Therefore, the vexation of war had to continue. If the spiritual struggle of the war was only about the North's conversion and positive reaction to the vexation, then it might be argued that, once fully converted to the national covenant, the North could abandon its war effort, allow the South to secede from the Union, then create that one nation under God that would welcome in and protect God's church. However, things were not so simple. This struggle indeed extended beyond Northern conversion; it also included a divine mandate to crush the rebellion. Based upon what we now know concerning the core of the Southern cause, had the South not been defeated, the American Covenant, despite any Northern conversion developing around it, would have remained threatened and perhaps would have eventually been lost. Let us now consider how Southern victory might have presented a dangerous threat to the development and sustainment of the national covenant and, by extension, to God's plan.

First, if the North had allowed Southern victory, and even if it had done so after having fully applied the national covenant to its new and approved northern nation, the blessings of the covenant would have still been threatened. Its new neighbor to the South—the Confederate States of America—would have maintained and proliferated the evil social order that threatened the cause of liberty and salvation. With a shared border, a shared culture, and a shared bloodline, the Confederate States of America would have maintained the ability to greatly influence the Northern government, causing the evils of oppression to seep back in. And if the South had reunited with the North, with slavery remaining intact (as some Northerners and Southerners favored) the nation would be no better off, as the constitutional amendments called for by the Prophet would not have come to light. Either way—whether Southern victory meant total independence or reunification with slavery intact —the evil practice and all the evils growing out of it would continue to attack God's plan. The evil system of the South, therefore, simply could not be tolerated in any form. It had to be disassembled and realigned with the North.

Second, if a truce and treaty created an environment where the Northern United States government attempted to co-exist on the continent with the newly independent Confederate States, conflict would have eventually ensued once again. With much of the western territories still unclaimed and in dispute, both sides would have moved to claim the undeveloped land and implement their competing ideologies therein. Not only would this have left open the opportunity for the evil, anti-gospel, social order of the South to spread, but such an adversarial relationship between the two American governments would not have been conducive to the covenant land designed by God to be a source of peace and security for His gospel. In fact, this adversarial relationship would have perpetually left the door open for subsequent and future civil wars to disrupt the land of promise.

Third, had the North given up, allowing the South to win its independence, there is no guarantee that those converted Northerners would have been able to influence the desired changes under God in the new and improved "Northern United States" government. Too many in the North, perhaps, had not yet been converted. Arguably, full Northern conversion to the principles of the covenant did not occur until the North witnessed God's hand in delivering victory to the North. It was this fuller witness of God's doing that provided the Union with the courage, strength, and moral authority to make sure the constitutional provisions called for by the Prophet would come to light and secure the covenant. In short, Southern victory might have prevented the vexation to run its full course, not only for Southerners but for Northerners as well.

Fourth, God had established *all* of America as His base of operations to serve His purposes under the covenant. Even if the North began to fully apply the covenant to itself, ignoring the South, how many millions of Americans in the South, unconverted to, and unaffected by, the national covenant, would have fallen short of their divine destiny? How many souls, then, might have been lost through Southern victory? Furthermore, consider all the good America has brought the world—freedom through strength. A divided nation would not have been able to generate such strength. A successful rebellion might have set a precedent that would have led other states to similarly rebel, creating many separate nations throughout the would-be United States. With so many independent nation-states, it might have looked today like Central America currently does. It might have, then, generated about as much power for good as Central America does today. Indeed, all of this would have further divided and weakened the power for good which God granted the world through the Constitution. Southern defeat was imperative, then, so the North could bring the covenant to *all* of America. Remember, God created the Union by the Constitution He Himself claimed to have influenced (see D&C 101:80). Was He just kidding? Did He not really intend to make this Union? Was it all the same to Him whether this Union remained or not—whether states left as they pleased in order to practice wickedness? "What therefore God hath joined together, let not man put asunder" (Mark 10:9).

Fifth, there is a moral obligation to cleanse the Promised Land of wickedness. The South spawned this wickedness against God's children and seemed to delight in it. How could the North be God's covenant nation and turn a blind eye to such wickedness in its own backyard, especially when they had the power to reach out and help? There was a moral obligation to bring the South back into the fold, cleansed and worthy, where it had always belonged. Remember, God had placed the South under the American Covenant as well as the North.

Finally, if the North had permitted Southern victory, then the nations of the world would have claimed victory over their guarded belief that democracies do not work. Democracy thereafter would have been a failed experiment not to be tested again, thus frustrating God's plan to spread a fullness of agency throughout the world in preparation for His Restoration.

All together then, leaving the South alone was not an option to the God-fearing North. The Union had to crush the rebellion for the eternal designs of the Almighty.

In Chapter 4, we discussed the Anti-Lincoln / Pro-South theorists, who believe (even today) that the South's defeat drastically weakened the nation and made us all less free. We pointed out how these theorists see freedom as the ability for states to do what they want without federal intervention. Their problem is that they somehow think that "states' rights" today (which is defined as states' freedom from the burden of federal intervention in things like healthcare, education, etc.), is the same thing as "states' rights" in the days of Joseph Smith and Abraham Lincoln (which was defined as states' freedom from the burden of federal intervention to liberate enslaved races and prevent the beating and killing of minority religionists like the Mormons). One definition (of today) represents something true and noble. The other (of the Civil War days) represents the exact opposite. That the theorists cannot see this clear difference—that they cannot see how the definition of "states' rights" has drastically evolved—explains their strange perspectives on the Civil War. And of these strange perspectives, nothing is stranger than their views on slavery.

We discussed how many of these theorists have drawn a neat little box and filled it with ideas concerning how things were always meant to be in America (e.g. states always have had the right to secede, the federal government should never have grown, etc.). But they have run into a problem. What do they do about slavery? History is clear that Southern motive for the war revolved around this evil practice, but recognizing this evil practice forces disruptions within the theorists' neat little boxes. The result produces one of the most ironic commentaries in American historical perspectives—that these liberty-loving / liberty promoting theorists argue against the mechanism that brought freedom to the most oppressed people ever to walk the land. It is the epitome of what Victor Hugo called "being ultra." As quoted earlier, Hugo defined it as "to champion things to the point of becoming their enemy; it is to be so pro you become con."[33]

So, what do the theorists do? They deny history. They deny slavery was the issue at hand. Contrary to the evidence put forth previously (and contrary to simple logic), they claim the Emancipation Proclamation did *nothing* to free slaves. They claim Lincoln was a racists who never wanted to free slaves. And, flying once again in the face of history, they claim that the virtuous and noble South was not fighting for slavery and was, in fact, going to free the slaves on their own.[34] Their evidence? They quote the Southern leadership who made these claims. What they do not tell you is *when* the Southern leadership made these claims. For, almost always, they made them *after* their defeat.

Apparently, the theorists do not stop to contemplate why the timing of these Southern commentaries are relevant. Though Jefferson Davis, and the others, had clearly stated their purpose for the war, *during* the war, what were they to say *after* the slaves were freed? It was fine for them to speak of slavery's benign normalcy while the slaves were still slaves. But, after witnessing an entire people achieving liberation out from under you, what do you say now? What do you say if you are Jefferson Davis? Do you declare, *Oh yes, our cause of enslaving people because of the color of their skin was great and righteous! Tearing children from the desperate, prying grips of their mothers and fathers was a fine system. Too bad we lost that war!*? Of course not. You wipe the egg off your face as soon as possible and scramble for another reason. You point out other real issues that had existed (like tariff disagreements) and place the entire emphasis of your war efforts on all things that are *not* slavery. Unless you do this, you cannot claim, as Jefferson Davis did some twenty years after the war, that "African servitude was in no wise the cause of the conflict, but only an incident."[35]

As summed up by historian Dwight Pitcaithy, "The South knew why it had to secede from the Union and said so through letters and speeches of its secession commissioners. With stunning clarity [we are reminded] that race and slavery were at the center of the march toward secession." All other justifications were, as historian Ron Andersen pointed out, "a medium to cover up their true designs."[36] Sadly, the theorists get duped by the tactic. Why they refuse to believe what the Southerners *themselves* said during the war is beyond comprehension.

Furthermore, as we already discussed, the Prophet Joseph prophesied of the Civil War, declaring that it would commence in

South Carolina. Joseph stated in the scripture that the war "would probably arise through the slave question. This a voice declared to me, while I was praying earnestly on the subject" (see D&C 130:12-13; 87:1-5). If the war really was not about slavery, as the theorists claim, then the Lord sure had a bizarre explanation for its commencement.

But, in order to find resolution to this dispute (still raging today), we do not need to justify whose position is correct based on who said *what when*. We need only consult our own hearts on the matter. During the Civil War, there were approximately 4,000,000 slaves in the South.[37] About one third of slave marriages ended in a greedy business decision by the master, and over one half of all slave children lost at least one of their parents (and many times both of their parents) for the same reason.[38] There is no more important institution to the Lord than the family. The Southern system obliterated families as a matter of state policy. And we can add to this iniquity the extreme physical and sexual abuse hurled upon the slaves throughout the land.

As a young man doing business in the South, Lincoln would have seen advertisements, such as the following (which actually existed): "I will at all times pay the highest cash price for Negroes of every description, will also attend to the sale of Negroes on commission, having a jail and yard fitted up expressly for boarding them." Another read, "For sale—several likely girls from 10 to 18 years old, a woman 24, a very valuable woman 25, with three very likely children."[39] Upon seeing this misery, the young Lincoln turned to his companion and stated, "Boy, let's get away from this. If ever I get a chance to hit that thing [slavery] I'll hit it hard."[40]

The theorists do not deny these atrocities happened, but they say that the Civil War was not the answer. They say that these atrocities would have died on their own? But *when*? *How*? There was no guarantee this would have happened, or happened very soon, especially on its own. So many (including Joseph Smith and Abraham Lincoln) had tried for a peaceful end to it all. And yet, the evil only grew. Joseph and Abraham finally concluded, like so many others, that something awful and drastic (like war) would be required.

Furthermore, some regions practiced slavery for centuries, while others still practice it today.[41] Who can say that America might not still be plagued by this sin today had it not been for the great vexation? After all, the evidence proves that the South fully intended to dig its heals in deeper than ever before to see that slavery had a powerful base from which to flourish. Or, if it truly was destined to peacefully pass away, *when*? *When* would the South have released its grip? One decade? Two? How long must the Promised Land endure this? Perhaps the Lord permitted some measure of tolerance for the first generation nation-builders. After all, the Founders *had* to tolerate it in order for the South to enter the Union. This was a necessary step, lest the North and the federal government never gain access to the suffering slaves within the newly formed Union.

The theorists cannot provide a time frame for *when*, and they do not seem to care much. I would ask them, what if it were *your* wife? *Your* child? Would you simply say, *well, at some point in the indefinite future the suffering will stop*. Of course not. You would do all you could to stop the suffering. You certainly would not let some vague, subjective interpretation of the Constitution stop you. In fact, the theorists would readily admit that to allow one's child to suffer this way is sinful, cold-hearted, and cruel. Yet, when it comes to slavery and the Civil War, the theorists side with those who took that sinful, cruel, and cold-hearted approach. The true answer, and the one the theorists blush to give, is: *well, it was not my wife. It was not my child*. But they *were* Heavenly Father's children. They were (and are) your brothers and sisters. Does this count for anything?

The theorists love to say they would be bound by the law. They quote from the Declaration of Independence, which states that "whenever any form of government becomes destructive of these ends, it is the right of the people to alter or to abolish it, and to institute new Government...in such a form, as to them shall seem most likely to effect their safety and happiness." It is true that the federal government had indeed threatened to be "destructive" to the form of government that provided the South with its "safety and happiness." And so, *independence*, yelp the theorists, *was theirs to proclaim*. The theorists ignore, however, that the thing that was destructive to Southern happiness was the idea that the federal government might steal their slavery away—that their state right to oppress might be stripped from them. Is this what the Founders intended by these words? Did God, who had inspired the Declaration of Independence, perceive that the South had appropriately applied this principle? Would the Lord really concede that His most important spiritual law "to love one another" is so easily trumped by a subjective interpretation of the political law He also provided? And yet, the theorists allow themselves to be duped yet again.

The way to achieve clarity on this matter is to view history through the lens of the national covenant. Doing so makes it impossible to hide behind so-called legal interpretations. Let us see clearly with the covenant in the forefront of our minds. This is what Lincoln and Seward did. Speaking about slavery, Seward declared, "There is a higher law than the Constitution, which regulates our authority over this domain, and devotes it to the same noble purposes." "Does it therefore follow," asked Seward, "that Congress may amend the ten commandments, or reverse the principles of Christ's Sermon on the Mount...? Man could not, by any law, make right what God and his own conscience [the Light of Christ] declared wrong."[42] Things will turn out bad if man attempts to amend or reinterpret the American Covenant.

In the end, slavery, in and of itself, was bad enough to justify the North's new vision for the war. It is enough, alone, to justify standing today with the North on the correct side of history. And yet, as noted above, there is even more reason to stand with the North. Adding insult to injury upon the theorists' position (especially the Mormon theorists' position), is the notion that slavery also led to the atrocities against all minorities—God's church and kingdom included.

The conclusion is as clear as it is tragic. Blinded by their preconceived notions, and ignoring both scriptural and historical evidence (not to mention conscience), the theorists continue to frame the war as North: oppressors of states' rights, versus South: noble freedom-fighters. Though all evidence points in the opposite direction. It was, in actuality, North: bearers of the covenant blessings of liberty, versus South: preservers of a state's right to rule with blood and horror over the innocent—to legally enslave a race and to legally issue an extermination order against the Saints of God. Indeed, it was a clear war of oppression versus freedom, as prophesied by scripture and as understood by the Prophet of the Restoration. It was an extension of the war in heaven.

God in the North: Eternal Victory By and For the Covenant

Upon recognizing the adversary's evil doings, designed to thwart God's plans and purposes for America, it becomes all the more clear why God intervened and facilitated the great American vexation. His plan was perfectly calculated. First, humble the North through the scourge of war, thus converting it to the cause of the covenant; and second, with the now humbled and converted North, eradicate the Southern system of government that threatened to obstruct the plan of salvation. As the North grew in its understanding and application of the covenant principles of *national repentance* and *universal agency*, it would not only gain the blessings of heaven to defeat the enemy, but would take these principles and with them consume the Evil One's stronghold. The North, under God, would consume this stronghold by breaking it down and then applying to it the covenant principles through the inspired constitutional provisions called for by the Prophet Joseph. (Though the South would not respond to the vexation as rapidly as the North, the South would eventually succumb and enter the covenant, as will be detailed later.) Then would the prophecy be fulfilled. Then would the covenant be strengthened and activated for the salvation of mankind.

With this big picture in mind, the true and eternal significance of the war is almost overwhelming. The Civil War truly was a struggle that transcended world history, for it had its roots and true beginnings in the pre-mortal existence and its consequences would extend into eternity. It was not just a war of the ages, but a war of the cosmos. As one influential Northerner, George Washington Julian, prophetically declared, it had become "a fight... between God and the Devil—between Heaven and Hell."[43]

Julian's declaration was not an isolated idea. It is clear that the born-again American Covenant-makers, within the now converted North, felt the heavenly power of what they were doing, particularly upon recognizing what evil the South represented. In the preceding chapter, we detailed how the North had become converted to the covenant principles. This conversion is summed up by a minister from Gettysburg who, in response to the Battle of Gettysburg, had this to say about the war's purpose: "The deadly war that is now waging, is, on the one hand, the price we are paying for past and present complicity with iniquity [*national repentance*]; on the other, it is the cost of...the realization of the grand idea enunciated in the Declaration of Independence [*universal agency*]." But it was not only seen as an internal issue that Northerners had to work out. It was also seen as an issue that equally involved the evil Southern system. The minister declared that this Southern system was the "mortal antagonist of Democratic Institutions," and that Northern victory would mean "a higher, purer, nobler national life and character"—a higher national life and character not only compared to the old Northern way, but especially as compared to the Southern system of evil. Concluded the minister, "God forbid" the war should "stop short of this glorious end."[44] These words, published by Robert Harper, indeed spoke for the Northern heart. The great Northern conversion would translate into action against the South.

The scholar Carwardine recognized how the North's conversion compelled its efforts against the South, writing that Southern rebellion had become for the North an "act of destruction that challenged God's Providence." James Moorhead agreed, opining that the war had become an effort "infused with a new moral significance...The holy Union that Northerners defended was no longer the compromise-tainted object of earlier years; it was democratic civilization in collision with an alien way of life."[45] As historians Larry Schweikart and Michael Allen put it, "America's Civil War was ultimately and overwhelmingly about the idea of freedom: whether one group of people could restrict the God-given liberty of others."[46]

As Lincoln was at the heart of Northern conversion, it is no surprise that he too understood how this conversion came with a mandate to destroy the adversary's system embedded in the South. Lincoln called the conflict "the eternal struggle," and even described it as a prophet might describe the War in Heaven. He explained that this struggle was about "two principles that have stood face to face from the beginning of time; and will ever continue to struggle. The one is the common right of humanity [God's gift of agency unto salvation] and the other is the divine right of kings [Satan's plan of obstruction]." Lincoln continued, "No matter in what shape it comes, whether from the mouth of a king who seeks to bestride the people of his own nation...or from one race of men as an apology for enslaving another race, it is the same tyrannical principle."[47] Lincoln would later add that the Confederacy's efforts were "an attempt to overthrow this government, which was built upon the foundation of human rights, and to substitute for it one which should rest exclusively on the basis of human slavery."[48]

The soldiers' and peoples' testimonies of the same naturally followed. According to Union soldier Abraham Irvine, an Irish immigrant whose family all lived in Europe, the conflict pitted "the defenders of freedom, the champions of liberty" against "those enemies of humanity, of Liberty, & God, who would tear to attoms [sic]...the best government that the world ever knew." It was, according to Irvine, a fight between "humanity and liberty" on one side and "despotism and oppression" on the other. It was a fight the North must win, not only for Americans, but for his family in despotic Europe as well. Irvine said Northern victory was for all "who would be free."[49] Another witness was Private Leigh Webber. He too understood that Northern victory meant the destruction of an evil system for a righteous one. "If all this untold expense of blood and treasure, of toil and suffering, of want and sacrifice, of grief and mourning is...to result in no greater good than the restoration of the Union as it was," wondered Private Webber in 1863, "what will it amount to?" It certainly would not, he concluded, amount to "real and lasting good." Fighting for "the Union under old construction" was, according to Private Thomas Covert, not sufficient anymore: "We now want a new one."[50]

Northern testimonies that the war truly was about a deep conflict that pitted good against evil continued further. Illinois Congregationalists told Lincoln that Southern rebellion equated "the revolt against the Divine scheme for the world's advance in civilization and religion."[51] A common message published in the North during the conflict was: "One God! One Union! One People...all the powers of hell are just now against us."[52] The Chicago Tribune hailed the war as "in its profoundest aspect, a religious contest...a war for Christian civilization, for God's pure truth." After Union victory, then, asserted the paper, nothing "shall prevent the American Union from being, henceforth the crowning national work of the Almighty, the wonder of the world."[53]

Julia Ward Howe
Courtesy of the Library of Congress

Another influential Northerner declared the conflict to be "Christ's doctrine of righteousness conflicting with evil."[54] One Ohio corporal wrote his wife that there was, what he called, a *"big Idea"* at stake in the war, namely "the principles of Liberty, of Justice, and of Righteousness which exalteth a nation."[55] Another Union soldier wrote his wife that "Everyday I have a more religious feeling, that this war is a crusade for the good of mankind."[56] The following poem was printed on commonly used Northern stationary during the war: "for right is right, as God is God / And right will surely win; to doubt would be disloyalty— / to falter would be sin."[57]

Orville Browning told Lincoln that the war was "God entering into judgment" with the South, and that the Union cause was "as holy...as ever engaged men's feelings." One U.S. Senator added that "God the Almighty must be with us."[58] And Wisconsin Wesleyans prophesied to Lincoln that Union victory would cause that "our light Shall break forth as the morning. Our health Shall Spring forth Speedily and the glory of the Lord Shall be our reward."[59]

One of the most powerful and enduring testimonies from the Civil War came from a Northern woman named Julia Ward Howe—a true prophetess of the American Covenant. Ms. Howe was very religious and had been watching the war and had been pondering and internalizing the war's purposes. One night she had a revelation. She explained:

> I awoke in the grey of the morning, and as I lay waiting for the dawn, the long lines of the desired poem began to entwine themselves in my mind, and I said to myself, 'I must get up and write these verses, lest I fall asleep and forget them!' So I sprang out of bed and in the dimness found an old stump of a pen, which I remembered using the day before. I scrawled the verses almost without looking at the paper.[60]

What she had written were the lyrics of the hymn we call today The "Battle Hymn of the Republic." But more than the inspired manner in which the lyrics came to be, the real power comes from the words themselves. They represent knowledge perhaps only attainable through revelation. Indeed, they echo the revelations of Joseph Smith. They appear to have fallen directly out of the D&C 101 prophecy explaining why the Lord must vex the nation.

For instance, the lyrics state that the Lord is "trampling out the vintage [the yield of wine during one season] where the grapes of wrath [the wicked] are stored." They further express how the Lord "hath loosed the fateful lightening of His terrible swift sword." They declare, "I have seen Him in the watch fires of a hundred circling camps; They have builded Him an altar in the evening dews and damps." The hymn continues, "I have read a fiery gospel," which declares and exhorts: "Let the Hero, born of woman, crush the serpent with His heel." Finally, "He is sifting out the hearts of men before His judgment seat; Oh, be swift, my soul, to answer Him! Be jubilant, my feet; Our God is marching on." And consider what the hymn concludes is the ultimate fruit of the war. From a gospel perspective, and in light of the reason God gave—in D&C 101—as to why He would bring the vexation, this climactic phrase is powerful indeed: "His truth is marching on!"

Perhaps most stunning is a single line that has since been adapted for a modern audience. After singing about Christ being "born across the sea" and how we access His atoning sacrifice "that transfigures you and me," we sing the phrase: "As he died to make men holy, let us live to make men free." Only, the original lyrics stated, "As he died to make men holy, let us *die* to make men free."[61] The North knew the correct version, and they marched to it in war. Consider what they understood. They knew there was an atoning sacrifice offered by the Savior of mankind, but that in order to fully access it, man must first be free. And so, they would fight against the Serpent's plan of oppression—they would "*die* to make men free." With the Southern system abolished, temples would at last be free to stand unburned and unmolested. Then, Christ's atoning sacrifice could be made available in its fullness.

The hymn was first published in February 1862, precisely when Lincoln was passing through his deep conversion to the covenant—precisely when his Willie was dying, when he possessed the Book of Mormon, and when he received his revelations. It was that precise time during which he experienced his "process of crystallization," a time during which he "constantly prayed."[62] The hymn was published with the title: "A Battle Hymn for the Northern Republic During the Civil War." During a public service, Army Chaplain Charles Caldwell McCabe sang the hymn. Lincoln was present and he watched and listened in awe. "The effect was magical, people shouted, wept, and sang together...and above the applause was heard the voice of Abraham Lincoln, exclaiming while the tears rolled down his cheeks, 'Sing it again.'"[63]

The North had learned its covenant purpose in the war. The boys in blue, and their righteous supporters, had received and born testimony that they were, in fact, fighting on the righteous side of a war "between God and the Devil—between Heaven and Hell."

Much of our analysis of the Civil War has thus far focused on statements, declarations, and testimonies that support themes related to the American Covenant (these include broad-brush themes such as *national repentance* and *universal agency*). However, in presenting a somewhat abstract and thematic analysis of Northern conversion, we have sacrificed the telling of the entire story in its chronological order and with its many key events that make up the impressive narrative. And yet this narrative (in its chronological outline) provides us with some of the finest evidence of the existence and power of the American

Covenant and God's firm placement in the Northern cause. The narrative tells the story of how the North's conversion translated into the reactivation of the American Covenant, which translated into blessings from Heaven, which enabled victory over the South and a dismantling of evil designs. This, of course, led to an even stronger covenant and to a larger measure of the covenant blessings that would supply the Restoration with what it needed to thrive. Our chronological narrative of the war left off (in preceding chapters) at the time of the North's conversion, which largely revolved around the issuance of the Emancipation Proclamation. We will now pick up the narrative from this point in history to see how the many themes we have discussed fit together with the historical events leading to the North's victory over the South and thus to God's victory over the adversary.

For a premise to this fascinating narrative, we turn to the great John Quincy Adams. Though he died some ten years before the Civil War, for all intents and purposes, Adams had been fighting this war his entire life. At age seventy-four, Adams defined this struggle when he accepted the call to defend a group of slaves who were being charged for having mutinied aboard the slave ship *Amistad*: "The world, the flesh, and all the devils in hell are arrayed against any man, who now, in this North-American Union, shall dare to join the standard of Almighty God, to put down the African-American slave-trade...what can I do for the cause of God and man? for the progress of human emancipation?...Yet my conscience presses me on."[64]

Unlike Adams, Lincoln and his Northern faithful had been placed in the rare position of being able to actually conquer hell on this matter. The eternal conflict had once again come to a critical juncture here in mortality, just as it had so many times before. And this time Abraham Lincoln and his faithful had taken center stage, particularly after the Northern war machine took aim directly at the adversary through the Emancipation Proclamation. It was one of those critical moments in which light meets dark, and as the eternal laws of physics command, both could not occupy the same space at the same time; or in Lincoln's prophetic words (borrowed from the Bible), "A house divided against itself cannot stand."[65]

Many of the final events leading to Northern victory were carried out by Lincoln's spiritual strength and resolve. Lincoln had received much of this spiritual power from the spiritual sentiments of the nation. There was, for example, the old preacher who (during this time of national realignment of purpose) prayed with arms lifted at a fast and prayer meeting just outside the White House: "O Lord command the sun & moon to stand still while your Joshua, Abraham Lincoln, fights the battle of freedom." There was similar encouragement from others. One White House visitor from Buffalo told Lincoln, "Up our way, we believe in God and Abraham Lincoln." Congressmen William Kelley declared that "the Lord has given us this man to keep as long as we can." The Methodist John Scripps reminded Lincoln that, by accepting the call as chief over the Union and over the conflict which rocked the nation, he had "voluntarily accepted the highest responsibility which any one not endowed with the Godhead can assume." Another minister told him, "It is your high mission under God to save us." Still others repeatedly offered Lincoln their belief that "God has raised [you] up for such a time as this." They left him with the blessed reminder, in the words of one correspondent, that "the daily prayer of millions" is that "Heaven give you and your Advisors the Wisdom for Our emergency."[66]

The people knew what their leader needed, and so they did what they could to endow him with spiritual strength. Lincoln's response to the nation was one of deep gratitude. He was grateful for "the effective and almost unanimous support," as he told a group of Baptists, "which the Christian communities are so zealously giving to the country."[67] These believers in God and covenant had certainly added to Lincoln's already oft-expressed belief that he humbly had become an "agent of divine providence."[68*] Lincoln often spoke of his "firm reliance upon the Divine arm," and readily acknowledged that he was "a humble instrument in the hands of our Heavenly Father."[69] His own

---

* As witnessed throughout this study, Lincoln often referred to himself as *an instrument in the hands of God*. There are more than ten instances in the Book of Mormon where servants of the Almighty are referred to as "instruments in the hands of God " (See 2 Nephi 1:24; 2 Nephi 3: 24; Mosiah 23: 10; Mosiah 27:36; Alma 1:8; Alma 2:30; Alma 17: 9, 11; Alma 26: 3, 15; Alma 29:9; Alma 35: 14). Conversely, this particular phraseology is nowhere to be found in the Bible.

recognition of the divine intent behind the conflict, and the growing national recognition of the same, was largely responsible for his now unwavering stance on God's purposes: "I expect to maintain this contest until successful, or till I die, or am conquered, or my term expires, or Congress or the Country forsakes me."[70] Lincoln's firm resolve—symbolically displayed by the clenched fist depicted in his statue at the Lincoln Memorial—was summed up by a Chicago city lawyer who declared, "You may depend upon it, the Lord runs Lincoln," to which a local Methodist preacher responded, calling that statement "the true theory and solution of this terrible war."[71]

Beyond his relentless war campaign from the beginning, we can certainly sense Lincoln's strong will and drive, under God, for the principles of civil and religious freedom. This unwavering will is evident throughout the remarkable events that occurred in the wake of emancipation and led the Union to final victory. A notable aspect of many of these key events was that Lincoln perpetuated them himself. He seemed to comprehend that his heaven-derived resolve would have to inspire the nation when nothing else could. As the war made its final turns, Lincoln stood firmly, as Carwardine put it, "gripping the strategic reins"[72] while others struggled to hang on to the wagon. Such endurance was imperative because—though much of the North had responded penitently to the war and had thus changed their hearts—the South had not yet been redeemed, making it necessary for the vexation and purge to continue until the entire nation was sufficiently pure.

The first of the key post-emancipation events, following chronologically, occurred in November 1862, just months after the crucial victory at Antietam—the battle which (in many ways) marked the birth of the Emancipation Proclamation. In a move that stunned America, Lincoln fired the hero-general of the battle, George B. McClellan. The firing came after Lincoln learned that McClellan refused to pursue the South aggressively. Perhaps Lincoln understood that McClellan's reticence stemmed from his deeply held opinion that slavery should not be eradicated. The general had, after all, at an earlier time, arrogantly and inappropriately informed the president that slavery should remain. He had so testified to Lincoln in an official memorandum.[73]

Furthermore, a Union Major named John Key, whose brother was a personal aide to McClellan, was found guilty by Lincoln of having perpetuated and supported a secret strategy. Key had believed that the object of the Union's refusal to pursue and destroy the Southern army, particularly in the wake of Antietam, was to ensure no great advantage for either side. This would produce a stalemate which would force the exhausted nation to compromise on slavery, permitting its continual existence. Once he had learned of the secret intent, Lincoln immediately dismissed Key from the Union army.[74]

With his mind and heart on human freedom, along with his belief that this was his new mission under God, how could Lincoln possibly allow the general, the major, or any others who might obstruct this divine mandate, to remain in a position of influence? Lincoln's bold action was yet another testament of the covenant he was fighting for.

It should be of little wonder then, that within months of this change-up, Lincoln issued one of the most powerful calls to the covenant ever given in America—the March 1863 call to *national repentance* cited in the previous chapter. It declared to the nation that the war was "a punishment inflicted upon us for our presumptuous sins" to realize "our national reformation as a whole people." Lincoln called upon the nation "to confess their sins" and remember that "those nations only are blessed whose God is the Lord."[75] That the people had accepted and internalized these sentiments, as a result of the national vexation, is evidenced by the testimonies provided in the previous chapter from the people themselves concerning their conversion to the covenant principle of *national repentance*.

Such an invocation of—and adherence to—the covenant would certainly call down the covenant blessings; and within a few months of Lincoln's powerful call to the nation, blessings indeed arrived in a powerful way. In early July 1863, the Union defeated the

South in the single battle that forever turned the tide of war in favor of the North—Gettysburg. Apart from providing a venue for Lincoln's great and gospel-connected speech on *universal agency*, Gettysburg was special for other spiritual reasons that reinforced Lincoln and reminded him whose cause he was really fighting for. In order to present these spiritual reasons within their proper context, it is important to understand the framework within which this crucial battle was fought.

General Lee had again led his Southern troops into Northern territory seeking the final blow to win his cause. He was eventually met by Union forces at and around the sleepy town of Gettysburg, Pennsylvania. Both sides had gathered together an enormous number of troops, and everybody knew that if Lee could push past his Union foes, there was nothing stopping him from marching into and taking Washington D.C. The fate of the Union, and by extension the godly freedoms it was to protect, literally hung on the outcome of this battle. Edward Everett, the keynote speaker of the Gettysburg National Cemetery dedication, concluded that the Battle of Gettysburg had determined if America "should live, a glory and a light to all coming time, or should expire like the meteor of a moment."[76] After three days of fierce fighting, which left countless bodies scattered across the countryside, the Union prevailed, causing Lee to retreat once again back into the South.

In light of the eternal consequences of Gettysburg, the following account of what Lincoln was experiencing in Washington D.C., even while the battle raged, is ever so significant. Lincoln offered the following personal account days after the battle to a then bedridden General Dan Sickles, who had lost a leg at Gettysburg and was now back at the capital struggling to recover. According to General Sickles (and General James Rusling, who was also present), Lincoln stated the following:

> In the pinch of the campaign up there [at Gettysburg] when everybody seemed panic stricken and nobody could tell what was going to happen, oppressed by the gravity of our

affairs, I went to my room one day and locked the door and got down on my knees before Almighty God and prayed to Him mightily for victory at Gettysburg. I told Him that this was His war, and our cause His cause...And I then and there made a solemn vow to Almighty God, that if He would stand by our boys at Gettysburg, I would stand by him. And he did stand by your boys, and I will stand by Him....Never before had I prayed with so much earnestness. I wish I could repeat my prayer. I felt I must put all my trust in Almighty God. He gave our people the best country ever given to man. He alone could save it from destruction. I had tried my best to do my duty and found myself unequal to the task. The burden was more than I could bear. I asked Him to help us and give us victory now....And after that, I don't know how it was, and I cannot explain it, but soon a sweet comfort crept into my soul. The feeling came that God had taken the whole business into His own hands and that things would go right at Gettysburg....I was sure my prayer was answered. I had no misgivings about Gettysburg.[77]*

Lincoln's prayer was a clear invocation, by the leader of a nation, of the national covenant with the Almighty. His prayer was answered. When Lincoln came to Gettysburg in the aftermath of battle to deliver his famous speech, it was altogether fitting that as he slowly walked through the death fields of Gettysburg and viewed the freshly dug graves through tear-filled eyes, he was heard saying, "I gave myself to God, and now I can say that I do love Jesus."[78] One of the greatest declarations and descriptions of the American Covenant is found in Ether 2:12, where America is called a "choice land" to be "free from bondage" as long as the people

---

* As Lincoln stood to leave General Sickles' bedside, the general related that "Mr. Lincoln took my hand in his and said with tenderness, 'Sickles, I have been told, as you have been told perhaps, that your condition is serious. I am in a prophetic mood today. You will get well." And he most certainly did. See Kunhardt, et al, *The American President* (New York: Riverhead Books, 1999), 336.

adhere to the "God of the land, who is Jesus Christ." Lincoln's quiet comment seems particularly relevant.

The American Covenant would become even more pronounced on that historic day. As Lincoln wiped the tears from his eyes and stood to deliver his most famous speech at Gettysburg, he touched the very core of this national covenant and challenged his countrymen to enter into it. As explained last chapter, the speech promoted the idea that the war's new purpose was the American Covenant principle of *universal agency*; and then came the invitation to the nation to reengage under this covenant and its principles: "It is rather for us to be here dedicated to the great task remaining before us—that from these honored dead we take increased devotion to that cause for which they gave the last full measure of devotion...that this nation, under God, shall have a new birth of freedom." The Gettysburg Address was a call to the covenant. And the covenant connection expanded even further as witnesses and scholars expressed a belief that Lincoln's speech was an effort to present a "vision of God's American Israel that reconnected it to God's original Israel."[79] Furthermore, as noted by these same witnesses and scholars, the people in the North responded to Lincoln's call to the covenant at Gettysburg by devouring his words and "immersing [themselves] in one fastening ritual, creating community."[80] They became a *covenant community*.

God further assisted the nation in its recognition and adherence to the covenant by providing a sign of its power and veracity. On the very day the Union achieved victory at Gettysburg, another simultaneous and significant Union victory occurred at the Battle of Vicksburg. The fact that both of these key Union victories—on opposite sides of an embattled America—occurred on July 4, 1863 (Independence Day) was received by the North, according Manning, as an announcement of "divine intervention and reawakened Union soldiers' millennial understanding of the war."[81] It was during this spiritually jubilant time that a surge in the religious and spiritual nature of the conflict began to congeal. As such, most of the quotes and examples (listed and noted previously) that refer to the North's newfound belief that the war was now about *national repentance* and *universal agency* under God, surfaced, most prominently, during this time.[82] Sgt J.G Nind summed up well these feelings in his own post-Gettysburg/Vicksburg reflections when he stated that now the "nation will be purified" and "God will accomplish his vast designs."[83]

Shortly after Gettysburg another incident occurred that reflected the divine purpose of the war and partially fulfilled the gospel prophecies of the war in dramatic fashion. It began on July 15, 1863, when Lincoln issued his Proclamation of Thanksgiving. In his proclamation, Lincoln encouraged Americans to pray and give thanks. In doing so, he invoked the "Holy Spirit…to change the hearts of the insurgents."[84] And who were the insurgents? Obviously they included the Confederates and those of the pro-slave movement in general. And certainly they should have *especially* included any group that aligned themselves with such oppressive movements *and* had wielded such oppression over God's church and kingdom. If the many aforementioned gospel prophecies concerning the socio-political elevation of the Church were fulfilled through the Civil War, then we should certainly expect to see those enemies of the Church, who caused its oppression, to be affected, humbled, and positively changed by the war.

In Chapter 3, we discussed these prophecies. Specifically, we discussed how the vexation would, according to D&C 121, single out those who had "lift[ed] up the heel against mine anointed" and who had "[sworn] falsely against my servants, that they might bring them into bondage." Indeed, the war would target those who had "driv[en], and murder[ed], and testif[ied] against them [the Saints]." In other words, the punishment would fall upon the same group of people that persecuted the prophet and his people. (In this same prophecy, the Lord provides further evidence that that same generation would suffer the vexation by stating that "in not many years hence…they and their posterity shall be swept from under heaven.") This punishment and corrective action would fall upon these "children of disobedience," even to the point that "their basket shall not be full," and that "their houses and their barns shall perish" (See D&C 121:11-24).[85]

We have already established that these principal insurgents against the Church resided in and around Jackson County Missouri, and that these offenders had suffered greatly during the war. As David McCullough pointed out, the Civil War in Missouri began some seven years before it began in the rest of the country: "It was a war of plunder, ambush and unceasing revenge. Nobody was safe. Defenseless towns were burned...Neither then nor later did the rest of the country realize the extent of the horrors."[86]

In particular, there was one stunning and dramatic event which occurred within weeks of Lincoln's appeal for corrective action to "change the hearts of the insurgents." It was called General Order No. 11. By August 1863, the Union army had recognized the mobocracy in Missouri that continually attacked those trying to support the Union and the eradication of slavery. It was this same mobocracy, perpetuated by the same groups of people, against freedom and liberty that had almost snuffed out the Saints years earlier. Indeed, it was the same evil spirit of oppression introduced by the adversary to limit eternal progression and to impede the gospel plan; and it was this very evil that had, therefore, become the principal target of God's vexation. That a hotbed of wicked rebellion was found in this region of the nation should be of little surprise—the adversary had set up camp there years earlier for the purpose of obstructing God's work in the sacred land of Zion. And the adversary had not, as-of-yet, vacated the premises. As one witness put it, "The Devil came to the border [state], liked it, and stayed awhile."[87]

This time around, the evil power was specifically directed at anti-slavery supporters, and the Union army had seen enough. And where exactly within Missouri did the Union army see this spirit of mobocracy and destruction against the innocent? The answer is almost too fitting: Jackson County, along with a few other surrounding counties. General Order No.11, issued on August 25, 1863, forced these residents from their homes "and commanded that their homes be burned"—which decree was carried out forthwith.[88] The D&C prophecy—that "their houses and barns shall perish"—had been fulfilled to the letter.

Evidence that this corrective action perhaps was successful is seen in General Order No. 20, issued months later. This order allowed all those who would take an oath of allegiance to the Union, and prove this allegiance, to return to their homes.[89]* In light of what we know the Union now stood for—even those principles of the American Covenant —Jackson County residents willing to enter this oath were, in a sense, entering the American Covenant. They were promising to stand behind a policy based upon the covenant principles of *national repentance* and *universal agency*. Whether they recognized it or not, the very same persecutors of Joseph Smith and the Church were now complying with the very principles Joseph had worked tirelessly to get them to comply with in his lifetime—the very principles God had promised to influence them to accept through His terrible vexation should they reject the efforts of His prophet. The vexation, once again, appeared to be doing its job. As these residents took their oaths, after having been swept from their homes, one wonders if they reflected upon "old Joe Smith." Did they remember that he had warned them that this very thing would occur to them should they choose not to repent? Did they recognize that he had told them all this could be avoided if they would but treat the Saints and others with civility? Did they comprehend that they had, by choice, fallen violently into the Prophet's prophecy?

The point of this story is not to suggest that the principal targets of the vexation were limited to any one group in any one state. We have seen how the entire nation was under condemnation for abandoning the covenant and thus abandoning the cause of God. Therefore, the war was, indeed, intended for all. The Prophet Joseph recognized this, which is why he directed his exhortations and warnings to the entire

---

* It was Lincoln's policy throughout the war to allow captured rebels to take "the oath of allegiance" to the Union and the Constitution. Lincoln explained that such oaths embodied "the Christian principle of forgiveness on terms of repentance" (See Richard Ellis, *To The Flag*, 210-11). Some believed that Lincoln's practice of allowing rebels to enter an oath and covenant to return to the Union was strange. However, this was a very common practice of the Book of Mormon commander-in-chief, Moroni (see Alma 44; 46:35; 62: 16-17). Lincoln would have read these accounts in his copy of the Book of Mormon.

nation. However, it is highly significant that the prophecies gave special attention to the insurgents in Missouri and that the proposed fulfillment of the prophecies (the vexation of the Civil War) gave special attention to these same insurgents, even touching the exact county wherein they resided. Add the fact that an inspired president called for the insurgents to change their hearts just weeks before this particular event, and we witness, once again, a stamp of historical authenticity upon the American Covenant and the divine role the Civil War played in connection to this covenant.

By the end of summer 1863, Lincoln was only becoming more dedicated to the new and inspired purpose of the war. During this time, Lincoln made several public comments reinforcing his position that "black freedom had become an objective of the war." In August he announced that "the promise [of freedom] being made must be kept," and by September he had ordered the Union military government of Tennessee (Tennessee had by then fallen to the Union) to write a permanent emancipation policy into the new state's constitution.[90]

Just months later, in October 1863, Lincoln pronounced "Thanksgiving" a permanent national holiday. (Though Washington had called for a similar day, like others would do after him, Lincoln was the first to make it a permanent fixture and recognized national holiday.) Recognizing the nation's responsibility to the American Covenant, Lincoln proclaimed: "It has seemed to me fit and proper that they [gifts of God] should be solemnly, reverently and gratefully acknowledged as with one heart and one voice by the American people." He then declared "the last Thursday of November next as a day of thanksgiving and praise to our beneficent Father who dwelleth in the heavens."[91] (Perhaps while we celebrate Thanksgiving today, we should reflect upon the context in which it was given and upon the true purposes for which it was originally designed. Perhaps we should make it a day in which we, as Lincoln proposed, recommit ourselves to the American Covenant.)

Further evidence of this mighty change of heart in America has to do with the sudden surge in Christian converts during the war, particularly among the soldiers on both sides of the conflict. Some

Union generals, such as William Rosecrans, refused to even fight on the Sabbath. General Oliver Howard (known as the "Christian General") regularly preached to his troops. The Union leadership even offered weekly religious services. It is estimated that, in addition to the already vast Christian population of recruits, some 200,000 Union soldiers were made Christians as a result of the national vexation.[92]

Though it would take the South several decades to experience significant internal change pursuant to the vexation (their compliance to the post-war constitutional corrections were initially based on compulsion, not conversion), certain stirrings towards God and truth were being felt under the surface, even in the midst of the war. For example, the two most famous Southern generals, Robert E. Lee and Thomas "Stonewall" Jackson, both active and outspoken Christians, offered Christian services to their own troops.*

The effect of such examples, underscored most prominently by the natural humility-producing effects of such a tragic war, helped to change the South. Though (strangely and sadly) most could not bring themselves to admit that enslaving innocent human beings was immoral, the natural surge in spirituality did encourage them to reexamine their lives. In general, the South, at this time, believed that God could not help them unless they improved the living conditions of their slaves. Consequently, many Southerners

---

* It should be noted that Lee believed that slavery was, in his own words, a "moral and political evil." He had even been an early critic of Southern secession and considered an initial offer to take command of the Union troops. However, as Virginia was his "country," he ultimately felt he was required to defend it. (see Bennett, *America*, Vol. I, 359). Additionally, as strange as it may seem, the Southern general "Stonewall" Jackson, who was killed during the war, was listed among the eminent men of Wilford Woodruff, whose temple work was done, pursuant to the miracle at the St. George Temple. He too did not join the cause in deference to any race, but for what he interpreted to be loyalty to his country. In fact, before the war, he had set up a Sunday school (at his own expense and at the risk of breaking certain laws and customs) for the religious instruction of black persons within his community. See Wilford Woodruff's journal and temple records, as quoted in Anderson, Preface, 226.

issued injunctions on the physical abuse of slaves, legalized slave marriages, and began preaching the Bible to their slaves.[93]

At least one Southerner, John Killian, who had returned from California for the express purpose of fighting in the war against Northern abolitionism, eventually came to the difficult (and brave) conclusion that perhaps he was on the wrong side: "I some times think that this is wrong to own a slave, for the Bible says that a man shall eat bread by his sweat of his brow."[94] We might presume the vexation caused other Southerners to entertain such thoughts. What we do know, however, is that by war's end, as many as 100,000 Southern troops had converted to Christ during the conflict.[95] All of this was at least a start.

As difficult as it was for the South to make the necessary change, ultimately—though painfully slow at first—they would. But for now, as the war raged on, the hope of a land fit for the restored gospel would fall principally on the Northern faithful and their noble leader. As 1863 came to a close, Lincoln once again emphasized to the nation what the war was meant to produce in America. In his December 1863 Annual Message, Lincoln declared that the "world must stand indebted" to the Union soldiers "for the home of freedom disenthralled, regenerated, enlarged, and perpetuated."[96]

Months later, a national symbol of the American Covenant was issued by the Congress of the United States—a symbol which has endured to the present day. On April 22, 1864, Congress passed an act mandating that the U.S. Mint Director place the following words on U.S. coins: IN GOD WE TRUST. The first appeal to apply such a divine invocation on the currency came a few years earlier by way of a letter from Reverend M.R Watkinson to Lincoln's Secretary of the Treasury, Salmon Chase. Rev. Watkinson declared to Secretary Chase that such an act was needed, as it "would place us openly under the divine protection we have personally claimed." It would also, he declared, help the nation achieve repentance, as "our national shame in disowning God" was "not the least of our present national disasters." Picking up on the covenant theme issued by the reverend, Secretary Chase perpetuated it with a statement of his own to the director of the Mint at Philadelphia: "Dear Sir, No nation can be strong except in the strength of God, or safe except in His defense. The trust of our people in God should be declared on our national coins." And so it was by 1864. IN GOD WE TRUST was later made, by an act of Congress, the national motto of the United States.[97] The covenant had been invoked once again.

Notwithstanding such powerful and continual recognitions and invocations of the covenant by the North, the question still remained—How many had (by then) been fully converted to the covenant? Were there enough to merit the full blessings of heaven? Enough to warrant a full Northern victory under God? The world would soon find out. The test would come in the form of the presidential election of 1864.

With the North entering its fourth year of the bloodiest conflict the nation had ever seen, Northern spirits appeared to dwindle in exhaustion, doubt, and fear. But Lincoln seemed more determined than ever to stay the course despite any personal or political consequences to himself. Just months before the 1864 presidential election, with the people now "wild for peace," the South sent delegates to meet Lincoln's men at Niagara Falls to discuss a peace treaty and a reunification. But an unrelenting Lincoln preempted the visitors with a demanding and startling message up front: before any treaty could even be discussed, something would be uncompromisingly required. It was a shock to many. As written in a memo by his own hand, he required the South's complete "abandonment of slavery."[98]

After the Southern politicians unsurprisingly rejected the terms, they leaked the president's memo to the press, after which Lincoln and his advisors concluded in a memo of their own that "it seems exceedingly probable that this administration will not be re-elected."[99] Even Lincoln's friend and anti-slavery supporter, Horace Greeley, tried to convince the president that "our bleeding, bankrupt, almost dying country also longs for peace—shudders at the prospect of fresh conscriptions, of further wholesale devastations, and of new rivers of human blood. And a wide-spread conviction that the Governemnt...[is] not anxious for Peace, and do not improve proffered opportunities to achieve it, is doing great harm."[100]

Indeed, it was difficult for anyone, including friends of the president, and his very own administration, to believe the North would be happy with Lincoln's decision to reject the peace treaty solely because he wanted to press for the universal eradication of slavery. He was, in effect, asking the North to continue dying, bleeding, and suffering, not only to restore the Union, as he had originally declared (for the South was now willing to discuss this), but to also enlarge freedom for minorities. Today, with the benefit of hindsight, we know and have evidence (as provided earlier) that the North, at this point, had been sufficiently converted to the cause and would stand by Lincoln. However, Lincoln and his people were not convinced of this as they entered the election; and so they feared the worst.

Despite the perception he had of the public's opinion on his refusal to concede on the point of human freedom, Lincoln was, at this point, immovable. He knew whose mission he was on and so he stayed the course. Even facing the probability of losing the presidency, Lincoln would trust in God and the people and move forward with faith. In fact, instead of downplaying the importance of emancipation during the presidential campaign, Lincoln instead seemed to become even more radical in his position. It was during this time that he himself began to organize an underground railroad from the South to assist runaway slaves.[101]

This is not to say Lincoln was not tempted to end the terrible war by compromising on emancipation. At one point in August 1864, shortly before the election, Lincoln responded to such a proposal by writing a memo that invited peace through reunification without requiring Southern abandonment of slavery. How easy it would be. How politically sensible it would be. It would perhaps save his presidential career. Furthermore, we might consider the immediate burden that would be released from the shoulders of the gentle statesman from Illinois, who hated violence and yet was perpetuating it through the endless war he presided over. This was an internal struggle that pulled at his tender heart daily. Yes, the temptation to compromise was there. And yet, as a reflection of his righteous resolve under such pressure, he refused to send the memo. As his secretaries explained, the letter "thereafter slept undisturbed, in the envelope in which he placed it, for nearly a quarter of a century" (presumably before one of the secretaries found it among Lincoln's papers).[102] He would ultimately obey the God he had given himself to. He would rather be right than be president. He would rather bear the unbearable burden than achieve the immediate relief of a quickened peace agreement. Lincoln knew, as he stated on numerous occasions, that God would rather the war continue than to permit human bondage of the innocent to remain in the Promised Land.

Lincoln's political opponent in the election, and the Democrat's nomination for president, was none other than the arrogant slave owner's apologist and the *former* Union general Lincoln had fired, George McClellan. The Democrats, under McClellan, were pushing for peace and reunification with the South at the sacrifice of emancipation. "Beware the Africanization of the North," they declared, while simultaneously promising that, if elected, America would happily have "the Constitution as it is, and the nigger where he was."[103] A McClellan victory certainly would mean the reinstitution of slavery, which would mean no Thirteenth Amendment and no Fourteenth Amendment. Indeed, they would have kept "the Constitution as it [was]." In addition to black freedom being severely threatened, so was the future and hope that the Church would gain its appropriate status and reap the blessings of the national covenant under the Fourteenth Amendment and the Civil Rights Act. The eternal cause of God again hung in the balance.

Several Union soldiers sensed this threat and thus warned: "[F]ailure now is failure forever." The soldiers declared that the election would become "the day of national judgment," and if McClellan won, they asserted, "We may write 'Ichabod' on the wall of its Temple of Liberty."[104] This particular warning, published in a Union paper, was especially poignant when considering the American Covenant and from whence that covenant had sprung. The Hebrew "Ichabod" translates into the phrase: "The glory is departed from Israel."[105]

With such eternal consequences at stake, some thought Lincoln should have frantically stumped around the nation seeking votes. However, he chose to make very few public appearances during this time.[106] Instead, Lincoln very naturally and calmly turned the nation once again to God, knowing that only the Almighty could convince the nation, voter by voter, to hang on and let His work and glory prevail in the matter. First on September 10, 1864, then again on October 20, 1864, Lincoln called for consecutive days of national fasting, prayer, and thanksgiving. Lincoln dedicated these sacred days in a public proclamation to "our Heavenly Father" in the hopes for "an ultimate and happy deliverance," and the triumph of "the cause of freedom and humanity."[107] These days of national humility unto God were bolstered by what many considered a gift from God delivered on September 2, 1864—General William T. Sherman shocked the nation by capturing Atlanta. Within a month of Lincoln's call to prayer and fasting, an elated North elected Lincoln as their president and as their guide to lasting victory.

Fittingly, as it was the soldier on the ground who had felt the pressure of Heaven's vexation, and who had thus gained a greater measure of the divine vision of the conflict, it was the soldier vote that pushed Lincoln to victory. Indeed, a remarkable eighty percent of those who suffered the most, voted to keep their commander-in-chief, knowing that such a vote would keep them on the bloody battlefield until victory was achieved.[108] It was an amazing testament to the converted state of the North. Lincoln had become the first president reelected to a second term since 1836.[109]

In the end, the election of 1864 was a referendum on the American Covenant and a testing ground to determine whether God's vexation on the nation had maintained its lasting intention. It most assuredly had. "In affording the people the fair opportunity of showing...the world this firmness and unanimity of purpose," declared the newly reelected Lincoln, "the election has been of vast value to the national cause."[110]

That God was still in the middle of events was not lost on Lincoln's most faithful. "There probably never was an election in all history into which the religious element entered so largely, and so nearly on one side," declared the nation's chief Methodist newspaper. Theodore Tilton added that Lincoln's victory was "nothing less than an over ruling Divine Hand outstretched to save the Republic."[111] The minister Gilbert Haven compared Lincoln voters to "an army of Christ, with the banner of the cross" who had "march[ed] to the ballot box."[112] Perhaps most visionary was the clergymen who hung a transparency over his door on election day, which read: "The angel of the Lord called unto Abraham out of heaven a second time."[113] Not surprisingly, it was in the midst of these spiritual undertones that we witness Lincoln's March 1865 Second Inaugural Address, in which he reiterated the covenant principle of *national repentance*. As detailed earlier, it was in this short address that Lincoln (after enjoying a miraculous burst of sunlight at the moment he stood to speak, during an otherwise stormy day) invoked God fourteen times, referred to prayer three times, and quoted or paraphrased the Bible four times.[114]

Perhaps more important than these general sentiments was the way in which they moved the people to action. Such action is powerfully represented by the fact that by war's end, of the more than two million troops serving under Lincoln, a mere fifty thousand were actually drafted. The rest signed-up, fought, and endured out of a desire within.[115] (This was in stark contrast to the Confederate army, who drafted a much higher percentage from among its Southern populace, and whose desertion rate clearly outnumbered that of the North.)[116] Significantly, among those volunteers were the thousands of black troops who—thanks to emancipation—also volunteered, thus tipping the sensitive scale of victory toward the Union.[117]

The North's conversion to the cause, and its obedience to God, culminated in a victorious event on April 2, 1865 (within one month of Lincoln's Second Inaugural), when the Confederate capital of Richmond, Virginia fell to Union forces.[118] (Before Union troops arrived, the Confederate government and a large portion of the populace had already evacuated. Before doing so, however, they had accidently set fire to much of their own city—reducing much of it to ruins—in their mad dash to burn supplies so as to keep them out of Union hands.)[119]

Days later, on April 4, Lincoln entered the city, and the scene that followed emphasized what great accomplishments had been secured. As Lincoln landed at Richmond by boat, he found himself surrounded by a growing group of now freed black men and woman who shouted, "Bress de Lord!... Dere is de great Messiah!...Glory Hallelujah!" The former slaves then, one by one, began falling on their knees in deep respect and utter emotion. They began kissing Lincoln's feet. Lincoln, shocked at the events transpiring before him, became emotional. He pled with the group, saying, "Don't kneel to me, that is not right. You must kneel to God only, and thank him for the liberty you will hereafter enjoy." The liberated ones then stood, joined hands, and began to sing a hymn of praise to God. The streets, which up until that point had been "entirely deserted," became alive with happiness and jubilee, as black people all around began "tumbling and shouting, from over the hills and from the water-side."[120]

One witness later reported to Lincoln that he had seen an elderly white-haired slave exclaim, "Massah Linkum, he eberywhar. He know eberyting. He walk de earf like de Lord!" Responding to the report, Lincoln became silent for several moments, then solemnly stated, "It is a momentous thing to be the instrument, under Providence, of the liberation of a race."[121]

With the liberated slaves all about him in the streets of Richmond, Lincoln spontaneously decided to do something extraordinary. Lincoln had become fully convinced of the reality of the American Covenant. In fact, it was this covenant that had allowed him to be where he was in that very moment. Fittingly, he wasted no time in calling the now liberated blacks to the same covenant. "I am but God's humble instrument," declared Lincoln, "but you may rest assured that as long as I live no one shall put a shackle on your limbs, and you shall have all the rights which God has given to every other free citizen of this Republic."

> My poor friends, you are free—free as air. You can cast off the name of slave and trample upon it...Liberty is your birthright...But you must try to deserve this priceless boon. Let the world see that you merit it, and are able to maintain it by your good works. Don't let your joy carry you into excesses. Learn the laws and obey them. [122]

The Union celebrations taking place in the newly conquered South were extended days later in Washington D.C., as the inevitable news arrived that Lee had surrendered to Grant. The war was officially over. Washington D.C. instantly became a city of gratitude to the God who had blessed the nation with Union victory. During those nights, the Capitol Building was lit, as were the homes of the citizenry. People took to the streets in celebration. An enormous gas-lit transparency, with oversized letters, was stretched across the entire length of the Capitol's western portico, for all to see. Borrowing words from the Bible, it read, "This is the Lord's doing; it is marvelous in our eyes." [123]

On April 11, Lincoln, now back at the White House, responded to the throng of friends and supporters who had gathered at the foot of his residence, longing to celebrate the news with him. As he entered the north portico of the White House, his face lit by a lantern held by his son Tad, Lincoln declared to the elated crowd, "We meet this evening...with gladness of heart...In the midst of this, however, He from whom all blessings flow, must not be forgotten...no part of the honor is mine." Lincoln then, in a forward-looking effort to begin the reconstruction of the nation, proposed, albeit informally, the induction of blacks, not only as citizens, but as voting citizens.[124] He spoke to the accomplishments America had made in recovering the covenant and its blessings. Indeed, he spoke to the implementation, under God, of a fullness of *national repentance* and a fullness of *universal agency*. In this quiet suggestion, in what would be his final public address, Lincoln summed up what victory had come to mean. As he had done so many times throughout the conflict, Lincoln shined a light along the path which would give oppressed minorities everywhere (from former slaves to persecuted religious groups) reason to hope for expanded liberty under a renewed constitution—under a renewed national covenant.

These sentiments not only reflected Lincoln's views, but those of the victorious North. As victors of the conflict, they could now assist the Lord in bringing to pass His purposes. The American Covenant would soon be supported by an amended Constitution. The covenant blessings would at last begin to be poured out in greater measure upon the nation and upon all the earth. *Liberty, protection* and *prosperity* would enable the Restoration and facilitate God's great gift to mankind—free agency unto eternal salvation.

In a symbolic gesture (perhaps from heaven itself) of this national renewal, an astonishing thing happened in Richmond, Virginia. The mostly evacuated former Southern capital had recently been all but burned to the ground (during the great evacuation). Then, just weeks after the Union had occupied the city, as reported by the *Richmond Times*, "the very floodgates of heaven seemed to open." The rains poured down violently. According to the *Times*, "Never within 'the recollection of the oldest inhabitant' has such a destructive rainstorm occurred in this city....And so great was its effect that the whole city was soon submerged in water, overflowing all the streams and washing from their banks a number of small houses, trees, [etc.]." Some believed all this (the fires, the occupation, the storms) were "a plague of almost biblical proportions," while others saw it as a baptism of sorts, and the dawning of a new era for America.[125]

Richmond was, at one time, the hub of American patriotism—a city of the covenant. It was in Richmond where, in 1775, George Washington and Thomas Jefferson witnessed, along with many others, Patrick Henry's spiritually gripping *Give Me Liberty or Give Me Death* address. It was in Richmond where Jefferson served as governor and where he and Madison had crafted the legislation that would inspiringly separate church and state, and which would one day help bring forth the First Amendment.[126] In light of this, its symbolic baptism—its cleansing, its rebirth, its renewal of purpose—was entirely fitting.

In the end, we see how adherence to the covenant not only blessed the North with victory, but created the environment in which the covenant blessings could reach all mankind in fulfilling the Almighty's work and glory. America became one nation under God.

Conclusion

The Prophet Joseph recognized the crumbling of the covenant in his day, as he and the Saints witnessed the plan of the adversary take shape and find a stronghold within the oppressive mobocracy that ruled the day. The plan of the Evil One had successfully kept the gospel fullness at bay by belittling and rendering useless the American Covenant promises as laid out in the Declaration of Independence and the Constitution. As a result, prophets had been murdered in cold blood and temples had fallen to tyrants. But now, the prophesied solution to the American Covenant crises had run much of its course. At last, as a result of the national vexation of war, the covenant blessings were emerging to protect and support God's gospel plan.

In light of how this Civil War narrative played out under God and covenant, the words of a young Abraham Lincoln, offered over twenty years before the war, have proven inspired—if not wholly prophetic. His speech, known as the Lyceum Address, was given at Springfield, Illinois in 1838. His words were significant in that they were given not far from the place where the Latter-day Saints were (at that very time) suffering severe persecution. But more importantly, the speech was directed at the very core of the problems plaguing the Church. Indeed, the speech called out the adversary's long-standing plans to obstruct the Father. His speech was a recognition of, and solution to, the tragedy of tyrannical mob rule over agency. More amazing still was the way Lincoln couched the solution to the national crises in the language of the American Covenant.

Lincoln began his speech with a recognition of the American Covenant blessings. He defined America as "the fairest portion of the earth," composed of the great promises of "civil and religious liberty," even a "political edifice of liberty and equal rights." He called these the "fundamental blessings" and proposed that it was incumbent upon the people to ensure these blessings were perpetuated. Lincoln then pointed out the dark slayer of these blessings, which he described as something of "ill-omen amongst us" that is represented through "accounts of outrages committed by mobs, from every-day news of the times. They have pervaded the country...it is common to the whole country." After pointing out how mob rule had violently affected various peoples of different races and locales throughout the land, he added that "strangers, from neighboring States, going thither on business, were, in many instances subjected to the same fate" (was he referring here directly to the Saints?). Lincoln specifically pointed out that "whenever the vicious portion of population shall be permitted to gather in bands of hundreds and thousands, and burn churches, ravage and rob provision-stores, throw printing presses into rivers, shoot editors, and hang and burn obnoxious persons at pleasure, and with impunity; depend on it, this government cannot last." (It seems as though he was referring to what had happened to his neighbors, the Latter-day Saints.)

Just as the Prophet Joseph had done, Lincoln recognized Satan's plan; and just as the Prophet Joseph had called for a national solution, Lincoln (his neighbor and contemporary from Springfield) was proposing the same one. "The question remains," asserted Lincoln in his speech, "how shall we fortify against it? The answer is simple." Then, in a stunning display of covenant language, Lincoln provided the inspired answer:

> Let every American, every lover of liberty, every well wisher of his posterity swear by the blood of the Revolution, never to violate in the least particular, the laws of the country; and never to tolerate their violation by others. As the patriots of seventy-six did to the support of the Declaration of Independence, so to the support of the Constitution and Laws, let every American pledge his life, his property, and his sacred honor;—let every man remember that to violate the law, is to trample on the blood of his father, and to tear the character of his own, and his children's liberty. Let reverence for the laws, be breathed by every American mother, to the lisping babe, that prattles on her lap—let it be taught in schools, in seminaries, and in colleges; let it be written in Primers, spelling books, and in Almanacs;—let it be preached from the pulpit, proclaimed in legislative halls, and enforced in courts of justice. And, in short, let it become the political religion of the nation; and let the old and the young, the rich and the poor, the grave and the gay, of all sexes and tongues, and colors and conditions, sacrifice unceasingly upon its altars.

Apart from the obvious allusions to covenant-making and covenant-living ("swear by the blood," "pledge his life," "remember," "preached from the pulpit," "political religion" "sacrifice...upon its alters"), Lincoln's suggestion that the Declaration of Independence and the Constitution were at the center of this covenant further connected his words to the American Covenant. We have detailed in previous chapters how these two documents, more than any others, embody the spirit and purpose of the covenant.

Later in his speech, Lincoln again referred to the Founders who brought us these documents and described their cause as "the noblest cause—that of establishing and maintaining civil and religious liberty." He described the Founders as "the pillars of the temple of liberty." Finally, in his closing statement, Lincoln not only emphasized the religious nature of America, but appropriately suggested that the national covenant was connected, yet subordinate, to that greater covenant of the gospel of Christ. Declared Lincoln, "Upon these let the proud fabric of freedom rest, as the rock of its basis; and as truly as has been said of the only greater institution, 'the gates of hell shall not prevail against it.'" [127]

Lincoln's Lyceum Address was highly significant for several reasons that speak to the power of the national covenant and its connection to the Civil War. First, Lincoln's ideas—from his recognition of the evils of mobocracy against agency, to his solutions based in the constitutional principles of the covenant—paralleled what the Prophet Joseph had said himself (see Chapter 3). Second, these two men, born within a few years of each other, made these warnings and exhortations during the very same time period. Lincoln's Lyceum Address and Joseph's national exhortations, warnings, and Civil War revelations occurred during the 1830's, within a few years of each other. Both men had made these declarations in enough time for the nation to change on its own and thus avoid the terrible vexation. Third (and perhaps most stunning and significant), when the Prophet's warnings went unheeded, thus prompting the godly solution of war, it was his silent partner, contemporary, and neighbor from Springfield, who would preside over it.

As a young man, some twenty years before the war, Lincoln had charted the course of the nation's solutions: a course that was (unbeknownst to him) tethered to the frightening prophecies issued at this same early time. Though Lincoln could never have imagined the manner by which his solutions would eventually be achieved, nor the prominent role he would play in seeing them achieved, the prophesied vexation would ultimately fulfill his every word and place him at the forefront of the fulfillment. It was the war that compelled the people to finally adhere to Lincoln's initial advice to turn toward the covenant and "sacrifice unceasingly upon its altars." It was the war that caused the people to carry out Lincoln's call to sacrifice with the intent of reapplying the Declaration of Independence and the Constitution, so as to forbid evil men from thwarting God's gift of agency.

Of course, more than his Lyceum Address itself, it was Lincoln's inspired role over the war effort, and it was his words and actions during the war, that gave power and meaning to his youthful address and confirmed his calling by God. As a result of it all, the nation would inherit the covenant blessings of the Declaration and the Constitution, just as Lincoln had suggested, just as Joseph had envisioned, and just as God had designed.

From the Lyceum Address to Union victory in war, we have seen the American Covenant shine forth boldly as it strived to fulfill its destiny in God's plan. But some of the most powerful evidence of the covenant's existence only began to appear as the war made its final turns toward fruition. This evidence is represented through the nation's reflections of who they really were in relation to the covenant. It is represented through the nation's tacit recognition that they were latter-day Israel. For example, Lincoln explained that the war had brought him to a place and time, "when I felt that slavery must die that the nation might live," to which, with the help of a scriptural allusion, he added that he had, at last, hearkened to "the groaning of the children of Israel whom the Egyptians kept in bondage."[128] This was a striking comparison considering that he was, in fact, indirectly freeing the most prominent representation of the House of Israel (which was, at that point, biding its time in the western territories, waiting for the "new birth of freedom" to reach and restore them).

Directly after this statement was issued, the scriptural symbolism inspiringly extended nationally, as soldiers and commoners began referring to their president as "Father Abraham."[129] As the Old Testament patriarch, Abraham is the eternal symbol and figurehead of the covenant, so it is fitting—and perhaps not coincidental—that this modern leader of the American Covenant shared the same sacred name and title.

This allusion to ancient Israel's connection to modern day America was no isolated incident. Like the inspired revolutionaries before them, the inspired Northerners also understood something of this divine connection. We have seen this connection in the Gettysburg Address, the Second Inaugural Address, and in other declarations. Yet it went even further. Secretary of War, Edwin Stanton, once declared in the midst of the conflict, that "our national destiny is as immediately in the hands of the Most High as ever was that of the Children of Israel."[130] Others would shout *amen* to the prayers outside the White House, which included the plea, "O Lord command the sun & moon to stand still while your Joshua, Abraham Lincoln, fights the battle of freedom."[131]

If his peers and colleagues had honored Lincoln with such sacred titles, it was because he had acted the part. Author William J. Wolf said this about Lincoln in his work, *The Almost Chosen People*:

> Lincoln is one of the greatest theologians of America—not in the technical meaning of producing a system of doctrine, certainly not as the defender of some one denomination, but in the sense of seeing the hand of God intimately in the affairs of nations. Just so the prophets of Israel criticized the events of their day from the perspective of God who is concerned for history and Who reveals His will within it. Lincoln stands among God's greatest latter-day prophets.[132]

The slaves also saw themselves as a latter-day version of the ancient Israelites in bondage, incessantly singing hymns—spirituals —about ancient Israel's enslavement and divine rescue. They too pulled from this old story a hope for their own Moses and for their own liberty under God and covenant.[133]

Henry Ward Beecher invoked the ancient covenant and applied it to the Civil War by preaching to Northerners that "Right before us lies the Red Sea of war. It is red indeed. There is blood in it. We have come to the very edge of it, and the word of God to us today is, 'Speak unto this people that they go forward.'"[134] What was this, but a declaration that the same national covenant of old had become the covenant of modern America?

Beecher would again invoke the covenant a few days after the South officially surrendered. On April 14, 1865, before a crowd of Union faithful celebrating victory in the re-conquered Fort Sumter (where the South had launched the first attack), Beecher expounded upon the flag of the United States, which had recently been hoisted up over the fort. Beecher explained that for the past four years the flag (a sign of the covenant) "lay brooding in darkness" just as Moses and the Israelites had to "brood in the wilderness" because of their disobedience. But now, having at last repented of its sin, the flag and covenant was unfurled once more, America having "dedicated itself to liberty."[135] As the ancient Israelites had repented and received the Promised Land, so had America done the same.

These many allusions and connections to the ancient covenant, recognized and applied by the converted North, were not insignificant nuances. They were at the core of the war's purpose and at the core of why the North achieved victory. As Volume I of this book explained (using scripture and history), the national covenant given to ancient Israel had been bestowed upon modern-day American Israel—and for the same purpose. It was given so that through righteousness, the blessings of *liberty*, *protection*, and *prosperity* would abound, thus paving the way for God's work and glory to prevail. Indeed, the ancient promises are clear in the book of Genesis that the American Covenant would thrive among Joseph's posterity (including those faithful American Ephraimites loyal to the Union), that they would thwart their enemies, even "the archers" that "shot at [them] and hated [them];" and that they would defeat them with their "bow abode in strength," made possible "by the hands of the mighty God of Jacob" (see Gen. 49: 1, 22-26).[136]

The promises were reiterated in the Book of Mormon, that if latter-day Americans would live worthy of their divine call and mandate, these covenant blessings would be theirs, as they partnered with God in bringing truth and salvation to the world.[137] It is what the Savior referred to when he told the Nephites that modern-day America would "be set up as a free people by the power of the Father...that the covenant of the Father may be fulfilled which he hath covenanted with his people, O house of Israel" (3 Nephi 21:4). Lincoln and his faithful had tapped into this covenant. They had taken on the evils of the South, as the Nephites of old had taken on their enemies in battle, for "they cried with one voice unto the Lord their God, for their liberty and their freedom from bondage" (Alma 43:49). We have documented in detail these cries to God and have seen in this final assessment God's positive response. As Union soldiers so inspiringly declared, "Lincoln could claim the divine blessing."[138] And so he did.

But more than declarations by Lincoln and the North connecting their cause with the ancient covenant, the most important evidence of this connection had come by way of something more powerful than mere words—national action. Indeed, the evidence of the covenant in America at this historic time is seen most prominently through the story we have just finished. It is a story of a sinful, yet chosen, people finding redemption through the humbling acts bestowed upon them by Heaven; it is a story of a people who, through trial and tribulation, learned the will of God, became converted to His national covenant, and thus took their place in the grand design of the grand plan. The scholar Manning helps us see how the scriptural purposes of the vexation were clearly fulfilled:

> By the Spring of 1865, the war had created a world almost
> no American could have recognized in 1861. White Union
> troops who might once have eschewed radical abolitionism

now took pride in fighting to redeem the nation from the sin of slavery [*national repentance*], and many took seriously the obligation to make ideals like freedom and equality into realities for black as well as white Americans [*universal agency*].[139]

The *national repentance* and *universal agency* America needed to accept and promote was at last being achieved. Though blacks in America were the most immediate and apparent beneficiaries of this liberation, it is important to understand that this liberation—through the shifts in social and political culture that followed the war—would extend itself to *all* minorities, including the Latter-day Saints. For after the Northerners had accepted and internalized the covenant principles, they brought them to the rest of the nation through conquering the evil therein and securely applying these righteous principles nationally.

In their concluding statement regarding the Civil War, renowned historians Schweikart and Allen speak to this claim and thus support this conclusion: "The Civil War finalized the contract and gave to 'all men' the promises of the Declaration of Independence and the purposes of the Constitution. And although thousands paid the ultimate price for completing that process, what emerged—truly 'one nation under God'—could never again be shattered from within."[140]

The war had securely applied the covenant principles, had finalized the contract, and had sealed up the Declaration and the Constitution (even those beacons of the covenant)—never again to be shattered from within. All of this was done in the wake of war through constitutional amendments (like the Fourteenth Amendment) and related legislation (like the Civil Rights Act) that took the newfound covenant principles of *national repentance* and *universal agency* and bound them to the supreme law of the land. Thus, the national covenant was redeemed and delivered just as the Prophet Joseph had called for. The Kingdom of God on earth would, at last, enjoy the constitutional support and protection God had designed for it in these latter-days. Using a metaphor from the scriptures, Lincoln once compared America's law and covenant to a silver picture frame protecting the imagery of an "apple of gold." This reinforced frame of silver would forever "adorn and preserve" the precious fruit of truth, light, and gospel.[141]

In light of what the war had offered to the Church, Latter-day Saints might envision themselves celebrating in spirit alongside the jubilant freed slaves on the streets of Richmond or with the elated victors within the walls of the re-conquered Fort Sumter in South Carolina (even the place that the Prophet Joseph had correctly revealed as the starting point of the vexation), or with the exuberant patriots under the north portico of the White House, listening to their president deliver his final address to the nation. Father Abraham and his faithful followers had most certainly done more than free a race; they had also stripped the chains off of all the other latter-day children of Israel through delivering the covenant and thus allowing these children of Israel to safely carry out their priesthood mandate to bring souls unto salvation. And thus was offered to America and the world a renewed opportunity for all to accept the gospel, or whatever else they might choose to accept, and work out their salvation accordingly. Such is the purpose of life. Such was the ultimate purpose of the Civil War.

ENDNOTES

[1] Mac and Tait, *Under God*, 89-90.

[2] David Goldfield, *America Aflame: How the Civil War Created a Nation* (New York: Bloomsbury Press, 2011), 183-196.

[3] James Swanson, *Bloody Crimes*, 54.

[4] Schweikart and Allen, *A Patriot's History*, 350.

[5] Schweikart and Allen, *A Patriot's History*, 350; See also Alan T. Nolan, "The Anatomy of the Myth," in Gallaghar and Nolan, eds., *Myth of the Lost Cause*, 11-34 (quote cited on 20).

[6] Schweikart and Allen, *A Patriot's History*, 298.

[7] Schweikart and Allen, *A Patriot's History*, 302.

[8] Schweikart and Allen, *A Patriot's History*, 302; William J. Davis, *Jefferson Davis: The Man and His Hour* (New York: HarperCollins, 1991), 495.

[9] For a more exhaustive account of how the Southern secession movement was based in the preservation of slavery, see the following: Schweikart and Allen, *A Patriot's History*, Chapter 9: The Crisis of the Union (with particular emphasis on the section entitled "The Confederate States of America;" David Goldfield, *America Aflame*, 183-196; and Lincoln's First Inaugural Address, available from multiple sources on the Internet.

[10] Miller, 243, 239.

[11] Schweikart and Allen, *A Patriot's History*, 302.

[12] Manning, 32. The scope of this study does not permit an exhaustive list of the many publications, sermons, and other communications in the South, which clearly prove that the Southern war cause was sustained by a passion to preserve the practice of slavery. For more on this, see David Goldfield, *America Aflame*, 183-196.

[13] Schweikart and Allen, *A Patriot's History*, 345; *Confederate States of America Congress, Minority Report* [on the recruitment of black troops] (Richmond: Confederate States of America, 1865), as discussed in Charles Wesley, "The Employment of Negroes as Soldiers in the Confederate Army," *Journal of Negro History*, July 1919, 239-53.

[14] Manning, 64.

[15] Manning, 36.

[16] Manning, 36-37.

[17] Manning, 61.

[18] Abraham Lincoln, as quoted in Leidner, 75.

[19] Lincoln, as quoted in Carwardine, 143.

[20] Frederick Douglas, given in an 1862 speech to the Emancipation League in Boston, as quoted in Wikipedia, accessed from http://en.wikiquote.org/wiki/ Frederick_Douglass.

[21] Ralph Waldo Emerson, as quoted in Neil Kagan and Stephen Hyslop, *Eyewitnesses to the Civil War* (Washington D.C.: National Geographic Society, 2006), 23.

[22] Schweikart and Allen, 301, 307, 325-326.

[23] Schweikart and Allen, 301, 307, 325-326.

[24] Stewart and Stewart, *Seven Miracles*, 161-163; Manning, 29.

[25] Lincoln, as quoted in Miller, 150.

[26] Certain details surrounding the assassination have been provided by Parley P. Pratt's son, Parley Pratt, and described as an addendum in Parley P. Pratt, *The Autobiography of Parley P. Pratt* (Salt Lake City, Deseret Book Co., 1938), 415.

[27] B.H. Roberts, *New Witness For God* (USA: Published by Lynn Pulsipher, 1986), 89-90, as originally published in Millennial Star 50: 440-447.

[28] Vetterli, 81.

[29] Bushman, *Rough Stone Rolling*, 357.

[30] Vetterli, 218.

[31] B.H. Roberts, *New Witness For God*, 88-90.

[32] Bushman, *Rough Stone Rolling*, 514.

[33] Victor Hugo, *Les Miserables* (New York: Penguin Books, 1987), 621-622. (Originally published in 1862).

[34] The theorists' arguments can be read and analyzed from the following sources: See the research of Stephen Pratt at http://www.libertyandlearning.com/downloads/an-heuristic-exploration-of-the-union. See also Stephen Pratt, "The Three Foundings" (video presentation), available at www.libertyandlearning.com/videos; and Stephen Pratt, "The Second Founding," video available at www.libertyandlearning.com. I encourage all to read Brother Pratt's conclusions on Lincoln and the Southern position and compare them with the research in this book. Other prominent sources which use similar allegations to paint Lincoln and the North in a very negative light, and which tend to downplay the hideous sin of slavery, include Thomas J. DiLorenzo, *Lincoln Unmasked: What You're Not Suppose to Know About Dishonest Abe* (New York: Three Rivers Press, 2006); Jeffrey Rogers Hummel, *Emancipating Slaves, Enslaving Free Men: A History of the American Civil War* (Chicago: Open Court, 1996); Allen Buchanan, *Secession: The Morality of Political Divorce from Fort Sumter to Lithuania and Quebec* (Boulder, CO: West view Press, 1991); Robert Higgs, *Crises and Leviathan: Critical Episodes in the Growth of American Government* (New York: Oxford University Press, 1987).

[35] Ron Andersen, 224; also quoted in Charles Dew, *Apostles of Disunion* (Charlottesville and London: University Press of Virginia, 2001), 17.

[36] Ron Andersen, 219.

[37] Chandra Manning, *What This Cruel War was Over* (New York: Alfred A. Knopf, 2007), 14.

[38] Manning, 49.

[39] Ron Andersen, 22.

[40] Ron Andersen, 22.

[41] Schweikart and Allen, 351.

[42] Goldfield, *America Aflame*, 67.

[43] Julian, as quoted in Carwardine, 122.

[44] Gabor Boritt, *The Gettysburg Gospel* (New York: Simon and Schuster, 2006), 17.

[45] Carwardine, 276.

[46] Schweikart and Allen, 351.

[47] Lincoln, as quoted in Miller, 404.

[48] Miller, 269-70.

[49] Manning, 151-152.

[50] Manning, 84.

[51] Carwardine, 224.

[52] Carwardine, 224-5.

[53] Carwardine, 302.

[54] Carwardine, 122.

[55] Carwardine, 288.

[56] Carwardine, 288.

[57] Carwardine, 288.

[58] Carwardine, 225.

[59] Carwardine, 276.

[60] Thomas R. Valletta, ed. *Great American Documents for Latter-day Saint Families* (Salt Lake City: Deseret Book, 2011), 135.

[61] Thomas R. Valletta, ed. *Great American Documents*, 139.

[62] Carwardine, 223.

[63] Thomas R. Valletta, ed. *Great American Documents*, 137.

[64] Jon Meacham, *God, the Founding Fathers, and the Making of a Nation* (New York: Random House, 2006), 126.

[65] Lincoln, as quoted in Carwardine, 76.

[66] Carwardine, 225, 279.

[67] Lincoln, as quoted in Carwardine, 282.

[68] Carwardine, 225.

[69] Lincoln, as quoted in Carwardine, 227.

[70] Lincoln, as quoted in Carwardine, 229.

[71] Carwardine, 279.

[72] Carwardine, 313.

[73] Goodwin, 451-52, 484-86.

[74] Miller, 217-218.

[75] Lincoln, as quoted in Leidner, 107-108; full speech available from Richardson ed, "A Proclamation by the President of the United States of America (March 30, 1863)," *Messages and Papers of the Presidents* (Washington DC: United States Congress, 1897), 164-165; also available at www.showcase.letin.net/web/creative/lincoln.speeches/fast.htm

[76] Boritt, 129.

[77] Lincoln, as quoted in Gingrich, *Rediscovering God in America,* 54; and as quoted in Philip P. Kunhardt Jr, Philip P. Kunhardt III and Peter W. Kunhardt, *The American President* (New York: Riverhead Books, 1999), 336; and as quoted in Chris and Ted Stewart, *Seven Miracles That Save America,* 190-191.

[78] Lincoln, as quoted in Carwardine, 320. Lincoln's quote here, though quoted by many, has never been fully substantiated.

[79] Feiler, *America's Prophet,* 165; see also the analysis in Chapter 5 of this book, under the subheading: *The Second Great Good: Universal Agency*

[80] Boritt, 122.

[81] Manning, 115.

[82] Manning, 119, 125.

[83] Manning, 157.

[84] Leidner, 108.

[85] Refer also to Chapter 3 of this book under the subheading, "The Prophet's National Warning and God's Fulfillment."

[86] David McCullough, *Truman* (New York: Simon and Schuster, 1992), 26-28.

[87] David McCullough, *Truman* (New York: Simon and Schuster, 1992), 26-28.

[88] General Order No. 11 (1863), available from http://en.wikipedia.org/wiki/General_Order_No._11_(1863).

[89] General Order No. 11 (1863), available from http://en.wikipedia.org/wiki/General_Order_No._11_(1863).

[90] Carwardine, 231.

[91] Gingrich, 55.

[92] Mac and Tait, *Under God,* 125.

[93] Manning,143-144.

[94] Manning, 171.

[95] Mac and Tait, *Under God*, 125.

[96] Lincoln, as quoted in Boritt, 149.

[97]From the official website of the United States Treasury, available at www.ustreas.gov/education/fact-sheets/currency/in-god-we-trust.shtml.

[98] Goodwin, 647.

[99] Goodwin, 648.

[100] Goodwin, 646.

[101] Miller, 384-5.

[102] Miller, 387.

[103] Carwardine, 305.

[104] Carwardine, 305.

[105] From *Easton's 1897 Bible Dictionary*, retrieved by http://dictionary.reference.com/browse/ichabod.

[106] Carwardine, 295.

[107] Carwardine, 298.

[108] Manning, 185.

[109] Miller, 377.

[110] Leidner, 120.

[111] Carwardine, 307-8.

[112] Carwardine, 297.

[113] Carwardine, 299.

[114] Gingrich, 52; Feiler, *America's Prophet*, 166.

[115] Carwardine, 282.

[116] Schweikart and Allen, 307.

[117] Carwardine, 232-33.

[118] Carwardine, 364.

[119] Swanson, *Bloody Crimes,* 28-29.

[120] Goodwin, 719; Swanson, *Bloody Crimes,* 44-46; Carwardine, 364.

[121] Leidner, 33-34.

[122] Swanson, *Bloody Crimes,* 45-46.

[123] Swanson, *Bloody Crimes,* 93.

[124] Swanson, *Manhunt,* 4-6; Carwardine, 364.

[125] Swanson, *Bloody Crimes,* 331-332.

[126] O'Reilly and Dugard, 38.

[127] The Lyceum Address is available in Abraham Lincoln, *The Collected Works of Abraham Lincoln*, Edited by Roy P. Basler (New Brunswick: Rutgers University Press, 1953), Vol. I, 108-115.

[128] Lincoln, as quoted in Bennett, *America*, Vol. I, 348.

[129] Bennett, *America*, Vol. I, 348.

[130] Carwardine, 225.

[131] Carwardine, 279.

[132] As quoted in Ron Andersen, *Lincoln: God's Humble Instrument*, 235.

[133] Feiler, 124-129.

[134] Feiler, 159.

[135] Feiler 170.

[136] Refer to Volume I, Chapter 2 of this book for more details.

[137] Refer to Volume I, Part I of this book.

[138] Carwardine, 288.

[139] Manning, 211.

[140] Schweikart and Allen, *A Patriot's History of the United States*, 352.

[141] Leidner, 45. See Proverbs 25:11.

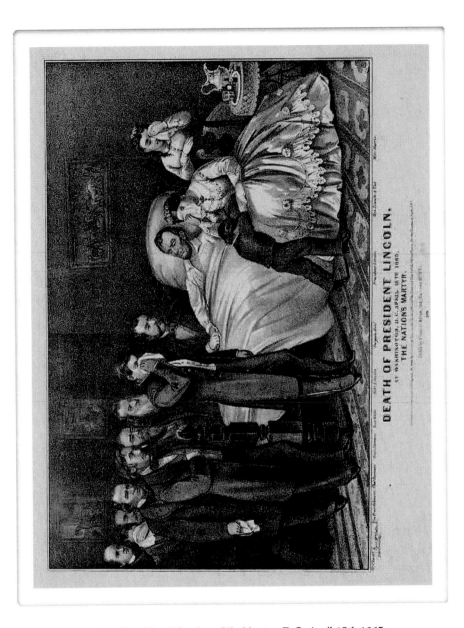

Death of President Lincoln at Washington D.C. April 15th 1865
by Currier & Ives (1865)

Courtesy of the Library of Congress

CHAPTER 7

SAINTS, SYMBOLS AND SACRIFICES: AN EPILOGUE TO WAR

I remember that thou hast said that thou hast loved the world,
even laying down thy life for the world....And now I know that
this love which thou hast had for the children of men is charity;
wherefore, except men shall have charity they cannot inherit that
place which thou hast prepared in the mansions of thy father.

—Moroni (Ether 12:33-34)

The Civil War was a most significant and powerful event in the history of the world, particularly in relation to the building up of the Kingdom of God in these latter-days. In the last few chapters, we have dissected the historical events that occurred in connection with the war. In so doing, we have presented an abundance of evidence that supports this bold gospel claim. However, there are other events and incidences related to the war which, while not fitting directly into the war's narrative, further connect the war to God, covenant, and the gospel. And so, before following the American Covenant story into post-war America, we will provide in this chapter an epilogue of sorts to the war in order to reveal these inspiring accounts—accounts that revolve around the independent, yet connected, themes of Saints, Symbols, and Sacrifices.

The Saints

As we have journeyed through the amazing narrative that is the Civil War, we have frequently mentioned the Latter-day Saints, who were biding their time on the outskirts of main America. They were awaiting the covenant blessings that would one day reach their cause of gospel restoration. As the Civil War would be a major event in furthering the Restoration, we should consider what relationship the early Saints had with Lincoln and the war. With the help of the restored gospel, and years of hindsight, we have witnessed in the past few chapters the great spiritual bond that connects Lincoln and the Saints. The bond we have witnessed is related to scripture and prophecy and, therefore, may require gospel light and historical hindsight to fully perceive. Yet notwithstanding the difficulty the early Saints might have had in fully recognizing their shared role with Lincoln in building the Kingdom of God, there is strong indication that an unusual and recognizable bond existed between them—even while they lived together in mortality. It was a bond that grew stronger and stronger as the historic times and seasons they witnessed together became ever more significant in God's plan. The existence of this unique relationship places yet one more stamp of validation on the American Covenant story, and once again shows God's hand in orchestrating the historic events that shaped the foundation of His restored gospel.

The first indication we have of Lincoln's recognition of the Church came, fittingly, about the time he offered his Lyceum Address (even that great speech that placed him in line with the Prophet Joseph's national pleas and prophecies). Expressing curiosity about the Church, Lincoln made reference to the Saints in writing, identifying them as the "strange new sect" moving into the state. Within a year of his recognition of the Saints, we know that

Lincoln and the Prophet were in the state's capital at the same time. Did they ever meet? They possibly did, as Lincoln once admitted that "Joseph Smith is an admirer of mine." In that same year (1840), Lincoln, then a state politician, assisted the Saints by helping push the Nauvoo charter through the Illinois legislature.[1] This would not be the first time Lincoln's actions would assist in the building up of Zion.

In 1842, the Lincolns resided in the same boarding house as Apostle Willard Richards and other leaders of the Church, which means the future president quite possibly dined and conversed with them and learned more of the "strange new sect." In 1843, for reasons unknown, Lincoln's wife, Mary Todd, attended the tragic extradition hearing of the Prophet Joseph. In response to Joseph's murder, Lincoln admitted to be "keeping abreast of the Mormon situation." Lincoln's cousin, Abram, would sit on the Grand Jury that indicted the Prophet's assassins, and Lincoln's secretary, John Hay, would write an account of the martyrdom for the *Atlantic Monthly*. Furthermore, we know that Lincoln had met and known Joseph's successor, Brigham Young. Whatever their relationship amounted to, we do know that on the day after the November 1860 presidential elections, Brigham turned to Wilford Woodruff and declared, "I hope that Abe Lincoln was elected president of the United States yesterday."[2]

Positive things had indeed occurred between Lincoln and the Saints. But as the divine vexation was poured out over the land, the relationship only grew stronger. When war broke out, it may have been expected that the Saints would have taken a very neutral, even uninterested, position. After all, the Saints had been driven out of their homes without any sympathy or protection from the negligent and unfeeling federal government. To make matters worse, two years before the Civil War, in response to false rumors and lies about the Saints, the same federal government had sent an army into Salt Lake to crush the Saints. Though this conflict had a peaceful ending, to say the Saints were, at this point, fed up with the U.S. government would be a severe understatement. And so when war broke out, the natural man would be thinking, *if the nation has shown us no support, why should we show support to the nation?*

Notwithstanding, just after the South began its fervent secession from the Union, the Church (instead of taking the path of the natural man) issued a policy which represented a spirit of forgiveness and benevolence toward the Union. The transcontinental telegraph line had recently been put into place at the Salt Lake City station, coincidentally during the war's commencement. President Young was given the opportunity to send the first message back to the eastern states. He could have said anything he wanted, but his chosen words were significant. "Utah has not seceded," he proudly declared, "but is firm for the Constitution and laws of our once happy country."[3]

President Young, in characteristic fashion, then backed his words with deeds. The Church responded enthusiastically to a request from Lincoln to guard, in the name of the Union, the western transcontinental telegraph and western transportation routes. The Saints also responded willingly to a request from Congress that the Utah Territory supply $26,982 annually toward the war effort—no small sacrifice for the struggling Saints. And finally, in the only direct military effort rendered by the Saints, President Young responded to a federal request in the spring of 1862 for a cavalry unit to be organized and dispatched to secure western routes. (Interestingly, at the time he received this request, President Young was no longer governor of the territory, and was acting only in his higher calling as a prophet of God.) Immediately, President Young organized a 120 man unit, which served its country well and later received highest compliments from a grateful nation—though no fighting had been required.[4]

Based on the Church's response, it seems likely that Brigham, and perhaps even some of the Saints, understood the divine nature and purpose of the war. If so, the bond between the Saints and Lincoln would grow stronger still. In Chapter 3, we discussed Brigham's participation in the revelations concerning this scourge and vexation to be poured out over the nation. Some fifteen years before the war, Brigham made it clear that it was coming as a result of the nation having killed the Prophet and having driven out the Saints. He called it a day of "calamity" and "sorrow" and said it could only be avoided if the nation "speedily repent, yea, very speedily" (see D&C 136:34-36). Brigham further commented that the nation's sins (turning away the servants of God and rejecting the principles of righteousness) would result in the country's attempt "to make Mason and Dixon's the dividing line; but they will not remain, for they will cross it to destroy each other, and the sword and fire will be prevalent in the land."[5] And so, when war broke out, Brigham knew for what purpose it would serve. He declared at the time, "our enemies, who sought to destroy us, are being humbled."[6] The Saints concurred that the war was "a judgment upon the nation for the murders of Joseph and Hyrum Smith, for not keeping the commandments of God, and for injustices inflicted upon the Saints in Missouri and Illinois."[7]

But if Brigham and the Saints had believed it was all just an act of vengeance, it seems they would have happily stayed out of the conflict and let it run its course. However, if they had believed it would accomplish something for the Kingdom of God, then they would naturally ally themselves with Lincoln and join in on the side of the Union. Perhaps their enthusiastic response to Lincoln and the Union indicated an understanding that the national humbling caused by the war would bring some good to the work and glory of God. Perhaps they even knew something of the constitutional changes that would come in the wake of war to support and uphold the Restoration. The Saints, particularly President Young, did, after all, have memory of, and access to, the many Civil War prophecies that had come through the Prophet Joseph. These prophecies clearly spoke of great changes to occur in the wake of the vexation— changes that would bring the Church the political support divinely intended for it.[8]

Furthermore, the Saints knew the Book of Mormon stories, which were abundantly clear on the idea that when God intervenes in the affairs of a sinful nation, He does so to compel humility and induce national obedience, so He can provide national blessings. If the Saints knew God's hand was in the war (which they did) then they naturally understood God had planned to redeem the nation through war in furtherance of His righteous designs.

Underlying the prophecies and general sentiments of the Saints at this time was the closely held belief that America and its Constitution had been created by God and given by covenant for the building up of His kingdom (see D&C 101: 80). So, when the prophet of God responded to Lincoln, based on his aforementioned declaration that the kingdom of God on earth was for the Union and "firm in the Constitution and laws of our once happy country," we can be sure that such dedication was derived from a gospel comprehension of what the war would be about. The entire relationship between the Saints and the nation at this time can be summed up in this strangely ironic commentary: While half the country was fighting, with rather bad reason, to leave the Union, the Saints, who actually had *good* reason to leave the Union, were fighting to get back in. It is well documented that Lincoln was the first president of the United States to earn the respect, admiration, and love of the Saints. Perhaps it was the Church's deeper understanding of the president and his divine mission that led to such sentiments.

If the Saints knew something of the divine to be found in Lincoln and his struggle, did Lincoln know something more profound about the Saints? Did he feel at all connected to the Saints, as they felt connected to him? We have certainly proven that Lincoln did become completely converted to the idea that God was behind this struggle and that this struggle was all about the covenant principles—the same covenant principles promoted and prophetically foreseen by the Prophet Joseph. Lincoln and his disciples even correctly connected these blessings to the ancient national covenant of the Hebrews. To conclude that Lincoln's understanding went beyond this already profound gospel comprehension would be speculative. However, that Lincoln felt a further gospel connection that directed him toward the Saints, and their destiny under God's vexation, might be entertained upon considering, once again, the fact that Lincoln checked out a Book of Mormon and had it with him in the White House during the precise months of his intense conversion to the covenant. (Furthermore, let us not forget the American Covenant prophecies of Isaiah, found in the Book of Mormon, which Lincoln relied upon when addressing the nation. These prophecies, as placed in the context provided by the Book of Mormon, would have been clearly understood by Lincoln as prophecies he was fulfilling in the Promised Land he presided over.)[9]

During this time, Lincoln also borrowed the following books: *Mormonism In All Ages, Mormonism: Its Leaders and Designs,* and *The Mormons or Latter-day Saints in the Valley of the Great Salt Lake: A History of their rise and progress, peculiar doctrines, present conditions, and prospects.*[10] Perhaps it was coincidence. Perhaps he was simply informing himself of the Saints in order to determine policy. Or perhaps—in light of the many aforementioned miraculous connections between God, Lincoln, the war and the gospel—it meant much more. Either way, it likely tightened the bond between Lincoln and the Saints.

Skeptics of the Lincoln-Saints bond will naturally point to the fact that in July 1862, Lincoln signed into law the Morrill Anti-Bigamy Act, which had clearly been directed at the Church and its practice of plural marriage. However, upon further examination, this law ironically brought to the surface further proof to the Saints that Lincoln felt compassion toward them. To begin with, it should be noted that the bill was conceived and passed by Congress before being sent to Lincoln for consideration. On principle, Lincoln rarely utilized the veto, and considering the understandably strong opinions the public maintained against the strange practice of plural marriage, Lincoln's refusal to utilize the veto in this case seems perfectly natural. However, it was Lincoln's position *after* the bill was passed that positively touched the Saints.

About one year after the bill had been passed, President Young sent T.B.H Steinhouse, of the *Deseret News*, to Washington

D.C. to inquire about Lincoln's intention toward the Saints, particularly in regards to the new legislation. Lincoln assured Steinhouse that he would not be enforcing this law, nor did he wish anything but peace upon the Saints: "Steinhouse," Lincoln began, "when I was a boy on the farm in Illinois there was a great deal of timber on the farms which we had to clear away. Occasionally, we would come to a log which had fallen down. It was too hard to split, too wet to burn and too heavy to move, so we plowed around it. That's what I intend to do with the Mormons. You go back and tell Brigham Young that...I will let him alone."[11]

Lincoln backed this promise with action. In June 1863, Lincoln fired the territorial governor of Utah, Stephen Harding, after learning that he was hard on the Church and had participated in persecuting Joseph Smith, even during Joseph's early days as a very young prophet in Palmyra. Lincoln promptly replaced Harding with James Doty, who Lincoln knew to be a "very discreet gentlemen" who would support Lincoln's policy of leaving the Saints alone.[12]

President Lincoln's tolerance towards the Saints (something they had rarely enjoyed from their government) allowed them to divert attention from politics, diplomacy, and conflict, and instead focus their efforts on missionary work. Not insignificantly, one of the great missionary surges in Church history occurred during the tenure of President Lincoln. In 1860 the Church established a European Mission, and between 1861 and 1868, over 16,000 recent converts, mostly foreigners, joined the Saints in Utah, and assisted greatly in the building up of the Church.[13]

In so many ways, Lincoln benefitted the Kingdom of God, both directly and indirectly. This was not lost on the Saints, even those living in Lincoln's day. For when Lincoln died, something happened in Zion that had perhaps never happened before in the history of Latter-day Israel—the Saints mourned their national leader. Upon hearing the news of their president's death, Brigham Young declared a day of mourning and held a memorial service for Lincoln in the Old Tabernacle.

Since then, Lincoln has been quoted in General Conference over two hundred times. Elder Hyrum M. Smith declared, "I believe Abraham Lincoln was raised up to do God's will." President Heber J. Grant declared: "Perhaps no other people in all the world look upon Abraham Lincoln as an inspired servant of God, a man raised up by God to occupy the presidential chair, as much as do the Latter-day Saints." And during the nation's bicentennial year, the First Presidency went so far as to ask members of the Church to read and ponder Lincoln's words regarding God's hand in the affairs of men.[14] Prophets and apostles certainly do not make such public declarations and invitations lightly. They would clearly need some powerful reason for doing so. In this case, they certainly possessed such a reason.

The Symbols

God teaches and reminds His children through symbols. Throughout the past chapters we have witnessed many symbols revealed during the Civil War that reflect and teach the war's deeper gospel purposes. For example: the official recognition of Thanksgiving, the advent of the national motto IN GOD WE TRUST, miracles on the battlefield, the breaking forth of sunlight as Lincoln stood to offer his Second Inaugural Address, speeches connecting America and its flag to the ancient covenant of Israel, and many, many others. There are additional Civil War symbols not directly conceived by the inspired actors of the war (which is why they were not mentioned in our war narrative). These symbols came to us under providential influence. Many of them sit among us. They are seen and felt by millions upon millions, and yet their connection to God and the covenant have been mostly lost through time.

One such symbol is the Statue of Liberty. Though few remember today, the French initiated the idea to build and gift the statue to America as a result of Northern victory and the tragic death of the man who presided over the victory. France recognized what

Lincoln lived and died for and wanted the message of liberty to beam from America.[15] The message beaming from the statue could not have resonated Lincoln's vision any better. It was not just a symbol of liberty, but a symbol of liberty through the covenant. Bestselling author Bruce Feiler has pointed out that the statue offers many symbols representing God and covenant. For example, the statue itself is but a representation of the great national covenant leader, even the Prophet Moses. Feiler gleaned such observations from the French historian Pierre Provoyeur, who taught that the statue was indeed emblematic of Moses and was made to be "a seer and a prophetess."

Fieler first points to the statue's crown, from which shoots seven pointed sun rays, perhaps representing the days of God's creation. But, according to Feiler, the rays mean more than just that: "The notion that light should envelop the head of an exalted figure is introduced first in the Hebrew Bible." As explained in Exodus 34, after his personal encounter with God, Moses returned to the Children of Israel with his face beaming and radiant, with what the Hebrew text calls "rays of light." Though the chief historian for the Statue of Liberty, Barry Moreno, admits he does not know for sure what the statue's creator intended with these symbols, he believes they came from "Judeo-Christian sources."

Feiler further connects the statue to the ancient covenant leader by pointing out that the statue is holding a tablet, not unlike that which Moses brought down from Sinai. According to Feiler, "Tablets were not common in classical art and were introduced into European art in conjunction with one story, Moses carrying the Ten Commandments." Chief Historian Moreno concurs, adding that the law on this American tablet represents more than Moses' law, but also the promises of "constitutional law." Engraved upon the tablet is the year 1776, which, according to Moreno, means that the promises of the Declaration of Independence are included as well. (We discussed in Volume I how the Declaration is but an iteration of the national covenant.)

The statue inspired by Lincoln and the Civil War indeed reflects the deep covenant principles that flow from Lincoln and the war. From the connections to the ancient covenant found in the symbols of Moses, to the connections to the modern-day covenant represented by the Constitution and the Declaration, the statue is an embodiment of the American Covenant renewed through God, Lincoln, and their joint effort in the war. The covenant principles reflected in these documents are, after all, the principles Lincoln fought to restore; this was the cause he openly declared under God, and then decisively accomplished under God. According to Moreno, freedom from "slavery, tyranny, any kind of oppression in the world...whether [in reference to] the Exodus or the Civil War, is one of the more subtle messages [of the statue]."[16]

Another oft-visited statue in America also carries the same symbolic meaning. Soaring high above Washington D.C., perched atop the United States Capitol Building, is the great bronze statue known as the Statue of Freedom. She is a female allegorical figure with a sword and shield and with elaborate robes draped over her shoulder. When the Civil War broke out, the Capitol Building was under construction, with the Statue of Freedom nowhere to be seen. As Lincoln gave his First Inaugural, inviting the South to return with slavery intact and the Constitution as it was, the dome of the Capitol —like the unconverted nation with its flawed constitutional interpretations—was conspicuously empty. Four years later, with the Civil War drawing to a close, the nation now converted, and the Constitution now being prepared to, at last, provide the blessings of the covenant as intended, Lincoln stood at the base of the Capitol to deliver his Second Inaugural Address. Standing proudly and strongly above him was the recently erected Statue of Freedom. Referencing the new statue's place at Lincoln's Second Inaugural, historian William Lee Miller explained, "Now the symbolism was completed as Liberty herself stretched toward the heavens."[17]

Of all the Civil War symbols that connect Lincoln to God, covenant, and gospel, one stands above the rest, and it happens to be the most visited spot in Washington D.C.—the Lincoln Memorial.

One need only visit the Memorial (particularly with the backdrop of night) to experience the power of the structure and feel its significance. Surrounded by such spiritual energy, one might feel as though they are standing outside a dedicated LDS temple. Fittingly, the etched words above the grand statue of Lincoln describe the Memorial as a "Temple."

But the covenant connection goes much deeper than this. Adorning the two inner walls on either side of the Lincoln Memorial are the words of the Second Inaugural Address and the Gettysburg Address, which, as detailed in Chapter 5, respectively capture and immortalize the covenant principles of *national repentance* and *universal agency*. Knowing what we do through the restored gospel about how these powerful themes—representative of Lincoln's inspired work—would play out in God's plan for His children, the symbolic murals accompanying these two speeches within the Memorial become ever-more remarkable, even astonishing.

Accompanying the words of the Second Inaugural Address (which speech outlines the theme of *national repentance*) within the Memorial is a giant mural depicting several personages involved in various activities. The U.S. National Parks Service (USNPS) describes the mural as depicting the "Angel of Truth" presiding over a ceremonial representation of reunification, which implies repentance and forgiveness. The angel figure is joining the hands of two former adversaries. The fruits of this repentance and reunification are depicted in a personage that symbolizes "Charity" and in the figures of "the Man and the Woman, symbols of the family developing the abundance of the earth." On either side of the family are the "vessel of wine and the vessel of oil, symbols of Everlasting Life." It is a perfect illustration of the American Covenant. As the nation applies *national repentance*, "Charity," even the pure love of Christ, is made manifest. Then, the nation becomes worthy of the covenant blessings, which include the "abundance of the earth." All of this leads to the opportunity for the family to gain "Everlasting Life."

On the opposite side of the Memorial are the words of the Gettysburg Address (which speech outlines the theme of *universal agency*). These words are also accompanied by a giant mural depicting several personages involved in various activities. According to the USNPS, this mural depicts the "Angel of Truth" freeing slaves from "the shackles of bondage." A second scene depicts how this new liberty is to be sustained. The "Guardians of the Law" are depicted holding "the torches of intelligence" and protecting a personage who sits in the "Chair of Law." This personage is holding "the Sword of Justice in one hand" and the "Scroll of the Law" in the other. She is accompanied by individuals whose job it is to correctly interpret the Law. Finally, a third group of figures depict a personage being crowned with immortality, with the "standing figures [of] Faith, Hope, and Charity" watching on. And "on either side are the vessels of wine and oil, the symbols of Everlasting Life."[18] Again, we have perfect imagery of the American Covenant: *universal agency* is at last being divinely protected by new law, which law will be interpreted correctly, thus allowing faith, hope and charity to reign. This, once again, facilitates "Everlasting Life."

The Sacrifices (Upon the Altar)

Upon learning of an 1864 report that a Mrs. Lydia Bixby had recently lost five sons in the war (she had actually lost two), Lincoln wrote her the following: "I pray that our Heavenly Father may assuage the anguish of your bereavement, and leave you only the cherished memory of the loved and lost, and the solemn pride that must be yours, to have laid so costly a sacrifice upon the altar of Freedom."[19] In the end, these words would speak for Lincoln himself, and his many faithful followers; for he, like many of them, laid himself upon this same altar, a sacrifice for God and man. But, as the gospel makes plain, such sacrifices bring forth the blessings of heaven. And so it has been for Lincoln and his faithful. As a most fitting epilogue to the preceding Civil War chapters, we will now review some of these sacrifices. We will reflect upon what these sacrifices meant, eternally, for both the bearers of the sacrifices and for all mankind.

Lincoln's personal journey through these sacrifices and towards eternal rewards ended tragically, but perhaps fittingly. Like so many of the Lord's anointed before him, Lincoln gave his life for this great cause of God. As Lincoln stood at the north portico of the White House (as described in the previous chapter) and discussed the great constitutional changes and enhanced liberties to come as a result of Union victory, John Wilkes Booth listened impatiently. After the speech he turned to his accomplice, David Herold, and said, "That means nigger citizenship. Now, by God, I will put him through." As he walked from the event in demonic hatred, he squealed to another accomplice, "That is the last speech he will ever give."[20]

Three days later on Good Friday, April 14, 1865 (just days after Union victory), Lincoln sat hand in hand with his wife, Mary, enjoying a play at Ford's Theatre. According to Mary, at one point during the play Lincoln leaned over and, as a reflection of the spiritual high he was experiencing, told her that he wanted "to visit the Holy Land and see those places hallowed by the foot-steps of the Savior."[21] Mary later said, "There is no city on earth he so much desired to see as Jerusalem."[22] Within moments of these whisperings to his dear wife, a shot rang out through the walls of the theatre. Booth had shot the president in the back of the head. Lincoln, who never regained consciousness, would be dead by early the next morning.

News of the assassination spread immediately and rapidly through the city that night. Lincoln's young child, Tad, was sitting with his caretaker in a nearby theatre watching the play *Aladdin*. A messenger took to the stage and emotionally revealed the tragic news (perhaps not knowing or remembering that Tad was in attendance). Tad was immediately ushered back to the White House where he collapsed into the arms of a staffer: "They've killed papa dead!" he cried out, "They've killed papa dead!"[23]

For Booth, the fatal decision was based on an evil desire to keep the black man where he was in relation to society. For the adversary, the violent act (in addition to forwarding Booth's evil designs) translated *also* into an effort to keep the Lord's latter-day church, even His restored Israel, in its obscure and oppressed place in relation to society. Both master and agent thought their shared goals might be possible if only they could obstruct the Emancipation Proclamation from advancing to a constitutionally untouchable level, even to the level of the Fourteenth Amendment and the Civil Rights Act, where freedom, equality, and redemption might reign and thus lift the downtrodden and oppressed. The rash act might just keep African Americans, Mormon Americans, and other minorities in chains; and the nation would remain unworthy and unready to play its part in God's plan of salvation. Perhaps the desperate effort to kill the man behind the great movement would accomplish the malicious goal.

On the contrary, however, as was said of the Prophet Joseph after his martyrdom,* so the same was publicly said of Lincoln, directly after his. In a remarkable tribute, connecting Lincoln to God and covenant, a Brooklyn Presbyterian declared: "A martyr's blood has sealed the covenant we are making with posterity," forever securing "the rights of men, the truth of the Gospel, the principles of humanity, the integrity of the Union, the power of Christian people to govern themselves, the indefensible equality of all creatures of God."[24]

Lincoln's death brought the nation closer to him. More importantly, it brought them closer to the covenant he had lived and died for. In "the largest and most magnificent funeral pageant in American history," Lincoln's funeral train traveled 1,600 miles from the capital to his final resting place in Springfield, Illinois. He was

---

*See D&C 135:3.

buried not too a far a distance from Nauvoo—where the Prophet Joseph was buried. Two martyrs for the same cause. More than one million people waited in endless lines to view the body of the president. Services were held in every major city along the route. Millions more, tears in their eyes, lined the train tracks just to catch a glimpse. Lincoln historian, James Swanson, summed up the funeral pageant best: "Lincoln's coffin became a kind of ark of the American Covenant."[25]

The nation seemed overcome by the solemn spirit of what Abraham Lincoln's death might really have meant in the eyes of God. Drawing on, and directly quoting from, the many eulogies that praised Lincoln directly after his death, Carwardine offers the following glimpse into the heart and mind of America at this time:

> Lincoln's religious credentials and role as liberator of an enslaved people cast him as a latter-day Moses (though one who had freed even more slaves than the Old Testament leader, "and those not of his kindred or his race"); he had taken "this Israel of ours" over "the blood-red sea of rebellion" and, like Moses, had been allowed to see, but not to enter, the Promised Land. More compelling still were the Christ-like characteristics of the murdered president. Vicarious sacrifice for his people on Good Friday succeeded a Palm Sunday on which Lincoln had in humble triumph entered the Confederate capital of Richmond: "As Christ entered Jerusalem, the city that above all others hated, rejected, and would soon slay Him…so did this, His servant, enter the city that above all others hated and rejected him, and would soon be the real if not the intentional cause of his death"….God had taken Lincoln, "the Saviour of his country," from the American people, just as he had taken Moses and Jesus when their tasks were done. In the future, urged Gilbert Haven [a religious historian and Lincoln peer], his death should be commemorated not on the calendar date, but on every Good Friday, as a "movable fast" to be kept "beside the

cross and the grave of our blessed Lord, in whose service
and for whose gospel he became a victim and a martyr."[26]*

The 1865 analogies offered and believed by a grieving
American people are today, particularly among secular historians,
written off as inflated, exaggerated, and over-dramatized examples
of a desperate nation in need of some spiritual connection, so as to
make sense of this tragedy. However, if the thesis of this book
regarding Lincoln and the war is true, then such sentiments laced
throughout Lincoln's eulogies may very well have been truly
inspired.

In light of such a spiritual perspective, perhaps Lincoln
(again like the Prophet Joseph) had an inkling that such a sacrifice
would be required of him, that he might seal his work and
immortalize his cause. He no doubt showed a willingness to suffer.
Indeed, the overwhelming burdens befalling him as the leader of a
country and a covenant falling to ruin had, alone, been bleeding him
slowly for the four years leading to his death. Yet, he pushed on for
a second term in spite of the pain. Noah Brooks attested to the fact
that the "happy-faced lawyer" from 1861 had evolved into a lowly,
sad, and stooped man, with a "sunken deathly look about the large,
cavernous eyes."[27] (A layman's viewing of Lincoln photograph
portraits from 1861, compared to those of 1865, definitively confirms
Brooks' point.)

But Lincoln was prepared to sacrifice further. While in
Lafayette, Indiana—during his famous 1861 trip into Washington
D.C. to take his post as president—Lincoln spoke of the importance
of preserving the American ideals of liberty and equality (not
insignificantly, the very things the Church needed more than
anything at that time). He called these founding principles the "hope
to the world for all future time," then concluded presciently that, "I
would rather be assassinated on this spot than surrender it."[28] He

---

* Modern studies of the Lincoln eulogies conclude that the president was compared
to Moses and/or the Savior in over one hundred and fifty separate speeches. See
Feiler, *America's Prophet*, 171.

would later tell Harriet Beecher Stowe that "whichever way [the war] ends, I have the impression I shan't last long after it's over."[29]

As an appendage to this thought, we might wonder if there was something inspired about a dream Lincoln had in the days before his death. In his dream he found himself in the East Room of the White House, whereupon he witnessed throngs of people gathered around a corpse being guarded by soldiers. The people were in deep mourning. Lincoln asked who is dead. A soldier responded, "The President, He was killed by an assassin." Lincoln awoke at the shock and was unable to fall back asleep. Three days before his death, Lincoln told his wife and William Lamon (who later reported the account) of the dream. Said Lincoln, "although it was only a dream, I have been strangely annoyed by it ever since."[30]

As shocking and tragic as it was, Lincoln's death does have a happy ending. This happy ending went beyond the national redemption that had, at last, culminated in the land. For the happy ending also included happiness, even joy, for Lincoln on a very personal level. As described above, Lincoln's relationship with the Saints, and with the restored gospel of Jesus Christ, seemed to grow closer and stronger as time went on. This trend apparently continued in death, even reaching a climax of sorts. For Lincoln was also listed among the choice spirits whose Priesthood covenants were performed in August 1877, as a result of the miraculous visitation at the St. George Temple. [31]

Whatever Lincoln's conversion to Christ and the national covenant had been in mortality, and whatever his understanding had been of his divine mission on earth, at this point in his eternal journey, it perhaps all came together for him. He had fought, cried, endured sleepless nights, suffered incessantly, and ultimately died so that America might have the government God designed. Now he knew why he had done what he had done. Now he knew why he had received the revelations he had received, why he had been given the spiritual gifts he had been given. Now he understood the miracles he had witnessed both on and off the battlefields of war. Now he understood why he had been required to seal his testimony of it all with his own blood. And that reason was in so many ways embodied in the grand edifice at St. George, that his spirit seemed deeply connected to in August 1877. For it was the new government and new covenant he had brought America that would provide the necessary foundations for the fullness of agency that allowed God's temples to exist unmolested by the adversary. He had indeed been an agent for God in bringing to pass the eternal life of man. So it seems altogether fitting that God would allow his son Abraham to partake of this most sacred and powerful gift.

According to Gideon Welles, Lincoln's Secretary of the Navy, the president had recounted something prophetic in a cabinet meeting on the very day he would be killed. Lincoln had told the cabinet that before "every great and important event of the War," he had experienced the same dream. Lincoln told the cabinet that some great event would soon occur, as he had experienced, once again, that dream the night before. Lincoln described the dream in these words (recorded by Welles in his diary): "[I] seemed to be in some singular, indescribable vessel...moving with great rapidity towards an indefinite shore."[32] Welles believed the president had, perhaps, prefigured his death on that day.[33] Perhaps he had. Perhaps the Lord was telling him that the day had come—he would, at last, arrive upon that "indefinite shore." He would arrive in the bosom of his Lord. He would arrive at a place where he might enter the temple of God.

This arrival, of course, could not occur until he had brought the nation safely into port. This he had done. He had served his mission and it was time to go home. At his funeral service, the reverend stood and declared, "There is no assassin strong enough and no weapon deadly enough to quench [the liberty Lincoln brought]...though our President is slain, our beloved nation is saved." Another minister, standing directly over Lincoln's coffin, declared, "I am the resurrection and the life, saith the Lord; he that believeth in me, though he were dead, yet shall he live; and whoever liveth and believeth in me shall never die."[34]

With this image in our minds of Lincoln with the Lord—with Lincoln in the temple—we might reconsider the grand memorial that consecrates his life and mission. As we stand in the great Lincoln Memorial—flanked on either side by the Second Inaugural Address (*national repentance*) and the Gettysburg Address (*universal agency*), with all the aforementioned gospel symbolism therein—and raise our eyes above the famous Lincoln sculpture, we read: "*In this temple*, as in the hearts of the people for whom he saved the Union, the memory of Abraham Lincoln is enshrined forever."

Notwithstanding Lincoln's great sacrifice for the cause, perhaps the greater sacrifice was that of Mary Todd Lincoln. Often ridiculed by history for her bouts of irrational rage against those around her (including her husband, who never seemed to respond in any other way but with humility and love), Mary's profound kindness and acts of charity have long gone unnoticed. She was, for example, daily present at the war hospitals in and around D.C., giving gifts and comforting the wounded and dying soldiers.[35] This makes it all the more difficult to ponder that, in addition to grieving with her husband over the war, and losing her precious young child, Willie, she also had to lose her husband in such a violent manner while sitting next to him, his hand in hers. All of this makes the lovely scene that occurred just hours before that fateful theatre trip all the more heart-wrenching. With the war finally over, and her husband finally reflecting something of a "boyish cheerfulness," he invited his wife for a carriage ride before leaving to Ford's Theatre. During the ride he revisited with her how "between the war and the loss of our darling Willie—we have both been very miserable. We must both be more cheerful in the future."[36]

A few short hours later, Mary's world would be turned upside down, once again. She sat close to her dying husband, as he lay unconscious in a small bedroom, in a bed too small for his elongated frame (he had been taken to a boardinghouse across the street from Ford's Theatre). Lincoln's closest advisors and friends were huddled around the bed, and they could hardly bear the miserable death scene they were witnessing. "Love," exclaimed

Mary, "live but one moment to speak to me once—to speak to our children." Her sobs were so distressing that she was carried out of the room. Hugh McCulloch, Lincoln's Secretary of the Treasury, remembered how the scene with Mary "pierced every heart and brought tears to every eye."[37]

Mary never recovered from her husband's death. "Each morning, on awakening, from my troubled slumbers," lamented Mary, "the utter impossibility of living another day, so wretched, appears to me, as an impossibility." Her only reason for living, she later said, was for her adolescent son, her "precious Tad," the two being "nearly inseparable." If not for him, said Mary, "[I] would gladly welcome death." Tad died a few years later at age eighteen from a heart condition. At that point, Mary's older, more distant, son felt compelled to commit the grieving woman to a state hospital for the insane (she hardly spoke to him again after that). Her sister later retrieved her and cared for her in the very house where she had met and married Abraham.[38]

Her long-awaited and hoped-for death at last took her home to her family in 1882. Mary died some five years after the St. George Temple miracle. But on February 12, 1909, on Lincoln's one hundredth birthday, Elder Matthias F. Cowley entered the Salt Lake Temple and helped perform the sealing ordinance for Abraham Lincoln and Mary Todd.[39]

Another powerful reunion occurred as a result of it all. It was a reunion that was reflected in mortality shortly after Lincoln's death. Before his funeral train left the D.C. station, a hearse had arrived from Oak Hill Cemetery in Georgetown. It carried the body of little Willie Lincoln. He was to travel with his father to Springfield, where they would be buried together.[40] Some three years earlier, upon Willie's death, Lincoln mourned deeply; but he mourned with hope. He often recited to himself: "I shall see my boy again."[41] He did. And he does. According to Church records, Willie was baptized and confirmed during his father's one-hundredth birthday celebration. He was then sealed to his mother and his father—even to his best friend in mortality.[42]

Another underrated sacrifice on the altar of the American Covenant, during the Civil War period, was that suffered by the oft-referenced William Seward family. As noted in Chapter 4, Seward, who ran against Lincoln in the presidential primaries, and was expected to win, at first believed the presidency should have been his. When Lincoln won instead, the president-elect did the odd and humble thing of inviting Seward to assume the most powerful position in the Cabinet: the position of Secretary of State. From that point on, Lincoln and Seward became the best of friends.

It was the kindly, good, and God-fearing Seward who saved the Union by keeping foreign powers from allying with the South; it was Seward who supported and assisted Lincoln in carrying out emancipation, when few others around him dared to hazard such a policy; and, perhaps most importantly, it was Seward who was Lincoln's friend when friends of the president were scarce during the dark days of war. Like Lincoln, Seward believed in what he called "higher laws" that trumped even the Constitution—laws "bestowed upon [us] by the Creator of the universe." [43] Because of this vision, Seward had the unique ability to see the soul of Lincoln and to understand who Lincoln was in the eyes of God. He called Lincoln "superhuman" and conceding that he is "the best of us." [44] Lincoln openly recognized that "Seward was the one man in the cabinet [he] could trust completely, the only one who fully appreciated his unusual strengths as a leader, and the only one he could call an intimate friend." [45] Though his wife would scold him for spending too much time chatting, joking, and relaxing at the Seward residence, Lincoln needed the strength and influence of his dear friend. [46]

At one point during the war, radical Republicans in the Senate were led to believe false rumors about Seward, which caused them to call for his dismissal. As an indication of how Lincoln felt about Seward, Lincoln himself declared that it was this event alone that left him more depressed than any other event in his life—and Lincoln was no stranger to life's tragedies. (Fortunately, Lincoln was able to convince the senators to leave Seward where he was.)[47] Lincoln and Seward were indeed brothers in the cause of God.

On the night Lincoln was assassinated, William Seward lay in critical condition in his Washington D.C. home, after suffering a carriage accident that nearly claimed his life. At about the time Lincoln was being shot, Booth's accomplice, Lewis Powell, pretending to be a courier with medicine from Seward's doctor, made his way into Seward's bedchamber. Powell attacked him, after attacking others in the house, with a large Bowie knife. Slicing through neck and cheek, he left Seward near death on the floor. Seward barely survived (a metal brace placed around Seward's neck after the carriage accident had, ironically and perhaps miraculously, prevented Powell from getting a clean stab into the neck).[48*]

As he lay near death, this most recent tragedy compounded with the first, news of Lincoln's murder was withheld from him, as doctors feared the shocking truth would do him in. Then, as reported by Noah Brooks, on Easter Sunday (two days after the attempt), Seward grimly pronounced to his attendant, "The president is dead." The attendant denied such a claim, only to be cut off by Seward: "If he had been alive he would have been the first to call on me, but he has not been here, nor has he sent to know how I am, and there's the flag." He pointed out his window toward the flagpole at Lafayette Park. It was at half mast. The room fell completely silent, as Seward lay back on his bed, "the great tears coursing down his gashed cheeks, and the dreadful truth sinking into his mind."[49]

As he lay there with tear-filled eyes, perhaps he was reflecting upon the last time he had seen the president. Days earlier, Lincoln had arrived from Richmond, after having experienced the fruits of the war there. Upon landing at the wharf, back at the capital, Lincoln did not go home. He did not go to report at the War Department. Instead he went straight to Seward's home. He could not wait to visit his convalescing friend to tell him first hand of the events at

---

*Lewis Powell escaped from the Seward home only to be caught shortly thereafter. He was later hung with other Booth conspirators for his part in the assassination attempt.

Richmond and to celebrate the end of the war. According to Seward's son, Lincoln spoke gently to his still critical and suffering father, casually stretching his elongated body out on Seward's bed with his hand supporting his tilted head. Lincoln stayed, conversing and encouraging, until his loyal friend and Secretary of State had drifted off to sleep.[50]

Seward would miraculously recover from both the carriage wreck and the assassination attempt, but he would lose both his wife and daughter to events springing from the attack.* After Lincoln's death, Seward's love and loyalty to Lincoln compelled him to carry Lincoln's torch after it was decided that he should remain in his position into the Johnson administration. Even when a majority of his party shunned the merciful way in which he planned to rehabilitate the South (as Lincoln would have done), he stuck to Lincoln's plan. For that, he was eventually forced out of public life.[51] Notwithstanding such

William Seward
Courtesy of the Library of Congress

---

* Frances Seward (the same wonderful companion who encouraged her husband early on, as aforementioned, to follow God's will and adopt a policy of full emancipation), could not deal with the tragedy that beset her home (her son and others were also almost killed by Powell that night). Overwhelmed by what she called her "vicarious suffering," she collapsed and died six weeks later. The Seward's daughter, Fanny, had also been physically attacked by Powell on that fateful night. Overcome by it all, Fanny fell ill and followed her mother in death shortly thereafter. "The assassin's blows passed by the father and son," so noted the *Washington Republic*, "and fell fatally on the mother and daughter." See Goodwin, 751; O'Reilly and Dugard, 201-202.

consequences, he did what he knew was right. He died surrounded by family in 1872. His parting words of advice to his loved ones, even spoken from his deathbed, were "Love one another."[52] His tombstone reads simply: "He was faithful."[53] He most certainly was.

Seward died a mere five years before the miraculous events of Elder Wilford Woodruff at the St. George Temple—just in time to participate himself. According to the apostle's records, Seward stood in the spirit alongside the other great Founders and protectors of the American Covenant. No doubt, rubbing shoulders with Seward that day in the temple, in a most joyous reunion, was Lincoln. (The work for Francis Seward was performed at a later date.)[54]

The thought of such an event makes the following words of John Hay, Lincoln's personal secretary, all the more powerful:

> The history of governments affords few instances of an official connection hallowed by a friendship so absolute and sincere as that which existed between these two magnanimous spirits. Lincoln had snatched away from Seward at Chicago [at the Republican National Convention] the prize of a laborious life-time, when it seemed within his grasp. Yet Seward was the first man named in his Cabinet and the first who acknowledged his personal preeminence....From the beginning of the Administration to that dark and terrible hour when they were both struck down by the hand of murderous treason, there was no shadow of jealousy or doubt [that] ever disturbed their mutual confidence and regard.[55]

As it was said of Joseph and Hyrum, so it might be said of Lincoln and Seward: "In life they were not divided, and in death they were not separated" (D&C 134).* Like the Lord had done for the

---

* John Hay, the same witness who wrote the referenced statement about Lincoln and Seward, had also written the account of Joseph and Hyrum Smith's martyrdom for the *Atlantic Monthly*. See Winder, 106.

Prophet Joseph, He had sent Lincoln an elder brother—an elder brother who would serve as the unsung hero to encourage and support like no other one could. There was indeed a powerful and inspired element to this relationship.

How wonderfully fitting that their final sacrifices upon the "altar of freedom" would eventually allow them the special access to the more significant, yet closely related, "altar of God"! It is, therefore, appropriate that we conclude our Civil War narrative with the image of Lincoln and Seward in the House of the Lord, receiving gospel covenants. In the end, it was for this gospel cause that these great men gave all that they did for the rest of us—not only that *they* might rejoice in the temple and its blessings, but that *mankind* might share in the same glorious gift from on high.

And, of course, we must not forget the other hundreds upon thousands that made the same sacrifice during this great and terrible war, which caused more death (over 600,000) than was suffered collectively in every American war from the Revolutionary War to World War II. To better understand this tragic number, we need only consider it in terms of our population today. As a percentage of total population, it would be like losing over five million people.[56] Not one home went unaffected.

One of the most moving and emotional memorials of this great sacrifice—and one which completely captures the divine motive, purpose, and ultimate blessings connected to the war—was a letter from a 32-year-old Union major named Sullivan Ballou to his wife, Sarah. The letter was written, along with two very similar letters to his two very young sons, days before Sullivan entered a bloody battlefield that claimed his life—days before he willfully made the ultimate sacrifice upon the altar of freedom. "My very dear Sarah:"

> The indications are very strong that we shall move in a few days—perhaps tomorrow. Lest I should not be able to write again, I feel impelled to write a few lines that may fall under your eye when I shall be no more..."Not my will,

but thine, O God be done." If it is necessary that I should fall on the battlefield for my Country, I am ready.

I have no misgivings about, or lack of confidence in, the cause in which I am engaged, and my courage does not halt or falter. I know how strongly American Civilization now leans on the triumph of the Government, and how great a debt we owe to those who went before us through the blood and sufferings of the Revolution. And I am willing—perfectly willing—to lay down all my joys in this life, to help maintain this Government, and to pay the debt...

I cannot describe to you my feelings on this calm Summer Sabbath night, when two-thousand men are sleeping around me, many of them enjoying perhaps the last sleep before that of death, while I am suspicious that death is creeping around me with his fatal dart, as I sit communing with God, my Country and thee. I have sought most closely and diligently and often in my heart for a wrong motive in thus hazarding the happiness of those I love, and I could find none. A pure love of my Country and of the principles I had so often advocated before the people— another name of Honor that I love more than I fear death, has called upon me and I have obeyed.

Sarah my love for you is deathless, it seems to bind me with mighty cables that nothing but Omnipotence could break; and yet my love of Country comes over me like a strong wind and burns me unresistably on with all these chains to the battlefield....I have, I know, but few and small claims upon Divine Providence, but something whispers to me—perhaps it is the wafted prayer of my little Edgar, that I shall return to my loved ones unharmed. If I do not my dear Sarah, never forget how much I love you, and when my last breath escapes me on the battle field, it will whisper your name....

But, Oh Sarah! if the dead can come back to this earth and flit unseen around those they loved, I shall always be near you; in the gladest days and in the darkest nights, advised to your happiest scenes and gloomiest hours, always, always, and if there be a soft breeze upon your cheek, it shall be my breath, as the cool air fans your throbbing temple, it shall be my spirit passing by. Sarah do not mourn me dead; think I am gone and wait for thee, for we shall meet again.

As for my little boys—they will grow up...and never know a father's love and care. Little Willie is too young to remember me long—and my blue eyed Edgar will keep my frolics with him among the dim memories of childhood. Sarah I have unlimited confidence in your maternal care and your development of their characters, and feel that God will bless you in your holy work.

....O! Sarah I wait for you there; come to me and lead thither my children. [57]

Many read these words and find it difficult to comprehend how this young husband and father could willfully and knowingly sacrifice the grandest, purest, and most joyful experiences of life: romance, love, and family. Only the light of the gospel, revealing what eternally enduring blessings would stem from the cause, could possible explain it. Sullivan clearly possessed this light. And so he bid farewell to his darling Sarah, his blue-eyed Edgar, and his precious little Willie. But let us never forget that he gave them up so that he might have them in eternity. And he most certainly has them today. For he, like Lincoln, fought for the cause of the covenant. He helped build the foundation that would protect God's gospel and facilitate the promises of eternal families, of eternal life. Sullivan's dearest hope and desire, which he expressed to his Sarah, telling her, "I wait for you there; come to me and lead thither my children," would prove to be prophetic—a promise made good. As Sullivan knew, so he declared: "We shall meet again."

Let us remember, *before* the vexation of war hit the land, God's temples burnt to the ground, as did the hope that the world would ever obtain the everlasting covenant. *After* the war, the nation changed. The Constitution was strengthened. The blessings of the land went forth. And the temples stood strong and unmolested. This is what Sullivan died for. Years later, with the dust of war settled at last, one such temple blessed the lives of Sullivan, Sarah, Edgar, and Willie. According to Church records, they were baptized members of the Church. Their temple work was done. They were sealed as an eternal family.[58]

This was also the case for Sullivan's faithful colleagues in the cause. We know they also were converted to the cause and willing to sacrifice for the same blessings. As detailed throughout these past chapters, Lincoln and his soldiers shared a special bond. They were the first to feel the vexation and recognize it for what it was, under God. These soldiers were the ones who voted overwhelmingly in 1864 to maintain "Father Abraham" as their leader, knowing such a vote meant the war would go on, leading many of them to their deaths. But death was worth it. They sacrificed as if to express to the world their understanding of the scriptural principle that they could be "joint-heirs with Christ; if so be that [they] suffer with him, that [they] may be also glorified together" (Romans 8:17).

These soldiers knew, loved, sang, and marched to the lyrics of the *Battle Hymn of the Republic*. The original lyrics, specifically written for the Union forces, read, "As Christ died to make men holy, let us *die* to make men free." (Only later were the words "*die* to make men free" changed to "*live* to make men free.") The Union soldiers knew the correct version; they knew they sacrificed their lives for *national repentance* and *universal agency*. They knew that Christ's sacrifice—His atoning sacrifice that "makes men holy"— could only be maximized if men were free. They "died to make men free," that eternal salvation might be made available to all God's children.[59] Based on this deeper gospel knowledge of the war, the oft-sung chorus of the beloved Civil War hymn perhaps takes on new meaning for us today: "Glory, glory hallelujah! His truth is marching on!"

As Lincoln and his faithful soldiers shared the pains and triumphs of the great vexation (in a way no outsider could possibly understand), it is no wonder they were the first and foremost to convert to the covenant principles and to the cause of God. Their vision was the same, their bond was unbroken. Lincoln loved his soldiers, and his soldiers loved him. One evening during the war, Lincoln traveled past a long line of ambulances, carrying dead and dying soldiers. Overcome with emotion, the president turned to his companion and lamented, "Look yonder at those poor fellows. I cannot bear it. This suffering, this loss of life is dreadful."[60]

According to the daughter of a Presbyterian minister (a minister who had befriended and worshipped with Lincoln during the war), the president called upon her father late one night (at 1:30 am). "Doctor," cried Lincoln, "you must come down and go to my room with me." The minister followed Lincoln back to the White House and into "Mr. Lincoln's room strewn with maps, where he was marking out the movements of the troops." Lincoln sent the minister into an adjacent room and asked him to pray. During this experience, according to the daughter, "Three times [Lincoln] came to my father's room and fell down on his face on the floor by his side and prayed mightily to God to bless the boys about to die for the Republic, and to save the Republic."[61]

The soldiers felt this love and concern. Even after Union victory, the soldiers found it difficult to celebrate upon pondering the death of their commander-in-chief. According to General Joshua Chamberlain, the hero of Gettysburg, they felt a bit empty during their final Union victory parade, as they passed the official reviewing stand and felt the void where Lincoln once stood and smiled down upon them. "We miss the deep, sad eyes of Lincoln," said Chamberlain, "coming to review us after each sore trial. Something is lacking in our hearts now—even in this supreme hour."[62]

Considering this bond, it is perhaps fitting that so many of these soldiers shared the same violent death as Lincoln. And how can we not suppose that they also shared the same glorious spiritual jubilee in the world beyond? We owe them a debt of gratitude for allowing us, all of God's children, the opportunity to pursue and receive the same great and eternal reward in the House of the Lord.

For it was them—all of them—who had achieved so much for the kingdom of God, and the fruits of such achievement would gloriously and eventually be felt directly by millions of beneficiaries in the years and decades that followed the great vexation. They had certainly made some of the first stitches in the arduous attempt to re-sew what the Prophet Joseph called the "heavenly banner," even the Constitution of the United States, or what we might also call the American Covenant. The principles they fought for and achieved would thereafter begin congealing and manifesting themselves in the long-awaited-for constitutional corrections called for by the Prophet. These constitutional corrections would secure the Saints in their mission to bring to pass the eternal life of man. They created the political foundations that would allow for the proliferation of God's temples and the subsequent establishment of God's covenants unto eternal life.

In the end, when Lincoln wrote to Mrs. Bixby of the sacrifice and blessings under our Heavenly Father, he was indeed speaking for himself, Seward, their wives, all the soldiers and their loved ones, and all those who had ever suffered or died for the American Covenant. It is up to the rest of us, the beneficiaries of their sacrifices, to express our thanks by also giving what we can to the same cause. In the end, their sacrifices have become our eternal rewards. That most of us today will not be asked to give our lives for the cause, as the Civil War soldiers did, is reflected in the lyric-change in the *Battle Hymn of the Republic*. And so, let us do today as the hymn (today) admonishes us—"As Christ died to make men holy, let us *live* to make men free."

In light of the fact that all these sacrifices under the scourge and vexation of war truly lead us all to the temple and its covenants, it is no coincidence that in describing how we should sacrifice to bring forth the blessings of heaven, Lincoln used the same three words. He used them in his prophetic Lyceum Address years before the war, and he used them again for the benefit of Mrs. Bixby in the final year of the war. Lincoln's repeated choice of metaphor was indeed remarkable: "upon the altar"!

ENDNOTES

[1] Winder, *Presidents and Prophets*, 105-106.

[2] Winder, *Presidents and Prophets*, 106-107.

[3] *Church History in the Fullness of Times*, 384.

[4] *Church History in the Fullness of Times*, 382.

[5] Brigham Young, as quoted in *Discourses of Brigham Young*, John Widtsoe (Salt Lake: Deseret Book, 1954), 365.

[6] *Church History in the Fullness of Times*, 382.

[7] *Church History in the Fullness of Times*, 381; a more detailed discussion of these Civil War prophecies and commentaries are found in Chapter 3.

[8] Consider references from Chapter 3, to include D&C 101:93-95 and 121:11-12.

[9] These prophecies are found in Isaiah 5 and in 2 Nephi 15. See Chapter 5 of this book, subheading, "Lincoln on National Repentance," for the details pertaining to how Lincoln might have utilized these scriptures.

[10] Winder, *Presidents and Prophets*, 107-108.

[11] *Church History in the Fullness of Times*, 383.

[12] Winder, *Presidents and Prophets*, 109-110.

[13] *Church History in the Fullness of Times*, 388-89.

[14] Winder, *Presidents and Prophets*, 111-112.

[15] Feiler, *America's Prophet*, 180.

[16] Feiler, *America's Prophet*, 177-187.

[17] Miller, *President Lincoln: The Duty of a Statesman*, 396-397.

[18] A depiction and the official description of the murals are available at the U.S. National Parks Service official website: www.nps.gov/linc/upload/memorialinside.pdf.

[19] Leidner, 112.

[20] Swanson, *Manhunt*, 6.

[21] Holland, *Bonds of Affection*, 252.

[22] Feiler, *America's Prophet*, 170.

[23] O'Reilly and Dugard, 214.

[24] Carwardine, 321.

[25] Swanson, *Bloody Crimes*, summary in inside jacket, 293.

[26] Carwardine, 320.

[27] Carwardine, 322-323.

[28] Carwardine, 146.

[29] Lincoln, as quoted in Neil Kagan and Stephen Hyslop, *Eyewitnesses to the Civil War* (Washington DC: National Geographic, 2006), 376.

[30] Ward Hill Lamon, *Reflections of Abraham Lincoln 1847-1865* (Lincoln: University of Nebraska Press, 1994), 116-117.

[31] Vicki-Jo Anderson, preface.

[32] Swanson, *Bloody Crimes,* 111-112.

[33] Swanson, *Bloody Crimes,* 111.

[34] Swanson, *Bloody Crimes,* 189-190.

[35] Goodwin, 456-459.

[36] Carwardine, 315.

[37] Swanson, *Bloody Crimes,* 120.

[38] Goodwin, 753-754.

[39] Goodwin, 753-754; Winder, 112.

[40] Swanson, *Bloody Crimes,* 208-209.

[41] Ron Andersen, 197.

[42] See http://new.familysearch.org. Search Abraham, Mary Todd, and William Wallace Lincoln (1850-1862).

[43] Seward, as quoted in Goodwin, 146.

[44] Goodwin, 364.

[45] Goodwin, 488.

[46] Goodwin, 387-388.

[47] Goodwin, 486.

[48] Goodwin, 735-37.

[49] Goodwin, 744-755.

[50] Goodwin, 724-725; Swanson, *Bloody Crimes,*78.

[51] Vicki-Jo Anderson, 346.

[52] Goodwin, 751.

[53] Vicki-Jo Anderson, 347.

[54] Vicki-Jo Anderson, preface, 343.

[55] Goodwin, 744-745.

[56] Schweikart and Allen, *A Patriot's History of the United States*, 306; Zinn, *A People's History of the United States,* 192.

[57] Sullivan Ballou, as quoted in Neil Kagan and Stephen Hyslop, *Eyewitnesses to the Civil War* (Washington DC: National Geographic, 2006), 72.

[58] See https://new.familysearch.org. Search for Sullivan, Sarah, Edgar, and Willie Ballou.

[59] Gingrich, 10; Carwardine, 288.

[60] Ron Andersen, 277.

[61] Ron Andersen, 277-278.

[62] Swanson, *Bloody Crimes,* 336-337.

Riot Police Protecting the Los Angeles Temple, November 6, 2008.

CHAPTER 8

THE COVENANT REDEEMED

America! America! God mend thine every flaw, Confirm thy
Soul in self control, Thy liberty in law.

—America the Beautiful (third verse)

How [did the Mormon church] go from being the
ultimate outcast to the embodiment of the
mainstream in two generations? It's a
breathtaking transformation.

—2007 PBS Broadcast

In hindsight we imagine how the Saints might have celebrated
along with black Americans in Richmond and Washington at the
time the Civil War was ending. However, the Saints perhaps had
little inclination to *fully* comprehend that a principal fruit of what
was occurring within their estranged United States was their own
liberation and, by extension, the development of the fertile ground
whereupon God's kingdom might thrive. Though they might have
connected the war to gospel prophecies, when or how the entire
event would touch them was likely unclear. But whatever the Saints'

perception was of the war, the afore-cited prophecies made it plain that the blessings of the war would eventually reach the Church. Indeed, something was bound to happen on the heels of the war that would forever improve the Church's position, elevating it to prominence in the world.

That this change occurred is obvious. As a journalist recently said on national television, "How do you go from being the ultimate outcast to the embodiment of the mainstream in two generations? It's a breathtaking transformation…[Mormons became] the embodiment of what it means to be America."[1] As indicated by the journalist, though the realization of this transformation is obvious, exactly *how* it happened is not. And so, it is the purpose of this chapter to tell this story. It is a story that connects the fulfilled prophecies of the Civil War to the present day. It is a story of how Joseph Smith's vision for America and the Restoration became a reality. It is a story about how *national repentance* and *universal agency* sealed the promises and redeemed the covenant.

Post-War Amendments

Lincoln himself had set forth the divine vision of what American reconstruction was to consist of. Specifically, he paved the way for the constitutional corrections that would seal the progress already made through emancipation. Lincoln knew his efforts would not be fully secured until they met the highest standard of the land—that is, until they transcended any legislative act, executive order, or judicial review, and became amended directly into the Constitution. The national conversion to this concept had gradually, but steadily, grown thanks to the national vexation.

One of Lincoln's military leaders summed up this conversion, stating, towards the end of the war, that "to have the Constitution as it is and the union as it was is an impossibility."[2] Another Union faithful wrote to his local newspaper that the Union was only "worth contending for" if Americans dedicated themselves to a higher "standard of liberty and freedom."[3] And yet another visionary, a New York private, declared, "By war, God is regenerating this Nation."[4]

The great change such inspired ones sought would certainly include constitutional amendments. At war's end, Lincoln might not be able to constitutionally justify the extension of the Emancipation Proclamation, as it was only legally justified under the Constitution as a war-time, defensive measure. Lincoln voiced particular concern that the Proclamation would be legislatively or judicially whittled down to include only "those who came into our lines" or that it would "have no effect upon the children of the slaves born hereafter."[5] He further spoke of the absolute necessity to secure the blessings of liberty for these children—or as he called them: "the unborn millions to come."[6] That is precisely why, from the time the Proclamation was issued, Lincoln began lobbying for a thirteenth amendment to bring his decision into an almost untouchable position. By January 1865, as Lincoln biographer Doris Goodwin pointed out, "[n]othing on the home front...engaged Lincoln with greater urgency than the passage of the Thirteenth Amendment." It would be, as Lincoln called it, "a King's cure for all the evils."[7]

Lincoln furiously lobbied for its passage before a hesitant Congress, and even began a campaign to convince the individual states to create their own version of emancipation amendments for their state constitutions.[8] The penitent nation helped convince Congress that Lincoln was correct. In an unprecedented event, the people (during the last year of the war) had gathered over 400,000 signatures on a petition demanding slavery be permanently abolished. The petition was sent to Congress.[9]

As the proposed amendment finally emerged victorious from both houses of the federal legislature, the news was rushed to Lincoln. According to one friend and witness, upon hearing the news, "it filled his heart with joy. He saw in it the complete consummation of his own great work, the emancipation proclamation."[10] Sadly, though Lincoln saw its safe passage through Congress, he was murdered before he could watch the proposal become a constitutional amendment, after achieving the required approval of three-fourths of all state governments. But before 1865 was out, an amendment it had become. America had taken giant steps forward off the platform created by the Proclamation. "And to whom is the country more immediately indebted for this vital and saving amendment?" shouted the great abolitionist William Lloyd Garrison, before a cheering crowd. "I believe I may confidently answer—to the humble railsplitter of Illinois—to the Presidential chain-breaker for millions of the oppressed—to Abraham Lincoln."[11]

The Thirteenth Amendment had freed the slaves and thus represented a powerful manifestation of the *national repentance* required to redeem the American Covenant. However, it did little, in and of itself, to provide for the general welfare of newly freed black Americans, or to provide the constitutional promises denied the Saints and other afflicted minorities. It fell short of offering the required *universal agency*. What it did provide, however, was the momentum for the next two amendments, which did offer these loftier blessings. As it was with the Thirteenth Amendment, Lincoln's vision set the stage for the Fourteenth and Fifteenth Amendments as well. These additional amendments overturned the wickedness of the *Dred Scott* decision and granted American citizenship and voting rights to all men, regardless of race or color. Remember, it was in Lincoln's final address—days before his death —that he promoted such ideas. *

And his death only inspired a national desire to carry on the fallen president's vision, or as Matthew Simpson declared, "to carry forward the policy...so nobly begun...to give every human being his

---

* Even as early as 1864, Lincoln seemed convinced that the nation would move toward universal citizenship. One account of the dealings between Lincoln and a black White House worker, William Johnson, is very telling. When Johnson passed away rather suddenly in 1864, Lincoln personally paid for his burial at Arlington Cemetery. Lincoln placed one very profound and bold descriptive word on Johnson's headstone, and in so doing broadcasted a message to the nation. The word was "Citizen." See Boritt, *The Gettysburg Gospel*, 170.

true position before God and man; to crush every form of rebellion, and to stand by the flag which God has given us."[12]

If the Saints were included as renewed beneficiaries under the "flag God has given" (which of course they were, even in ways nobody comprehended at the time), then these following amendments, particularly the Fourteenth Amendment, were especially remarkable and relevant to God's work and glory. For not only did the Fourteenth Amendment grant citizenship, but it did what the Prophet Joseph had pled for some thirty years earlier. It took the warped application of the "states' rights doctrine" by the horns, and compelled all states to respect and adhere to the divine laws governing moral agency. Under the Fourteenth Amendment, states would be forced by the federal government to adhere, not only to the new amendment, but also to other amendments defined by the Bill of Rights.

This expansive requirement was placed in the Amendment because Congress knew that without it the Southern states would say to their black neighbors what Missouri had said to the Saints— that the Bill of Rights can't trump state law. But all this had now changed. Overturning judicial misapplications, such as those stemming from decisions like that found in the aforementioned *Barron v. Baltimore* (1833), which gave states a justification for rejecting the Bill of Rights, the new amendment demanded: "No State shall make or enforce any law which shall abridge the privileges or immunities of citizens of the United States, nor shall any State deprive any person of life, liberty, or property, without due process of law, nor deny any person within its jurisdiction the equal protection of the laws."

The Constitution, through this amendment, had literally "incorporated" the Bill of Rights directly into every state and local government, thus guaranteeing once and for all such God-given liberties to all men.[13] It was a grand recognition that Americans are citizens, not only of states, but of the United States; and therefore, they are entitled—no matter what—to the covenant blessings of the Constitution. The Court even emphasized that, while this amendment grew out of Union victory over slavery in the Civil War, and thus carried the intent to elevate black Americans, it most certainly applied to all other minority groups as well.[14] No longer, then, could the president or congress tell a prophet of God that, though his cause is just, the federal government's hands were tied, as the state governments controlled all matters of religious freedom. No longer could a county judge or state governor tell the Lord's people that the First Amendment or other constitutional rights were only guaranteed under federal and not state matters. No longer could an evil state or local government confiscate the Saints' arms, deny them the vote, or force them into exile, simply because they believed a certain way.

If the Constitution had not "cover[ed] the whole ground," as Joseph alleged in his day, it certainly did now. Indeed, the states had been called to the carpet, just as Madison had argued they should have been from the beginning.* And if a state ever attempted such a stunt again, the federal government now had a sure and absolute constitutional mandate to come to the rescue. The amendment itself concludes with the words, "Congress shall have the power to enforce...the provisions of this article." Speaking of the blessings such constitutional changes might bring, one African American newspaper declared, (as the Saints might have just as easily declared), that we are "determined to hold every step which has been given to us as citizens of the United States...for our elevation which represents justice, the purity, the truth, and aspiration of heaven."[15]

In the fashion of a true American Covenant-maker, Congressman Robert Bingham, who officially proposed the Fourteenth Amendment, declared that the new amendment included "all the sacred rights of person—those rights dear to

---

* James Madison, the "Father of the Constitution," perhaps foreseeing such potential problems as those faced by the Saints, argued unsuccessfully that the First Amendment's religious clause should specifically call out the states and compel them to adhere. See Monk, 215.

freeman and formidable only to tyrants—and of which the fathers of the Republic spoke, after God had given them victory."[16]

Admittedly, by the time the Fourteenth Amendment fell upon the land in the post Civil War era (it was proposed in 1866 and ratified in 1868), the Saints had long since abandoned their place in the promised land of Missouri. The Amendment, it would appear, came a few decades too late. However, the Church was not to remain in isolation forever. It would, by prophecy, fill America and the world. As such, it *would* return, not only to Missouri, but every other state that had (or otherwise would have) employed the "states' rights doctrine" to oppress and destroy God's work. The war had changed America forever, just as the Doctrine and Covenants prophecies explained that it would. And the Fourteenth Amendment took its place among the most prominent of these changes. As noted by the renowned legal scholar, Linda Monk, "many constitutional scholars believe that, through its wide scope and promise of equality, the Fourteenth Amendment created a new Constitution."[17] Indeed, the Fourteenth Amendment was a direct fulfillment of gospel prophecy. The Fifteenth Amendment (ratified in 1870) only bolstered the Fourteenth Amendment by emphasizing the right of all men to vote, regardless of race.

By 1896, Utah was granted statehood, and this time, as the Saints reintegrated into America, their constitutional rights—so long denied them—were beginning to take shape.* The *universal agency*

---

* It should be noted that, though these constitutional corrections have benefited the Church immensely, there was a period leading up to statehood in which the Church was denied all their rights due to violations of federal anti-polygamy laws. Members were denied their right to vote, own property, and, in some cases, were imprisoned. And though this government persecution (and the anti-polygamy law in general) seemed to violate several constitutional rights, the Lord solved the problem—this time not by a national vexation—but through a revelation to the Church, through the prophet, Wilford Woodruff, to cease the practice of plural marriage. For, if they did not, the Lord revealed that the temples would fall into gentile hands and God's work would be obstructed. Once the Church complied with the revelation and the law, and thus became a state, the Constitution (complete with the added amendments) did, in fact, begin to bless the Church like it never had in its past, and continues to bless the Church today. See *Church History in the Fulness of Times*, 439-443.

and *national repentance* born of the Civil War, and developed in its aftermath, were restoring the American Covenant. The Kingdom of God would roll forward more rapidly and powerfully than ever before.

The Civil Rights Movement

As great and beneficial as the post-war amendments were to minorities, they did not completely solve the constitutional problems that plagued the country. Such problems were most prominently displayed in the Southern states, which found all loopholes possible to violate the spirit of the new amendments, if not the letter. Most of these loopholes centered around laws, known as the *Jim Crow Laws*, which segregated—and thus discriminated against and persecuted—black Americans. The Klu Klux Klan and other organizations developed terror strategies to keep black Americans down. The Klan also targeted Jews, Catholics, and Republicans* during this time.[18]

With so many minority groups being targeted, it is clear that the restored gospel would not have fared well even if it had maintained a strong presence in post-war America. Indeed, the Lord was not ready to bring the Saints out of obscurity quite yet. The lynch mobs, which were responsible for at least 4,735 documented lynchings from the end of the Civil War until the Civil Rights Act, represented the cancer in America that still needed to be purged before America could fulfill its mandate as host-nation of the Restoration. These tragic attacks, of which 1,294 were targeted at whites, were an all too familiar reminder to the Saints of their recent history in the nation created for their divine mission.[19]

---

* Though many modern pundits try to hide this fact, in the 26 major civil rights votes after 1933, a majority of Democrats opposed civil rights legislation in over 80 percent of the votes. The Republican majority, by contrast, favored civil rights in over 96 percent of the votes. See http://www.congresslink.org/civil/essay.html and http://www.yale.edu/ynhti/curriculum/units/1982/3/82.03.04.x.html. Naturally, Martin Luther King Jr was, himself, a member of Lincoln's party—he was a registered Republican. It was President Ronald Reagan who made Dr. King's birthday a national holiday. See http://www.nbra.info/index.cfm?fuseaction=pages.blackgop#martinlutherkingjr.

That America had more growing to do before this divine mission could advance is further reflected in the horrendous Supreme Court decision in *Plessy v. Ferguson* (1896) that legitimized such discrimination and wickedness. In an attempt to maintain the evils of segregation, and still shrewdly dawn the appearance that the wicked policy was consistent with the new constitutional requirement of "equal protection" (Fourteenth Amendment), the Courts simply announced in *Plessy* that "separate is equal."

If such misinterpretations and misapplications still existed in deference to black Americans, then the Saints or any other minority group could not expect more for themselves. The Saints—who gained statehood in the very year that *Plessy* was decided—certainly continued to feel skittish about the Constitution's application during this same period; for it was in this same period, even in the years leading right up to Utah's statehood, that the Church felt the heavy hand of the government fall upon their perceived constitutional right to practice plural marriage. And this was merely in addition to its longer and more brutal history of such governmental injustices. In the spirit of the Prophet Joseph, the Church still recognized the need for more. At this point, this need for more had nothing to do with plural marriage, which had already been abandoned by the Church, but simply equal protection under the law to exist and grow. Indeed, more specific legislation, enforcement, and inspired judicial decisions would be needed before the country was sufficiently free and worthy, and thus fully redeemed, to carry out its divine mandate. And many would step forward and pick up the torch lit by Lincoln, and carry it onward in furtherance of this national redemption.

In the post Civil War era these torch carriers, by and large, consisted of the brave black Americans who fought for such additional constitutional corrections. At one point, after the Emancipation Proclamation had been issued, Lincoln asked black leaders if he could help them with a voluntary migration to Central America, or elsewhere, where the newly liberated men and women might feel more comfortable living their lives. Inspiringly, they

vehemently turned down the offer.* Instead, these brave souls—
many of which included the nearly 190,000 blacks who directly
contributed to Northern military victory—would stay and fight to
change America.[20] Had they left, then the black generations that
stood on their shoulders would not have been there to make the
even greater political changes that they, along with the Saints and
others, would one day enjoy.

To be sure, these souls had taken up the cause of God in a
way nobody could have comprehended at the time. But in the end,
the effort directly contributed to the spreading of God's restored
gospel, as the Civil Rights Movement provided the specific laws and
enforcement the Church needed. Black Americans, in fighting for
freedom, truly were American Covenant-makers. Such an idea is
especially poignant upon considering that they seemed to
understand this all along. They connected their plight and their
hope to ancient Israel, as they sang those spirituals of Moses,
freedom, and the covenant with God. "When Israel was in Egypt's
land," they would sing, "Let my people go."[21] At the news of the
passage of the Thirteenth Amendment, they similarly sang, "Sound
the loud timbrel o'er Egypt's dark sea, Jehovah has triumphed, His
people are free."[22]

Like Lincoln, these inspired African Americans knew they
were on God's mission. Consider, for example, Sojourner Truth
(1797-1883), the former slave turned preacher and abolitionist. "Is
God dead?" she would rhetorically ask the famous Frederick
Douglas during a public speech in which he showed signs of
pessimism for black Americans' future. Ms. Truth taught Christ's
gospel to the nation, turned hearts toward heaven, and clearly knew
whose mission she was on.[23] These black Americans understood
well that the recent vexation was, as one black sergeant commented,
"a medium through which God is helping us."[24] Another black

---

* It was clear that Lincoln made this offer, not as a means to banish former slaves,
but rescue them from an America that would persecute them. See William Lee
Miller, *President Lincoln: The Duty of a Statesman*, 299.

soldier, and one-time Union recruiter, told how his black colleagues had "entered the field for 'Liberty,' and are holding the starry emblem, dear to our hearts as a precious jewel, never to trail in the dust." Another Northern black man, during this time, proclaimed that his people would fight to "preserve that glorious Union which our fore fathers had preserved for us," and which promised "our country's rights; our rights, our people's rights."[25] And yet another black soldier testified that, even after the war, it would take the continual interventions of God to bring about "equal right and justice to all men in the United States."[26]

Though the earliest attempts to effectively apply the new amendments in post-war America were slow at best, some advancements had been made. For example, President Ulysses S. Grant had signed the Klan act, outlawing the KKK.[27] In most instances of mass lynchings and riots, National Guard troops were sent in to protect and restore minority rights, such as what occurred in the great Springfield riot of 1908.[28] Consider what joy the Prophet Joseph would have experienced if a government official had sent troops into Missouri or Illinois to protect the Saints in their days of distress. That conditions had changed enough so as to permit such federal action on behalf of the oppressed is proof-positive that the Lord's vexation was already producing fruit. But more would be needed. As one black Civil War veteran understood, and explained in words that the Saints might have borrowed at the time, "God in his own good time will batter down this barrier...and open the hearts of the people to the justness of our claim."[29]

One of the greatest American Covenant-makers who helped develop the fruits of liberty during this era was Theodore Roosevelt. As President of the United States, he understood the road to national redemption. He recognized sins past and opened doors for the downtrodden. A true Northern Unionist (from the time he was a small child), Roosevelt captured the divine intention of the Civil War. As president, he took bold and refreshing measures to make it clear that he was for equal rights, no matter one's color. "The only wise and honorable and Christian thing to do," he declared, "is to treat each black man and each white man strictly on his merits as a man." He told of how he had fought in Cuba side by side with black soldiers and he testified of their worth. He promised to get them a "square deal." To the chagrin of many, Roosevelt opened the White House to Black Americans, taking no issue (as his predecessors had) with entertaining them along with white Americans. He was praised by black leaders. "The administration of President Roosevelt," stated one prominent black preacher, "is to the Negro what the heart is to the body. It has pumped life blood into every artery of the Negro in this country."[30]

Roosevelt's role as American Covenant-maker expanded further in that he was one of the first to build America into a power and influence the entire world began to recognize. He thrust America into the limelight through, for example, expanding its military power and parading it before the family of nations. America's influence was being felt. The bridges he built in this effort would facilitate the American principles of liberty to reach out and touch these foreign nations one day, thus paving the way for the restored gospel of Christ to follow.

In that he possessed an understanding of American Covenant principles, it is altogether fitting that Roosevelt had an intimate knowledge of, and high admiration for, the Church of Jesus Christ of Latter-day Saints. According to historian Michael Winder, "no President did more than Theodore Roosevelt to bestow national legitimacy on the LDS Church."[31] In 1902, President Roosevelt promised the Church he would "do anything he could" for it. He immediately made good on that promise. Upon learning of Mormon missionaries who were suffering persecution in Germany, Roosevelt pledged to intervene on their behalf.

During this time, Roosevelt also served as a proactive proponent of Mormon Senator (and Apostle) Reed Smoot, who was facing persecution by a prejudiced Senate. Many Senators believed that a Mormon (though legitimately elected) should not be honored with a Senate seat and were fighting to keep him out. Apart from showing much personal love and support to the suffering Smoot,

Roosevelt publicly declared, "By all that's holy, I say to you that Reed Smoot is entitled to his seat in the Senate." Roosevelt even appointed the chief counsel for the anti-Mormon faction in the Senate to a federal judgeship in Ohio in order to get him out of Washington. The president was doing all he could to disrupt this oppressive and wicked movement against the Mormons. Roosevelt visited Salt Lake City in 1903, becoming the first U.S. president to speak in the Tabernacle. Roosevelt also defended the Mormons against discriminatory attacks, writing an article in a national publication in which he praised the Church's "unusually high" morals. Roosevelt did all of this for the Church, even though advisors told him it would "cost you moral support" of the large anti-Mormon movement, which was by now "cussing Roosevelt up-hill and down-dale" for his Mormon association.[32]

Notwithstanding the consequences, Roosevelt seemed to act on a deeper understanding of what America was suppose to be. And he knew the Church was part of the grand design. Shortly before securing the presidency, Roosevelt met Ben E. Rich, the Mormon Mission President for the Southern States Mission. Roosevelt took a liking to him and invited him for a visit on his private train car. Roosevelt expressed an interest in the Church, and the two stayed up all night, and into the early morning hours, discussing the Restoration. President Rich bore his testimony and gifted a Book of Mormon to Roosevelt. When President Rich stood to excuse himself for the night, the soon-to-be President of the United States declared that he had "never listened to a more interesting account of a great people and a great religion."[33] Did this incident prompt his deep commitment to the Church? Whatever it did, Roosevelt's actions thereafter had a profound effect on the Saints and their ability to grow the Kingdom.

Years after his presidency, and shortly before his death, Roosevelt called on Elder Smoot (who had, at last, been given his Senate seat). The sickly and dying former president told the Apostle that he believed his time on the earth was nearing its end. He then bore the following testimony to Elder Smoot: "I have tried to live a

Christian life, I believe in God, I have tried to wrong no man. I expect to continue my work beyond."[34] Upon Roosevelt's death in 1919, Elder Smoot was one of the few to be invited to his small and private funeral. The only song at the service was Roosevelt's favorite Hymn, *How Firm a Foundation*.

At the General Conference following Roosevelt's death, Elder Richard L. Lyman declared, "I recognized, long before the death of Theodore Roosevelt, that the Lord raised him up to stir the hearts of men to civic righteousness, as perhaps no man could have stirred them." President Heber J. Grant said, "I believe that Roosevelt felt that we were right. I think he was nearer converted to the truth than any man who ever occupied the presidential chair." Soon after, Elder Smoot served as Roosevelt's proxy and had his temple work done.[35] Like so many leaders before him, God had placed Roosevelt in a position to assist in the great work. And like the others, in addition to his clear vision of American Covenant principles, there was also a tender connection to the restored gospel.

The Lord was clearly doing what He could to ensure that the fruit of the great and terrible vexation was coming to light. Another event that helped the Lord in His quest was World War II. Like the Civil War, this war also humbled the nation, keeping it on a divinely appointed track. Theodore Roosevelt's cousin, President Franklin Delano Roosevelt, recognized this trend and tried to facilitate it for the benefit of God and man. Shortly before D-Day, Roosevelt and British Prime Minister Winston Churchill sat through a sermon in Alexandria, Virginia, in which the Reverend Edward Welles invoked the American Covenant: "I believe that this present world struggle is at its core a spiritual struggle, and that much of the evil is on our side. We Americans need to be purged and cleansed individually and nationally before we are worthy to survive...and we must repent and turn to God if we are to be saved."[36]

Roosevelt took the message to heart. On the eve of America's D-Day invasion, he led the nation, via radio broadcast, in a prayer. In the prayer, he pled for America's victory in its effort to "preserve our Republic, our religion and our civilization, and to set free a suffering humanity." But the president knew that for the Lord to bless America, America had to make greater strides in redeeming itself from its national sin. The prayer concluded, "Help us to conquer the apostles of greed and racial arrogances. Lead us to the saving of our country...[and to] a peace that will let all men live in freedom, reaping the just rewards of their honest toil. Thy will be done Almighty God, Amen."[37] Like Lincoln and Washington before him, Roosevelt invoked the American Covenant. He knew the key to unlocking it was further *national repentance* and a policy and culture of *universal agency*—even a development of the young fruit produced from God's vexation.

That World War II did, in fact, have a positive effect on America and her covenant is evidenced by the clear socio-political changes that evolved immediately following the war. Whether fighting abroad or assisting at home, whether black or white, Christian or Jew, the nation had been forced to join hands against a common enemy. Thus was forged a closer bond and understanding among Americans. Some nine hundred black Americans had enlisted in the armed forces. This prompted a newfound respect for minorities in the post-war era, particularly as their white comrades-in-arms brought home the message that blacks and whites both bleed the same red. The returning black soldiers vocalized the same: "I spent four years in the Army to free a bunch of Dutchmen and Frenchmen," declared a black corporal upon his return, "and I'm hanged if I'm going to let the Alabama version of the Nazis kick me around when I get home."[38]

President Harry Truman, who had led America to final victory after Roosevelt's death, immediately responded to this benevolent wind of change by desegregating the armed forces. Truman further responded by becoming the most vocal president since Lincoln on the issue of civil rights.[39] He even recognized that civil rights included the betterment of all minorities, including religious ones; for, at the same time he desegregated the armed forces, he also pressed Congress to work for anti-discrimination legislation in protection of Catholics and Jews (a comforting sentiment for all religious underdogs, including the Saints). Truman admitted that the Fourteenth Amendment had been ignored, and that the federal government had the responsibility to protect "individual liberties and equal protection under the laws" so that *all* Americans might see the government's "faith in the free way of life." When asked where his unpopular rhetoric stemmed—which rhetoric he knew might cost him his reelection—he simply responded "the Constitution and the Bill of Rights."[40]

The Southern states responded with belligerence and threats, citing the "state's rights doctrine" as protection against such federal intervention, just as Missourians had done when the Prophet Joseph called on Washington D.C. But this time, armed with the post-vexation amendments, along with a post-WWII surge of spiritual enlightenment, Truman—who ironically hailed from Jackson County, Independence, Missouri—stood boldly in opposition to them. Echoing the aforementioned words of the Prophet Joseph, who had declared that the "states' rights doctrine" was a "stink offering in the nose of the Almighty,"[41] Truman's ally in the cause, Hubert Humphrey, declared in 1948 that it was time to "get out of the shadow of states' rights and walk forthrightly into the bright sunshine of human rights."[42] These sentiments reflected the already developing post-war American culture that fostered both the repentance for past sins of discrimination and the desire to make things right through increased freedom and equal empowerment to minorities.

Truman's American Covenant vision perhaps compelled him to view the Latter-day Saints with much fondness. As a native of Independence, Missouri, Truman apologized to the Church for the "prejudice" that had existed there against the Saints.[43*]

---

* When Truman visited Utah in 1948, he told a crowd of his fondness for Mormon Congressman Walter K. Granger. He then related a humorous exchange between the two of them: "Congressman Granger...told me that he had become so fond of me that when the Mormons moved back to Independence, he was going to let me stay. I thought that was the greatest compliment that could be paid to anybody." See Winder, 265.

Truman asked Church leaders for a Book of Mormon, which was sent forthwith. The Prophet George Albert Smith included a letter outlining Mormon doctrine. Elder James Talmage sent additional literature. Within the year, Truman got word that President Smith was visiting Washington D.C. and summoned him to the White House. During the Oval Office visit, Truman opened his desk drawer, took out the Book of Mormon, and said, "Look, President Smith, I've got my Book of Mormon right here."[44]

Truman, an active Freemason, was indeed an American Covenant-maker. "I do not think that anyone can study the history of this nation of ours," declared Truman, "without becoming convinced that Divine Providence has played a great part in it."

> I have a feeling that God has created us and brought us to our present position of power and strength for some great purpose. It is not given to us to know fully what that purpose is. But I think we may be sure of one thing. And that is that our country is intended to do all it can, in cooperation with other nations, to help create peace and preserve peace in the world. It is given to us to defend the spiritual values—the moral code—against the vast forces of evil that seek to destroy them.[45]*

The progress made by the American Covenant during this era was not only propelled by the executive branch, but from the judiciary as well. The Supreme Court has no enforcement arm of its own (outside the executive branch), and therefore must rely on the people's acceptance of their decisions to maintain credibility. It is, therefore, easy to find cultural changes reflected in its decisions. Such was the case in the Court's decision in *Brown v the Board of Education of Topeka, Kansas* (1954). The decision at last recognized the

---

* Harry Truman felt a bond with Israel. In May 1948, when Israel declared itself a free and sovereign state, President Truman was the first national leader to recognize the new state of Israel. Much of the rest of the world followed his example, and Israel, at last, had been given a seat at the table of the family of nations.

true meaning of the Fourteenth Amendment and ruled that segregating educational facilities (Linda Carol Brown had been forced to attend a segregated and thus substandard school) was in no way "equal," as the minority facilities were clearly underdeveloped. The decision essentially overturned the segregation of *Jim Crow, Plessy,* and the evil parts of the states' rights doctrine, and truly enlivened the inspired Fourteenth Amendment. Indeed, it bolstered the constitutional principle of equal rights.

As Cheryl Brown, sister of the plaintiff, commented years later, "We don't pretend that *Brown* was completely and solely about public schools. It wasn't. It was about changing the nature of things [and] holding this country to its constitutional promise."[46] Martin Luther King described the Brown decision in true American Covenant fashion. "One day, through a world-shaking decree by nine justices of the Supreme Court of America," he said, "the Red Sea was opened, and the forces of justice marched through to the other side."[47]

The Lord clearly inspired leaders (like Truman) and utilized events (like World War II) to further shape and mold the people, influencing them to come unto the covenant. Upon recognizing the people's will on the matter, the Court more easily ruled as it did in *Brown*. But it appeared to many that the Lord had done even more to influence this important judicial decision. When the case first came before the Court in December 1952, it had little chance of sustaining the Brown family's argument, as Chief Justice Vinson was set on influencing the Court in favor of discrimination. His opponents, however, managed to delay the decision, and asked for time to research the matter. Just months before the case was to be reheard, Vinson suffered a major heart attack and died, thus turning the tide of the Court in favor of equality. Vinson's colleague on the court, Justice Felix Frankfurter, interpreted the Chief Justice's sudden death as "the first indication I have ever had that there is a God."[48] Whether God took Vinson for His purposes or not, one can hardly deny the Heavenly influence in the final outcome. After all, the Fourteenth Amendment—which was so necessary for the further constitutional protection of the restored gospel—had, through *Brown,* landed on the high ground where it belonged. Clearly, the fertile soil of a free and worthy America, intended for the growth of gospel restoration, had once again been enriched.

In light of how the Court often reflects society, it is interesting to note the stark contrast between the *Dred Scott* decision (1858), which practically defined blacks as sub-human, and the *Brown* decision (1954), which ruled in the opposite direction. The bridge that gaps these opposing opinions was, notably, nothing less than the foretold vexations of the Lord. Such an idea only further validates the prophecies as presented by this study. God had caused the people to change, and the Court was a reflection of it.

In spite of this progress, however, too many Americans still refused to acknowledge or respect *Brown* or the Fourteenth Amendment, and remained determined to segregate and discriminate. Certain state politicians even publicly pronounced that they would not obey these constitutional corrections and continued to enforce discrimination.[49] Notwithstanding, as it was the American Covenant that hung in the balance, the Lord would continue to inspire His chosen ones to advance His cause. Though the stories of the Lord's hand in such advancements are too vast for this study to include them all, we will consider a few.

There was, for example, the tragic 1955 death of the young black boy Emmit Till, who, after showing off in front of a white woman in Mississippi (as many 14 year-olds do), was summarily kidnapped, tortured, and murdered by the woman's family. Emmit's mother, Mamie, explained how she had turned to the Lord to discover what she should do. In a strange revelation, it was shown to her that she must reveal to the world photographs taken of the tortured and battered dead body of her baby, so the world could see and thus deal with the national cancer that still needed purging. "With God's guidance," explained Mamie, "I made a commitment to rip the covers off Mississippi, USA—revealing to the world the horrible face of race hatred."[50] It worked. Americans rose to the occasion and elevated their efforts to make America that nation God had intended.

Approximately one hundred days after the murder, with this new surge of national awareness, a little woman in Montgomery, Alabama named Rosa Parks refused to give her seat up on the bus because of the color of her skin. And again, as it was God's covenant with America that was at stake, it was God who encouraged Rosa. Rosa later reflected, "I felt the presence of God on the bus and heard His quiet voice as I sat there waiting for the police to take me to the station. There were people on the bus that knew me, but no one said a word to help or encourage me. I was lonely, but I was at peace. The voice of God told me that He was at my side." Rosa's actions led to a major bus boycott which shook Montgomery and the nation. Rosa legally challenged the law that had got her arrested and, months later, the Supreme Court heard her case and agreed with her.[51]

A similar story is that of Ruby Bridges, the six-year-old black child who, in 1960, challenged Southern non-compliance of the *Brown* decision by matriculating into a previously all white school. In the midst of screaming and protesting Southerners, the small girl in the white dress, accompanied by four husky U.S. Marshals, made her way to class. She stopped briefly and bowed her head, then continued on her way. A child psychiatrist, Dr. Robert Coles, who had been observing Ruby and offered his services to the family, later asked her about what she had been doing (Ruby's teacher, who witnessed it, had told Coles that it looked like Ruby had stopped to talk to the protesters). "I wasn't talking to them," she replied, "I was just saying a prayer for them...I pray for me, that I would be strong and not afraid. I pray for my enemies that God would forgive them."[52] She astonished the doctor, her teacher, and the nation.

Through people like Mamie Till, Rosa Parks, and little Ruby Bridges, all of whom felt and testified that they were on God's errand, the nation took one more step (during this post-WWII enlightened environment) toward the required *national repentance* and *universal agency*. Such inspiring stories of change only gave more credence and power to the enlightened work of advancements like the Fourteenth Amendment and the *Brown* decision. To be sure, unlike Joseph Smith's America, much had already changed in the socio-political environment.

These changes at last justified and encouraged the very solution the Saints had called for when they found themselves up against an unjust faction, just as their black brothers and sisters did at this time in American history. Indeed, whereas the president and the federal government had refused to act on behalf of the Saints, the proof-positive that these days were over, and that the prophesied changes had arrived, had manifested itself in Rosa's favorable *federal* court decision and in Ruby's *federal* escort. And underlying it all, of course (as the principal players attested to), was the spirit and influence of God. Adding to the list of federal action, President Dwight Eisenhower—the same president who appointed a true apostle of God (Elder Ezra Taft Benson) to serve on his cabinet—sent the 101st Airborne Division into Little Rock, Arkansas to enforce these constitutional rights for black students being denied an education.[53] Could not, then, the Saints expect the same reaction if ever such injustice fell upon them again in their efforts to bring the gospel's salvation to the world? Again, what affects one, affects all.

The religious freedom and tolerance that naturally accompanied this Civil Rights Movement continued to manifest itself. For example, for decades Catholics in America had been discriminated against and abused, just as the Baptists in colonial Virginia had been before them. But, during the 1960 presidential election, a Catholic candidate, John F. Kennedy, seemed to be the rising star. In spite of his success, however, he was constantly being attacked by the many intolerant judgments against his faith. Kennedy finally responded to the attacks in a speech given before the Greater Houston Ministerial Association on September 12, 1960. Kennedy identified himself as "the victim" of the nation's social ills, which had for too long "ripped the fabric of our harmonious society." He said he looked forward to the day when the nation would "refrain from those attitudes of disdain and division which have so often marred their works in the past, and promote instead the American ideal of brotherhood."[54] He continued, "This is the kind of America for which our forefathers died, when they fled here...when they fought for the Constitution, and [the] Bill of Rights."[55] Americans largely responded to the speech by recognizing the truth of what Kennedy declared, and collectively pushed to achieve further progress in religious tolerance. That such progress was achieved is perhaps best illustrated by the fact that Kennedy was elected president some two months later.

Fittingly, this "American ideal of brotherhood" achieved even greater heights under the Kennedy White House. In 1963, it sponsored a bill that effectively combined, shored up, and specified the above-referenced civil rights amendments, court decisions, and executive orders, and placed them into what would become the most comprehensive civil rights legislation to date: The Civil Rights Act of 1964. And while many associate this legislation exclusively with black rights—as blacks were, in fact, the most obvious recipients—it equally and specifically includes religious groups and promises to protect them from persecution. Further, it mandates that the federal government intervene in any state where such religious intolerance might be present. Pulling constitutional authority from both Article I (the interstate commerce clause) and from the Fourteenth Amendment (which charges the federal government to intervene in states where civil rights are being violated), the Civil Rights Act provides much sought-after federal protection.[56] As detailed in previous chapters, it was the precise solution that the Prophet Joseph had called for over one hundred years earlier. To quote him again: "The only fault I find with the Constitution is, it is not broad enough to cover the whole ground."

> Although it provides that all men shall enjoy religious freedom, yet it does not provide the manner by which that freedom can be preserved, nor for the punishment of Government officers who refuse to protect the people in their religious rights, or punish the mobs, states, or communities who interfere with the rights of the people on account of their religion. Its sentiments are good, but it

provides no means of enforcing them. It has but this one fault.[57]

At last, this "one fault" was being corrected.

As we have already discussed, Joseph was commanded to seek out such constitutional change at the *federal* level (D&C 101:88), which he tried so tirelessly (but unsuccessfully) to do. So, the Lord, as promised, took matters into His own hands (D&C 101:89-90). After over one hundred years, and after much bloodshed, toil, tears, and humbling, which resulted in righteous, yet still incomplete, constitutional amendments, congressional acts, court decisions, and executive orders, the nation at last was achieving that which the prophet of the Restoration had called for. Thus, the prophesied change (D&C 101:93-95; 121: 11-12) came closer and closer into focus and began to reach out and touch the Saints and expand the Restoration.

But, like every socio-political movement, it would take additional time and further inspired leadership for this crowning legislation to take effect. In fact, Kennedy did not live to see the Civil Rights Act passed (the Senate blocked its vote with the infamous filibuster). Notwithstanding, his vision for civil rights was correct, if not prophetic. On September 26, 1963, two months before his tragic and abrupt death, Kennedy linked this vision to the American Covenant like few had before. He did so in a speech, which he later said was "one of the best speeches" he had ever given. Fittingly, it occurred in the Mormon Tabernacle, with the Prophet David O. McKay at his side. President Kennedy declared the following:

> Let us remember that the Mormons of a century ago were a persecuted minority, harried from place to place, the victims of violence and occasionally murder, while today, in the short span of 100 years, their faith and works are known and respected the world around, and their voices heard in the highest councils of this country. As the Mormons succeeded, so America can succeed, if we will

not give up or turn back....Tonight I speak for all
Americans in expressing our gratitude to the Mormon
people—for their pioneer spirit....But I am particularly in
their debt tonight for their successful battle to make
religious liberty a living reality—for having proven to the
world that different faiths of different views could flourish
harmoniously in our midst.[58]

As part of his speech, Kennedy also recited the inspired
words of Joseph Smith, as recorded in the 11th Article of Faith: "We
claim the privilege of worshipping Almighty God according to the
dictates of our own conscience, and allow all men the same
privilege, let them worship how, where, or what they may."[59]

Following the speech, the Mormon Tabernacle Choir sang the
Battle Hymn of the Republic, even that hymn which more than any
other reflected the American Covenant, particularly during the Civil
War. Gordon B. Hinckley (then an Apostle) witnessed this event and
testified of its power with the "presence in this building of the chief
executive of the nation...touching the emotions of everyone here
assembled." Elder Hinckley remembered, "I felt a catch in my throat
and a tingle in my spine." On another occasion, Elder Hinckley
recalled, "I was seated near [President Kennedy] when he spoke in
the Salt Lake Tabernacle not long ago...It was a stirring thing to hear
his plea."[60]

The Mormon cause was the American cause. And the chief
proponent of the Civil Rights Act knew it. And so he would, per the
covenant, push for further protection for minorities like the Saints.
Kennedy invited future apostle James Faust to join his Lawyer's
Committee for Civil Rights. The president also invited the Prophet
to Washington to consult on the issue. President McKay sent the
General Relief Society President to represent the Church. Also
significant was the fact that Mormon Congressman Ralph Harding
hand-delivered a copy of the Book of Mormon (even that most
prominent book outlining the principles of the American Covenant)
to President Kennedy.[61]

Beyond his firm grasp of American Covenant principles at home, Kennedy was perhaps even more passionate about these principles as applied to evil abroad. As if he understood how the War in Heaven had extended to earth below, Kennedy famously declared in his Inaugural Address that "the rights of man come... from the hand of God," and that America "will pay any price [and] bear any burden...for the success of liberty."[62] He stated that "here on earth God's work must truly be our own."[63] Hugh B. Brown, of the First Presidency, stated the following at a Church memorial service for Kennedy shortly after his death: "It was our good fortune to live at a time when a world leader was raised up to chart the way and to inspire...the youth of our land and of the world. God bless his memory."[64]

While Kennedy had done much to fulfill the Prophet Joseph's dream of civil rights legislation, it had not yet been accomplished. The reins would be passed to another to finish the job —President Lyndon B. Johnson. Johnson pushed the bill through successfully and signed it into law in July 1964. Not insignificant was the fact that, directly leading up to the moment of signing, hundreds of believers lined the halls of Congress during the bill's final debates, praying with the nation for its safe and secure passage.[65] The prayers had decisively been answered. In his 1965 inaugural address, Johnson recognized, like those before him, that the Civil Rights Movement was something connected to a national covenant composed of *national repentance, universal agency* and the Lord's will: "They [the early Americans] came here," declared a newly sworn-in Johnson, "to find a place where a man could be his own man. They *made a covenant with this land.* Conceived in justice, written in liberty, bound in union, it was meant one day to inspire the hopes of all mankind: and it binds us still. If we keep its terms we shall flourish."[66]

Such covenant-based, spiritually–derived themes (which sound more like Book of Mormon scripture than political speech) only increased in Johnson as he continued his fight for increased liberty by pushing for the Voting Rights Act of 1965. (In spite of the

Civil Rights Act, Southern state's found loopholes to deny blacks the vote.) In a nationally televised speech to a joint Congress, he declared that the fight for civil rights was the same fight that began at "Lexington and Concord" (the Revolutionary War), was carried on through "Appomattox" (the Civil War), and continued on in his day through events like the recent "Bloody Sunday" attack by state troopers on peaceful black protesters marching at Selma, Alabama. (We might add that it was the same fight fought at places like Haun's Mill, Missouri in October 1838.)

Indeed, as Lincoln had suggested, the entire struggle was bigger than any one man or race—it was about growing and protecting the liberty and agency God desires for His children. And though few, if any, made this gospel connection at the time, it was true. Johnson dedicated his words and actions on civil rights to "the dignity of man and the destiny of democracy" and asked "Americans of all religions and of all colors" to "join me in that cause." "We shall overcome," he demanded.[67]

During this speech, Johnson, in the spirit of Lincoln, even went beyond the theme of *universal agency*, and suggested that *national repentance* was also an issue at stake. Applying a scriptural principle to the entire nation, Johnson asked his fellow Americans, "What is a man profited if he shall gain the whole world and lose his own soul." And finally, he ended the speech fittingly, by stating that "[God] really favors the undertaking that we begin here tonight."[68] Though marred forever by other issues—like the debacle that was Vietnam, unhealthy growth via the New Deal, campus riots, rampant inflation, political assassinations, etc (it seemed the adversary was trying his best to deflect a great work in progress at this time)—Johnson, in the area of civil rights, was one of the greatest presidents. This was especially true in light of the fact that the freedom and repentance he helped encourage in America would directly support God's church on the earth—it would directly support modern-day Israel and the American Covenant.

As such, it is rather fitting that religionists in America connected the struggles and achievements surrounding civil rights legislation to the struggles and achievements of enslaved ancient Israel longing to be free. Author Theodore White compared Johnson's ultimate civil rights victory to the same Old Testament story. "It was as if Kennedy, a younger Moses, had led an elder Joshua [Johnson] to the height of Mount Nebo and there shown him the promised land which he himself would never enter but which Joshua would make his own." In an apparent confirmation of this idea, President Johnson uttered the following spine-chilling declaration in his 1965 Inaugural Address: "The American covenant called on us to help show the way for the liberation of man."[69]

But the connections between Johnson and the gospel do not end there. According to Winder, "Without question, the friendship between Lyndon B. Johnson and David O. McKay was the strongest bond between a Church president and U.S. President in history."[70] The relationship began ordinarily enough with Johnson making a pair of courtesy political visits (as John Kennedy's vice president) to President McKay beginning in 1960. But clearly Johnson felt something profound and unusual in these visits. Two months after Kennedy was assassinated, placing the burden of the presidency on Johnson, he called the Prophet.

The Prophet David O. McKay with President Lyndon B. Johnson, Courtesy of LDS Church Archives

"I wonder if you feel like coming down to Washington and see me sometime in the next week or two?...I don't have anything emergency, but I just need a little strength and I think that would come from visiting with you an hour or so." President McKay arrived in Washington within days and consulted with Johnson. President McKay was the first religious leader invited to the Johnson White House. Johnson explained that he had called the Prophet on an "impulse." Edwin B. Firmage, an aide to Johnson, found the connection unique. He explained that the Administration did not expect to ever carry Utah in any presidential election. The President's deep desire to speak to the Prophet seemed genuine. McKay's secretary recalled that after that initial visit, President Johnson contacted the Prophet "all the time...He would have ideas, and would want to talk them out...He really liked President McKay." [71]

Johnson once told the Prophet that when he was a boy dealing with the stresses of life he had his mother's shoulder to rest his head on. He told President McKay that he needed him to be "another shoulder to rest on."[72] On that same occasion he told the Prophet, "I feel that the spiritual and moral fiber of this country needs strengthening, and we need it badly. I would like to ask you, President McKay, if you can tell me how to get it. I have been out to see you on two or three occasions before and each time I left you I came away inspired." On another occasion, Johnson stated, "I could not fly over Utah without stopping to see President McKay. I always feel better after I have been in his presence." And on yet another occasion, Johnson admitted, "I don't know just what it is about President McKay. I talk to...all of the others [preachers from other faiths] but somehow it seems as though President McKay is something of a father to me. It seems as though every little while I have to write him a letter or something."[73]

For obvious reasons, LDS chaplains serving in the military reflect something of the American Covenant. During the 1960's, the military had created a policy that made it impossible for LDS chaplains to serve. The Prophet brought this problem to President Johnson. Being the good American Covenant leader he was, Johnson immediately remedied it. In a phone call to a military bureaucrat, who was attempting to defend the old policy, President Johnson barked back, "Listen here, these Mormons, from the minute they are out of their mothers' womb, have been praying and teaching and leading one another, and then they go out on missions. I would rather have one of their boys than one of the preachers you get out of the seminary, so you fix it up so that they can get their chaplains." He then added, "I cannot have Dr. McKay out in Salt Lake City sitting there thinking I am not doing the thing he has asked me to do, so you do it."[74]

One of the most telling symbols of Johnson's powerful relationship with the Prophet occurred during Johnson's presidential inauguration ceremony in 1965. Johnson had invited the Mormon Tabernacle Choir to perform at the inaugural ceremony, which set the spiritual tone. It was during his speech at the ceremony that Johnson made his aforementioned comment about how the liberation of man was provided under what he called "The American covenant." Amidst all the business of the day, two hours after his speech, Johnson called the Prophet. "Dr. McKay," said Johnson, "I want you to know that I was thinking of you during the time I was delivering my address." Johnson spoke briefly to the Prophet's wife, Emma Ray, telling her, "Take care of my good friend President McKay." Johnson followed up the phone call with a letter, telling the Prophet that Inauguration Day "was marred only by your absence, but the personal strength we have taken from you in the past was present—and very real—for both Mrs. Johnson and me." Three flags flew over the U.S. Capitol during Johnson's inauguration. He kept one for himself, offered one to his vice president, but saved the third one for the Prophet of God.[75]

This powerful relationship between Prophet and President has made many wonder if it represented a fulfillment of a prophecy put forth by Brigham Young's first counselor in the First Presidency: "The President of the United States," declared Heber C. Kimball, will "come and consult with authorities of this Church to know what is best to do for his people."[76] It was indeed a relationship reminiscent of other prophets and national leaders of antiquity, who similarly worked together for the benefit of God's national covenant. (Consider, for example, the ancient king of Israel and Elisha the

Prophet, or Captain Moroni and the Prophet Alma.)[77] But the thing which binds this relationship even closer, making it a true reflection of the American Covenant, is that it occurred under the American Administration which brought us the single piece of legislation called for and prophesied over by Prophet Joseph, and which was miraculously delivered by the Lord. It brought us the Civil Rights Act.

We might conclude that amidst the many private interviews and correspondence that occurred between Johnson and President McKay (we do not know the half of what went on between them),[78] perhaps they discussed the importance of the Civil Rights Movement. However, linking President McKay to the Civil Rights Act requires careful consideration. For, many of the Brethren serving under and advising President McKay warned him that this legislation was nothing but a move by communists to take over the nation. Others claimed that it represented a violation of the states' rights doctrine.[79] (This argument was especially ironic, as it was the precise justification given to the Prophet Joseph as to why the federal government could not help the suffering Saints.) President McKay listened to the warnings intently, but remained mostly quiet when the issue arose before the general councils of the Church. The Prophet did, however, make one single move that perhaps reflects his final decision on the matter. In 1961, while the debate over civil rights raged, President McKay did something that had not been done since the presidency of Brigham Young. He called a third counselor into the First Presidency. His choice was Hugh B. Brown, a staunch proponent of Civil Rights legislation.[80]

In October General Conference, 1963, President McKay had President Brown read a profound statement. President McKay later had this statement re-published in the *Deseret News* as a confirmation that this was the Church's "official" position on Civil Rights.[81]

> [T]here is in this Church no doctrine, belief, or practice that
> is intended to deny the enjoyment of full civil rights by any

person regardless of race, color, or creed...[W]e believe that all men are the children of the same God and that it is a moral evil for any person or group of persons to deny any human being...We have consistently and persistently upheld the Constitution of the United States, and as far as we are concerned that means upholding the constitutional rights of every citizen of the United States. We call upon all men everywhere, both within and outside the Church, to commit themselves to the establishment of full civil equal equality for all God's children. Anything less than this defeats our high ideal of the brotherhood of man.[82]*

Within one year of this statement, President Johnson signed the Civil Rights Act into law. Many in the LDS community were not for the Civil Rights Act and were slow when it came to elevating African Americans in Utah society.[83] Perhaps they did not (or could not) comprehend the fact that this piece of legislation seemed directly tied to scripture, prophecy, and the building of the Kingdom. But they did not need to immediately understand. When it came to civil rights legislation, this was a matter that the American Covenant-makers in the United States government needed first and foremost. And the Lord blessed these civil servants with this knowledge. For the rest of us, hindsight is twenty-twenty. Though President McKay confessed that there were "some" problems with the legislation (certainly it was not perfect), he did accept President Johnson's invitation to

---

* President McKay stated clearly that the LDS priesthood ban on blacks "is a practice, not a doctrine, and the practice will some day be changed. And that's all there is to it." See Prince and Wright, 79-80. According to Joseph Smith Biographer Richard Bushman, the exclusion of black men from the Priesthood was not a church policy until after the death of the Prophet Joseph. Furthermore, blacks were permitted to participate in temple worship under Joseph's administration. Also, we know of at least one black member and friend of Joseph, Elijah Abel, who had been ordained an Elder under Joseph's administration. See Richard Lyman Bushman, *Joseph Smith, Rough Stone Rolling*, 289.

serve on his national committee for civil rights.[84] Also, a few months after the Civil Rights Act became law, a strange and telling thing occurred in Utah. It broke with its long-standing tradition and voted decidedly for the Democrat's nominee for president. Utahans voted for the incumbent, Lyndon B. Johnson—the champion of the Civil Rights Act.[85]

The story of the Civil Rights Movement, and its connection with the American Covenant, would not be complete without discussing the one man who worked harder than any other to get it passed—Dr. Martin Luther King Jr.* Though, again, most people associate his success exclusively with the advancement of black Americans, Dr. King himself understood that he was working toward something more inclusive. On Sunday, March 31, 1968, he stood at the pulpit of the National Cathedral in Washington D.C. and stated the following before an audience of mixed races and religions: "We are tied together in the single garment of destiny, caught in an inescapable network of mutuality. And whatever affects one directly affects all indirectly. For some strange reason, I can never be what I ought to be until you are what you ought to be. This is the way God's universe is made."[86] In other words, whatever advances toward liberty and opportunity that have been (or will be) made by black Americans through God and His inspired leaders, will likewise benefit and elevate *all* minorities, to include God's restored church on earth. And history proves that such was the case.

Fittingly, displayed within the panels of the pulpit from which he spoke was a scene depicting the issuance of the Magna Carta—that original British document which symbolizes the beginnings of transfer of power from kings and tyrants to the people. It is a symbol and great affirmation of the very agency needed for gospel existence and personal progress. King truly assisted in the furtherance of such liberty to all. Also fitting was the manner in which King concluded his remarks, especially in light of what we know to be the origins of our national covenant. King

---

* It is surprising to some that Martin Luther King was a registered Republican. However, it is only logical that he would be a member of the party of Abraham Lincoln.

asserted that America was to be "a new Jerusalem*...a new day of justice and brotherhood and peace. And that day the morning stars will sing together, and the sons of God will shout for Joy. God bless you." [87]

Days later, King stood before a crowd in Memphis at a Masonic Temple. "[God] has allowed me to go up to the mountain," he declared, "and I've looked over and seen the Promised Land! And I may not get there with you, but I want you to know tonight that we as a people will get to the promised land!...Mine eyes have seen the glory of the coming of the Lord." [88] How prophetic, considering how much he had done to stabilize the very political foundation upon which the Lord *would* come to millions through His restored gospel. The following day, King was shot and killed for the cause he fought for.

It is also significant to note that King understood even deeper principles underlying the national covenant. He understood that these great blessings from God were conditional upon worthiness. "We usually think of freedom *from* something, but freedom is also *to* something. It is not only breaking loose from some evil force, but it is reaching up for a higher force. Freedom from evil is slavery to goodness." [89] On another occasion, he expounded upon our national obligations under the covenant. "One day we will have to stand before the God of history," King warned, "and we will talk in terms of things we've done."

> Yes, we will be able to say we built gargantuan bridges to span the seas. We built gigantic buildings to kiss the skies. Yes, we made our submarines to penetrate oceanic depths. We brought into being many other things with our scientific and technological power. It seems that I can hear the God of history saying "That was not enough! But I was hungry, and ye fed me not. I was naked, and ye clothed me not. I was devoid of a decent sanitary house to live in, and ye provided no shelter for me. And consequently, you cannot enter the kingdom of

---

* See The Articles of Faith, verse 10 in the *Pearl of Great Price*, 61.

greatness. If ye do it unto the least of these, my brethren, ye do it unto me." That's the question facing America today.[90]

King's most memorable speech, which perhaps sums up best the many godly constitutional changes born of the Civil War and developed through the Civil Rights Movement, came a few years earlier. While famously standing on the steps of the Lincoln Memorial (surely it was no coincidence that King chose the Lincoln Memorial—for in the end, these two men fought and died for the same eternal cause), King pronounced, "I have a dream." He then recited several scenarios which would take place in this dream, all having to do with an American socio-political evolution into freedom and justice for all. This was, in fact, the same dream pursued by the Prophet Joseph in his day. King further described his dream as one in which "all God's children...will be able to join hands and sing in the words of the old Negro spiritual, "Free at last! Free at Last! Thank God Almighty, we're free at last."

In light of how this freedom would extend to all religious minorities (including those desirous to spread the priesthood and truth to all the world), it is altogether fitting that King and his followers constantly invoked the Almighty, referring to their cause as the cause of Christ.[91] King wrote from jail, after being arrested for peaceful protest, that "[w]e will win our freedom because the sacred heritage of our nation and the eternal will of God are embodied in our echoing demands."[92] They were more correct than they knew; indeed, they were more intimately aligned with the cause of God than perhaps they ever realized. King, most fittingly, was in attendance, right behind President Johnson, when he signed the Civil Rights Act into law.[93]

As powerful as King's above-cited words were at the Lincoln Memorial, the most striking part of the speech, as it related to the restored gospel and the American Covenant, came as he recited Isaiah 40:4-5. This particular part of his speech was later carved into the granite approach to the Lincoln Memorial:

> I have a dream that one day every valley shall be exalted, and every hill and mountain shall be made low, the rough places will be made plain, and the crooked places will be made straight and the glory of the Lord shall be revealed and all flesh will see it together.[94]

Is this not prophetic and profound? When the Prophet Joseph sought for the constitutional changes needed by the Church—that the "rough places be made plain" and the "crooked places be made straight," etc—did the Lord not say He would make it so? And did the Lord, through a series of events (spanning from the Civil War through the Civil Rights Movement), not direct these changes, which ultimately provided the socio-political foundation whereby the restored gospel has come out of obscurity, that the "glory of the Lord shall be revealed"? How appropriate that this speech, and this scriptural reference, have been immortalized forever at the memorial of the man who was the founder of these constitutional changes— even at the temple of *national repentance* and *universal agency*.*

Conclusion: Fruits of Redemption

The journalist may genuinely ask in wonderment how Mormons went "from being the ultimate outcast to the embodiment of the mainstream in two generations?" Though he could not explain it, he knew it was "a breathtaking transformation." Indeed, it was breathtaking when we think of the Saints in Missouri and Illinois— their wives and children being run out into the freezing wilderness,

---

* After the Church recently assisted a humanitarian organization led by Martin Luther King III (Dr. King's son), he visited Salt Lake City. "I originally came to express my appreciation to the Church for their humanitarian support," he said, "but I quickly learned that the essence of who you are is much deeper and profound. Between the Humanitarian Center, Welfare Square, and the temple open house, I now have a greater appreciation for why you do what you do." See Quentin L. Cook, "Stewardship—A Sacred Trust," October General Conference 2009.

their prophets and leaders being beaten, jailed, and assassinated, and their temple being burned to the ground. Yet, in the years that followed, we have seen the states of Illinois and Missouri make public and official apologies to the Church.[95] We have seen Mormon leaders in the U.S. Congress and other prominent government positions. We have seen a prophet of God receive the highest honor bestowed upon any citizen—the United States Medal of Freedom given by President George W. Bush to President Gordon B. Hinckley.* These examples are but few of the many signs of a miraculous transformation. It was a transformation that took the Kingdom of God and placed it in its rightful and preordained place as a powerful and protected entity under the Constitution—under the American Covenant.

No event in recent history illustrates this powerful change in America better than the events that occurred in Los Angeles, California on November 6, 2008. In protest to the Church's moral position on Proposition 8 (California's marriage amendment), more than one thousand rioters gathered around the Los Angeles Temple, threatening both the sacred edifice and the Saints working therein. Though in days past, the temple might have been left to the will of the mob (as it was with the Kirtland and Nauvoo temples), in this case the American Covenant came to the rescue. Police officers in raid gear landed powerfully upon the temple grounds, prepared to defend it by force if necessary.[96] (Though it was largely state officers who came to the rescue, this does nothing to belittle the importance of the Fourteenth Amendment and the Civil Rights Act. Remember, it was those laws that compelled states to act, and which stand as a backup, should the states fail to act.) It was a perfect illustration of the purpose of America and her covenant—to protect and defend

---

* The official written citation accompanying this award stated, "His tireless efforts to spread the word of God and to promote good will has strengthened his faith, his community and our nation. The United States honors Gordon B. Hinckley for his devoted service to his church and to his fellow-man." See Winder, 394.

freedom of religion, to protect and defend the Kingdom of God. It represented the American Covenant in action.*

Though it is a mystery to many how America elevated the Church from its Nauvoo Temple status (a burned temple) to its Los Angles Temple status (a rescued temple), it is no mystery. It is spelled out in prophecy delivered by the Prophet Joseph Smith. The Lord warned that if the people chose not to fulfill their divine mandate as protectors of the gospel, then He would intervene and "set his hand and seal to change the times and seasons," that He might "proceed to pass [His] act, [His] strange act, and perform [His] work, [His] strange work (see D&C 121:12; D&C 101: 95; and Chapter 3). In the last several chapters we have seen, through scripture and history, how God fulfilled the prophecy through the Civil War, the post-war amendments, and the Civil Rights Movement. And we have clearly seen that at the core of all these events was God and His American Covenant, even that covenant which provided the fertile ground for His gospel restoration. At last, the many wonderful endorsements given to the Constitution by patriots and prophets could be fully justified. Joseph's dream of having a Constitution that fulfilled its divine mandate—that was the "Heavenly Banner" he sought—was finally realized.

But God's restored church was not the only beneficiary. For, all boats were elevated in this glorious rise of the tide. All men gained freedom, and thus gained the privilege to progress within their respective spheres. One grand example of the silent partnership between minorities that grew under God and through the American experience was manifested in the 2008 presidential election. For the first time in history, a Mormon candidate and a black candidate were serious contenders. (The same pattern is being repeated for the 2012 presidential election.) When we consider that pre-Civil War America emphatically placed black Americans and

---

* When President David O. McKay dedicated the Los Angeles Temple, he offered a powerful dedicatory prayer. In that prayer he thanked God for the Constitution, which had made the Restoration possible. See Rex E. Lee, "The Constitution and the Restoration," BYU Devotional, January 15, 1991, available at www.speeches.byu.edu.

Mormon Americans together in the adversary's crosshairs, the transformation and progression we see amongst both groups today is stunning.[97]

Through the acceptance and adoption of new law (e.g. the Fourteenth Amendment, the Civil Rights Act, etc), the covenant requirements (defined by the Book of Mormon) of repenting of sin and serving God had indeed been filled. The cancers of America—religious persecution and slavery—had been crushed. *National repentance* and *universal agency* had, in at least one sense, hit an astonishing peak. *Liberty, protection* and *prosperity* at last began to more fully inundate the nation, thus causing agency unto salvation to flourish further. God had painstakingly, but very successfully, fulfilled the prophecy and redeemed the covenant through these constitutional changes—through this divinely derived law. The famous spiritual plea sung in the hymn *America the Beautiful* had been answered: "America, America, God mend thine every flaw; Confirm thy soul in self control, Thy liberty in law."

ENDNOTES

[1] "The Mormons," produced and directed by Helen Whitney, PBS Special: American Experience, Frontline; airdate: April 30, 2007, program available at http://www.pbs.org/mormons/.

[2] Sgt. David Blair, September 1864, as quoted in Manning, 188.

[3] Captain Henry Riggs, October 1864, as quoted in Manning, 188.

[4] Private John Foote, September 1864, as quoted in Manning, 188.

[5] Goodwin, 686.

[6] Goodwin, 687.

[7] Goodwin, 686.

[8] Carwardine, 237-8.

[9] Zinn, *A People's History of the United States, 192.*

[10] Goodwin, 689.

[11] Goodwin, 690.

[12] Matthew Simpson, as quoted in Carwardine, 321.

[13] Monk, 215.

[14] Monk, 219.
[15] From the *Christian Recorder,* June 1863, as quoted in Manning, 96.

[16] Waldman, *Founding Faith,* 189.

[17] Monk, *The Words We Live By,* 213.
[18] Mac and Tait, 208.

[19] Mac and Tait, 108.
[20] Carwardine, 211; 233.

[21] Feiler, 124-125.

[22] Ron Andersen, *Lincoln: God's Humble Instrument,* 289.

[23] Mac and Tait, 172-175.

[24] Manning, 125.

[25] Manning, 125-26.

[26] Manning, 196.

[27] Mac and Tait, 208.

[28] Mac and Tait, 249.

[29] Manning, 197.

[30] See Political Positions of Theodore Roosevelt, available online at http://en.wikipedia.org/wiki/Political_positions_of_Theodore_Roosevelt#cite_note-7.

[31] Michael Winder, *Presidents and Prophets* (American Fork: Covenant Communications, 2007), 183.

[32] Winder, 183-194.

[33] Winder, 187-188.

[34] Winder, 192.

[35] Winder, 196.

[36] Edward Welles, as quoted in Meacham, 163.

[37] FDR, as quoted in Meacham, 170.

[38] Justin Ewers, "Making History," *US News and World Report*, March 22-29, 2004, 77.

[39] McCullough, *Truman*, 569.

[40] McCullough, *Truman*, 587.

[41] Bushman, *Rough Stone Rolling*, 514.

[42] McCullough, *Truman*, 639.

[43] Winder, 270.
[44] Winder, 267.

[45] Vaughn E. Hansen, *Whence Came They: Israel, Britain and the Restoration* (Springville: Cedar Fort, 1993), 127.

[46] Ewers, 80.

[47] Feiler, 245.

[48] Ewers, 80.

[49] Ewers, 80.

[50] Mac and Tait, 281-283.

[51] Mac and Tait, 63-66.

[52] Mac and Tait, 71-72.

[53] Monk, 221.

[54] JFK, as quoted in Meacham, 184-185.

[55] JFK's speech in its entirety is available online at http://www.npr.org/templates/story/story.php?storyId=16920600.

[56] Monk, 49, 222, 228.

[57] Joseph Smith, as quoted in Joseph Fielding Smith, ed, *Teachings of the Prophet Joseph Smith* (Salt Lake: Deseret Book, 1976), 326-327.

[58] Winder, 292; See also Rick Walton, "What Famous People Have Said About Mormons," *Mormon Times*, Saturday, July 30, 2011.

[59] The Articles of Faith, *The Pearl of Great Price* (Salt Lake: The Church of Jesus Christ of Latter-day Saints, 1986), 61.

[60] Winder, 292.

[61] Winder, 286, 288-290.

[62] From John F. Kennedy's Inaugural Address, January 20, 1961, Washington D.C., available at www.jfklibrary.org.

[63] JFK, as quoted in Robert Putnam and David Campbell, *American Grace, How Religion Divides and Unites Us* (New York: Simon and Schuster, 2010), 518.

[64] Winder, 296.

[65] Bennett, *America, The Last Great Hope,* Vol. II, 366.

[66] LBJ, as quoted in Meacham, 191-192.

[67] Meacham 196-7.

[68] Meacham 196-7.

[69] Feiler, *America's Prophet*, 257, 277.

[70] Winder, 301.

[71] Gregory Prince and Wm. Robert Wright, *David O. McKay and the Rise of Modern Mormonism* (Salt Lake City: University of Utah Press, 2005), 353- 354.

[72] Prince and Wright, 354.

[73] Winder, 304, 305, 308.

[74] Prince and Wright, 357.

[75] Prince and Wright, 355; Winder, 307.

[76] Winder, 301.

[77] See 2 Kings 6:8-10; Alma 43:23.

[78] Winder, 304, 306.

[79] Prince and Wright, 63-64, 67, 70.

[80] Prince and Wright, 67-68.

[81] Prince and Wright, 71.

[82] Prince and Wright, 69-70.
[83] Refer to Chapter 4, Prince and Wright.

[84] Prince and Wright, 71.

[85] Prince and Wright, 354.
[86] MLK, as quoted in Meacham, 203.
[87] Meacham, 204.

[88] Bennett, *America, The Last Great Hope*, Vol II, 392; Feiler, 265-266.

[89] Feiler, 248.

[90] Meacham, *American Gospel*, 203-204.

[91] Meacham, 192.

[92] MLK, in his *Letter from a Birmingham jail*, available at http://www.africa.upenn.edu/Articles_Gen/Letter_Birmingham.

[93] Bennett, *America, The Last Great Hope*, Vol. II, 367.

[94] As referenced in Gingrich, 53.
[95] Melissa Sanford, "Illinois Tells Mormons It Regrets Expulsion," *New York Times*, April 8, 2004; "Mormon Massacre and Apology," *Branson Missouri News, http://bransonmissouri.missourinetizen.com/2008/09/mormon-massacre-and-apology.html.*

[96] Jessica Garrison, "Prop. 8 Protesters Target Mormon Temple," *Los Angeles Times*, November 7, 2008, available at www.latimes.com/news/local/la-me-protest7-2008nov07,0,3827549.story; For images of police in riot gear protecting the temple, see www.youtube.com, video number 0EtD0Bu9Bie.

[97] No matter ones personal politics, when President-elect Obama was sworn into office, his hand upon the Bible Lincoln himself used at his inauguration, a sense of the miraculous transformation set in. Further illustrating the progress America has made in liberty and opportunity is the fact that the First Lady's great-great-great grandmother was an American slave. Rachel Swarns and Jodi Kantor, "In First Lady's Roots, Complex Path From Slavery," *New York Times,* October 8, 2009.

Celebration of Statehood
Courtesy of Special Collections Dept., J. Willard Marriott Library, University of Utah

In celebration of Utah's statehood (1896), a giant U.S. flag was draped over the wall of the Salt Lake Temple. The flag was placed backwards in what military and law enforcement entities call a "charging flag" formation. The charging flag indicates that the flag is moving forward, being carried by a charging standard bearer. The forward momentum causes the stars and stripes to stream back. U.S. flag patches worn on military and law enforcement uniforms are often placed in the "charging flag" formation.

CHAPTER 9

A CHARGE TO KEEP:
LIVING THE COVENANT TODAY

A small child holds a miniature American flag in the air. Together with throngs of people—of differing backgrounds, races, and religions—she watches the Fourth of July parade. An Army band plays *The Battle Hymn of the Republic*. Cheers are heard as United States fighter jets fly close overhead in dramatic and stunning formation. A good-hearted civil servant walks and waves to the crowd. School children march and sing *God Bless America*. Civic and Charitable organizations follow with smiles on their faces. *The Pledge of Allegiance* is recited, even that sacramental symbol of the covenant which bonds us together "under God." An invocation is given in the name of the God of the land, and is received by audible voices declaring reverently, "amen." This is America. A sense that we are an almost chosen people is felt. The Spirit testifies. We believe the sacred truth that "the Spirit of God…is also the spirit of freedom" (Alma 61:15). But what is at the core of this American spiritualism? Though we seek an explanation, do we comprehend the magnitude of it all?

Do we comprehend that what we feel has its roots in ancient prophecy—prophecy derived from Abraham, Jacob, Moses, Jeremiah, Isaiah and many others? Do we understand that no land in the history of the world has been seen more in vision—has been so long-awaited for—than this land America? Do we internalize the fact that an ancient American prophet, even Nephi of old, saw details concerning the discovery, the settlement, the Revolution, and the making of this nation? Do we oft consider that all of this occurred by the hands of the Almighty, that He might have a place to initiate "a marvelous work among this people, even a marvelous work and a wonder"? (Isaiah 29:14). Indeed, He established this choice land so that His children might achieve eternal life and fill the measure of their creation. He established the land as a major power source for His latter-day kingdom seen in ancient prophecy, even that "kingdom which shall never be destroyed," which was "a stone cut out of the mountain without hands" and was destined to become "a great mountain, and fill the whole earth" and "consume all [other] kingdoms" (Daniel 2:34-35, 44-45).

The restoration of the gospel represents the crowning event of world history. However, it is larger than the story (great as it is!) of a prophet and his small band of disciples, building the Kingdom of God. It is larger than the story of nineteenth century pioneers who settled in the West and grew Christ's true church. For, as seen in this study, the scriptures also testify often and powerfully of the national covenant which brought to bear this Restoration. Too often we merely recognize, but only with a glance and nod, this American Covenant story and all that it implies. However, in that the national covenant holds a preeminent place in the scriptural account, it should also hold a preeminent place in our hearts. As we read the scriptures, may we see with new eyes the powerful role this national covenant plays.

LDS scholars have pointed out that the Old Testament "is a book directed to, and recorded for, the Israelite nation in general—not the worthy Saints who may have been among them. The words of the prophets in it are public pronouncements to their wayward society, not their private teachings to those who had risen above the sins of their generation." This, accordingly, "explains why 'the solemnities of eternity' (D&C 43:34) are not as apparent."[1] Indeed, the Old Testament is the national covenant, which explains why the Founding Fathers of America, while building the nation, quoted it more than any other source (including literature from the Classical and Enlightenment periods). More particularly, the Founders' most quoted book of scripture was Deuteronomy (which does more to lay out the covenant law and obligation, as connected to the "Promised Land," than any other).[2] The New Testament is largely a record of gospel principles and ordinances pertaining to the Saints (more than the nation they were a part of). And, most significantly for us today, the Book of Mormon is a clear combination of both national covenant principles and gospel/priesthood principles.

In that the national covenant element clearly represents a large portion of the canonical scripture, perhaps it is time we pay closer attention to it. There is, after all, a reason the Book of Mormon came to light in the place and at the time that it did. For the Book of Mormon, with its powerful combination of both national and gospel/ priesthood covenants, was written for a people who would need to understand both. It was written for a people who would largely live out Book of Mormon history all over again and would therefore benefit from the lessons learned anciently.

Indeed, what is American history if not Book of Mormon history? American history, after all, is the story of a chosen people, with ties to the blood and promises of Israel (largely through Joseph and Ephraim), who were given a promised land by covenant. It is a story of this people's struggle to live righteously as a nation so as to be blessed with the covenant blessings (*liberty, protection* and *prosperity*) required to realize God's work and glory. It is a story of war against evil and oppression. It is a story of divine scourge and punishment, of national humiliation and national repentance. It is also a story of miracles and conversions. It is a story where prophets of God share the stage with political and military leaders. It is a story of prophecy and fulfillment, a story of God's efforts to save His people. At the pinnacle of this story are the temples of God, even those portals to eternity and eternal life (this pinnacle is largely summed up by the Founding Founders' visit to the St. George Temple). And at the core of this story is the one thing that ties all elements together, the one thing that, if adhered to, will allow the blessings of *liberty, protection* and *prosperity* to thrive, thus securing these temples, and securing mankind's ability to fulfill God's ultimate purposes. At the core of this story is the American Covenant.

If this latter-day American story were to be recorded by a prophet and placed into the side of a hill, to be recovered by another prophet thousands of years later, what would be the end result? What would that prophet of the future be holding in his hands? Scripture. The question is, *do we realize this?* For years we have gloried in America, celebrating its history as if staring at the image of beautifully splashed colors—red, white and blue—of an autostereograph ("magic eye" image), but only seeing it in two dimension. This book was written with the intention of encouraging the reader to stare intently enough to realize there is a deeper image, a multi-dimensional image. Beyond seeing this image, it is hoped that the reader will further realize that he/she is not only looking, but standing squarely inside. Indeed, we are living scripture. Did the Nephites generally understand that they were living scripture when they made decisions that led to their demise? If we fail to realize it ourselves, might our ultimate fate look like theirs?

The American Covenant story we have journeyed through—from the discovery of the land to the present day—is not yet over. And it will not end until the restored gospel has "penetrated every continent, visited every clime, swept every country, and sounded in every ear, till the purposes of God shall be accomplished, and the Great Jehovah shall say the work is done."[3] So what do we, as Americans, do now? We draw on the lessons from the scriptures, particularly from the Book of Mormon, and from our own national history, and we *live* the covenant. The lessons are vast and profound, and are left to the reader to flesh out completely. However, we offer here seven principles to be followed.

1. Keep the Commandments and Serve the God of the Land

The Book of Mormon cannot lay it out any clearer to the nation. As detailed throughout this two-volume work, if we keep the commandments, by maintaining a level of righteousness, and as we serve God, by maintaining the blessings and Constitution He has provided, we will receive *liberty*, *protection*, and *prosperity* in furtherance of His plan of salvation. Latter-day prophets have interpreted this level of righteousness to at least mean adherence to the Ten Commandments.[4] These are standards easily understood and accepted through the Light of Christ, which is given to all men— standards that can be accepted by all, regardless of personal religion.

President Gordon B. Hinckley issued his own prophetic call to the American Covenant. In his 2000 book, *Standing for Something*, published by Times Books, with endorsements by non-LDS civic leaders and a non-LDS senator, it was directed not at the Church, but at the nation. Commenting on the nation's moral decline, the Prophet warned that "blessings will come only as we deserve them...If we are to continue to have the freedoms that evolved within the structure that was the inspiration of the Almighty to our Founding Fathers, we must return to the God who is their true Author."[5] Then, in the spirit of the Thirteenth Article of Faith, he offered detailed instructions on how the nation might pull itself out of the mire by employing the following godly principles: Love, Honesty, Morality, Civility, Learning, Forgiveness, Thrift and Industry, Gratitude, Optimism, and Faith.[6]

On another occasion, this same prophet, backed by the First Presidency and Council of the Twelve Apostles, addressed not only the Church, but the nation and all mankind, in *The Family: A Proclamation to the World*. Invoking the national covenant and warning that blessings would be lost upon disobedience, the Proclamation calls on the nation and world, (specifically calling on "citizens and officers of government") to adhere to righteous principles pertaining to marriage and family.

God has called the nation, even in our day, to the covenant. And He expects adherence. In that His gospel plan, even His entire purpose for the creation of this world, hangs on the ability to provide eternal life, He will have a worthy nation wherein His priesthood and temples might dwell. As such, He has made clear what will happen to us if we fail. He has made clear how He will humble us to influence compliance. "And thus we see that except the Lord doth chasten his people with many afflictions, except he doth visit them with death and with terror, and with famine and with all manner of pestilence, they will not remember him" (Helaman 12:3).

If we fail to be righteous, He has declared that "he will cease to preserve [us] by his miraculous and matchless power" (Helaman 4:25). Even the very last words of Alma, before he walked into the sunset, never to be heard of again, were concerning the national covenant: "Cursed shall be the land, yea, this land, unto every nation, kindred, tongue, and people, unto destruction, which do wickedness...for this is the cursing and the blessing of God upon the land" (Alma 45:16). Even among those most famous verses in Ether, Chapter 2 (that describe the American Covenant), we find the same warning. Directing the warning squarely at latter day America (see verse 11), we are told, "this is a land which is choice above all other lands; wherefore he that doth posses it shall serve God or shall be swept off" (verse 10). Even prophets from our own generation made plain, in *The Family: A Proclamation to the World*, that failure to comply with the covenant will bring "upon individuals, communities, and nations the calamities foretold by ancient and modern prophets."[7]

There is no conceivable reason Book of Mormon prophets would have included these warnings in a book intended for the latter-days—and there is certainly no reason modern prophets would repeat them—if such warnings were not applicable today. God has fulfilled these warnings at least once in America (between the years 1861-1865). There is no reason He would not do so again, if necessary. It is our choice.

2. Promote Separation of Church and State, Not Separation of God and State

The one being, above all other beings, who cherishes mankind's right to choose its own destiny, is God the Eternal Father. Consider what He has done, the sacrifices He has made, for agency to reign. To take Him out of government, for fear that somehow His existence there might threaten liberty (as secularists claim), represents one of the most ironic and wrongheaded political suggestions of all time. Only *with* Him will agency exist. Without His blessings and protection, the adversary will take the reins. Then we shall see how the secularist likes his "liberty."

Joseph Smith, who declared he was ready to die for any man's right to practice whatever religion he so desired, declared, "It has been the design of Jehovah, from the commencement of the world, and is his purpose now to take the reins of government into his own hand."

> This is the only thing that can bring about the "restitution of all things, spoken of by all the holy prophets since the world was"...Other attempts to promote universal peace and happiness in the human family have proved abortive; every effort has failed; every plan and design has fallen to the ground; it needs the wisdom of God, the intelligence of God, and the power of God to accomplish this.[8]

The Prophet called it a *Theodemocracy*, "where God and the people hold the power to conduct the affairs of men in righteousness. And where liberty...and the protection of life and property shall be maintained inviolate, for the benefit of ALL."[9]

The Founders understood this. They understood that the great constitutional separation had to do with building a wall between government and any one denomination—for any one religion in the hands of the government would certainly prove a useful tool of oppression. However, to misrepresent these constitutional restraints (as secularists do), claiming that it was the Founders' intent to keep God out of government, is simply mindboggling for the sane, and frankly embarrassing for the one making such a claim. George Washington accused anyone unwilling to recognize God in American government as "worse than an infidel."[10]*

This book need add nothing more here than the enormous amount of evidence already offered with regards to the Founders' belief about God's place in American history and government. To understand it as the secularist does today not only denies history, but represents nothing less than ignorance in its fullness—ignorance that if left to fester will destroy the American Covenant. To fight this ignorance, we must reintroduce God's place in American history books, rather than follow the trend to take Him and His many miracles out. We need to follow the instruction of President Ronald Reagan: "[Americans] must seek Divine guidance in the policies of their government and the promulgation of their laws."[11]

Many readers of this book might have, at one point or another in their lives, wondered how it was possible for the Nephites to so easily forget the wonders and signs that God had blessed them with (such as the miraculous star signaling Christ's birth). Within a few generations, these signs were somehow cast away and all but lost. We might say to ourselves, *well, I would never have forgotten such miracles.* And yet, how many of us have forgotten our own miracles? How many of us have read accounts in this book wondering why they had never heard them before? The sad truth is, we are forgetting as the Nephites did.

And so, we must fight to put God back into our history where he belongs. For without Him, we have no history—at least not one that makes any sense. Let us follow the example of presidential hopeful, Governor Mitt Romney, who declared, "I will

---

* One of the great tributes to Washington and his understanding of God and government is found in a small chapel within the U.S. Capitol Building. The chapel is a private chamber for U.S. legislators for their use in "prayer and meditation." The existence of this chapel within the halls of congress is the perfect symbolic reminder of what it means to be one nation under God. On the wall of the chapel is a depiction of Washington kneeling in prayer, under the inscription, "In God We Trust." A prayer is inscribed in the window: "Preserve me, God, for in Thee do I put my trust." See Gingrich, *Rediscovering God in America*, 82.

take care to separate the affairs of government from any religion, but I will not separate us from 'the God who gave us liberty.'"[12]

3. Participate in Government

Declared President David O. McKay, "Next to being one in worshipping God there is nothing in this world upon which this Church should be more united than in upholding and defending the Constitution of the United States."[13] Upon considering what America and the Constitution mean to the Restoration, this rather bold statement does not seem so bold after all. However, democracy is a living government, just as the Constitution is a living document, able to change for better or worse, per the decisions of the people. Therefore, our righteous political participation is paramount to America's success. Consequently, our righteous political participation is also paramount to the Restoration's success. We have seen in this book what happens to the Kingdom of God when the nation is ruled in unrighteousness. For this reason, the first revealed temple dedicatory prayer in this dispensation includes the plea that "the Constitution of our land...be established forever" (D&C 109:54).

Like all worthy prayers, this one requires action. We must participate in the governing of the national covenant. There is a reason the First Presidency and other modern apostles have repeatedly asked us, and all Americans, to study the Constitution and adhere to—and oppose infringements of—its principles.[14] Furthermore, there is a reason the Lord commands us to "seek ye out of the best books words of wisdom, seek learning even by study and also by faith... obtain a knowledge of history, and of countries, and of kingdoms, of laws of God and man, and all this for the salvation of Zion" (D&C 93:7, 53). Again, the Lord admonishes us to study and teach "things which are at home, things which are abroad; the wars and perplexities of the nations, and the judgments which are on the land" (D&C 88:79).

With this knowledge, we are to then participate. We are commanded to elect "honest men and wise men" into government positions (D&C 98:10). Almost every election cycle, we are counseled by the First Presidency, via a letter in Sacrament Meeting, to participate in elections, utilizing the Spirit to vote our beliefs. The First Presidency has even addressed our generation, asking us to "be willing to serve" in public office, in the party of our choice.[15]

President Hinckley made clear our responsibility today:

> We should earnestly and sincerely and positively express our convictions to those given the heavy responsibility of making and enforcing our laws. The sad fact is that the minority who call for greater liberalization, who peddle and devour pornography, who encourage and feed on licentious display make their voices heard until the legislatures may come to believe that what they say represents the will of the majority. We are not likely to get that which we do not speak up for. Let our voices be heard.[16]

4. Do Not Legislate Immorality

In order to maintain the freedom to choose, we should not legislate morality, except in cases where *not* doing so puts innocent people in harm's way. Likewise, we should *never* legislate immorality. In the name of liberty and equal rights, many have favored legalizing (and thus recognizing and approving) what the God of this land has deemed sinful behavior. While always careful to supply as much freedom to all Americans as possible, let us be mindful of what happened to the nation the last time we legislated, codified, and slapped our national seal on immoral behavior. It led to the heaven-backed scourge and vexation of civil war. This is a God-ordained government, and God will not be mocked.

5. Be Slow to Political Wrath

While we need to stand resolute on the principles that should govern our land, let us check our emotions and be slow to wrath against our brothers and sisters of the covenant, who may sit on the opposite side of the political aisle. The building and improving of our nation is not some sort of sporting event where biased and unfounded fault-finding and "trash talking" is accepted and encouraged. This is a covenant with the Lord, and should be dealt with respectfully and reverently. At times righteous indignation may be required, but too often we create "straw man" arguments that falsely accuse and incite hate and revenge. We then lay these false accusations upon those we deem political enemies, then we tear our opponents down. This behavior is both dishonest and unhelpful. It never ceases to amaze me that when "our guy" is in office, we are appalled at the wicked slurs laid at his feet, then when "their guy" is elected, we do the same in our turn.

I often tell my political science students that the key to a successful argument (and to an "A" paper) is to get to the root of your opposing argument. Consider what your political opposite would argue, and give that argument a fair and honest try. You will most likely still disagree, which is fine. Our nation was, after all, built on debate. However, you might also come to realize why the opposition believes the way they do. You may come to realize that your political opposite ("their guy") is not the evil villain you once thought him to be. If we would but study opposing viewpoints (based not on what some pundit says, but on primary sources), we will find that rarely is there an American government official in high position, even one who has been elected by the generally righteous "voice of the people" (Mosiah 29:26), who sincerely maintains wicked-intent and is plain evil.

We must work together as brothers and sisters of the covenant, finding commonalties for progress when possible and voting out of office those better suited for different employment.

However, let us not obstruct the entire process (as we so often do) simply because we adhere not to the council of James: "Let every man be swift to hear, slow to speak, slow to wrath: For the wrath of man worketh not the righteousness of God" (James 1:19-20). Said the Christ: "For verily, verily I say unto you, he that hath the spirit of contention is not of me, but is of the devil (3 Nephi 11:29).

The last thing we need as we build upon our national covenant is to invite the Evil One, who has, since the days of discovery and settlement, been doing all he can to get into the ring. And yet we invite him in daily, as political contention opens his cage. Once free to roam, he will blind us to our covenant purposes. As President George Albert Smith declared at General Conference, "Whenever your politics cause you to speak unkindly of your brethren, know this, that you are upon dangerous ground."[17]

Throughout the past chapters of this American Covenant story, there have perhaps been characters that you, the reader, may not have voted for nor fully supported—characters that were, nonetheless, influenced by God to further His purposes in some way. With this in mind, let us do as Brigham Young counseled, and always "pray for [our political leaders] and give them our faith and influence to do the will of God and to preserve themselves and the people in truth and righteousness."[18] President Hinckley added, "I know of no better way to inculcate love for country than for parents to pray before their children for the President and the Congress."[19]

6. Deliver the Book of Mormon

While we have proven that the national covenant has been written into the hearts of the citizenry, past and present, too many details concerning the covenant blessings and obligations have not yet found access to the populace in general. They need the Book of Mormon. Conversion to the Book of Mormon, in addition to the blessings of personal salvation, carry also the added benefit of delivering the words of the national covenant, thus encouraging the living of this covenant. As American historian Richard Bushman explains:

> The Book of Mormon also makes religion a public concern. Its religion has a broader scope than the salvation of individuals. Sermons are directed to kings and cities with the intent of converting whole societies. Mormon charts the spiritual health of the whole Nephite people, knowing their fate hangs on their corporate faith. The rise and fall of civilization over a thousand-year period depends on national righteousness. Individuals suffer in the concluding debacles—Mormon, Moroni, Coriantumr, Ether—but the epic tragedy is the obliteration of two nations. The Nephites and the Jaredites are ultimately the book's protagonists. They illustrate the books' main point that submission to God is necessary for society to survive. The Book of Mormon shows an Old Testament—or Puritan—concern for national sin and the fate of entire peoples.[20]

Let us consider this upon contemplating our missionary efforts. Let us get the Book of Mormon into as many hands as possible, that the national covenant might be better lived.

7. Take the Blessings Unto Every Nation

In that this book so closely connects the gospel to America alone, the critic might feel we are being a bit myopic with our approach to the Restoration—for the Restoration was not designed for one land only, but for *all* the world. The critic is correct. The nations of the world have a preeminent place in this entire story, though their place falls outside the scope of this particular study. So much could be said of this worldwide story that it is worthy of its own book—a book that should be written.[21] The prophecies and promises of the national covenant do, after all, pertain to all of God's children everywhere.

Isaiah, who saw America and the Restoration, spoke of this worldwide vision. After describing latter-day America and describing a latter-day temple "established in the top of the mountains" where "all nations shall flow," the great prophet prophesied: "For out of Zion [America] shall go forth the law" (See Isaiah 2:2-5). President Harold B. Lee prophetically interpreted Isaiah's words in his commentary about a significant portion of the Idaho Falls Temple dedicatory prayer. The prayer stated the following:

> We thank thee that thou hast revealed to us that those who gave us our constitutional form of government were wise men in thy sight and that thou didst raise them up for the very purpose of putting forth that sacred document [the U.S. Constitution]....We pray that kings and rulers and the peoples of all nations under heaven may be persuaded of the blessings enjoyed by the people of this land by reason of their freedom and under thy guidance and be constrained to adopt similar government systems, thus to fulfill the ancient prophecy of Isaiah.[22]

This prayer and prophecy, according to what President Lee said he had learned at the dedicatory service, was a direct reflection of Isaiah's prophecy that "out of Zion shall go forth the law."[23]

The dedicatory prayer was issued in 1945—on the heels of World War II. Since that landmark era of United States history, the sacred law has indeed gone forth from the United States. It has gone forth (and continues to go forth) to South America, to Asia, to Russia, to the Middle East, and everywhere in-between. It has and is filling the earth. And when it enters these nations, history has taught us that it leaves temples of God in its glorious wake. The law has gone forth through U.S. influence, sometimes by example, sometimes by diplomatic encouragement, and other times by war (when necessary). Some of the most powerful American Covenant experiences are found in the accounts that make up these miraculous events.

Too many fail to see this vision. They fail to understand the scriptural principle that the Constitution was created not for America alone, but "belongs to all mankind" (D&C 98:5), that it was delivered by heaven "for the rights and protection of all flesh, according to just and holy principles" (D&C 101:77). They fail to recognize that Satan has brought his war over agency and salvation to the earth, that (as promised) he has bought up armies and navies to oppress with blood and horror. They do not see that God has, in these latter-days, called a righteous army (a literal military force) of His own to defeat this spiritual and physical threat to His plan. And they fail to secure the vision and compassion possessed by the Prophet Joseph, who plainly declared, while commenting on the divine purpose of the Constitution, "I am always ready to die for the protection of the weak and oppressed in their just rights."[24]

Perhaps we do a disservice to ourselves and our covenant by failing to always include the singing of the third verse of the National Anthem:

> *Oh, thus be it ever, when free men shall stand*
> *Between their loved homes and war's desolation!*
> *Blest with victory and peace, may the heaven-rescued land*
> *Praise the Power that hath made and preserved us a nation!*
> *Then conquer we must, when our cause it is just*
> *And this be our motto: "In God is our trust!"*

One of our greatest American Covenant leaders was Ronald Reagan. He understood this principle clearly. He manifested his knowledge of the covenant when he declared the following as President of the United Stated before a nationwide television audience:

How that cry echoes down through the centuries, a cry for all children of the world, a cry for peace, for a world of love and understanding. And it is the hope of heeding such words—the call for freedom and peace spoken by a chosen people in a promised land, the call spoken by the Nazarene carpenter....Let us then thank God for all his blessings to this nation, and ask Him for his help and guidance so that we might continue the work of peace and foster the hope of a world where human freedom is enshrined.[25]

On another occasion Reagan similarly declared, "I, in my own mind, have thought of America as a place in the divine scheme of things that was set aside as a promised land....I believe that God... has always...kept an eye on our land and guided it as a promised land."* He concluded, "I believe we were preordained to carry the torch of freedom for the world."[26] These verbalized thoughts were certainly not the exception to his normal rhetoric on America's place in the world. He spoke often of this vision. More importantly, he turned his words and vision into action. Utilizing the covenant blessings of the land, he brought freedom to the world. He paved the way, under God and covenant, for gospel principles to penetrate lands that had been hijacked for years by the adversary. Temples now stand in some of those lands.

Our covenant, namely the Constitution, is as Elder Dallin H. Oaks recently stated, "this nation's most important export."[27] Through this export, the gospel has found fertile ground in which it has and will flourish, bringing eternal salvation to all mankind everywhere. Let us, therefore, cut through the godless misrepresentations and half truths surrounding American foreign policy—let us support righteous efforts to fight tyranny and export the sacred law, that it might go forth out of Zion.

---

* During his inaugural ceremony, Reagan raised his arm to square to take his presidential oath of office. He placed his hand upon the following Biblical passage: "If my people, which are called by my name, shall humble themselves, and pray, and seek my face, and turn from their wicked ways; then will I hear from heaven, and will forgive their sin, and will heal their land" (2 Chronicles 7:14). See Paul Kengor, *God and Ronald Reagan*, 158.

Notwithstanding the existence of the covenant, with all its blessings and obligations, do we have hope that it can be sufficiently lived? Do we have hope that America can be that nation God intended for it to be? Unfortunately, we live in a time of despair. Many good Americans tend to believe that we should just hunker down with our food storage and accept the inevitable: that this nation is in decline, that the end is near. *Let if fall,* they say, and hasten the Second Coming of Christ. But this is wrong! The Lord did not give this land and this covenant with the expectation that we should ever give up. To the contrary, His only commandments relevant to this issue charge us to maintain and build upon the nation—to build upon the covenant.

Let us ever be mindful that when the Christ comes again, His reign will be both a spiritual *and* political one. He will govern the land, even the world, under "just and holy principles" (D&C 101:77) —principles He has already largely provided by inspiration to the latter-day Promised Land (D&C 101:76-80). Let us prepare for His coming, not by giving up on these principles, but by strengthening them—that when He comes again, we will have done all in our power to facilitate His reign. Let us make Zion, even the nation of America, the millennial capital it was intended to be.

President Ezra Taft Benson, while frequently making mention of the threat to the national covenant—repeatedly pointing out the moral decline within the land—never failed to lose this vision. He never failed to lose hope for America. After reviewing all the Lord has done to create this nation—all the miracles, all the heavenly efforts—President Benson declared, "No, God's base of operations will not be destroyed." He boldly claimed, "It may cost us blood before we are through. It is my conviction, however, that when the Lord comes, the Stars and Stripes will be floating on the breeze over this people."[28]

Let us have hope! After all, despite our many ills, America is still a land worthy of hope. The most recent data suggests that 83 percent of Americans belong to a religion, 59 percent pray regularly, 80 percent are absolutely sure there is a God, and 60 percent are absolutely sure there is a heaven.[29] These statistics, it should be noted, drastically stand out in a world of nations (our European cousins among them) whose numbers in percentages struggle to reach half of those reported for America (as cited above).[30]

In June 2002, when a federal judge ruled that the "under God" clause in the Pledge of Allegiance was unconstitutional, the nation was outraged. Both houses of the U.S. Congress immediately halted important business and drafted a resolution condemning the decision. The resolution was passed unanimously in the Senate, and almost unanimously (with the exception of three members) in the House. But that was not all; members of Congress also immediately gathered upon the steps of the Capitol to recite, with pride, the Pledge "under God." This only reflected the sentiments all around the nation. The ruling was, needless to say, overturned.[31]

Furthermore, statistics are clear that Americans put their faith into action. For example, charitable donations in the United States (not including the colossal amount of service hours offered by Americans) was twice as much as the next most charitable nation (the United Kingdom).[32] And need we even mention the amount of blood and treasure America has spent over the years in fighting world oppressors and delivering freedom to the innocent everywhere, all under God's plan of agency and salvation? Indeed, there is reason to hope for America's future under the covenant.

Before concluding this book, we must first recognize one final charge that has been given, one final mandate to remember, in connection with the American Covenant. It is a word of counsel especially for the Latter-day Saints, who are striving to maintain and build the Kingdom of God on earth. Let us remember the reason for which the national covenant was given. Consider the astonishing prophecy of Nephi, in which he saw everything from Columbus to the Pilgrims to the patriots of the America Revolution (see 1 Nephi 13). This prophecy was not given just to be given. There is a mandate for us today. For the prophecy culminates in us! It ends with the Saints of the Restoration. Through Nephi's vision, we discover that all the great and glorious work God administered on behalf of latter-day America, He did for this final gospel purpose. He did it so that He could deliver the Book of Mormon, even "much of [his] gospel, which shall be plain and precious." He did it so that He could provide "other books, which came forth by the power of the Lamb," which books "shall make known the plain and precious things which have been taken away" (1 Nephi 13: 34, 39-40).

> And in them shall be written my gospel, saith the Lamb, and my rock and my salvation. And blessed are they who shall seek to bring forth my Zion at that day, for they shall have the gift and the power of the Holy Ghost; and if they endure unto the end they shall be lifted up at the last day, and shall be saved in the everlasting kingdom of the lamb; and who shall publish peace, yea, tidings of great joy, how beautiful upon the mountains shall they be (1 Nephi 13: 36-37).

The same prophetic pattern and message is later repeated. The resurrected Lord spoke of the American Covenant to the Nephite people, and He declared that in the last days, America would "be set up as a free people by the power of the Father" (3 Nephi 21:4). He then expounded upon the covenant (in the very last verses of the chapter), warning these future inhabitants of the land that they must repent and be worthy to receive the blessings; only then might His gospel plan be carried out (see 3 Nephi 21: 21-29). Immediately following His admonition (in the very next chapter), he quoted a very significant prophecy from Isaiah (who, as detailed above, was no stranger to the visions of latter-day America and her covenant). In this prophecy (also recorded in Isaiah 54), Isaiah saw that latter-day Israel would "break forth on the right hand and on the left" and would "inherit the [lands of] the Gentiles." Then the Kingdom of God would be built: "Enlarge the place of thy tent," says Isaiah to the Church, "lengthen thy cords and strengthen thy stakes" (3 Nephi 22:2-3).

The message from the Savior, through His own words and those of Isaiah, is clear. It is the same message given throughout the entirety of this book. The Founders established the land, the nation, the covenant. They prayed, they cried, they suffered, bled and died. Consider Washington on the run, death at his back, with his small band of soldiers, invoking God and receiving miracles. Think of the old man Franklin, tired and weary, yet standing up (when he could hardly stand) risking it all for God's Revolution. Consider the sacrifices of Jefferson and Adams, who gave up their lives, who sought the Restoration. Consider Lincoln and the boys who died under this same cause of God. Think of Major Sullivan Ballou, who bid farewell to wife and children, that he might lay himself down, a sacrifice upon the altar of the American Covenant. The examples go on and on. And this they did, that we might stand upon their shoulders and build God's Kingdom—that we might preach the gospel, perfect the Saints, and redeem the dead. Let us not cower from the cause. Let us pick up the torch given to us by our Fathers, and with their zeal, let us *lengthen our cords and strengthen our stakes.**

In conclusion, let us, as a nation, adhere to the American Covenant. May we stand by our covenant leaders, who have throughout our history, admonished us again and again. As a representative sample of such invocations, consider the words from Moses' farewell

---

* Further proof that the Saints are to work their work under the foundation and protection of the national covenant is witnessed in the final verse of Isaiah's prophecy: "No weapon that is formed against thee shall prosper...This is the heritage of the servants of the Lord, and their righteousness is of me, saith the Lord" (3 Nephi 22:17 and Isaiah 54:17).

address to *his* nation under the same covenant (from Deuteronomy 30), which has been repeated for America. In the spirit of all our covenant leaders, these words have indeed been continually repeated by the likes of John Winthrop (while standing in 1630 on the ship that brought the first latter-day Israel covenant-makers to America), by patriots of the American Revolution (particularly after they secured independence), by Martin Luther King Jr. (who repeated these words the night before he was killed in 1968), and by the great Ronald Reagan (who boldly repeated this covenant language at the base of the Statue of Liberty on its centennial birthday in 1986):

> See, I have set before you this day life and good, death and adversity. For I command you this day to love the Lord your God, to walk in his ways, and to keep his commandments. But if you turn away, you shall certainly perish; you shall not long endure on the soil that you are crossing the Jordan to enter. I have put before you life and death, blessing and curse. Choose life—that you and your offspring shall live. That you may love the Lord your God, and that you may obey his voice, and that you may cleave unto him: for he is your life, and the length of your days: that you may dwell in the land which the Lord swore unto your fathers, to Abraham, to Isaac, and to Jacob. [33]

ENDNOTES

[1] Kent P. Jackson, "Foretelling the Coming of Jesus," Richard Neitzel Holzapfel and Thomas Wayment, ed, *The Life and Teachings of Jesus Christ, Volume I* (Salt Lake City: Deseret Book, 2005), 8.

[2] Bruce Feiler, *America's Prophet, Moses and the American Story*, 92-93.

[3] From Joseph Smith, *The Wentworth Letter,* available at www.lds.org.

[4] See Ezra Taft Benson, "America at the Crossroads," *New Era*, July 1978, 36.

[5] Gordon B Hinckley, *Standing for Something* (New York: Times Books, Random House, Inc., 2000), xviii.

[6] Gordon B. Hinckley, *Standing for Something*, xxiii.

[7] Read by President Gordon B. Hinckley at the General Relief Society Meeting, September 23, 1995, in Salt Lake City.

[8] Bushman, *Joseph Smith: Rough Stone Rolling*, 522.

[9] Bushman, *Joseph Smith: Rough Stone Rolling*, 522.

[10] Michael and Jana Novak, *Washington's God*, 126.
[11] Reagan, as quoted in Paul Kengor, *God and Ronald Reagan* (New York: Regan Books, 2004), 171.

[12] Mitt Romney, Speech Given on Religious Liberty, December 6, 2007, available at www.humanevents.com.

[13] Quoted from Gerald Lund, *The Coming of the Lord* (Salt Lake: Bookcraft, 1971), 59.

[14] From First Presidency letter of 15 January, 1987, as referenced and affirmed in Elder Dallin H. Oaks, "The Divinely Inspired Constitution," *Ensign*, February 1992, 68-9. President Ezra Taft Benson quoted a First Presidency statement from 1973, which reads: "We urge members of the Church and all Americans to begin now to reflect more intently on the meaning and importance of the Constitution, and of adherence to its principles," as quoted in Ezra Taft Benson, "The Constitution—A Glorious Standard," *Ensign*, May 1976, 91. As an apostle, President Benson personally asked us to read the Constitution so that we "can sustain it and the free institutions set up under it," as quoted in Ezra Taft Benson, "America at the Crossroads," *New Era*, July 1978, 36. This is but a sample of such official instruction given by the Church.

[15] Bruce C. Hafen, *A Disciple's Life: The Biography of Neal A. Maxwell* (Salt Lake City: Deseret Book, 2002), 492.

[16] Gordon B. Hinckley, "In Opposition to Evil," *Ensign*, September 2004, 5.

[17] Quoted from Elder Robert Wood, "Instruments of the Lord's Peace," General Conference Address, April 2006, *Ensign*, May 2006.

[18] Brigham Young, as quoted in John Widtsoe, *Discourses of Brigham Young* (Salt Lake City: Deseret Book, 1954), 358.

[19] Gordon B. Hinckley, Conference Report, April 1963, 127-28.

[20] Richard Bushman, *Joseph Smith, Rough Stone Rolling,* 107.

[21] The author is currently working on a manuscript detailing this story.

[22] The Old Testament, LDS Student Manuel 1Kings-Malachi (Salt Lake City: The Church of Jesus Christ of Latter-day Saints, 1982), 138-9.

[23] The Old Testament, LDS Student Manuel 1Kings-Malachi (Salt Lake City: The Church of Jesus Christ of Latter-day Saints, 1982), 138-9.

[24] Joseph Smith, as quoted in Joseph Fielding Smith, *Teachings of the Prophet Joseph Smith* (Salt Lake City: Deseret Book, 1976), 326.

[25] Reagan, as quoted in Paul Kengor, *God and Ronald Reagan*, 181.

[26] Reagan, as quoted in Paul Kengor, *God and Ronald Reagan*, 95.

[27] Dallin H. Oaks, "Religious Freedom is at Risk," speech given at BYU Idaho, as reported in *Church News*, Week Ending October 17, 2009, 6.

[28] Ezra Taft Benson, as quoted in Douglas Brinley, *America's Hope*, 208-210.

[29] Robert Putnam and David Campbell, *American Grace* (New York: Simon and Schuster, 2010), 7.

[30] Chris Stewart and Ted Stewart, *Seven Miracles That Saved America*, 290-291.

[31] Richard Ellis, *To The Flag* (Lawrence: University Press of Kansas, 2005), Preface.

[32] Chris Stewart and Ted Stewart, *Seven Miracles That Saved America*, 290.

[33] From Deuteronomy 30:15-20; as quoted in Bruce Feiler, *American Prophet*, 25-26, and as quoted in Cleon Skousen, *The Majesty of God's Law*, 14-16.

BIBLIOGRAPHY

SCRIPTURES

The Bible. 1986. Salt Lake City: The Church of Jesus Christ of Latter-day Saints. Authorized King James version with explanatory notes and cross references to the standard works of The Church of Jesus Christ of Latter-day Saints.

The Book of Mormon: Another Testament of Jesus Christ. 1986. Salt Lake City: The Church of Jesus Christ of Latter-day Saints.

Doctrine and Covenants of The Church of Jesus Christ of Latter-day Saints (abbreviated in this work as D&C). 1986. Salt Lake City: The Church of Jesus Christ of Latter-day Saints.

The Pearl of Great Price. 1986. Salt Lake City: The Church of Jesus Christ of Latter-day Saints.

BOOKS AND ARTICLES

Adams, Charles Frances. *The Works of John Adams, Second President of the United States.* Boston: Little Brown and Company, 1854.

Address of George Washington, Preparatory to His Declination. Baltimore: George and Henry S. Keating, 1796.

Ambrose, Stephen. *To America, Personal Reflections of an Historian.* New York: Simon and Schuster, 2002.

Andersen, Ron L. *Lincoln: God's Humble Instrument.* Salt Lake City: Millennial Mind Publishing, 2010.

Anderson, Vicki Jo. *The Other Eminent Men of Wilford Woodruff.* Malta: Nelson Book, 2000.

Baigent, Michael, Richard Leigh and Henry Lincoln. *Holy Blood, Holy Grail.* New York: Bantam Dell, 2004.

———. *The Temple and the Lodge.* New York: Arcade Publishing. 1989.

Basler, Roy P. et al., eds. *The Collected Works of Abraham Lincoln,* 9 vols. New Brunswick, NJ: Rutgers, 1953.

Bennet, William J. America, *The Last Best Hope, Volume I: From the Age of Discovery to a World at War.* Nashville: Nelson Current, 2006.

———. *America, The Last Best Hope, Volume II: From a World at War to the Triumph of Freedom.* Nashville: Nelson Current, 2007.

———.*The Spirit of America.* New York: Simon and Schuster, 1997.

Benson, Ezra Taft. "America at the Crossroads," *New Era,* July 1978, 36.

———."Beware of Pride," *Ensign* , May 1989, 4.

———. "Our Divine Constitution," *Ensign,* Nov. 1987, 4.

———. "The Constitution-A Glorious Standard" *Ensign,* May 1976, 91.

———. "The Lord's Base of Operations *The Improvement Era* 65, no. 6. 1962, 454-56.

Bernstein, William J. *The Birth of Plenty.* NewYork: McGraw-Hill, 2004.

Boritt, Gabor. *The Gettysburg Gospel, The Lincoln Speech That Nobody Knows.* New York: Simon and Schuster, 2006.

Bowman, John. *The History of the American Presidency.* North Dighton: World Publication Group,1998. (Revised edition 2008.)

Brinley, Douglas. *America's Hope.* Salt Lake City: Deseret Book, 2005.

Brookhiser, Richard. *What Would the Founders Do?* New York: Basic Books, 2006.

Brough, R. Clayton . *They Who Tarry.* Bountiful: Horizon Publishers, 1976.

Brown, Matthew B. *All Things Restored.* American Fork: Covenant Communications, 2000.

———. *Exploring the Connection Between Mormons and Masons.* American Fork: Covenant Communications, 2009.

Burlington, Michael and John R. Turner Ettlinger, eds., *Inside Lincoln's White House: The Complete Civil War Diary of John Hay.* Carbondale: South Illinois University Press, 1997.

Burr, Nelson. *A Critical Biography of Religion in America,* Vol.4. Princeton, N.J.: Princeton University Press, 1961.

Burstein, Dan, ed. *Secrets of the Code.* New York: CDS Books, 2004.

Bushman, Richard L. *Joseph Smith: Rough Stone Rolling.* New York: Alfred A. Knopf, 2005.

———. "1830: Pivotal Year in the Fulness of Times," *Ensign.* September 1978, 9.

Butler, Jon. *Awash a Sea of Faith: Christianizing the American People*. Cambridge: Harvard University Press, 1992.

Callister, Tad. *The Inevitable Apostasy and the Promised Restoration*. Salt Lake City: Deseret Book, 2006.

Carwardine, Richard. *Lincoln: A Life of Purpose and Power*. New York: Alfred A. Knopf, 2003.

Childress, David Hatcher. *The Lost Cities of North and Central America*. Kempton: Adventures Unlimited Press, 1998.

Christofferson, D. Todd. "Moral Discipline," General Conference Address, October 2009.

Church History in the Fulness of Times. Salt Lake City: Church of Jesus Christ of Latter-day Saints, 2000.

Columbus, Christopher. *Libro de las profecias*. Translated by Delano C. West and August King. Gainesville: University of Florida Press, 1991.

Columbus, Ferdinand. *The Life of Admiral Christopher Columbus by His Son Ferdinand Columbus*. New Brunswick: Rutgers University Press, 1959.

Connell, Janice T. *The Spiritual Journey of George Washington*. New York: Hatherleigh Press, 2007.

Cowley, Mathias F. *Wilford Woodruff: History of his Life and Labors*. Salt Lake City: Bookcraft, 1964.

Cummings, Milton C., Jr. and David Wise. *Democracy Under Pressure*, 10th ed. Toronto: Thomson-Wadsworth, 2005.

Davis, William J. *Jefferson Davis: The Man and His Hour*. New York: HarperCollins, 1991.

Davies, Peter R., George J. Brooke and Phillip R. Callaway. *The Complete World of the Dead Sea Scrolls*. New York: Thames and Hudson, 2002.

DeBardeleben, Joan. "Russia," *Introduction to Comparative Politics*, ed. Mark Kesselman, et al. New York: Houghton Mifflin Co., 2007.

Dew, Charles. *Apostles of Disunion*. Charlottesville and London: University Press of Virginia, 2001.

Doctrine and Covenants Student Manual, Religion 324-325. Salt Lake City: The Church of Jesus Christ of Latter-day Saints, 1981.

Don and Virginia Fehrenbacher, ed. *Recollected Words of Abraham Lincoln*. Stanford: Stanford University Press, 1996.

D'Souza, Dinesh. "Created Equal: How Christianity Shaped the West," *Imprimis*, Volume 37, Number 11, November 2008, 4.

Duyckinck, Evert A. *Portrait Gallery of Eminent Men and Women.* New York: Henry Edwards III, George C. et al, *Government in America.* New York: Pearson-Longman, 2004.

Edwards, Lester. *The Life and Voyages of Vespucci.* New York: New Amsterdam Books, 1903.

Ehrman, Bart. *Lost Christianities: Christian Scriptures and the Battle over Authentication.* Chantilly: The Teaching Company, 2002.

————. *Lost Scripture.* New York: Oxford University Press, 2003.

Ellis, Joseph J. *His Excellency.* New York: Alfred A. Knopf, 2004.

————.*First Family.* New York: Alfred A. Knopf, 2010.

Ellis, Richard. *To The Flag.* Lawrence: University Press of Kansas, 2005.

Evans, Michael D. *American Prophecies.* New York: Warner Faith, 2004.

Ewers, Justin. "Making History," *US News and World Report*, March 22-29, 2004.

Family Home Evening Lessons for the Bicentennial of the Constitution. Salt Lake City: The Church of Jesus Christ of Latter-day Saints, 1987.

Faust, James E. "The Restoration of All Things," *Ensign*, May 2006, 62.

Feiler, Bruce. *America's Prophet: Moses and the American Story.* New York: HarperCollins, 2009.

Ferling, John. *Adams vs. Jefferson, The Tumultuous Election of 1800.* New York: Oxford University Press, 2004.

Fiske, John. *The Critical Period of American History: 1783-1789.* Boston and New York: Houghton, Mifflin & Co., 1898.

Fleming, Thomas "Unlikely Victory," *What If? The World's Foremost Military Historians Imagine What Might Have Been.* New York, Penguin Putnam Incorporated, 1999, 162-163.

Foster, Marsha, and Mary Elaine Swanson. *The American Covenant, The Untold Story.* Thousand Oaks: The Mayflower Institute, 1981.

Francis, Richard. *Judge Sewall's Apology.* New York: Harper Collins Publishers, 2005.

Gay, Sidney Howard. *American Statesman: James Madison.* New York: Houghton Mifflin Co., 1898.

Gee, John. *A Guide to the Joseph Smith Papyri.* Provo: BYU/FARMS, 2000.

Gingrich, Newt. *Rediscovering God in America.* Nashville: Integrity House, 2006.

Givens, Terryl. *By the Hand of Mormon.* Oxford: Oxford University Press, 2002.

Gladwell, Malcolm. *Outliers, The Story of Success.* New York, Little, Brown and Co., 2008.

God Bless America: Prayers &Reflections For Our Country. Grand Rapids: Zondervan, 1999.

Goldfield, David. *America Aflame: How the Civil War Created a Nation.* New York: Bloomsburry Press, 2011.

Goodwin, Doris Kearns. *Team of Rivals.* New York: Simon and Schuster, 2005.

Greene, Steven D. *The Tribe of Ephraim.* Springville: Horizon Publishers, 2007.

Haag, Michael. *The Templars, The History and the Myth.* New York: Harper, 2009.

Hafen, Bruce C. *A Disciple's Life: The Biography of Neal A. Maxwell.* Salt Lake City: Deseret Book, 2002.

Hall, Timothy L. *Separating Church and State.* Chicago: University of Illinois Press, 1998.

Hall, Verna M. *The Christian History of the Constitution of the United States of America.* San Francisco: Foundation for American Christian Education, 1975.

Hansen, Gerald, Jr. *Sacred Walls: Learning From Temple Symbols.* American Fork: Covenant Communications, 2009.

Hansen, Vaughn E. *Whence Came They: Israel, Britain and the Restoration.* Springville: Cedar Fort, 1993.

Henry, William Wirt. *Patrick Henry: Life Correspondence and Speeches.* Vol.1. 1891.

Hieronimus, Robert. *Founding Fathers, Secret Societies.* Rochester: Destiny Books, 2006.

Hill, Donna. *Joseph Smith, The First Mormon.* Midvale: Signature Books, 1977.

Hinckley, Gordon B. "An Unending Conflict, A Victory Assured," *Ensign,* June 2007.

———. "In Opposition to Evil," *Ensign*, September 2004.

———. *Standing for Something.* New York: Times Books. Random House, Incorporated, 2000.

History of The Church of Jesus Christ of Latter-day Saints, 7 volumes, edited by Brigham H. Roberts. Salt Lake City: Deseret Book, 1957.

Holland, Matthew S. *Bonds of Affection.* Washington D.C.: Georgetown University Press, 2007.

Hosmer, William."Remember Our Bicentennial—1781," *Foundation for Christian Self-Government Newsletter.* June 1981, 5.

Hunter, Michael J. *Mormon Myth-ellaneous.* American Fork: Covenant Communications, 2008.

Hyde, Orson. "Celebration of the Fourth of July," *Journal of Discourses,* 6:368.

Irving, Washington. *The Life and Voyages of Christopher Columbus,* Vol. 6. New York: Peter Fenelon Collier, 1897.

Isaacson, Walter. *Benjamin Franklin, An American Life.* New York: Simon and Schuster, 2003.

Jackson, Kent P. "Foretelling the Coming of Jesus," Richard Neitzel Holzapfel and Thomas Wayment, ed, *The Life and Teachings of Jesus Christ,* Volume I. Salt Lake City: Deseret Book, 2005.

Jeffers, H. Paul. *The Freemasons in America.* New York: Citadel Press, 2006.

Jenkins, Timothy. *The Ten Tribes of Israel.* Colfax: Hay River Press, 2005. Originally published 1883.

Jensen, De Lamar. "Columbus and the Hand of God," *Ensign,* October 1992.

Journal of Discourses, 26 vols. Liverpool, Eng.: FD Richards, 1855-86.

Kagan, Neil and Stephen Hyslop. *Eyewitnesses to the Civil War.* Washington DC: National Geographic, 2006.

Kengor, Paul. *God and Ronald Reagan.* New York: Regan Books, 2004.

Knight, Christopher, and Robert Lomas. *The Hiram Key: Pharaohs, Freemasons and the Discovery of the Secret Scrolls of Jesus.* New York: Barnes and Noble Books, 1996.

Kunhardt, Philip P., Jr., Philip P. Kunhardt III and Peter W. Kunhardt. *The American President.* New York: Riverhead Books, 1999.

Lamon, Ward Hill. *Reflections of Abraham Lincoln 1847-1865.* Lincoln: University of Nebraska Press, 1994.

Leidner, Gordon. *Lincoln on God and Country.* Shippensburg: White Mane Books, 2000.

Lester, Edward. *The Life and Voyages of Americus Vespucius.* New York: New Amsterdam Book Company, 1903.

Let Freedom Ring, The Words That Shaped Our America. New York: Sterling Publishing Company, Incorporated, 2001.

Lossing, Benjamin. *Signers of the Declaration.* New York: J.C. Derby Publisher, 1856.

Ludlow, Daniel H., ed. *Encyclopedia of Mormonism.* New York: Macmillan, 1992.

Lund. Gerald N. *The Coming of the Lord.* Salt Lake City: Deseret Book, 1971.

Lund, John. *Mesoamerica and the Book of Mormon.* Salt Lake: The Communications Company, 2007.

Mac, Toby, and Michael Tait. *Under God.* Minneapolis: Bethany House, 2004.

MacNulty, Kirk W. *Freemasonry: A Journey Through Ritual and Symbol.* New York: Thames and Hudson, 1991.

Madsen, Truman. *Joseph Smith, The Prophet.* Salt Lake City: Deseret Book, 2008.

Mann, Charles. *1491-New Revelations of the Americas Before Columbus.* New York: Alfred A. Knopf, 2006.

Manning, Chandra. *What This Cruel War was Over.* New York: Alfred A. Knopf, 2007.

Marshal, Peter, and David Manuel. *The Light and the Glory.* Grand Rapids: Revell, 2009.

Mathisen, R. *The Role of Religion in American Life.* Washington D.C.: University Press of America.

McCollister, John C. *God and the Oval Office.* Nashville: W Publishing Group, 2005.

McConkie, Bruce R. *Mormon Doctrine.* Salt Lake City: Bookcraft, 1995. (Originally published 1966.)

McCullough, David. *1776.* New York: Simon and Schuster, 2005.

———. *John Adams.* New York: Simon and Schuster, 2001.

———. "The Glorious Cause of America," *BYU Magazine,* Winter 2006, 48-49.

———. "What the Fog Wrought," *What If? The World's Foremost Military Authorities Imagine What Might Have Been.* Edited by James Cowley. New York: Penguin Putnam, Incorporated, 1999.

McGavin, E. Cecil. *Mormonism and Masonry.* Salt Lake: Bookcraft, 1956.

McPherson, James M. "If The Lost Order Hadn't Been Lost," from Robert Cowley, ed., *What If? The World's Foremost Military Historians Imagine What Might Have Been.* New York: Penguin Putnam Inc, 1999.

Meacham, Jon. *American Gospel: God, the Founding Fathers, and the Making of a Nation.* New York: Random House, 2006.

Miller, William Lee. *President Lincoln, The Duty of a Statesman.* New York: Alfred A. Knopf, 2008.

Monk, Linda. *The Words We Live By.* New York: Hyperion, 2003.

Nathanial Greene to Nicolas Cooke, Jan. 10, 1777. *The Papers of General Nathanial Greene.* Vol. 2. Showman, Richard K., and Dennis Conrad, ed. Chapel Hill: University of North Carolina Press, 1980.

Nibley, Hugh. *Temple and Cosmos.* Salt Lake City: Deseret Book Company, 1992.

Nicolay, John G. and John Hays, eds, *Complete Works of Lincoln,* Vol. 6. New York: Francis D. Tandy, 1905.

Noonan, John. *The Lustre of Our Country: The American Experience of Religious Freedom.* University of California, Berkeley, CA, 1998.

Novak, Michael. *On Two Wings Humble Faith and Common Sense at the American Founding.* San Francisco: Encounter Books, 2002.

Novak, Michael, and Jana Novak. *Washington's God.* New York: Basic Books, 2006.

Oaks, Dallin H. "Love and Law," *Ensign,* November 2009.

———. "Religious Freedom is at Risk," *Church News,* Week Ending October 17, 2009, 6.

———. "The Divinely Inspired Constitution," *Ensign,* Feb 1992, 68.

Old Testament Seminary Student Guide. Salt Lake City: The Church of Jesus Christ of Latter-day Saints, 2002.

Old Testament Student Manuel: 1Kings-Malachi, 2nd Edition, Religion 302 Student Manual. Salt Lake City: The Church of Jesus Christ of Latter-day Saints, 1982, 141.

O'Reilly, Bill and Martin Dugard: *Killing Lincoln* (New York: Henry Holt and Company, 2011), 112.

Ovason, David. *The Secret Architecture of our Nation's Capital.* New York: HarperCollins, 2000.

Packer, Boyd K. *The Holy Temple* .Salt Lake: Bookcraft, 1981.

Parry, Donald. "The Dead Sea Scrolls Bible: Puzzles, Mysteries and Enigmas" *BYU College of Humanities Alumni Magazine,* Spring 2009, 9-11.

Partridge, E.D. "An Experience of One of Columbus' Sailors," *The Improvement Era.* Vol. 12, June, 1909.

Paul. Jeffers, H. *The Freemasons in America*. New York: Kensington Publishing Corp, 2006.

Perry, Donald, Jay Perry, and Tina Peterson. *Understanding Isaiah*. Salt Lake City: Deseret Book, 2009.

Pigott, David. "What We Hold So Dear," *Prelude to the Restoration*. Salt Lake City, Deseret Book, 2004.

Porter, Bruce, and Rodney Meldrum. *Prophecies and Promises, The Book of Mormon and the United States of America*. Mendon. NY: Digital Legend, 2009.

Pratt, Parley P. *The Autobiography of Parley P. Pratt*. Salt Lake City, Deseret Book Co., 1938.

Presidents of the Church: Joseph Smith. Salt Lake: Church of Jesus Christ of Latter-day Saints, 2007.

Prince, Gregory, and Wm. Robert Wright. *David O. McKay and the Rise of Modern Mormonism*. Salt Lake City: The University of Utah Press, 2005.

Putnam, Robert and David Campbell. *American Grace: How Religion Divides and Unites Us*. New York: Simon and Schuster, 2010.

R, Sergeant. "Battle of Princeton," Vol. 20. *Pennsylvania Magazine of History and Biography*, 1896, 515-516.

Ridley, Jasper. *The Freemasons: A History of the World's Most Powerful Secret Society*. New York: Arcade Publishing, 2001.

Rice, Allen T. *Reminiscences of Abraham Lincoln by Distinguished Men of His Time*. New York: North American Review, 1888.

Richards, LeGrand. *A Marvelous Work and a Wonder*. Salt Lake City: Deseret Book Company, 1976.

Richardson, H.L. "A Most Uncivil War," Vol. 17, No. 1. *California Political Review*, Jan/Feb 2006.

Richardson, James D. *A Compilation of the Messages and Papers of the Presidents*. Washington D.C.: by Authority of Congress, 1899, Vol. I, March 4, 1815.

———. ed. "A Proclamation by the President of the United States of America (March 30, 1863)," *Messages and Papers of the Presidents*. Washington DC: United States Congress, 1897.

Roberts, B.H. *New Witness For God*. U.S.A: Published by Lynn Publisher, 1986.

Roy, Basler, P., ed. *The Collected Works of Abraham Lincoln*, Vol. 7. New Brunswick, N.J.: Rutgers University Press, 1955.

Rutland, Robert A. *The Papers of George Mason.* Chapel Hill, NC: University of North Carolina Press, 1970.

Sanford, Melissa. "Illinois Tells Mormons It Regrets Expulsion," *New York Times*, April 8, 2004.

Scharffs, Gilbert W. *Mormons and Masons.* Orem: Millennial Press, 2006.

Schweikart, Larry, and Michael Allen. *A Patriot's History.* New York: Sentinel, 2004.

"Secrets of the Masons," *US News and World Report: Mysteries of History: Secret Societies.* Collectors' Edition, 2008, 32.

Seely, David Rolph. "Words 'Fitly Spoken,' Tyndale's English Translation of the Bible," *Prelude to the Restoration.* Salt Lake City: Deseret Book Company, 2004.

Seitz, Don. *Uncommon Americans.* The Bobbs-Merrill Company, 1925.

Sheldon, H. and Robert T. Handy, et al. *American Christianity, An Historical Interpretation with Representative Documents.* Vol.1: 1607-1820. New York: Charles Scribner's Sons, 1960.

Shugarts, David. *Secrets of the Widow's Son.* New York: Sterling Publishing, *2005.*

Skinner, Andrew C. "Forerunners and Foundation Stones of the Restoration," *Prelude to the Restoration.* Salt Lake City: Deseret Book Company, 2004.

———. *Temple Worship.* Salt Lake City: Deseret Book, 2007.

———. "The Dead Sea Scrolls and Latter-day Truth," *Ensign*, February 2006, 44-49.

Skousen, W. Cleon. *The Five Thousand Year Leap.* Washington D.C.: The National Center for Constitutional Studies, 1981.

———. *The Majesty of God's Law.* Salt Lake City: Ensign Publishing, 1996.

Smith, Joseph Fielding. *Doctrines of Salvation.* Compiled by Bruce R. McConkie. 3 vols. Salt Lake City: Bookcraft, 1954-56.

———. *Gospel Doctrine.* Salt Lake City: Deseret Book, 1986.

———. *Teachings of the Prophet Joseph Smith.* Salt Lake City: Deseret Book, 1976.

———. *The Progress of Man.* Salt Lake City: Deseret News Press, 1952.

Smith, Joseph, Jr. History of The Church of Jesus Christ of Latter-day Saints, 7 volumes, edited by Brigham H. Roberts. Salt Lake City: Deseret Book, 1957.

Snow, Erastus. *Journal of Discourses* 23:186-187, May 6, 1882.

Sora, Steven. *The Lost Colony of the Templars.* Rochester: Destiny Books, 2004.

Sorenson, John L. *The Geography of Book of Mormon Events,* Provo: FARMS, BYU, 1990.

Stewart, Chris and Ted Stewart. *Seven Miracles That Saved America.* Salt Lake: Shadow Mountain, 2009.

———. *Seven Tipping Points That Saved the World.* Salt Lake City: Shadow Mountain, 2011.

Stewart, John J. *Thomas Jefferson and the Restoration of the Gospel of Jesus Christ.* U.S.: Mercury Publishing, 1959.

Steyn, Mark. "Helium Diplomacy," *National Review,* May 4, 2009.

Swanson, James. *Bloody Crimes.* HarperCollins Publishers, 2010.

———. *Manhunt: The 12-Day Chase for Lincoln's Killer.* New York, HarperCollins Publishers, 2006.

Swarns, Rachel and Jodi Kantor, "In First Lady's Roots, Complex Path From Slavery," *New York Times,* October 8, 2009.

Talmage, James. *The Great Apostasy.* Salt Lake City: Deseret Book Company, 1978.

Teachings of President's of the Church, Spencer W. Kimball. Salt Lake: The Church of Jesus Christ of Latter-day Saints, 2006.

Thompson, Kenneth W. *The U.S. Constitution and the Constitutions of Latin America.* New York: University Press of America, 1991.

———., ed. *Constitutionalism: Founding and Future,* Vol. I. Lanham, University Press of America, 1989.

Utah Genealogical and Historical Magazine, Vol.11. July 1920, 107.

Valletta, Thomas R., ed. *Great American Documents for Latter-day Saint Families.* Salt Lake City: Deseret Book, 2011.

Vaughn E. Hansen, *Whence Came They? Israel, Britain and the Restoration.* Springville: Cedar Fort, 1993.

Vespucci, Amerigo. *Mundus Novus.* Translated by George Tyler Northrup. New Jersey: Princeton University Press, 1916.

Vetterli, Richard. *Mormonism, Americanism and Politics.* Salt Lake City: Ensign Publishing Company, 1961.

Waldman, Steven. *Founding Faith: Politics, Providence and the Birth of Religious Freedom in America.* New York: Random House, 2008.

Wallace, Tim, and Marilyn Hopkins. *Templars in America:* Boston: Weiser Books, 2004.

Wardle, Lynn D. "The Constitution as Covenant," *BYU Studies* 27, no. 3. 1987.

———. "Seeing the Constitution as Covenant," *Ensign*, September 1989, p. 7.

Wasserman, Jacob. *Columbus, Don Quixote of the Sea.* Translated by Delno C. West, and August Kling. Gainesville, FL: 1991.

Watts, Pauline Moffat. "Prophecy and Discovery: On Spiritual Origins of Christopher Columbus' Enterprise to the Indies," *American Historical Review* Feb.1985, 95.

Webster's College Dictionary. New York: Random House, 2000.

Weems, Mason Locke. *A History of the Life, Death, Virtues and Exploits of George Washington.* Philadelphia: Lippencott, 1918.

Wesley, Charles. "The Employment of Negroes as Soldiers in the Confederate Army," *Journal of Negro History*, July 1919. 239-53.

Whitchurch, David. "Thomas Bilney, A Prelude to the Restoration." *Prelude to the Restoration.* Salt Lake City, Deseret Book, 2004.

Whitney, Orson F. "The Gospel—A Global Faith," *Ensign*, Nov. 1991.

Widtsoe, John A. *Discourses of Brigham Young.* Salt Lake City: Deseret Book, 1954.

Wilbur, William H. *The Making of George Washington.* DeLand: Patriotic Education, Incorporated, 1970.

Williams, Roger. *The Great Prologue: A Prophetic History and Destiny of America.* Salt Lake City: The Church of Jesus Christ of Latter-day Saints, 1976.

Winder, Michael K. *President's and Prophets.* American Fork: Covenant Communications, 2007.

Winthrop, John. "A Model of Christian Charity". *Winthrop Papers, 1498-1649.* Vol. 2. Boston: The Massachusetts Historical Society, 282-295.

Wood, Gordon S. "Evangelical America and Early Mormonism," *New York History* 61. October 1980.

———. *Revolutionary Characters.* New York: Penguin Press, 2006.

———. *The Creation of the American Republic: 1776-1787.* Chapel Hill: The University of North Carolina Press, 1969.

Wood, Robert. "Instruments of the Lord's Peace," General Conference Address, April 2006. *Ensign*, May, 2006.

Woodruff, Wilford. *Wilford Woodruff's Journal, 1833-1898.* Typescript. Edited by Scott G. Kenney. Midvale, Utah: 1985.

Worthington, Ford C. and Gaillard Hunt, et al, eds. "Fast Day Proclamation of the Continental Congress, December 11, 1776." *The Journals of the Continental Congress, 1774-1789* .Vol.6. Washington, D.C.: Government Printing Office, 1904-37.

Zinn, Howard. *The People's History of the United States of America.* New York: Harper Collins, 1999.

SPECIAL COLLECTIONS AND ONLINE SOURCES

Bushman, Richard. Speech given at the Pew Forum on Religion and Public Life, May 14, 2007, available at http://Pewforum.org.

Custom House Library.www.oldnycustomshouse.gov/history

Ellis, Joseph J. *Patriots, Brotherhood of the American Revolution.* Lectures recorded by Recorded Books, Inc, and Barnes and Noble Publishing: 2004.

Journal of Discourses, 26 vols. Liverpool, Eng.: FD Richards, 1855-86.

Kennedy, John F. Inaugural Address, January 20, 1961, Washington D.C., available at www.jfklibrary.org.

King Jr, Martin Luther. *Letter from a Birmingham Jail,* available at http://www.africa.upenn.edu/Articles_Gen/Letter_Birmingham.

Liberty and Learning (Stephen Pratt), www.libertyandlearning.com.

Library of Virginia, www.lva.virginia.gov/whatwedo/k12/bor/vsrftext.htm.

Los Angeles Times. www.latimes.com/news/local/la-me-protest7-2008nov07,0,3827549.story; For images of police in riot gear protecting the temple, see www.youtube.com, video number 0EtD0Bu9Bie.

Madsen, Truman G., *The Presidents of the Church,* recorded lecture series (Salt Lake City, Bookcraft).

Papers from the Continental Congress, from the Library of Congress *American Memory* collection—memory.loc.gov/ammem/collections/continental/bdsdcoll2.html.

"President Jackson's Proclamation Regarding Nullification," (December 1832), *The Avalon Project,* Yale Law School, available at http://avalon.law.yale.edu/19th_century/jack01.asp.

Romney, Mitt. Speech Given on Religious Liberty, December 6, 2007, available at www.humanevents.com.

Smith Jr., Joseph. *The Wentworth Letter,* available at www.lds.org.

The Avalon Project at Yale University—www.yale.edu/lawweb/Avalon/.

The Church of Jesus Christ of Latter-day Saints--http://lds.org

The Emancipation Proclamation, Online Source: http://www.archives.gov/exhibit_hall/ featured_documents/emancipation_proclamation/transcript.html

The George Washington Papers, from the Library of Congress *American Memory* collection —lcweb2.loc.gov/ammem/gwhtml/gwhome.html.

The Mormons, produced and directed by Helen Whitney, PBS Special: American Experience, Frontline; airdate: April 30, 2007, program available at http:// www.pbs.org/mormons.

The Papers of George Washington—http://gwpapers.virginia.edu/documents/constitution/ index.html.

The Writings of George Washington, Volume 4, Electronic Text Center, University of Virginia —http://etext.virginia.edu/toc/modeng/public/WasFi04.html.

The Writings of James Madison, The Online Library of Liberty, A Project of Liberty Fund, Inc, available at http://oll.libertyfund.org/title/1940/119377.

U.S. National Parks Service official website: www.nps.gov/linc/upload/memorialinside.pdf

ABOUT THE AUTHOR

TIMOTHY BALLARD

After completing a Church mission to Chile, Timothy Ballard graduated Cum Laude from Brigham Young University in Spanish and Political Science, then went on to receive a MA (Summa Cum Laude) in International Politics from the Monterey Institute of International Studies.

Tim has worked for the Central Intelligence Agency and is currently a Special Agent for the Department of Homeland Security, where he spends time as an overseas operative to dismantle crime rings threatening the United States. For the last eight years, he has worked as an adjunct professor in American and International Politics at San Diego State University and at Imperial Valley College. Tim is also a book reviewer for The Association for Mormon Letters.

A frequent youth and fireside speaker in matters dealing with national and spiritual security, Tim lives in Southern California with his wife and six children.

For more information, visit **www.theamericancovenant.com**

* *The views and opinions expressed in this book are those of the author and do not necessarily represent the views of the Department of Homeland Security or the United States government.*